New Perspectives on

Blended HTML, XHTML, and CSS

2nd Edition

Introductory

New Perspectives on

Blended HTML, XHTML, and CSS

2nd Edition

Introductory

Henry Bojack

Farmingdale State College

COURSE TECHNOLOGY
CENGAGE Learning

Australia • Brazil • Japan • Korea • Mexico • Singapore • Spain • United Kingdom • United States

COURSE TECHNOLOGY
CENGAGE Learning

New Perspectives on Blended HTML, XHTML, and CSS, 2nd Edition—Introductory

Vice President of Publishing: Nicole Jones Pinard

Executive Editor: Marie Lee

Associate Acquisitions Editor: Brandi Shailer

Senior Product Manager: Kathy Finnegan

Product Manager: Leigh Hefferon

Associate Product Manager: Julia Leroux-Lindsey

Editorial Assistant: Zina Kresin

Director of Marketing: Cheryl Costantini

Senior Marketing Manager: Ryan DeGrote

Marketing Coordinator: Kristen Panciocco

Developmental Editor: Dan Seiter

Senior Content Project Manager: Jill Braiewa

Composition: GEX Publishing Services

Art Director: Marissa Falco

Text Designer: Steve Deschene

Cover Designer: Elizabeth Paquin

Cover Art: Bill Brown

Copy Editor: Mary Kemper

Proofreader: Kim Kosmatka

Indexer: Alexandra Nickerson

Library of Congress Control Number: 2009938739

ISBN-13: 978-0-538-74633-5

ISBN-10: 0-538-74633-5

Course Technology
20 Channel Center Street
Boston, MA 02210
USA

Some of the product names and company names used in this book have been used for identification purposes only and may be trademarks or registered trademarks of their respective manufacturers and sellers.

Disclaimer: Any fictional URLs used throughout this book are intended for instructional purposes only. At the time this book was printed, any such URLs were fictional and not belonging to any real persons or companies.

Microsoft and the Office logo are either registered trademarks or trademarks of Microsoft Corporation in the United States and/or other countries. Course Technology is an independent entity from the Microsoft Corporation, and not affiliated with Microsoft in any manner.

Cengage Learning is a leading provider of customized learning solutions with office locations around the globe, including Singapore, the United Kingdom, Australia, Mexico, Brazil, and Japan. Locate your local office at:
www.cengage.com/global

Cengage Learning products are represented in Canada by Nelson Education, Ltd.

To learn more about Course Technology, visit **www.cengage.com/coursetechnology**

Purchase any of our products at your local college store or at our preferred online store **www.ichapters.com**

Printed in the United States of America
2 3 4 5 6 7 14 13 12 11 10

Preface

The New Perspectives Series' critical-thinking, problem-solving approach is the ideal way to prepare students to transcend point-and-click skills and take advantage of all that HTML, XHTML, and Cascading Style Sheets (CSS) have to offer.

In developing the New Perspectives Series, our goal was to create books that give students the software concepts and practical skills they need to succeed beyond the classroom. We've updated our proven case-based pedagogy with more practical content to make learning skills more meaningful to students.

With the New Perspectives Series, students understand *why* they are learning *what* they are learning, and are fully prepared to apply their skills to real-life situations.

book provides detailed
nations and examples
for students just
ning to delve into this
t matter. The case
s reinforce concepts
elp students under-
how they apply to
vorld situations."
—Catherine White
Kaplan University

About This Book

This text offers a new approach to teaching HTML, XHTML, and Cascading Style Sheets (CSS).

- Presents an easy-to-understand, non-technical style that lets novice learners quickly grasp the material
- Builds a strong foundation in Cascading Style Sheets (CSS) so that students can migrate to and learn about HTML editors such as Microsoft Expression Web and Adobe Creative Suite 4 Web Standard
- Focuses on achieving page layouts through CSS positioning, which more closely reflects the way "real-world applications" are created
- Integrates CSS right from the start so that students feel confident about their knowledge of CSS when they complete the course
- Emphasizes accessibility, including tips for making Web pages accessible
- Features new coverage of creating fixed and liquid layouts and HTML 5.0 compatibility

System Requirements

This book assumes a typical installation of Microsoft Windows Vista (or Windows Vista Home Premium or Business edition) and Internet Explorer 7 (or higher) or Mozilla Firefox 3.5 (or higher). Note that you can also complete the tutorials in this book using Windows XP; you will notice only minor differences if you are using Windows XP.

The New Perspectives Approach

Context

Each tutorial begins with a problem presented in a "real-world" case that is meaningful to students. The case sets the scene to help students understand what they will do in the tutorial.

Hands-on Approach

Each tutorial is divided into manageable sessions that combine reading and hands-on, step-by-step work. Colorful screenshots help guide students through the steps. **Trouble?** tips anticipate common mistakes or problems to help students stay on track and continue with the tutorial.

InSight

InSight Boxes

InSight boxes offer expert advice and best practices to help students better understand how to work with the software. With the information provided in the InSight boxes, students achieve a deeper understanding of the concepts behind the software features and skills.

Tip

Margin Tips

Margin Tips provide helpful hints and shortcuts for more efficient use of the software. The Tips appear in the margin at key points throughout each tutorial, giving students extra information when and where they need it.

Reality Check

Reality Checks

Comprehensive, open-ended Reality Check exercises give students the opportunity to practice skills by completing practical, real-world tasks, such as creating and submitting an online resume.

Review

In New Perspectives, retention is a key component to learning. At the end of each session, a series of Quick Check questions helps students test their understanding of the concepts before moving on. Each tutorial also contains an end-of-tutorial summary and a list of key terms for further reinforcement.

Apply

Assessment

Engaging and challenging Review Assignments and Case Problems have always been a hallmark feature of the New Perspectives Series. Colorful icons and brief descriptions accompany the exercises, making it easy to understand, at a glance, both the goal and level of challenge a particular assignment holds.

Reference Window

Reference

While contextual learning is excellent for retention, there are times when students will want a high-level understanding of how to accomplish a task. Within each tutorial, Reference Windows appear before a set of steps to provide a succinct summary and preview of how to perform a task. Each book includes a combination Glossary/Index to promote easy reference of material.

Our Complete System of Instruction

Coverage To Meet Your Needs

Whether you're looking for just a small amount of coverage or enough to fill a semester-long class, we can provide you with a textbook that meets your needs.

- Brief books typically cover the essential skills in just 2 to 4 tutorials.
- Introductory books build and expand on those skills and contain an average of 5 to 8 tutorials.
- Comprehensive books are great for a full-semester class, and contain 9 to 12+ tutorials.

So if the book you're holding does not provide the right amount of coverage for you, there's probably another offering available. Go to our Web site or contact your Course Technology sales representative to find out what else we offer.

CourseCasts – Learning on the Go. Always available…always relevant.

Want to keep up with the latest technology trends relevant to you? Visit our site to find a library of podcasts, CourseCasts, featuring a "CourseCast of the Week," and download them to your mp3 player at http://coursecasts.course.com.

Our fast-paced world is driven by technology. You know because you're an active participant—always on the go, always keeping up with technological trends, and always learning new ways to embrace technology to power your life.

Ken Baldauf, host of CourseCasts, is a faculty member of the Florida State University Computer Science Department where he is responsible for teaching technology classes to thousands of FSU students each year. Ken is an expert in the latest technology trends; he gathers and sorts through the most pertinent news and information for CourseCasts so your students can spend their time enjoying technology, rather than trying to figure it out. Open or close your lecture with a discussion based on the latest CourseCast.

Visit us at http://coursecasts.course.com to learn on the go!

Instructor Resources

We offer more than just a book. We have all the tools you need to enhance your lectures, check students' work, and generate exams in a new, easier-to-use and completely revised package. This book's Instructor's Manual, ExamView testbank, PowerPoint presentations, data files, solution files, figure files, and a sample syllabus are all available on a single CD-ROM or for downloading at www.cengage.com.

Blackboard

Online Content

Blackboard is the leading distance learning solution provider and class-management platform today. Course Technology has partnered with Blackboard to bring you premium online content. Content for use with *New Perspectives on Blended HTML, XHTML, and CSS, 2nd Edition, Introductory* is available in a Blackboard Course Cartridge and may include topic reviews, case projects, review questions, test banks, practice tests, custom syllabi, and more.

Course Technology also has solutions for several other learning management systems. Please visit www.cengage.com/coursetechnology today to see what's available for this title.

Acknowledgments

I'd like to thank Marie Lee, Executive Editor, and Leigh Hefferon, Product Manager, for seeing this project through since its inception and recommending the second edition for publication. Their guidance and leadership were invaluable to the success of this project. I want to especially thank Christian Kunciw, Manuscript Quality Assurance Supervisor; John Freitas and Serge Palladino, Manuscript Quality Testers; and Mary Kemper, copy editor, for their special efforts in assuring that this text is a work of superior quality.

Of course, this project would not have been a success without the untiring and extraordinary efforts of Dan Seiter, Developmental Editor. There are not enough superlatives in the dictionary to describe his work. His diligence and dedication to this project were nothing short of phenomenal, and I owe him an immense debt of gratitude for his unflagging efforts.

I also want to thank Victoria Legier, Associate Project Manager, GEX, for her tireless efforts at ensuring the success of this project. In addition, I'd like to thank these very talented individuals at Cengage Learning for their assistance with this project: Jill Braiewa, Senior Content Project Manager; Brandi Shailer, Associate Acquisitions Editor; Julia Leroux-Lindsey, Associate Product Manager; Zina Kresin, Editorial Assistant; Kathy Finnegan, Senior Product Manager; Kate Russillo, Product Manager; Ryan DeGrote, Senior Marketing Manager; Kristen Panciocco, Marketing Coordinator; and Marissa Falco, Art Director.

I'd also like to thank the reviewers of the 2nd edition, whose comments and suggestions were invaluable: William Frankhouser, Everett Community College; Diana Kokoska, University of Maine at Augusta; Ron Robertson, Tidewater Community College; and Catherine White, Kaplan University.

I'd like to dedicate this book to the most beautiful woman I know—my loving and supportive wife, Liliana; my talented and handsome son, Mark; and my cherished "favorite" daughter, Lauren.

—Henry Bojack

Brief Contents

Table of Contents

Using XHTML to Create Web Pages

Creating and Formatting a Basic Web Page

Case | Nyce Paints

Andy Nyce founded Nyce Paints in Boston, Massachusetts. Since 1999, Nyce Paints has differentiated itself from its competition by focusing on selling exterior paint of only the highest quality. Andy worked for many years as a chemical engineer, and he spent more than two decades developing exterior paints that would stand up to the demands of coastal New England's harsh winter weather. In independent product testing, Nyce Paints are often judged as being the best exterior paints. Andy is seeking your assistance in developing a Nyce Paints home page so that he can advertise his products on the Web. Andy believes that a good Web page should be attractive yet simple; you will work with him to design a Web page that meets his company's needs.

Starting Data Files

Tutorial.01 → **Tutorial**
nyce.htm
nycelogo.gif

Review
stores.htm

Case1
shop.htm

Case2
brick.htm
bricklogo.gif

Case3
beth.htm
bethlogo.gif

Case4
warming.htm
warminglogo.gif

Session 1.1

Defining Blended HTML, XHTML, and CSS

Before we start, let's define the terms used in the title of this text. **HTML** is the language used to create Web pages. Using HTML, you create code to describe the structure of a Web page in terms of paragraphs, lists, tables, forms, and so forth. **XHTML** is a variation of HTML that more strictly defines how HTML code should be written and structured. **CSS** is a language used for describing the presentation of Web pages, such as the colors and fonts you see when the Web page appears in the browser. By separating the structure of a Web page from the presentation, it is easier to modify and share the code so that the same code can be used to create and format many Web pages.

This text takes a blended approach to teaching these three languages. The term "blended" describes how you will be taught to create Web pages: you will learn about the three languages at the same time, rather than one at a time.

You have made a wise decision to learn about this subject. What you learn in this text will serve as the foundation for creating and developing Web pages. A **Web page designer** is a person who designs Web pages, and a **Web page developer** writes programming code to add greater functionality to Web pages. (Increasingly, employers are looking for a **Web page "devsigner,"** a person who has both development and design skills.) Web page designers frequently work with software such as Microsoft Expression Web, Microsoft Expression Design, Adobe Dreamweaver, or Adobe Photoshop. Web page developers work with programming languages such as JavaScript, PHP, Perl, and MySQL.

What you learn in this text will make your study of Web page design or development much easier and far more understandable. This text will launch your study of becoming a successful Web page designer, developer, or devsigner.

Learning About the Internet and the World Wide Web

Whether you are interested in creating Web pages for personal use or you are training to become a professional Web developer or designer, you first need to know how the Internet and World Wide Web work. Let's start by briefly examining the technologies that make the Internet and World Wide Web what they are today.

The **Internet** is a global network of computers linked by high-speed data lines and wireless systems. The Internet was established in 1969 as a collaborative project between the U.S. Department of Defense and several colleges on the West Coast. National security concerns during the Cold War era had sparked interest in developing better communications systems. At that time, the concept of a local area network was a new one, and the idea of linking individual networks to create a "network of networks" was uncharted territory. During the 1970s and 80s, the primary users of the Internet were educational and research institutions. Back then, people at these institutions freely shared and exchanged research information by using their computer terminals to send and receive text-only messages, similar to the way you would send a text message to a friend using a wireless device today. The use of the Internet certainly has changed. Hundreds of millions of people now use the Internet to transfer not only text, but data, voice, images, and video.

The **World Wide Web** (or **WWW** for short) is one of several services provided by the Internet. The software you use to view and browse, or "surf," Web pages is called a Web **browser**. This software lets you navigate from one topic, page, or Web site to another.

Until the early 1990s, the Internet had a character-based, nongraphical user interface. In other words, you interacted with the software by typing commands. The Internet did not begin to enjoy widespread popularity until Mosaic, the first browser with a

Tip

The words "Internet" and "Web" are usually capitalized.

Windows-like graphical user interface, was introduced in 1993. A year later, Marc Andreessen, the main developer of Mosaic, introduced Netscape Navigator, the first commercially available browser. Today, the **contemporary browsers** are Microsoft Internet Explorer, Mozilla Firefox, Apple Safari, and Google Chrome. The Opera browser is popular in several European countries.

Exploring Hypertext and Markup

To display a Web page in a browser, the text and graphics must be formatted using **Hypertext Markup Language** (HTML). **Hypertext** is a way to organize information so that you can click links and view Web content in a nonsequential manner. Instead of viewing Web pages from the first page through the last, the way you read a book, you can view topics or pages on the Web in any order, according to your preferences. **Markup** refers to the symbols in HTML code that indicate how the content of a Web page should appear in a browser. Although *language* is part of HTML's name, it's not correct to say that HTML is a programming language. HTML does use computer code and it has **syntax**—specific rules for the way code should be written—but HTML is just a series of instructions that **renders** (displays an exact likeness of) the content of your Web page in a browser. There have been several versions of HTML; version 4.01 is the most recent as of this writing. Each version has added new features to HTML.

The **World Wide Web Consortium** (the **W3C**) is an organization whose full-time staff works to develop standards for the many languages used on the World Wide Web, including the HTML standard. As of this writing, the W3C had approximately 400 members, including businesses, nonprofit organizations, universities, and government entities. You can visit the W3C Web site at *www.w3.org*. To view the current member list, see *www.w3.org/consortium/member/list.php3*.

InSight	**Designing Web Pages for Multiple Browsers**

If you open the same Web page in different browsers, you might see a slight difference in the left and right margins, whether a vertical scroll bar appears at all times, and what fonts and font sizes are used. You want as many visitors to your Web site as possible, and you don't want them to have problems viewing your Web pages. Therefore, when designing your Web pages, you should always test the pages in several browsers to see if they are displayed in the manner you intended. Test your pages in at least the three most popular browsers, and in both the current and preceding versions of those browsers.

Introducing XHTML

XHTML is an acronym for **Extensible Hypertext Markup Language**. Version 1.1 is the current version. XHTML specifies that the code to display content on Web pages must follow certain rules. Most people refer to HTML and XHTML interchangeably, but these two languages are not the same. Prior to the introduction of XHTML, Web page developers did not have a strict standard for how to enter HTML Web page code. For example, in HTML, it's okay to type code using a mixture of uppercase and lowercase letters, but in XHTML, you must type code in lowercase.

To complicate matters, Netscape and Microsoft were the two major browser vendors in the 1990s, and they were in heated competition with each other. Each of these two companies created its own HTML **extensions**, code that would work only in their own browser, but not both—a situation known as **cross-browser incompatibility**. The intent of these extensions was for one company to obtain a competitive advantage over the other.

A draft of a newer version of HTML (version 5.0) is currently being developed by the W3C. When the W3C finalizes a draft, it is called a **recommendation**. Even after the W3C makes HTML 5.0 a recommendation, you probably will have to wait several months or longer before you can confidently use HTML 5.0. New versions of browsers must be developed that will **support** (make use of) the new features of HTML 5.0. In the past, browser vendors have supported new features of HTML and XHTML only incrementally (not entirely) with each new release of browser software. As of this writing, it is not known whether there will be an XHTML 2.0. Although it is difficult to predict what the W3C will enact, a likely scenario is that HTML 4.01 and XHTML 1.1 will both be replaced by HTML 5.0, and that HTML 5.0 will retain the stricter means of writing code found in XHTML.

Understanding What XHTML is Not

Tip

Notepad++ is not a Microsoft product. A good site to learn more about Notepad++ is *http:// notepad-plus. sourceforge.net/*.

The sole focus of XHTML is to uniformly and consistently deliver Web page content. Complex text formatting, composing images, and manipulating data are not features of XHTML. Even simple formatting instructions such as line spacing and tab indents don't exist in XHTML, nor do footnotes, headers and footers, or automatic column and table layout. To compose and edit a Web page in XHTML, you need a text editor such as Microsoft Notepad. You can use WordPad for larger files or you can use a more advanced text editor such as Notepad++.

If you use an Apple Mac, you might use BBEdit or TextEdit as your text editor. You also can use more advanced XHTML editing software such as Adobe Dreamweaver or Microsoft Expression Web. Other useful Web page tools are a photo editor such as Adobe Photoshop and a graphics editor such as Adobe Illustrator or Microsoft Expression Design.

Creating a Web Page with Basic XHTML Tags

You meet with Andy to discuss his goals for the Nyce Paints Web page. At the top of the page, he wants to feature the Nyce Paints logo and slogan. In the center of the page, he wants to explain what makes his company different from other paint manufacturers. He also wants to provide contact information at the bottom of the page. Before you start composing a Web page using XHTML, it's useful to create a **mock-up**—a hand-drawn or typed plan for the page. You collaborated with Andy to create the typed mock-up shown in Figure 1-1.

Figure 1-1 The mock-up for the Nyce Paints Web page

[NYCE PAINTS COMPANY LOGO WILL GO HERE]

Nyce Paints

Always Demand a Nyce Paint Job

Nyce Paints has been the **market leader** in exterior paint for more than a decade. All of our paints have been extensively tested, so you know that our paints can stand up to the toughest weather. Sun, sea, salt, snow, and rain are no match for Nyce Paints. We beat them all!

In independent laboratory[1] tests, our *NyceGuard Supreme*® paints have been chosen as the market leader for durability. Nyce Paints were formulated to withstand snow and rain. In addition, our paints have been determined the least likely to fade after months — and even years — of blazing summer sun. If you want the best exterior paint on the market, choose the one that the experts say is the best and the one that the professionals choose year after year. *Get a Nyce paint job for your home today*.

[1]Tests were conducted at Sheffield State University.

Our Newest Paint Colors

- Phoenix Red
- Seacrest Blue
- River Green

Our Most Popular Paint Colors

1. Boston Beige
2. Gloucester Gray
3. Winter White

Call us now at 613 420-2505 to get our *ASAP* service.

Mr. Andy Nyce
4708 N. Washington Avenue
Sheffield Ridge, MA 61361

An XHTML **element** creates structure on a Web page, conveys formatting instructions to the browser, or conveys information about the Web page to the browser or search engines. A **tag** is a representation of an element in XHTML code. For example, em is an element that emphasizes text when the Web page is displayed in the browser. By default, the em element makes text appear in italics. In XHTML code, the em element is represented as <em>. The element is enclosed by left- and right-facing angle brackets.

The em element conveys formatting instructions to the browser. Likewise, the meta element is an example of an element that conveys information about the Web page to the browser and search engines. The div element creates structure on a Web page. You will learn all about these elements—and many more—throughout the book. Some Web developers consider the terms "element" and "tag" interchangeable, but you can see they are not.

erence Window | **Typing the Code for XHTML Tags**

- To type the code for an element that has both a start tag and an end tag, use the following format: <start tag>*content*</end tag>.
- To type the code for an empty element, use the following format: <tag />.
- To nest tags, use the following format: <tag1><tag2>*content*</tag2></tag1>.

Most tags are paired—they have both a start tag and an end tag, and content is entered between them. End tags have a forward slash before the element name:

`<em>Nyce Paints</em>`

It is good coding practice to type the start and end tags side by side, and *then* type the content between the tags. By typing the tags first, you are less likely to accidentally omit the end tag after typing the content. If you begin by typing the start and end tags side by side, it's also easier to notice typographical or syntax errors in the tags themselves.

An **empty element** does not have any content. Empty elements have only a start tag; they do not have an end tag. For example, the **break element**, which is used to create a new line, looks like this in XHTML code: <br />. Note there is just a single break tag, which ends with a space, a forward slash, and the right-facing angle bracket.

Sometimes tags are used together to create more complex formatting. For example, you probably have used word-processing software to create text that is both bold and italic. To produce the same formatting in an XHTML document, you nest elements. A **nested element** is an element that appears within another element. For example, to make text italic, you would type the following XHTML code:

`<em>Nyce Paints</em>`

To make the same text appear as bold text, you would type this XHTML code:

`<strong>Nyce Paints</strong>`

To make text appear as both bold and italic, you would type this XHTML code:

`<strong><em>Nyce Paints</em></strong>`

When you nest elements, the order of the elements does matter. The elements should be a mirror image of themselves. For example, it would be incorrect to type the following XHTML code:

`<strong><em>Nyce Paints</strong></em>`

Managing Your Files

Store all your files in the same storage location, such as a folder on your hard drive or a flash drive. If your Web page uses image files or other file types, by default the browser looks for those files in the same location where you stored the XHTML document. Before you begin working with this text, make sure to download the student Data Files from the publisher's Web site, as you may have been instructed in class. Store your revised files in the same folder as the original source file.

InSight | **Viewing File Formats**

In this text, especially in the first few tutorials, you will often open a pair of documents to work with: an XHTML file to revise and a .gif image to insert into the XHTML file. By default, Windows Explorer lists filenames without displaying filename extensions. To make it easier to tell the difference between your XHTML files and your image files, which might have the same or similar names, consider changing the default option in Windows Explorer so that when you use the program, you can see both the filename and the filename extension. To change this option, double-click the Computer icon on your desktop, if there is such an icon. (You can also click the Start button, and then click Computer on the menu.) When Windows Explorer opens, click the Organize list arrow. Click Folder and Search Options. In the Folder Options dialog box, click the View tab. In the Advanced settings, click the "Hide extensions for known file types" check box to uncheck the box. Click the OK button. Both the filename and filename extension will now appear in Windows Explorer.

You are ready to show Andy how to create a basic Web page for Nyce Paints. Because Andy will use Notepad as his text editor, you will show him how to create a desktop shortcut for Notepad so he can open it easily each time he uses his computer. After Notepad is open, you'll show Andy how to make sure the Word Wrap option is selected so that lines of text wrap on the screen, just as they do in a word-processing program.

To create a desktop shortcut to Notepad in Windows Vista:

▶ **1.** Click the **Start** button 🍀 on the taskbar, then point to All Programs. The **All Programs** menu opens.

▶ **2.** Click **Accessories**, right-click **Notepad**, point to **Send To** on the shortcut menu, and then click **Desktop (create shortcut)**. A shortcut icon for Notepad appears on the Windows desktop.

▶ **3.** Double-click the **Notepad** shortcut icon on the desktop. The Notepad window opens. Maximize the Notepad window.

▶ **4.** Click **Format** on the menu bar. If the Word Wrap command is not checked, click **Word Wrap**. See Figure 1-2.

Figure 1-2 ▶ Word Wrap is selected

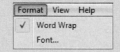

5. Click in the Notepad document area.

With Notepad open and the Word Wrap option checked, you're ready to create the XHTML document. Before you do, you want to explain to Andy the purpose of the tags that should appear at the beginning of every XHTML document.

Typing the Basic XHTML Tags

Each XHTML document should begin with a **Document Type Declaration**, which is an instruction that associates a particular Web page with a Document Type Definition. A Document Type Declaration looks like this:

```
<!DOCTYPE html PUBLIC "-//W3C//DTD XHTML 1.0 Strict//EN"
  "http://www.w3.org/TR/xhtml1/DTD/xhtml1-strict.dtd">
```

The **Document Type Definition** (DTD) is an instruction to the browser that determines the extent to which the Web page should follow the XHTML standard. In the preceding example, the Document Type Definition is "DTD XHTML 1.0 Strict." The DTD is preceded and followed by a pair of forward slashes. There are several DTDs, but the two most commonly used in Web page code are "transitional" and "strict." The transitional DTD renders all elements, including **deprecated** code, which is code the W3C has determined should no longer be used. The strict DTD, on the other hand, renders only code that exactly conforms to XHTML syntax—deprecated code is not allowed. The document you will help Andy create follows the strict DTD. The letters "EN" after the DTD tell the browser that the default language for the Web page is English. The URL in the second line of the Document Type Declaration points to a file that specifies this standard. The URL is a secure Web location that is open only to W3C members. You can type all of the code for the Document Type Declaration on one line, but it's common practice to type the declaration on two lines, with the URL on its own line.

As you can see, the Document Type Declaration contains quite a bit of code for you to type. However, all of the student Data Files you will use in this text already have the code for a Document Type Declaration. If you later decide to learn about an advanced XHTML editor such as Microsoft Expression Web or Adobe Dreamweaver, the code for the Document Type Declaration is automatically generated when you create a new Web page. Currently, the Document Type Declaration is optional, but if your Web page does not have one, the page will be displayed in **quirks mode**, which means that different browsers may render your Web pages differently. However, if your document has a Document Type Declaration, the document will be displayed in **standards mode**, which ensures that it will appear as consistently as possible in all browsers. Because quirks mode can be so problematic, you should always create your Web pages in standards mode by using a Document Type Declaration.

The **html element** is the **root element**, the container for all the other elements on the Web page. You type the start <html> tag below the Document Type Declaration. Although only the start <html> tag itself is required, contemporary Web pages have additional code entered as part of the tag:

```
<html xmlns="http://www.w3.org/1999/xhtml" lang="en" xml:lang="en">
```

This additional information also points to a URL on the Web, but this time it is to a Web site that anyone can access.

After the start <html> tag, the document's head section comes next. The **head section** contains XHTML code that does not appear in the browser's **document window**, which is the part of the browser window where Web pages appear. Think of the head section as a container for information about the document. The start <head> tag is typed on its own line just below the start <html> tag. The head section usually contains **metadata**—information about the document itself, such as its keywords, the author of the Web page, and a description of the content on the Web page. An example of metadata in the <head> section looks like this:

```
<head>
<meta http-equiv="Content-Type" content="text/html; charset=ISO-8859-
1" />
</head>
```

The preceding line of metadata code specifies the content information, which in this instance is a text file that contains XHTML code. ISO-8859-1 is a **character set**, one of many standardized ways to represent characters for communication and storage. ISO-8859-1 is the default character set for most browsers. Another commonly used character set is UTF-8, the universal Unicode standard that provides a larger set of characters to be used and rendered than ISO-8859-1.

The <meta> tags are followed by the start <title> and end </title> tags, which contain the text for the title of the Web page. The <title> tags and its content are typed on a separate line:

```
<title>Nyce Paints</title>
```

The content between the <title> tags appears in the title bar at the top of the browser window, not in the browser's document window, so the page title should be short and accurately describe the content of the page. Although there is no set length for the page title, it's a good coding practice to limit the title to not more than 70 characters (including spaces); otherwise, the page might be ignored by some Web search engines, or the title content might be ignored past the 70th character. After entering the content for the title, type the end </title> tag on the same line. If you fail to follow the title text with an end </title> tag, or if you incorrectly type the code for the end </title> tag, the Web page will appear blank in the browser. Assuming no other code follows the </title> tag, an end </head> tag follows the title on its own line:

```
<title>Nyce Paints</title>
</head>
```

The start <body> tag comes next. The **body element** is the container for all of the page content—the code, the text, and the images for your document that appear in the document window in the browser. Leave a blank line before the start <body> tag so that the tag stands out.

Blank lines and indenting are examples of **white space**, which is any part of the page that does not have content. In your text editor, you create white space by pressing the Spacebar, the Tab key, or the Enter key. Generally, you enter white space to make the code and content easier to read. However, when you enter white space in a text editor, you are not creating white space that will appear in the browser. You have to type code for white space into your text editor to see white space on your Web page. Of course, spaces you enter between words in your text editor do appear in the browser.

In general, you will type most start tags at the left edge of the screen, establishing what is known as an **eye line**, a vertical area of code where you can easily see the start tags. Creating an eye line makes it easier to find the XHTML code in your document because you only have to focus on one part of the screen.

The last two tags you must type at the end of every HTML document are the end </body> tag, which closes the body content area, and the end </html> tag, which ends the document.

```
</body>
</html>
```

At the very least, every XHTML file should include the following tags.

```
<!DOCTYPE html PUBLIC "-//W3C//DTD XHTML 1.0 Strict//EN"
  "http://www.w3.org/TR/xhtml1/DTD/xhtml1-strict.dtd">
<html xmlns="http://www.w3.org/1999/xhtml" lang="en" xml:lang="en">
<head>
<meta http-equiv="Content-Type" content="text/html; charset=ISO-8859-1" />
<title></title>

</head>
<body>

</body>
</html>
```

File servers are the computers that store the files you see on the Web. Many file servers use an operating system called UNIX. Unlike Windows, some versions of UNIX limit the length of filenames. Therefore, it's a good coding practice to limit your Web filenames to not more than eight characters. It's conventional to use only lowercase letters for Web filenames, but you are required to use only letters and numbers when naming Web files; you cannot include spaces or punctuation marks. Never save your Web page files with the filename extension of .txt; instead, use .htm or .html. Files that have a .txt extension will not appear correctly in the browser. The contents of the page will appear as plain text, not as a Web page.

Next, you'll show Andy how to begin creating the Nyce Paints Web page by entering the required XHTML tags. Then you will show him how to save the file under a new filename with an .htm extension. You will use a file named nyce.htm, which already has the Document Type Declaration and some metadata as well. You will start by showing Andy how to open the nyce.htm file, which is located in the student Data Files.

To open the nyce.htm file and save it with a new filename:

1. Make sure you have created your copy of the Data Files and that your computer can access them.

   Trouble? If you don't have the student Data Files copied to your flash drive or hard drive, you need to get them before you can proceed. Your instructor will either give you the Data Files or ask you to obtain them from a specified location (such as a network drive). If you have any questions about the Data Files, see your instructor or technical support person for assistance.

2. If necessary, insert your flash drive into the computer. Wait for the computer to recognize the flash drive.

3. Start your browser, and then start your text editor.

4. In your text editor, click **File** on the menu bar, and then click **Open**. The Open dialog box appears.

5. Navigate to the storage location of the Tutorial.01\Tutorial files on your flash drive.

6. If necessary, click the document type list arrow to the right of the File name text box, and then click **All Files**.

7. Locate and then double-click the **nyce.htm** filename. The **nyce.htm** file appears. See Figure 1-3.

Figure 1-3	The nyce.htm file in Notepad

8. Click **File** on the menu bar, and then click **Save As**.

9. Navigate to the storage location of your Tutorial.01\Tutorial folder.

10. In the File name text box, type **nycenew.htm**.

11. Click the **Save** button. The file is saved in the Tutorial.01\Tutorial folder.

Now that you have opened and saved the nyce.htm file with a new filename, you will show Andy how to type the page title between the two <title> tags.

To type the page title:

▶ **1.** Click between the <title> </title> tags. Type the following text, as shown in Figure 1-4:

    <title>**Nyce Paints**</title>

Figure 1-4   **The page title**

```
<!DOCTYPE html PUBLIC "-//W3C//DTD XHTML 1.0 Strict//EN"
  "http://www.w3.org/TR/xhtml1/DTD/xhtml1-strict.dtd">
<html xmlns="http://www.w3.org/1999/xhtml" lang="en" xml:lang="en">
<head>
<meta http-equiv="Content-Type" content="text/html; charset=ISO-8859-1" />
<title>Nyce Paints</title>


</head>

<body>


</body>
</html>
```

ge title is inserted

▶ **2.** Proofread your code and correct any errors you find.

▶ **3.** Click **File** on the menu bar, and then click **Save**.

It's a good idea to document your work by adding comments to your code as you develop your XHTML document. You'll show Andy how to enter comments next.

Entering Comments

Comments are used to explain how the code was written, to indicate an unusual or particular circumstance, or to otherwise include information that helps you or other Web developers to better understand the code on a Web page. You can include comments anywhere in a document, including within the <head> tags or the <body> tags. Comments do not appear in the browser.

---

erence Window | **Including Comments in an XHTML Document**

- On a new blank line in an XHTML document, type the start code for a comment: <!--
- Type the text for the comment.
- Type the end code for a comment: -->

XHTML comments use the following syntax:

```
<!-- comment -->
```

For example, the following comment indicates the placement of an image within an XHTML document:

```
<!-- image of Nyce logo is below -->
```

If you fail to close a comment with the correct end comment code (two hyphens followed by an angle bracket), then it's possible that none of your document will be displayed beyond that comment. You want Andy to establish the habit of including

Tip

You can enter the system time and date in Notepad by pressing the F5 key.

comments in his code, so you'll show him how to add a comment to the nycenew.htm document.

To add a comment to the XHTML document:

▶ **1.** Click after the end </title> tag and then press the **Enter** key twice to insert a new blank line in the document.

▶ **2.** Type the following lines of code, as shown in Figure 1-5, substituting your name and today's date where noted.

```
<!-- Tutorial 1
     Author: Your First and Last Name
     Date: Today's Date
-->
```

Figure 1-5 ▶ Adding a comment to the head section

```
<!DOCTYPE html PUBLIC "-//W3C//DTD XHTML 1.0 Strict//EN"
    "http://www.w3.org/TR/xhtml1/DTD/xhtml1-strict.dtd">
<html xmlns="http://www.w3.org/1999/xhtml" lang="en" xml:lang="en">

<head>
<meta http-equiv="Content-Type" content="text/html; charset=ISO-8859-1" />
<title>Nyce Paints</title>

<!-- Tutorial 1
     Author: Your First and Last Name
     Date: Today's Date
-->

</head>

<body>


</body>
</html>
```

comment code in the <head> area

▶ **3.** Save the file.

▶ **4.** If you are continuing to the next session, keep your text editor and browser open. Otherwise, close all open windows.

The nycenew.htm file you created can serve as a template file for any XHTML document. A **template file** can be used as the starting point for creating new Web pages. In your template file, you must change the comment and title text to that of your current XHTML project. You have shown Andy how to create the structure for an XHTML document. In the next session, you will show him how to enter and format content for the Web page.

1. What element is the root element for the Web page?
2. Where will text typed between the <title> tags appear in the browser?
3. What would happen if you did not enter the code for the end </title> tag properly?
4. What two tags serve as a container for all the content that will appear on the Web page?
5. What two tags are always typed at the end of an XHTML document?
6. What would you type to enter your name as an XHTML comment?

Session 1.2

Formatting Text on a Web Page

No doubt you have used word-processing software to create typed documents such as term papers and letters. When it comes to formatting text on a Web page, word-processing software offers many more formatting features than XHTML. Don't despair—in later tutorials you will learn how to format Web pages using many of the features you have come to expect from word-processing software. In the meantime, you will show Andy the basic formatting features of XHTML.

Creating Headings

The **heading elements** are used to bring attention to important topics on the page. By default, headings change the text size and make text appear in bold. Headings also have a default margin, so white space is created before and after a heading.

Text size is commonly measured in points. In typography, 72 points is equal to one vertical inch. The word *point* is abbreviated as *pt*. In XHTML, there are six heading elements: h1, h2, h3, h4, h5, and h6. Each heading changes the text size; h1 headings are the largest text size and h6 headings are the smallest. Each of the six heading elements has both a start heading tag and an end heading tag. Here are some examples of code for the heading tags:

```
<h1>Nyce Paints</h1>
<h2>Always Demand a Nyce Paint Job</h2>
```

Typing the Code for XHTML Headings

- To create the heading code, type the following, where *n* is a value from 1 through 6 and *content* is the heading text:
    ```
    <hn>content</hn>
    ```

The heading elements are one of the best ways to illustrate the differences between XHTML and word-processing software. In a word-processing program such as Microsoft Word, you have extensive control over the size of text. You can change the size to 22 pt, 48 pt, 72 pt, or many other sizes. However, unlike word-processing software, XHTML offers only six text sizes. The heading size h1 produces the largest text (24 pt), and the heading size h6 produces the smallest text (8 pt). See Figure 1-6. In a later tutorial, you will learn about other ways to express text size and use CSS to overcome this type size limitation.

Figure 1-6 ▸ **Heading sizes**

Heading Element	Point Size
h1	24 pt
h2	18 pt
h3	14 pt
h4	12 pt
h5	10 pt
h6	8 pt

Tip

Be careful not to use the lowercase letter l as the number 1. These two characters look alike, but they have different values.

Although you do not have to use heading sizes in order, and you can repeat the same heading size as often as you want, it is logical to use the h1 heading only once on a Web page, as a banner or a headline, and to decrease the size of the headings as you add more content to the Web page. Therefore, an h1 heading would be followed by an h2 heading, and one or more h3 headings would follow an h2 heading. Use the h1 and h2 headings sparingly; save them to call attention only to the most important content on the Web page. Of course, which heading size you start with depends on how much room there is for the text content on the Web page. Don't start with an h1 heading if it will overwhelm the rest of the text on the page.

Now you can begin showing Andy how to add formatting characteristics to the Nyce Paints Web page. Andy has told you he wants an image at the top of the page, so you'll show him how to enter the code for a comment as a reminder of where to place the image later.

To insert a comment in the body section:

▸ **1.** If necessary, open the **nycenew.htm** file in your text editor.

▸ **2.** Position the insertion point below the start <body> tag.

▸ **3.** Insert the following code, as shown in Figure 1-7.

```
<!-- image of Nyce logo is below -->
```

Figure 1-7 ▸ **Inserting a comment in the body section**

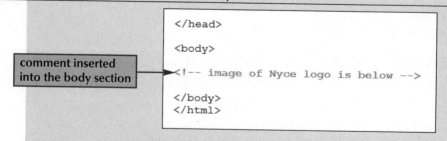

```
</head>

<body>

<!-- image of Nyce logo is below -->

</body>
</html>
```

comment inserted into the body section

▸ **4.** Press the **Enter** key twice after you type the comment.

▸ **5.** Save the file.

Now that you have typed the comment as a reminder to insert the code for an image, you'll next show Andy how to type the code and the content for two headings, which will be the first lines of text for the Web page.

To insert headings:

▶ **1.** Below the comment, type the following code, as shown in Figure 1-8.

```
<h1>Nyce Paints</h1>
<h2>Always Demand a Nyce Paint Job</h2>
```

Figure 1-8	The heading 1 and heading 2 code

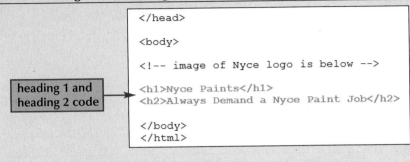

```
</head>

<body>

<!-- image of Nyce logo is below -->

<h1>Nyce Paints</h1>
<h2>Always Demand a Nyce Paint Job</h2>

</body>
</html>
```

heading 1 and heading 2 code

▶ **2.** Save the file.

Now that you have some content that will appear in the browser's document window, it's a good time to show Andy how to open the file in the browser and view the current Web page.

Displaying a Web Page in a Browser

Recall that you should test your Web pages in more than one browser as you develop the XHTML code. This testing ensures that most or all of your visitors can view the page as you had intended. Each time you make changes in your text editor, you should save them and then refresh the page in the browser to make sure it displays the current version of the file. Each browser has a Refresh (or Reload) command or button. In Internet Explorer, for example, you can press the F5 key or click the Refresh button ⟳ to refresh the page.

eference Window | Displaying a Web Page in a Browser

- After creating the XHTML document in your text editor, save the file.
- Start your Web browser, and then open the XHTML document.
- Whenever you edit the XHTML code in your text editor, save the file.
- Use the taskbar to switch back to your browser, and then refresh the page to view the revisions.

Tip

u can also press the rl+R keys to refresh the owser in both Internet plorer and Firefox.

You should display your Web page in a browser periodically to make sure the code is correct. The following steps use Internet Explorer to display the nycenew.htm Web page, but you can use any browser. You do not need to be connected to the Internet to view the page.

You'll show Andy how to use a Web browser to display the Web page you created. You will switch back and forth between your text editor and the browser frequently, so don't close either program. Instead, use your taskbar at the bottom of the screen to switch between your text editor and browser.

To view the Nyce Paints Web page:

▶ **1.** Start Internet Explorer or the browser of your choice, and wait for the home page to appear.

Trouble? If a dialog box opens and explains that you are not connected to the Internet, close the dialog box.

▶ **2.** Click **File** on the menu bar, and then click **Open**. Click the **Browse** button and navigate to the storage location of your nycenew.htm file.

Trouble? If the menu bar does not appear by default in Internet Explorer, press the Alt Key to display the menu bar.

▶ **3.** Double-click the **nycenew.htm** filename.

▶ **4.** Click the **OK** button to open the file from the Tutorial.01\Tutorial folder. Your browser displays the Web page shown in Figure 1-9.

Figure 1-9 ▶ **The file in the browser**

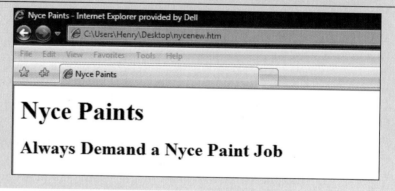

So far, you've created an XHTML document that contains the required XHTML codes, and then you inserted some comments. Next, you'll continue creating the Web page by adding body text, an image, and a list.

Creating Body Text

Now that you have developed an XHTML template document and started a Web page by inserting headings, you can type code in your text editor to create white space that will appear in the browser. You create white space by using the paragraph element and the line break element. Paragraph tags look like this:

`<p></p>`

The start <p> tag precedes each paragraph; the end </p> tag ends each paragraph. Together, the tags create a blank line between paragraphs. As such, the paragraph tags are equivalent to pressing the Enter key twice to create a blank line in a word-processing document. You type paragraphs in a text editor the same way you would in a word-processing document, which is by letting the text wrap as you type. At the end of the paragraph, type the code for the end </p> tag, and then press the Enter key twice to create some white space in your text editor. When you type paragraph text, enter a space after you type any terminal punctuation mark—a period, an exclamation point, or a question mark. XHTML ignores extra space in the browser, so if you type two spaces after a period in your text editor, only one space will appear after the period in the browser. A paragraph typed in your text editor will look like this:

```
<p>Nyce Paints has been the market leader in exterior paint for more
than a decade. All of our paints have been extensively tested, so you
```

know that our paints can stand up to the toughest weather. Sun, sea, salt, snow, and rain are no match for Nyce Paints. We beat them all!</p>

Now you'll show Andy how to enter paragraph text.

To enter paragraph text:

1. Switch to the **nycenew.htm** file in your text editor.

2. Click below the <h2> heading and then press the **Enter** key to insert a new blank line.

3. Type the code and the text shown in Figure 1-10, but do *not* press the Enter key at the end of each line; let the text wrap as it would in a paragraph in a word-processing document. Your line endings may be different from those in Figure 1-10. Press the **Enter** key twice after you type the first paragraph. Type the second paragraph, and then press the **Enter** key.

   ```
   <p>Nyce Paints has been the market leader in exterior paint for more
   than a decade. All of our paints have been extensively tested, so
   you know that our paints can stand up to the toughest weather. Sun,
   sea, salt, snow, and rain are no match for Nyce Paints. We beat them
   all!</p>

   <p>In independent laboratory tests, our NyceGuard Supreme paints
   have been chosen as the market leader for durability. Nyce Paints
   were formulated to withstand snow and rain. In addition, our paints
   have been determined the least likely to fade after months and even
   years of blazing summer sun. If you want the best exterior paint on
   the market, choose the one that the experts say is the best and the
   one that the professionals choose year after year. Get a Nyce paint
   job for your home today.</p>
   ```

Figure 1-10	The paragraph text

```
<body>

<!-- image of Nyce logo is below -->

<h1>Nyce Paints</h1>
<h2>Always Demand a Nyce Paint Job</h2>

<p>Nyce Paints has been the market leader in exterior paint for more than
a decade. All of our paints have been extensively tested, so you know that
our paints can stand up to the toughest weather. Sun, sea, salt, snow, and
rain are no match for Nyce Paints. We beat them all!</p>

<p>In independent laboratory tests, our NyceGuard Supreme paints have been
chosen as the market leader for durability. Nyce Paints were formulated to
withstand snow and rain. In addition, our paints have been determined the
least likely to fade after months and even years of blazing summer sun. If
you want the best exterior paint on the market, choose the one that the
experts say is the best and the one that the professionals choose year
after year. Get a Nyce paint job for your home today.</p>

</body>
</html>
```

4. Save the file.

5. Switch to the **nycenew.htm** file in your browser and refresh the page. Your document should look similar to the one in Figure 1-11.

Figure 1-11

The paragraph text in the browser

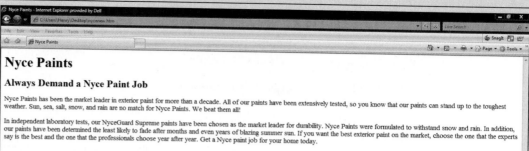

InSight | Learning XHTML

If there are more advanced tools for creating Web pages, such as Adobe Dreamweaver and Microsoft Expression Web, why bother to learn XHTML? While XHTML editing software makes code entry more efficient, these programs assume that you already are familiar with XHTML and CSS, and they use both types of commands extensively. It is difficult to attempt to learn these programs without knowing XHTML and CSS. In addition, if you plan to learn more about Web development languages, such as XML, JavaScript, and PHP, your knowledge of XHTML and CSS will help. Also, don't forget that most text editors, such as Notepad, are free. Notepad is a portable tool; it is installed with the Windows operating system. There is no additional software to purchase and periodically upgrade. Your best strategy is to learn XHTML and CSS first, and then graduate to other Web development languages or Web page editing software. This approach is much easier than trying to learn XHTML, CSS, and the operation of advanced XHTML editing software simultaneously.

The paragraph element and all six heading elements are all examples of **block-level elements**—the browser automatically creates a blank line above and below their content. In addition, block-level elements have internal padding (internal white space), a border, and an external margin. In a later tutorial about Cascading Style Sheets, you will use padding, borders, and margins to improve the appearance of your Web pages.

Making Text Bold or Italic

It is very common to make text bold or italic. The **strong element** makes text appear in bold, and the **em element** makes text appear in italics. You can combine both elements to make text appear as both bold and italic. Both elements are examples of an **inline element**, which means it is contained within a block-level element.

Creating Text Emphasis

- To create bold text, type the following:
  `<strong>`*content*`</strong>`
  where *content* is the text to be made bold.
- To create italic text, type the following:
  `<em>`*content*`</em>`
  where *content* is the text to be italicized.
- To create bold and italic text, type:
  `<strong><em>`*content*`</em></strong>`
  where *content* is the text to be made bold and italic.

Andy wants to emphasize some text in the Nyce Paints Web page. He'd like to display the "market leader" text in bold in the first paragraph so that readers notice that text immediately. He also wants to display the "NyceGuard Supreme" text in italics in the second paragraph so visitors understand it is a special name for that brand of Nyce paints. You'll show him how to use the <strong> and <em> tags to format the text.

To format text as bold or italic:

▶ **1.** Switch to the **nycenew.htm** file in your text editor. Type the code shown in Figure 1-12.

Figure 1-12 The code for the bold and the italic text

```
<body>

<!-- image of Nyce logo is below -->

<h1>Nyce Paints</h1>
<h2>Always Demand a Nyce Paint Job</h2>

<p>Nyce Paints has been the <strong>market leader</strong> in exterior
paint for more than a decade. All of our paints have been extensively
tested, so you know that our paints can stand up to the toughest weather.
Sun, sea, salt, snow, and rain are no match for Nyce Paints. We beat them
all!</p>

<p>In independent laboratory tests, our <em>NyceGuard Supreme</em> paints
have been chosen as the market leader for durability. Nyce Paints were
formulated to withstand snow and rain. In addition, our paints have been
determined the least likely to fade after months and even years of blazing
summer sun. If you want the best exterior paint on the market, choose the
one that the experts say is the best and the one that the professionals
choose year after year. Get a Nyce paint job for your home today.</p>

</body>
</html>
```

bold text

italic text

▶ **2.** Save the file.

▶ **3.** Switch to your browser, refresh the screen, and then compare your file to Figure 1-13.

| Figure 1-13 | The bold text and the italic text in the browser |

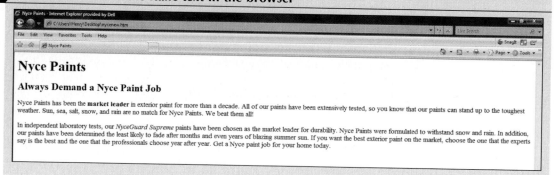

Andy would like to call special attention to the last sentence of the second paragraph. For this sentence, you will show Andy how to nest tags. You will nest the em element inside the content for the strong element.

To format text as both bold and italic:

▶ **1.** Switch to the **nycenew.htm** file in your text editor.

▶ **2.** Type the XHTML code shown in Figure 1-14.

| Figure 1-14 | The nested tags for bold and italic text |

```
<p>In independent laboratory tests, our <em>NyceGuard Supreme</em> paints
have been chosen as the market leader for durability. Nyce Paints were
formulated to withstand snow and rain. In addition, our paints have been
determined the least likely to fade after months and
even years of blazing
summer sun. If you want the best exterior paint on the market, choose the
one that the experts say is the best and the one that the professionals
choose year after year. <strong><em>Get a Nyce paint job for your home
today</em></strong>.</p>

</body>
</html>
```

▶ **3.** Save **nycenew.htm** in your text editor.

▶ **4.** Switch back to your browser, refresh the Nyce Paints page, and then compare it to Figure 1-15.

| Figure 1-15 | The bold and italic text in the browser |

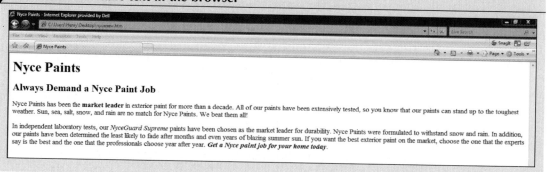

You and Andy examine the Nyce Paints Web page, looking for text that needs to be revised or refined. You'll show Andy how to use other special formatting codes next.

Identifying Deprecated Elements

Recall that a deprecated element is one that the W3C has determined should no longer be used. Deprecated elements include the center element, which was used to center text; the font element, which changed the appearance, size, and color of text; and the underline element. Because underlined text could be confused as text used with a link, Web page designers are now encouraged to emphasize text with bold or italic rather than underlining.

A number of other elements have not been deprecated, but they have clearly fallen out of favor with Web page designers because there are better alternatives. For example, the horizontal rule (hr) element has largely been replaced by the CSS border property and by images designed to appear as a rule.

Other elements that you seldom see in XHTML code today are the bold ("b") element and the italic ("i") element. The strong and em elements are now used instead, respectively. Initially, the address element was used to italicize an e-mail address (usually to the Webmaster) at the bottom of the home page. Over the years, however, the **site footer** area, the area at the bottom of the Web page, has become much more complex. The forthcoming HTML 5.0 standard makes more robust use of the address element.

The blockquote element is used to cite a long quotation, and is a block-level element. (The q element is an inline element used to cite short quotations, generally within a sentence.) The blockquote element formats text to be indented on the left and right by approximately one inch. Used correctly, blockquote text would appear in the XHTML code like this:

```
<blockquote>
<p>Four score and seven years ago our fathers brought forth on this
continent, a new nation, conceived in Liberty, and dedicated to the
proposition that all men are created equal.</p>

<p>The world will little note, nor long remember what we say here, but
it can never forget what they did here.</p>
</blockquote>
```

Unfortunately, too many Web page authors have used the blockquote element as a way to indent any type of text, but the element should only be used for a long quoted passage.

HTML 5.0 also has a new category of deprecated elements, which are called **not-supported elements**. Elements in this category are not to be used; you should make every effort to remove these elements from your Web pages. Some of the not-supported elements are frameset, frame, big, and acronym. To learn more about deprecated code in HTML 4.01/XHTML 1.1, and what will be deprecated and not-supported code in HTML 5.0, go to the W3C Web site at *http://www.w3.org*. For an unofficial summary of what most Web developers currently consider deprecated code, go to *http://webdesign.about. com/od/htmltags/a/bltags_deprctag.htm*.

This text does not use deprecated XHTML 1.1 code, nor any code that will become deprecated in the forthcoming HTML 5.0 standard.

Inserting Special Characters

In most cases, a **special character** is one you cannot enter from the keyboard. A few special characters can be entered from the keyboard, such as < > (angle brackets) and & (ampersand), but they are reserved for writing code. In XHTML, special characters are referred to as **character entities**. You can enter character entities into your code by using a name (a named character reference) or a number (a numeric character reference). A **named character reference** is a combination of symbols, including a suggestion of the special character's name. A named character reference is preceded by an ampersand (&) and followed by a semicolon. For example, to have the copyright symbol appear in the browser, you would enter the following code in your text editor:

```
&copy;
```

Reference Window | Inserting Special Characters

- A named character reference has the following form, where *name* is the named character reference:

  `&name;`

- A numeric character reference has the following form, where *number* is the numeric character reference:

  `&#number;`

Note the semicolon after the character reference. In the browser, the copyright symbol would look like this: ©. Not all special characters can be referred to by name. See the Appendices for the complete list of character entities.

When you refer to a special character by a **numeric character reference**, you are referring to the special character's position in the ISO (International Standards Organization) character set. The character number is preceded by both the ampersand and pound (#) symbols, and followed by a semicolon. For example, to have the registered trademark symbol appear in the browser, you would enter the ® special character.

All special characters can be entered into your code by a numeric character reference, but not all special characters can be entered by using a named character reference. Named character references are case sensitive. Figure 1-16 shows the code for some commonly used special characters.

Figure 1-16 ▶ **Commonly used special characters**

Named Reference	Numeric Reference	Appears in the Browser as	Description
&amp;	&#38;	&	Ampersand
&lt;	&#60;	<	Less than or left angle bracket
&gt;	&#62;	>	Greater than or right angle bracket
&dagger;	&#134;	†	Dagger
&Dagger;	&#135;	‡	Double dagger
&bull;	&#149;	•	Raised, large bullet
&ndash;	&#150;	–	En dash
&mdash;	&#151;	—	Em dash
		(a space)	Space
&pound;	&#163;	£	Pound sterling
&cent;	&#162;	¢	Cent sign
&yen;	&#165;	¥	Yen sign
&sect;	&#167;	§	Section sign
&copy;	&#169;	©	Copyright
&reg;	&#174;	®	Registered trademark
&deg;	&#176;	°	Degree
&middot;	&#183;	·	Raised, small bullet
&sup1;	&#185;	^{1}	Superscript 1
&sup2;	&#178;	^{2}	Superscript 2
&sup3;	&#179;	^{3}	Superscript 3

One special character that Web developers sometimes overuse is   (nonbreaking space), which is used to enter a space into a Web page. Recall that XHTML ignores redundancies. If you press the Spacebar twice after a period, for example, only one space will appear in the browser. However, when you use the   character in your code, the browser will display the space. In later tutorials, you will learn how to enter white space in your documents properly using CSS styles. Never use a string of non-breaking space special characters to create areas of white space to indent or position text on a Web page.

Andy wants to use some solid dashes in the third sentence of the second paragraph. A short solid dash is an "en dash," and a long solid dash is an "em dash." You will show Andy how to enter the code for the em dash character, which in XHTML is represented (by name) as "—".

To create special characters:

▶ **1.** Switch back to the **nycenew.htm** file in your text editor. In the third sentence of the second paragraph, position the insertion point after the letter "s" in "months." Press the **Spacebar** once.

▶ **2.** Type the following code:

```
&mdash;
```

▶ **3.** In the same sentence, position the insertion point after the letter "s" in "years." Press the **Spacebar** once.

4. Type the following code:

```
&mdash;
```

5. Your code should look similar to that in Figure 1-17.

Figure 1-17 ▶ **The em dash code**

```
<p>In independent laboratory tests, our <em>NyceGuard Supreme</em> paints
have been chosen as the market leader for durability. Nyce Paints were
formulated to withstand snow and rain. In addition, our paints have been
determined the least likely to fade after months &mdash; and even years
&mdash; of blazing summer sun. If you want the best exterior paint on the
market, choose the one that the experts say is the best and the one that
the professionals choose year after year. <strong><em>Get a Nyce paint job
for your home today</em></strong>.</p>

</body>
</html>
```

6. Save the file.

7. Switch to your browser and refresh the screen. Figure 1-18 shows the long, solid dash as it appears in the browser.

Figure 1-18 ▶ **The em dashes in the browser**

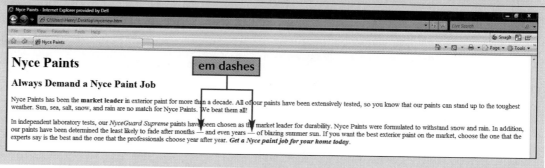

Next, you will work with Andy to create characters that are either raised or lowered in relation to the current line of text.

Creating Superscripts and Subscripts

You don't often see superscripts and subscripts on Web pages, probably because most Web users do not often read formal research or scientific documents. The **sup element** creates a superscript, which raises a character by one-half a line of type. Similarly, the **sub element** creates a subscript, which lowers a character by one-half a line of type. Superscript and subscript characters are useful when you need to include footnotes, endnotes, or mathematical and scientific notations in your Web pages. The sup and sub elements are inline elements. In a later tutorial, you will also learn how to use CSS to create superscripts and subscripts.

Andy wants to enter a footnote number after the word "laboratory" in the second paragraph. He then wants to enter the footnote text following the second paragraph. He also would like to have the registered trademark symbol appear in superscript after the word "Supreme" in the first sentence of the second paragraph. You will show Andy how to enter the code to create these superscripts and the footnote text.

To create the superscripts:

▶ **1.** Switch to the **nycenew.htm** file in your text editor.

▶ **2.** Type the code shown in Figure 1-19.

Figure 1-19	**The superscripts and the footnote text**

```
<p>In independent laboratory<sup>1</sup> tests, our <em>NyceGuard Supreme
</em><sup>&reg;</sup> paints have been chosen as the market leader for
durability. Nyce Paints were formulated to withstand snow and rain. In
addition, our paints have been determined the least likely to fade after
months &mdash; and even years &mdash; of blazing summer sun. If you want
the best exterior paint on the market, choose the one that the experts say
is the best and the one that the professionals choose year after year.
<strong><em>Get a Nyce paint job for your home today</em></strong>.</p>

<p><sup>1</sup>Tests were conducted at Sheffield State University.</p>

</body>
</html>
```

▶ **3.** Save the file.

▶ **4.** Switch to your browser and refresh the file. Figure 1-20 shows how the superscripts and registered trademark symbol appear in the browser.

Figure 1-20	**The superscript and footnote text in the browser**

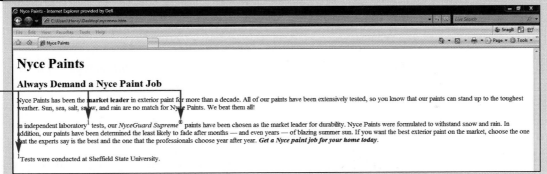

superscripts

▶ **5.** If you are continuing to the next session, keep your text editor and browser open. Otherwise, close all open windows.

Now that Andy has gained some familiarity with XHTML code, you will give him some tips for entering XHTML code correctly, regardless of which text editor he uses.

Tips for Typing XHTML Code in a Text Editor

At this point, you have entered much of the code that makes up the basic Web page for Nyce Paints. The following list contains tips and hints for keeping your XHTML code error-free.

• **Type all code in lowercase**. Type your HTML or XHTML code in lowercase, but type content as you normally would. Filenames should also be typed in lowercase.

- **Create an eye line**. With the exception of the <title> tags, don't wrap the tags for an XHTML document. You are trying to create an "eye line" in which most of the XHTML tags are entered at the left edge of the screen. Use the following style:

```
<html>
<head>
<title>Your page title goes here</title>
</head>
```

The following example, which shows code written in "paragraph style," is a poor coding practice:

```
<html><head><title>your title goes here</title></head>
```

- **Use white space**. Leave a blank line before and after the start <body> tag, as shown in the following code:

```
</head>

<body>

<p>Here is the first paragraph of the document.</p>
```

Enter paragraph text as follows, and let the text wrap. Do not place the start or end paragraph tags on separate lines, but do create a blank line between paragraphs.

```
<p>Here is the first sentence of the first paragraph. You want to
leave some white space between paragraphs so that you can easily
read and debug your code.</p>

<p>Here is another paragraph. Space once after any mark of terminal
punctuation, such as a period, exclamation point or question
mark.</p>
```

When you type a block-level element in a text editor, leave a blank line before the block-level element, just as you would if you were typing paragraphs in a business letter:

```
<body>

<h1>Reducing Code Errors</h1>
<p>Here is the first paragraph of text. Note that there is only
one space at the end of each sentence. XHTML eliminates extra
space.</p>
```

At the end of each document, leave a blank line before the </body> and </html> tags, as follows:

```
<p>Here is the end of the document.</p>

</body>
</html>
```

- **Insert break (<br />) tags at the beginning of a line of code, not at the end**.

See the following example:

```
<p>Mr. John Doe
<br />28 Smith Street
<br />Santa Fe, CA 30039</p>
```

Don't enter your <br /> tags like this:

```
<p>John Doe<br />
28 Smith Street<br />
Santa Fe, CA 30039</p>
```

- **Don't use deprecated tags**. For example, don't use underline tags. Use the em element instead of the underline element.

- **Don't use tags that are purely presentational, such as the <b> tag or the <i> tag.** Use the strong element to make text bold and use the em element to make text italic.
- **Format terminal punctuation properly.** Insert one space rather than two after a colon, and add one space after any terminal punctuation mark (the period, exclamation point, and question mark). Extra spaces are deleted in the browser.
- **Beware of quotation marks from pasted text.** If you are cutting, copying, and pasting text from a word-processing document or other program into your text editor, look to see if any of the text has quotation marks. Notepad, for example, only uses straight quotes (" "), not curly quotes (" "). If quotation marks do not appear properly in the browser, delete all the quotation marks from the pasted text and type straight quotes in their place.

Review | **Session 1.2 Quick Check**

1. What set of tags display text in the largest size of type?
2. In addition to making text larger or smaller, what other formatting is created by heading tags?
3. What set of tags makes text bold?
4. What set of tags makes text italic?
5. What does it mean if an element is deprecated?
6. What is a special character?

Session 1.3

Using Images on a Web Page

Prior to this century, transmission speeds were very slow. Because it took quite a while for a Web page to download, many Web pages were text-only. With the greater use of high-speed broadband transmission, Web pages today commonly display many images. Images are a great way to add variety and interest to your Web pages; however, using too many images can be distracting and can even make the page look amateurish. In a later tutorial, you will learn how to create a smaller image that links to a page that displays a larger version of the same image.

Understanding Image Files and File Types

Most images used on the Web today are either photos or drawings, such as clip art. Clip art and photos are typically stored in two different file formats. Clip art drawings use the **Graphics Interchange File** format and have the filename extension of .gif (pronounced most often with a hard "g" sound and not as "jif"). Gif files are **compressed**, which means that the file is reduced to a much smaller size. Although the compressed image loses some detail and clarity, the image downloads faster. Photos are most often stored as .jpg files. JPG, pronounced "jay peg," is an acronym for **Joint Photographic Experts Group**.

PNG (pronounced "ping"), is a new image file format. PNG files use **Portable Network Graphics**—a file format chosen by the W3C to replace .gif files. PNG files have better file compression than .gif files.

Bitmap files, which have a .bmp extension, are standard Windows graphics files. In general, avoid using bitmap files on your Web pages because they tend to be much larger than other file formats and therefore take longer to download.

Acquiring Images

Be judicious in your use of images, because they affect the overall file size and download time of your Web pages. If the image will enhance the appearance of the page or convey useful information, then include the image. Displaying a page that consists mostly of images and very little text is considered amateurish and should be avoided. On the other hand, a text-only page is also undesirable because it doesn't have much visual interest.

You can use your digital camera or cell phone to capture images for your Web pages, but you also can obtain images from several other sources. Many Web sites offer free clip art and photographs in .gif and .jpg file formats. You can also buy images and clip art on CDs or DVDs, or you can obtain images from the Microsoft Office suite or image editing software such as Adobe Photoshop. However, be mindful of copyright and use restrictions. If you find an image for a Web page that you want to use, make sure you have permission to use the image on the Web—you might otherwise be violating United States copyright law.

InSight | **Obtaining Public Domain Images**

Although it is simple to copy an image from a Web site, you should not. You don't want to violate any copyright restrictions. For school use, several Web sites offer photos that are in the public domain; these photos are free for people to use and copy. For example, browse to *www.wikipedia.org* and search for "public domain image resources." Another popular Web site where you can learn more about public domain photos is *www.pdphoto.org/*.

Using the Image Element

The **image element** is used to insert an image on a Web page. The image element is an empty element (it has no content), so in the XHTML code, the image tag ends with a space followed by a forward slash, like this: <img />. Images are also inline elements. Because every inline element should be inside a block-level element, if the image is not already within a block-level element, precede the code for the <img /> tag with the code for a block-level element, such as a start <p> tag, and follow the image code with the appropriate end tag, such as </p> in this instance. By default, the image is aligned at the left edge of the browser window, but text does not wrap around the image. In a later tutorial, you will learn how to position an image anywhere on the Web page and how to wrap text around an image.

Reference Window | **Inserting an Image**

- To insert an image, use the following code:
  ```
  <img src="imagename.filetype" alt="alternatetext"
  width="widthvalue" height="heightvalue" />
  ```
  where *img* is the image element, *src* is the source attribute, *imagename* is the filename of the image, *filetype* is the type of image file (such as .jpg or .gif), *alt* is the alt attribute, *alternatetext* is the description of the image, *width* is the width attribute, *widthvalue* is the width of the image in pixels, *height* is the height attribute, and *heightvalue* is the height of the image in pixels.
- The image code must be within the code for a block-level element.

Tip

 are many depre-
 attributes as well,
as bgcolor and
 ground.

An **attribute** defines a change to an element. Each attribute has (takes) a **value** that describes the extent to or manner in which the element will be changed. You can think of attributes as nouns and values as adjectives. All values must be enclosed in quotation marks. In your code, you type the element, an equals sign, and then the value. Don't insert a space either before or after the equals sign.

Whenever you type quotation marks in your XHTML code, it's a good coding practice to type both quotation marks first so that you avoid the mistake of omitting the closing quotation mark. For example:

""   Type both quotes first.

"|"   Position the insertion point between the quotes.

"value"   Then type the value between the quotes.

The img element uses several attributes. First, it must have the src (the source) attribute. The value of the source attribute is the name of the image file that should appear on the Web page. Values must always be enclosed by quotation marks. For example, the following code displays the Nyce Paints logo image:

```
<p><img src="nycelogo.gif" /></p>
```

If you have many images for your Web site, it's a good idea to create a separate folder for the images (the folder is usually named "images"). Store all your images in this folder so you can easily locate the image files used for your Web site. If you save an image file in a different folder from the one you used to store the XHTML file, you must specify the path to the image, like this:

```
<p><img src="../images/nycelogo.gif" /></p>
```

Another attribute used with images is the alt attribute, which provides a brief description of the image. The words associated with the alt attribute appear before the image downloads. Also, when you pass your mouse pointer over the image, the alternate text appears in some browsers as a **ScreenTip**, a small rectangular box that contains the text. Some Web developers refer to ScreenTips as Tooltips (or tool tips), but the term ScreenTip is more correct for what you see in the browser window. A Tooltip works like a ScreenTip; it displays text inside a small rectangular box when you pass the mouse pointer over an object on the screen. However, a Tooltip is designed to display one or two words that describe the purpose of an icon or button in a program's toolbar.

Web page accessibility describes the extent to which a Web page is accessible by as many people as possible despite visual or motor skill impairment. It is a good coding practice to always use the alt attribute (and include a descriptive value) whenever you enter the code for an image, even though the alt attribute is not required, because the alt text is read aloud by a screen reader. A **screen reader** is software that uses a synthesized voice to read aloud the text in the browser's document window.

Tip

 page developers
 to Web page acces-
 y simply as
 ssibility."

Try to use meaningful alternate text. For example, instead of using "car image" as alternate text, use a description such as "image of 1959 red Cadillac with enormous tail-fins and massive, gleaming chrome bumpers."

Technically, the order of the attributes and values does not matter, but it's a good coding practice to list the src attribute first. The alternate text should be brief but descriptive, as in the following example:

```
<p><img src="nycelogo.gif" alt="Nyce Paints logo" /></p>
```

You must include the end quote after the alt text. Without the end quote, the browser will treat all subsequent text in the file as alt text! This means it will not display the rest of the document. If you don't want to provide alt text, you don't have to; the alt attribute can have an empty value (for example, alt=""). But, for the reasons already mentioned, you should always provide alternate text.

Recall that cross-browser incompatibility occurs when different browsers don't display XHTML code in the same way. For example, the alt attribute displays a ScreenTip in

Internet Explorer, but not in the Firefox browser. In the Firefox browser, you see the alternate text only if the image fails to download. To display a ScreenTip in all browsers, you must use the title attribute:

```
<p><img src="nycelogo.gif" alt="Nyce Paints logo" title="Nyce Paints
logo" width="760" height="200" /></p>
```

In the preceding example, the same text was used as the value for both the alt attribute and the title attribute. If you take this approach, only the value for the title attribute will appear when you pass the mouse pointer over the image. See Figure 1-21.

Figure 1-21 | **The ScreenTip in the browser**

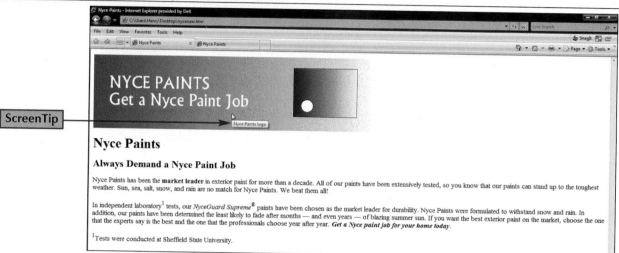

If the browser can't load the image file specified in the image tag, a placeholder icon appears in some browsers in place of the image. The **placeholder icon** substitutes an alert icon for the image, indicating that an image should appear in its place. The alternate text also appears next to the placeholder icon. See Figure 1-22.

Figure 1-22 | **The placeholder icon**

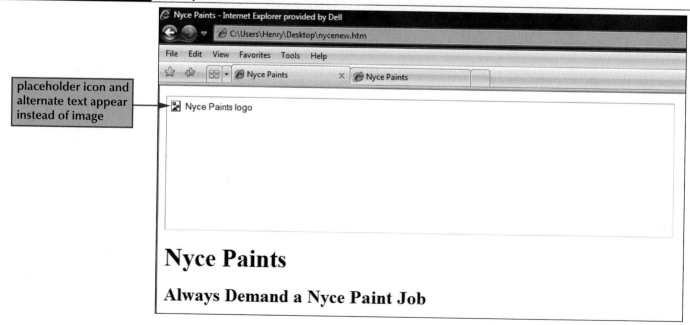

If you see the placeholder icon instead of an image, check your source code to make sure you typed the <img> tag and the associated XHTML code correctly. Be particularly mindful of images that have the numbers 0 and 1 in their filenames—they might be the letters "O" and "l". Also check the image tag code; a common error is to type <img scr> instead of <img src>. Additionally, check to make sure that the file type is correct. If you typed <img src="logo.jpg"> and the file actually is a .gif file, the placeholder icon appears. Finally, confirm that the image file and the XHTML file are in the same folder and storage location; or, if they are in a separate folder, confirm that you have specified the path to the image in the code.

Using the Width and Height Attributes

You use the **width attribute** and **height attribute** to specify the dimensions of an image, usually in pixel values. By including the width and height attributes in your code, the browser reserves the correct space for the image even before it downloads, so your page will download faster. You can determine the width and height of an image by using Microsoft Paint or any other image-editing software. You can also use Windows Explorer to find the dimensions of the image. If you have saved the image to your desktop, you can hover the mouse pointer over the image and read the dimensions of the image from the ScreenTip.

You must use caution when scaling an image because if you enlarge the image too much, it might look grainy and distorted in the browser. Also be aware of the **aspect ratio**, which is the relationship between the width and the height of the image. To **scale** an image means to change its width or height. If you scale the image by reducing the height only or the width only, the image becomes distorted. For example, if the original image had a width of 400 pixels and height of 200 pixels, and you want the image to be half its original size, scale both the width and height of the image to be 200 × 100 pixels. If you omit the width and height attributes, the image generally scales to its original size, which may not be desirable, especially if the image is quite large. You type the code for the width and height attributes as in the following example:

```
<p><img src="nycelogo.gif" alt="Nyce Paints logo" title="Nyce Paints
logo" width="760" height="200" /></p>
```

Don't forget to close the image tag code with the space-forward slash combination and follow the image with an end </p> tag.

You are ready to show Andy how to insert the nycelogo.gif image into the Nyce Paints Web page. The nycelogo.gif image is stored in your Tutorial.01\Tutorial Data Files folder.

To insert the image code:

▶ 1. Switch to your **nycenew.htm** file in your text editor.

▶ 2. Position the insertion point in the <body> section after the comment code for the image, and if necessary, press the **Enter** key to create a blank line after the comment. Type the following image code, as shown in Figure 1-23.

```
<p><img src="nycelogo.gif" alt="Nyce Paints logo" title="Nyce
Paints logo" width="760" height="200" /></p>
```

Figure 1-23 | The image code

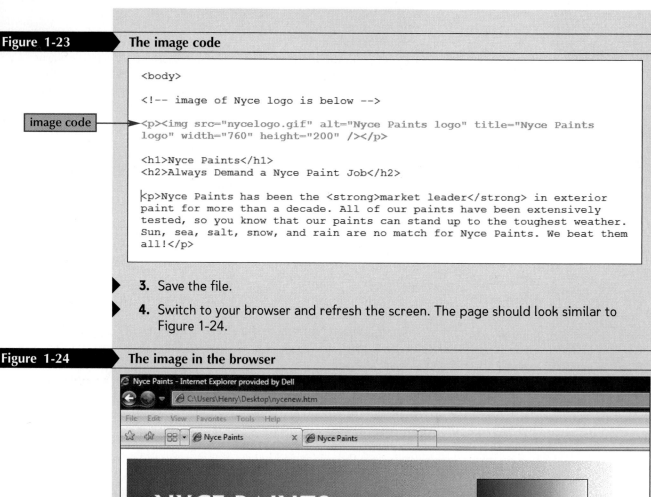

```
<body>

<!-- image of Nyce logo is below -->

<p><img src="nycelogo.gif" alt="Nyce Paints logo" title="Nyce Paints
logo" width="760" height="200" /></p>

<h1>Nyce Paints</h1>
<h2>Always Demand a Nyce Paint Job</h2>

<p>Nyce Paints has been the <strong>market leader</strong> in exterior
paint for more than a decade. All of our paints have been extensively
tested, so you know that our paints can stand up to the toughest weather.
Sun, sea, salt, snow, and rain are no match for Nyce Paints. We beat them
all!</p>
```

image code

3. Save the file.

4. Switch to your browser and refresh the screen. The page should look similar to Figure 1-24.

Figure 1-24 | The image in the browser

Looking over the Web page, Andy decides he'd like to include a list of Nyce Paints' new colors below the footnote. You will show him how to create a list next.

Creating Lists

XHTML has three types of lists. You can create an **unordered list** (a bulleted list), an **ordered list** (a list with numbers or letters), and a **definition list** (a list with a hanging indent format). The XHTML code for creating unordered and ordered lists is nearly identical, but the code for creating definition lists is quite different. Most commonly, you will see unordered and ordered lists on the Web. Definition lists, because they have a special purpose, are less common. Although the lists you will show Andy how to create are quite simple, later tutorials explain how lists can be styled to have a much greater visual appeal. You will start by showing Andy how to create an unordered list.

Creating an Unordered List

Use an unordered list when its items can appear in any order. For example:

- Banana
- Apple
- Orange

erence Window | **Creating an Unordered List**

- To create an unordered list, type the following, where *first item*, *second item*, and so on are the list items:

```
<ul>
    <li>first item</li>
    <li>second item</li>
. . .
</ul>
```

You begin the unordered list with the start <ul> tag. On separate lines, you include each list item, which is preceded by the start <li> tag and followed by the end </li> tag. Although it is not required, it's a good coding practice to indent the code for the list items by two or three spaces. Indenting the list item code has no effect on its appearance in the browser, but indenting in your text editor clearly shows where the list starts and ends and therefore makes the code more readable. The ul element is a block-level element, so the start <ul> and end </ul> tags will create a blank line before and after the list, respectively. In the following example code, an h3 heading precedes the unordered list, just to call attention to the list and identify it.

```
<h3>Our Newest Paint Colors</h3>
<ul>
   <li>Phoenix Red</li>
   <li>Seacrest Blue</li>
   <li>River Green</li>
</ul>
```

You will show Andy how to enter the code for an unordered list below the footnote text in the document. The list will be preceded by an h3 heading that identifies the subject of the list.

Tip

u fail to end the list
the </ul> tag, the
that follows the list in
file will be indented.

To insert the code for the h3 heading and the unordered list:

▶ **1.** Switch to your **nycenew.htm** file in your text editor.

▶ **2.** Position the insertion point after the </p> at the end of the line of footnote text.

▶ **3.** Press the **Enter** key twice to create a blank line after the footnote text.

▶ **4.** Type the following code shown in Figure 1-25.

```
<h3>Our Newest Paint Colors</h3>
<ul>
   <li>Phoenix Red</li>
   <li>Seacrest Blue</li>
   <li>River Green</li>
</ul>
```

▶ **5.** Press the **Enter** key after you type the end </ul> tag.

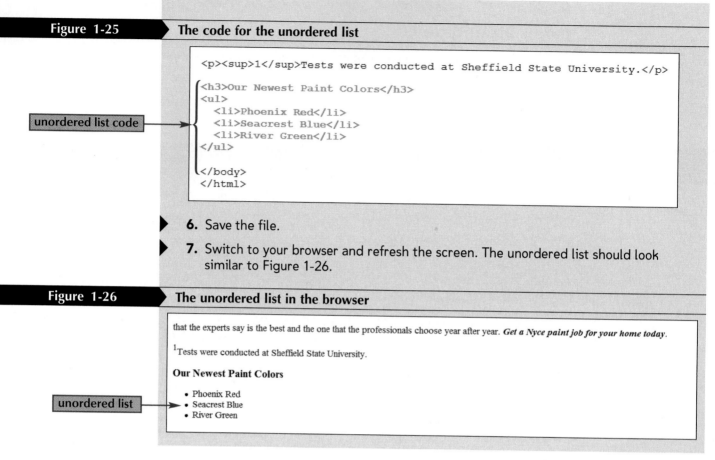

Figure 1-25 The code for the unordered list

```
<p><sup>1</sup>Tests were conducted at Sheffield State University.</p>

<h3>Our Newest Paint Colors</h3>
<ul>
   <li>Phoenix Red</li>
   <li>Seacrest Blue</li>
   <li>River Green</li>
</ul>

</body>
</html>
```

unordered list code

6. Save the file.

7. Switch to your browser and refresh the screen. The unordered list should look similar to Figure 1-26.

Figure 1-26 The unordered list in the browser

that the experts say is the best and the one that the professionals choose year after year. *Get a Nyce paint job for your home today.*

[1]Tests were conducted at Sheffield State University.

Our Newest Paint Colors

- Phoenix Red
- Seacrest Blue
- River Green

unordered list

Next, you will show Andy how to create an ordered list.

Creating an Ordered List

Use an ordered list when the items in a list have a particular order of importance or should appear in sequence. An ordered list would appear like this:

1. Preheat the oven to 450 degrees.
2. Bake for 30 minutes.
3. Remove from oven and let cool.

Reference Window | **Creating an Ordered List**

- To create an ordered list, type the following, where *first item, second item,* and so on are the list items:

```
<ol>
    <li>first item</li>
    <li>second item</li>
. . .
</ol>
```

You begin the ordered list with the start <ol> tag. Like the unordered list, each item in the list is preceded by the start <li> tag and its content is followed by the end </li> tag. At the end of the list, you type the end </ol> tag. Ordered lists are block-level elements, so the start <ol> and end </ol> tags create a blank line before and after the list, respectively. The code for an ordered list would look like the following. Again, an h3 heading precedes the list, just to identify its content:

```
<h3>Our Most Popular Paint Colors</h3>
<ol>
  <li>Boston Beige</li>
  <li>Gloucester Gray</li>
  <li>Winter White</li>
</ol>
```

Ordered lists appear with Arabic numbers (1, 2, 3, etc.) by default, but you can also use Roman numerals, uppercase letters, or lowercase letters. You will learn how to change the list style type in a later tutorial.

Andy wants to list the most popular colors that Nyce Paints offers. You'll show him how to add an ordered list to the Nyce Paints document. First, you'll insert an h3 heading to introduce the list, and then you'll show him how to enter the code for the ordered list.

To insert the code for the h3 heading and the ordered list:

1. Switch back to your **nycenew.htm** file in your text editor.

2. If necessary, position the insertion point below the end </ul> tag for the unordered list.

3. Type the following code, as shown in Figure 1-27.

```
<h3>Our Most Popular Paint Colors</h3>
<ol>
  <li>Boston Beige</li>
  <li>Gloucester Green</li>
  <li>Winter White</li>
</ol>
```

4. Press the **Enter** key after you type the end </ol> tag.

Figure 1-27 **The code for the ordered list**

```
<h3>Our Newest Paint Colors</h3>
<ul>
  <li>Phoenix Red</li>
  <li>Seacrest Blue</li>
  <li>River Green</li>
</ul>

<h3>Our Most Popular Paint Colors</h3>
<ol>
  <li>Boston Beige</li>
  <li>Gloucester Green</li>
  <li>Winter White</li>
</ol>

</body>
</html>
```

ordered list code

5. Save the file.

6. Switch to your browser and refresh the screen. Your document should look similar to Figure 1-28.

Figure 1-28 — The ordered list in the browser

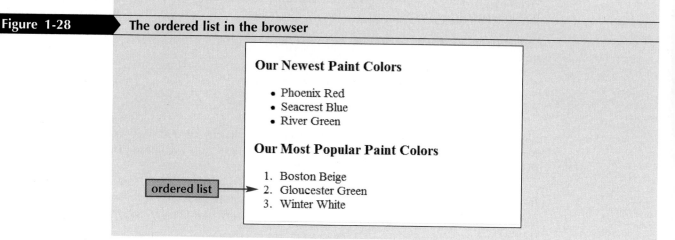

Our Newest Paint Colors

- Phoenix Red
- Seacrest Blue
- River Green

Our Most Popular Paint Colors

ordered list →

1. Boston Beige
2. Gloucester Green
3. Winter White

XHTML has one other type of list that you'd like Andy to know about. A definition list is used to create a hanging indent.

Creating a Definition List

A third type of XHTML list is the definition list, which is a way to create a list formatted as a hanging indent. Definition lists are commonly used to create a **chronology**, which is a list of events in time order, or a **glossary**, an alphabetic list of terms and their definitions. Definition lists can also be used to create a Works Cited page that lists author names and citations in alphabetic order, and to create a "question and answer" layout in which the question is entered on one line and the answer is entered on the next line. Definition lists can also be used to format scripts for plays and other theatrical, television, or movie productions. The definition list indicates the shift between one actor's lines and another's.

Reference Window | **Creating a Definition List**

- To create a definition list, type the following code, where *term1, term2*, and so on are the defined terms and *description1, description2*, and so on are the definition data:
  ```
  <dl>
      <dt>term1</dt>
      <dd>description1</dd>
      <dt>term2</dt>
      <dd>description2</dd>
      . . .
  </dl>
  ```
- Optionally, follow the start <dt> tag with a <strong> tag and precede the end </dt> tag with an end </strong> tag to make the defined term appear in bold as follows:
  ```
  <dt><strong>term1</strong></dt>
  ```

An example of a definition list (in this instance, some glossary entries) follows:

Los Angeles Dodgers

Moved from Brooklyn in 1958. Celebrated their 50th anniversary year several years ago by winning the National League Western Division title.

New York Yankees

The storied franchise recently replaced their legendary stadium, often called "The house that Ruth built," with a new stadium that cost more than $1.5 billion to construct.

In the XHTML code, a definition list begins with the start <dl> tag, which is followed by the text for the **defined term**, the text that will be flush with the left margin. It's a good idea to make the defined term bold text as well, so that it stands out. The defined term is preceded by a start <dt> tag and followed by an end </dt> tag. The definition data comes next. The **definition data**, the text that will be indented from the left margin, is preceded by a start <dd> tag and followed by an end </dd> tag. An end </dl> tag comes last. Similar to other lists, the definition list element is a block-level element, so entering the start <dl> and end </dl> tags will generate a blank line before and after the definition list. The code for the preceding definition list would look like this:

```
<dl>
<dt><strong>Los Angeles Dodgers</strong></dt>
<dd>Moved from Brooklyn in 1958. Celebrated their 50th anniversary
year several years ago by winning the National League Western
Division title.</dd>
</dl>
```

Next, you'll show Andy how to add abbreviations to the Nyce Paints Web site so customers can understand industry-specific jargon.

Using the Abbreviation Element

An **acronym** is a group of letters that stands for several words, such as "USA" for "United States of America." An **abbreviation** is a shortened form of a noun. The <acronym> and <abbr> tags produce an explanatory ScreenTip when the user hovers the mouse pointer over a word that has one of these sets of tags. The **abbreviation element** has replaced the deprecated acronym element, and is now used for both acronyms and abbreviations.

The abbreviation element displays an abbreviation in the Firefox browser with a dotted underline (a **tracer**), which helps draw attention to the abbreviation. Firefox displays ScreenTips as black text on a white background, and with a shadow effect.

erence Window | **Using the Abbr Element**

- To display a ScreenTip that defines either an acronym or an abbreviation, use the <abbr> tag and the title attribute, as follows:

<abbr title="*complete word or phrase*">*abbreviation*</abbr>

Tip

net Explorer 6.0 and versions do not support the <abbr> tag, but do support the onym> tag.

You enter the text for the <abbr> tag ScreenTip by using the title attribute. All values must be enclosed in quotation marks. The following example shows the code for the acronym "ASAP" and its resulting ScreenTip. Note in the following code that there is no space before or after the equals sign.

```
<p>Call us now at 613 420-2505 to get our <em><abbr title="As Soon As
Possible">ASAP</abbr></em>service.</p>
```

Andy would like to add a sentence at the end of the document about his special ASAP service. This seems a good spot to show him how to use the abbr element.

To enter the code for the abbr element:

1. Switch back to the **nycenew.htm** file in your text editor.

2. Click below the end </ol> tag. Press the **Enter** key.

3. Type the following code, as shown in Figure 1-29.

```
<p>Call us now at 613 420-2505 to get our <em><abbr title="As
Soon As Possible">ASAP</abbr></em> service.</p>
```

Figure 1-29 The abbreviation code

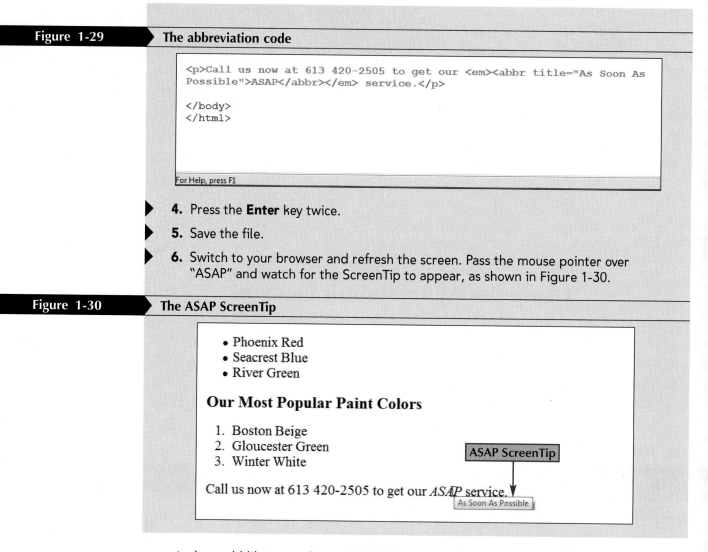

```
<p>Call us now at 613 420-2505 to get our <em><abbr title="As Soon As
Possible">ASAP</abbr></em> service.</p>

</body>
</html>
```

For Help, press F1

▶ **4.** Press the **Enter** key twice.

▶ **5.** Save the file.

▶ **6.** Switch to your browser and refresh the screen. Pass the mouse pointer over "ASAP" and watch for the ScreenTip to appear, as shown in Figure 1-30.

Figure 1-30 The ASAP ScreenTip

- Phoenix Red
- Seacrest Blue
- River Green

Our Most Popular Paint Colors

1. Boston Beige
2. Gloucester Green
3. Winter White

Call us now at 613 420-2505 to get our *ASAP* service.

ASAP ScreenTip

As Soon As Possible

Andy would like to put his mailing address at the bottom of the document, so you will help him with that task next.

Using the Break Element

The break element is used to end a line short of the right margin. It's equivalent to pressing the Enter key in a word processor once to end a line. For example, if you were typing the inside address in a letter, you would type one line of the address, press the Enter key, type the next line of the address, press the Enter key, and so forth. The break element is an empty element; it doesn't have any content. In your code, the break tag ends with the combination of a space and a forward slash:

```
<br />
```

Enter the code for the <br /> tag at the beginning of a line, rather than at the end. This makes it easier to find <br /> tags. The break element is an inline element, so always include the break element inside block-level element tags, such as the <p> tags. Use the break tag when you want to end a line before the right margin without wrapping text:

```
<p>Mr. Andy Nyce
<br />4708 N. Washington Avenue
<br />Sheffield Ridge, MA 61361</p>
```

Andy likes to have people write to him at company headquarters in Sheffield Ridge, Massachusetts and comment about his products. You will show Andy how to use the break element to create the lines for the mailing address.

To enter the mailing address:

▶ **1.** Switch back to the **nycenew.htm** file in your text editor.

▶ **2.** Type the following code, as shown in Figure 1-31.

```
<p>Mr. Andy Nyce
<br />4708 N. Washington Avenue
<br />Sheffield Ridge, MA 61361</p>
```

Figure 1-31 ▶ The code for the mailing address

```
<p>Call us now at 613 420-2505 to get our <em><abbr title="As Soon as
Possible">ASAP</abbr></em> service.</p>

<p>Mr. Andy Nyce
<br />4708 N. Washington Avenue
<br />Sheffield Ridge, MA 61361</p>

</body>
</html>
```

▶ **3.** Save the file.

▶ **4.** Switch to your browser and refresh the file to view the address. See Figure 1-32.

Figure 1-32 ▶ The mailing address in the browser

> **Our Most Popular Paint Colors**
>
> 1. Boston Beige
> 2. Gloucester Green
> 3. Winter White
>
> Call us now at 613 420-2505 to get our *ASAP* service.
>
> Mr. Andy Nyce
> 4708 N. Washington Avenue
> Sheffield Ridge, MA 61361

Recall that some of the metadata you include in the head section of an XHTML document is used by search engines to locate and list your document. Next, you'll show Andy how to help search engines include your Web page in their search results.

Entering Code for Metadata

One of the most useful aspects of the Web is the ability to quickly find Web pages on any topic. By entering one or more keywords in a search box, you can find Web pages that match those keywords. **Keywords** are words that best identify the content of a site. The **meta element** is used to contain metadata. When you view the source code for an XHTML page, you often see one or more <meta> tags within the <head> tags. One use of <meta> tags is to help **search engines**, such as Google, find your Web site based on the keywords you have entered in the head area on the home page. The <meta> element is an empty element, so it needs to end with the space-forward slash combination.

You can help search engines find your site by listing an effective set of keywords for your Web pages. Also include common misspellings and a variety of capitalization options to anticipate how users might enter the keywords. You can list the keywords on one line or several lines within the <meta> tags, as shown in the following example:

```
<meta name="keywords" content="Nyce, nice, paint, interior, exterior" />
```

You might see other values for the name attribute, including generator, which identifies the program used to generate the XHTML code, and author, which identifies the author of the Web page. The description and its content value appear when a browser generates the list of hits for a particular search topic. An example of the description would look like this:

```
<meta name="description" content="This is the home page for Nyce
Paints, maker of the finest exterior paints in New England." />
```

You will show Andy how to enter some metadata below the metadata tag in the head section of the document.

To insert the metadata into the head section:

▶ 1. Switch to your **nycenew.htm** file in your text editor.

▶ 2. Position the insertion point before the start <title> tag.

▶ 3. Press the **Enter** key once, and then press the **Up arrow** key once.

▶ 4. Type the following code, as shown in Figure 1-33.

```
<meta name="description" content="This is the home page for Nyce
Paints, maker of the finest exterior paints in New England." />
<meta name="keywords" content="Nyce, nice, paint, interior,
exterior" />
```

▶ 5. Press the **Enter** key once.

Figure 1-33 | The metadata code

```
<!DOCTYPE html PUBLIC "-//W3C//DTD XHTML 1.0 Strict//EN"
    "http://www.w3.org/TR/xhtml1/DTD/xhtml1-strict.dtd">
<html xmlns="http://www.w3.org/1999/xhtml" lang="en" xml:lang="en">
<head>
<meta http-equiv="Content-Type" content="text/html; charset=ISO-8859-1" />
<meta name="description" content="This is the home page for Nyce Paints,
maker of the finest exterior paints in New England." />
<meta name="keywords" content="Nyce, nice, paint, interior, exterior" />

<title>Nyce Paints</title>

<!-- Tutorial 1
     Author: Your First and Last Name
     Date: Today's Date
-->
```

▶ **6.** Save the file.

InSight | **Tips for Working With XHTML Documents**

Just as you should know what to code in your XHTML documents, you should know what to avoid when entering the code. The following list will help you avoid making some common errors.

- Save your file in your text editor and preview the file in the browser frequently. Don't wait until you've entered the code for an entire Web page before you view it in the browser. If you save and preview often, you will catch errors when they occur, and you won't have to debug an entire page of code at a time.
- Proofread your code and content carefully. Check for typographical errors and misspellings. A Web page should be error free.
- Check for syntax errors. Are any angle brackets missing? Are any quotation marks missing? Are any end tags missing?
- If your document does not appear in the browser at all, check for the absence of important end tags such as </title> and </head>. Also check those end tags for syntax and typographical errors, such as <title /> or </hhead>.
- If part of your document does not appear in the browser, you might be missing the end comment code (- ->) at the point where the text or images stop appearing.
- If a portion of text looks too large, check to see whether you entered the code for the applicable end heading tag or if you entered the code incorrectly.
- If your Web page does not appear as you intended, convert a line of code in the document to a comment (a technique known as "commenting out" the code). Then check to see the effect of hiding that code in the document when viewed in the browser. Insert a begin comment code before the code you are trying to debug and insert an end comment code after the code. Commenting out code is a good way to isolate an area that might contain errors.

With the work now completed on the Nyce Paints file, you are ready to show Andy how to ensure that the XHTML code in the file is correct. You will show him how to use a free XHTML validation service available from the World Wide Web Consortium.

Validating the Completed File

Now that the document is complete, you are ready to **validate** the file, which is the process of checking the file for syntax errors. Validating the file does not check for spelling, typographical, or grammar errors; it checks only to see if the code complies with the XHTML standard. Validating a file is optional, but because this is Andy's first attempt at creating a Web page, you want to show him how to check his work when you are no longer there to assist him.

Reference Window | **Validating a File for XHTML**

To validate a file to see if the XHTML code meets standard:

- Open your browser and navigate to *http://validator.w3.org*.
- If necessary, click the Validate by File Upload tab.
- Click the Browse button. Navigate to the storage location of the file to be validated.
- Double-click the filename to enter it into the File text box.
- Click the Check button.

The W3C maintains a site that has a free XHTML validator service; you can find it at *http://validator.w3.org*. In a later tutorial, you will work with a CSS validation service, which is located at a different W3C Web site.

After you go to the W3C XHTML validation page, you will see two methods for validating a document that has not been posted to a Web server: Validate by File Upload and Validate by Direct Input. When you choose Validate by File Upload, you navigate to the storage location of the file you want to validate, and then you click the Check button. If you choose Validate by Direct Input, you have to copy and paste (or type) the code into the text box on the validation page, and then click the Check button. The Validate by Direct Input method, however, assumes a character encoding of UTF-8. The nycenew document you helped Andy create has a character encoding of ISO-8859-1. If you were to validate the nycenew document using the direct input method, the validation software would generate at least one error regarding UTF-8 character encoding. You decide to show Andy how to validate the nycenew.htm file by using the Validate by File Upload method.

To validate the nycenew file:

► **1.** Open your browser and navigate to ***http://validator.w3.org***.

The W3C Markup Validation Service site opens, as shown in Figure 1-34.

Figure 1-34 **The W3C Markup Validation Service Web site**

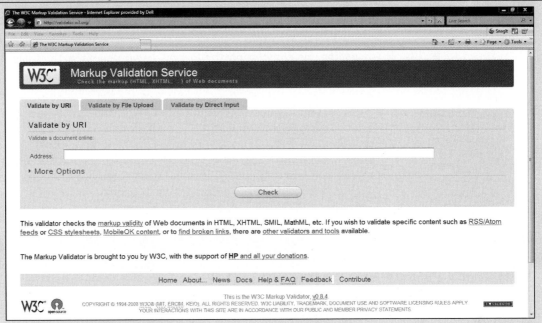

▶ **2.** If necessary, click the Validate by File Upload tab.

▶ **3.** Click the **Browse** button.

▶ **4.** Navigate to the storage location of your nycenew.htm file.

▶ **5.** Double-click the **nycenew.htm** filename to insert it in the File text box.

▶ **6.** Click the **Check** button. The document is checked as valid, as shown in Figure 1-35.

Figure 1-35 **The result of the validation**

Trouble? If the document does not pass validation, note the errors and debug your document accordingly.

▶ **7.** Submit the results of the **nycenew.htm** file to your instructor, either in printed or electronic form, as requested.

▶ **8.** If you will not be completing the Review Assignments or the Case Problems, close your text editor and your browser.

In this session, you learned how to insert an image into a file. You also learned about the importance of always providing alternate text for an image. You learned how to create both an unordered list and an ordered list. You used the abbreviation element to produce a ScreenTip. You also learned how to use the break element to end a line short of the right margin, how to add metadata to the head section so that browsers can locate your file on the Web, and how to validate a Web page to ensure that your code was entered according to the XHTML standard.

Review | Session 1.3 Quick Check

1. What attribute must always be used with the image tag?
2. What does it mean to scale an image?
3. What attributes are used to scale an image?
4. What is the aspect ratio?
5. What are the two most common types of lists?
6. How can you tell if your XHTML code is correct?

Review | Tutorial Summary

In this tutorial, you learned how the Internet and the Web work. You were introduced to the concepts of elements and tags. You learned about the basic XHTML elements required for every Web page. You also learned about elements that are used to format the appearance of text in Web pages. You learned about attributes that can further customize an element, how to include images on Web pages, and how to create unordered and ordered lists. You entered metadata into your XHTML documents and learned how to check the accuracy of the XHTML code by validating the document.

Key Terms

abbreviation
abbreviation element
acronym
aspect ratio
attribute
block-level element
body element
break element
browser
character entities
character set
chronology
comments
compressed
contemporary browsers
cross-browser incompatibility
CSS
defined term
definition data
definition list
deprecated
Document Type Declaration
Document Type Definition
document window
element
em element
empty element
Extensible Hypertext Markup
    Language
extensions
eye line

file servers
glossary
Graphics Interchange File
head section
heading elements
height attribute
HTML
html element
hypertext
Hypertext Markup Language
image element
inline element
Internet
Joint Photographic Experts
    Group
keywords
markup
meta element
metadata
mock-up
named character reference
nested element
not-supported elements
numeric character reference
ordered list
placeholder icon
Portable Network Graphics
quirks mode
recommendation
renders
root element

scale
screen reader
ScreenTip
search engines
site footer
special character
standards mode
strong element
sub element
sup element
support
syntax
tag
template file
tracer
unordered list
validate
value
W3C
Web page accessibility
Web page designer
Web page developer
Web page designer
white space
width attribute
World Wide Web
World Wide Web Consortium
WWW
XHTML

| Practice | **Review Assignments** |

Take time to practice the skills you learned in the tutorial using the same case scenario.

Data File needed for the Review Assignments: stores.htm

Andy has asked you to revise a different Web page at the Nyce Paints site. He would like to add some ordered lists that give directions to some of the new Nyce Paints stores. A preview of the Web page appears in Figure 1-36.

Figure 1-36

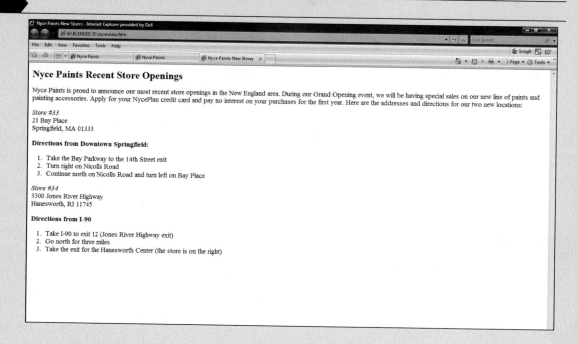

Complete the following:

1. Use your text editor to open the file named **stores.htm**, which is provided in your Data Files in the Tutorial.01\Review folder.
2. Save the file as **storesnew.htm** in the same folder.
3. Between the <title> tags, type **Nyce Paints New Stores**.
4. In the <head> section below the page title, create a comment with the following information:
   Your First and Last Name
   Tutorial 1, Review Assignment
   Today's Date
5. Format the words "Nyce Paints Recent Store Openings" as an h2 heading.
6. Below the h2 heading, enter tags before and after the text to format that text as a paragraph.
7. Format "Store #33" to appear as italic text.
8. Format the two lines below "Store #33" so that they appear on separate lines (use the break tag to create this formatting).
9. Format "Directions from Downtown Springfield" to appear as an h4 heading.
10. Format "Store #34" to appear as italic text.
11. Format the two lines below "Store #34" so that they appear on separate lines (use the break tag to create this formatting).
12. Format "Directions from I-90" to appear as an h4 heading.
13. Format the three lines of directions to Store #33 as an ordered list.

14. Format the three lines of directions to Store #34 as an ordered list.

15. Save your **storesnew.htm** file, and then open the file in your browser.

16. Submit the results of the preceding steps to your instructor, either in printed or electronic form, as requested.

> **Trouble?** If the file does not appear correctly in your browser, use the taskbar to switch back to your text editor. Make your corrections as needed and save the file. Switch to your browser, refresh the screen, and observe the result.

17. If you are not completing the next assignment, close your text editor and your browser.

Apply	**Case Problem 1**

the skills you
ed in the tutorial
date a basic Web
for a supermar-
hain.

Data File needed for this Case Problem: shop.htm

Shopping Good Supermarkets   The Shopping Good supermarket chain operates primarily in the Rocky Mountain regions of Wyoming and Idaho. Shopping Good favors regional suppliers as a way to keep prices low and remain competitive with other supermarkets in the region. Marketing director Janet Ruiz wants your help in creating a Web page that lists the top sale items. A preview of the Web page appears in Figure 1-37.

Figure 1-37

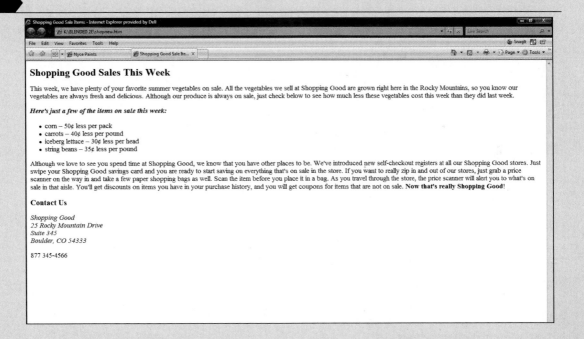

Complete the following:

1. Use your text editor to open the file named **shop.htm**, which is provided in your Data Files in the Tutorial.01\Case1 folder.

2. Save the file as **shopnew.htm** in the same folder.

3. Within the <title> tags, type **Shopping Good Sale Items**.

4. Within the <head> section, enter a comment with the following information:

   Your First and Last Name

   Tutorial 1, Case Problem 1

   Today's Date

5. In the <body> section, format "Shopping Good Sales This Week" as an h2 heading.

6. Format "Here's just a few of the items on sale this week" as text that appears as both bold and italic.

7. Format the next four lines below the bold and italic text as an unordered list.

8. After each of the vegetable names in the unordered list, insert the code for an en dash character (use a named character reference.)

9. In each of the lines in the unordered list, delete the word "cents" and insert the code for the cent special character (use a named character reference).

10. In the last paragraph, format the words "Now that's really Shopping Good" to appear in bold.

11. Format the words "Contact Us" as an h3 heading.

12. Format the four lines of text in the Shopping Good address to appear in italics.

13. Save the **shopnew.htm** file, and then open the file in your browser.

   Trouble? If the file does not appear correctly in your browser, use the taskbar to switch back to your text editor. Make your corrections as needed and save the file. Switch to your browser, refresh the screen, and observe the result.

14. Submit the results of the preceding steps to your instructor, either in printed or electronic form, as requested.

15. If you are not completing the next assignment, close your text editor and your browser.

Apply | Case Problem 2

Use the skills you learned in the tutorial to create a Web page for a supplier of masonry materials.

Data Files needed for this Case Problem: brick.htm and bricklogo.gif

Bent Brick and Stone Bent Brick and Stone has sold masonry supplies in the greater Atlanta area for more than 75 years. The company's name comes from its specialty of producing rounded brick in a variety of colors that are not extensively sold in the southern United States. Until now, the store has relied on in-person business as its only source of revenue. Ben Provo, the owner of Bent Brick and Stone, has asked you to develop a Web site that he hopes will attract more customers. A preview of the Web page appears in Figure 1-38.

Figure 1-38

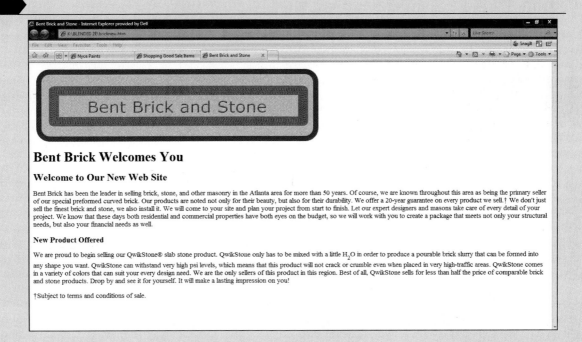

Complete the following:

1. Use your text editor to open the file named **brick.htm**, which is provided in your Data Files in the Tutorial.01\Case2 folder.

2. Save the file as **bricknew.htm** in the same folder.

3. Within the title tags, enter **Bent Brick and Stone** as the title.

4. Within the <head> section, enter a comment with the following information:
   Your First and Last Name
   Tutorial 1, Case Problem 2
   Today's Date

5. Just below the comment in the <body> section and between the tags, enter the code for the bricklogo.gif image. Use "Bent Brick and Stone logo" as the alternate text. The image has a width of 780 pixels and a height of 200 pixels.

6. Format "Bent Brick Welcomes You" to appear as an h1 heading.

7. Format "Welcome to Our New Web Site" to appear as an h2 heading.

8. Format "New Product Offered" to appear as an h3 heading.

⊕ **EXPLORE**   9. At the end of the fourth sentence of the first paragraph, enter the code for a single dagger symbol after the word "sell" (use a numeric character reference).

10. In the first sentence of the second paragraph, insert the registered trademark symbol after the word "QwikStone." Use a named character reference.

⊕ **EXPLORE**   11. In the second sentence of the second paragraph, insert the code to create a subscript for the number 2 in the chemical formula H_2O.

⊕ **EXPLORE**   12. In the third sentence of the second paragraph, insert the code for a ScreenTip to appear for an abbreviation for "psi," which is short for "pounds per square inch."

13. Following the second paragraph, enter the code for a single dagger character and type **Subject to terms and conditions of sale** as the text of the footnote. Enter a start <p> tag before the dagger character. Enter an end </p> tag after the footnote text.

14. Save your **bricknew.htm** file, and then open the file in the browser.

15. Submit the results of the preceding steps to your instructor, either in printed or electronic form, as requested.

16. If you are not completing the next assignment, close your text editor and your browser.

| Challenge | **Case Problem 3** |

Use what you've learned, and expand your skills, to create a Web page for a bridal shop.

Data Files needed for this Case Problem: beth.htm and bethlogo.gif

Beth's Budget Bridal Beth's Budget Bridal is a small chain of bridal shops on Long Island, New York. Beth's has achieved its success by knowing what customers want during tough economic times. Brides want a great gown at a great price. Over the last year, Beth's Budget Bridal has also begun offering wedding planning services; again, their idea is that a wedding should be a happy event that does not place a steep financial burden on the bride and groom. Beth Morrison, the owner of the chain, has asked for your assistance in creating a Web site for her stores. A preview of the Web page appears in Figure 1-39.

Figure 1-39

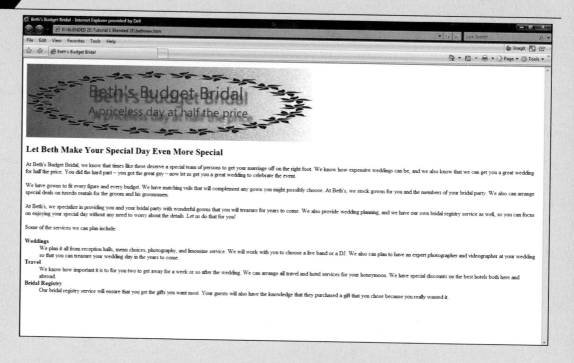

Complete the following:

1. Use your text editor to open the file named **beth.htm**, which is provided in your Data Files in the Tutorial.01\Case3 folder.

2. Save the file as **bethnew.htm** in the same folder.

3. Within the title tags, enter **Beth's Budget Bridal** as the title.

4. Within the <head> section, enter a comment with the following information:
   Your First and Last Name
   Tutorial 1, Case Problem 3
   Today's Date

5. Just below the comment in the <body> section and between the tags, enter the code for the bethlogo.gif image. Use "image of Beth's Budget Bridal logo" as the alternate text. The image has a width of 780 pixels and a height of 200 pixels.

⊕ EXPLORE

6. In the <head> section, insert a <meta> tag that provides the following description of the Web site: Beth's Budget Bridal is the only stop you have to make on the way to the altar.

⊕ EXPLORE

7. Create a definition list using "Weddings," "Travel," and "Bridal Registry" as defined terms. Have each of the defined terms appear in bold. Format the text below each of the defined terms as definition data.

8. Save your **bethnew.htm** file, and then open the file in the browser. View the result.

⊕ EXPLORE

9. In your browser, navigate to the *http://validator.w3.org* site. Click the Validate by File Upload tab. Click the Browse button, navigate to the storage location of your bethnew.htm file, and then double-click the filename. Click the Check button and then observe the result of the validation.

10. Submit the results of the preceding steps to your instructor, either in printed or electronic form, as requested.

11. If you are not completing the next assignment, close your text editor and your browser.

| Research | **Case Problem 4** |

with the skills e learned and he Internet to rch global ing and create formational page.

Data Files needed for this Case Problem: warming.htm and warminglogo.gif

Hemispheric Research   Tony Tamblino founded Hemispheric Research in Jacksonville, Florida, to study global warming and its effects on weather, sea levels, and species habitat. He recently hired you to assist him in his research and to produce Web pages that educate and inform interested users. Use the Web or other resources to research the topic of global warming and create an informational Web page for Hemispheric Research. In this case problem, you will create a new file.

Complete the following:

1. Use your favorite search engine to find and read at least three Web sites or online articles about global warming.

2. Prepare for creating the Hemispheric Research Web page by developing or finding the following material:

   a. At least four paragraphs about global warming and its effects on the Earth.

   b. Headings that will precede each paragraph.

   c. A quote from your research that you can use on the Web page and cite using a footnote reference.

   d. A list of the four leading factors contributing to global warming.

3. Open your browser and your text editor.

4. In your text editor, open the **warming.htm** file.

5. Within the <title></title> tags, give your page a descriptive page title.

6. Within the <head> section, enter a comment with the following information:

   Your First and Last Name

   Tutorial 1, Case Problem 4

   Today's Date

7. In the <body> section, include examples (in any order) of the following:
   - A comment
   - Bold text
   - Italic text
   - The use of an image (and its attributes and values)
   - A superscript or a subscript
   - An ordered or unordered list
   - Four or more paragraphs of text
   - An abbreviation or an acronym (use the <abbr> tag and create a ScreenTip)
   - At least two examples of headings
   - The break tag
   - A special character (use a numeric character reference)
   - The *correct* use of the blockquote element
8. Save your file as **warmingnew.htm** in the Tutorial.01\Case4 folder.
9. Open warmingnew.htm in your browser, review the Web page, and make any changes as necessary.
10. If no further changes to your file are necessary, close warmingnew.htm in your text editor.
11. In your browser, navigate to *http://validator.w3.org.*
12. Validate the warmingnew.htm document by using the Validate by File Upload method.
13. Submit the results of the preceding steps to your instructor, either in printed or electronic form, as requested.
14. Close your text editor and your browser.

| Review | **Quick Check Answers** |

Session 1.1

1. html
2. In the title bar at the top of the screen
3. Nothing would appear on the Web page.
4. <body> </body>
5. </body> </html>
6. <! - - your name - - >

Session 1.2

1. <h1></h1>
2. They add a blank line above and below the heading, and make text bold.
3. <strong></strong>
4. <em></em>
5. It should no longer be used.
6. Generally, a character that cannot be typed from the keyboard

Session 1.3

1. The src attribute
2. To specify the width and height of an image
3. Height and width
4. The ratio of the width to the height
5. Ordered and unordered
6. Have the document validated

Ending Data Files

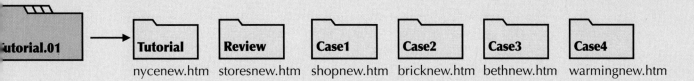

Tutorial.01

Tutorial — nycenew.htm

Review — storesnew.htm

Case1 — shopnew.htm

Case2 — bricknew.htm

Case3 — bethnew.htm

Case4 — warmingnew.htm

Creating Hyperlinks

Using Links to Navigate Documents on the Web

Case | Winter Water

Winter Water is one of the nation's oldest bottlers of natural spring water. The company was founded by Lionel Wynter in East Rock, Montana, more than a century ago. Wynter Water, as the brand was known then, was originally sold as a health tonic throughout Montana. In the late 1980s, Wynter Water officially changed its name to Winter Water and began marketing its products throughout the United States. Two years later, Winter Water introduced its first flavored water. Winter Water is preparing to launch the marketing of two new flavors: allspice and vanilla. Travis Green, who works in the sales and marketing department, has asked for your help in launching a new home page for the Winter Water Web site that reflects the new flavors.

Starting Data Files

Tutorial.02 →

Tutorial
allspice.htm
allspice.jpg
allspice_small.jpg
arrow.gif
cinnamon.gif
cinnamon.htm
cinnamon.jpg
cinnamonlogo.gif
nutmeg.htm
nutmeg.jpg
spices.gif
vanilla.htm
vanilla.jpg
winter.htm
winterlogo.gif

Review
cinnamon.htm
cinnamon.jpg
cinnamonlogo.gif
contest.pdf

Case1
barker.htm
barkerlogo.gif
leftarrow.gif
week.htm
week.jpg
week_small.jpg

Case2
club.htm
clublogo.gif

Case3
clothing.htm
clothinglogo.gif
home.gif
piechart.gif
regions.htm

Case4
college.htm

Understanding Communications Technology

The popularity that the World Wide Web enjoys today is due largely to its ability to let you locate and view information in a nonlinear manner—you do not have to read one page after another in a specific order. Many people use the terms "Internet" and "World Wide Web" interchangeably, but they are not the same. Viewing documents on the World Wide Web is just one of several services provided by the Internet. Other Internet services include file transfer and sending electronic mail.

To make information accessible in a nonlinear manner, Web pages use links. A **link** is text or graphics that, when clicked, displays another place on the same Web page (an internal link), another Web page in the same site, or another Web site (an external link). By convention, text links are generally blue and underlined. With links, visitors can choose the topics that interest them and can view those topics in any order. Before you show Travis how to create links, you want to explain some of the underlying technologies that make links work.

Using Protocols

A **protocol** is a standard for sending and receiving data over phone lines, cable, or by satellite. These standards are important. For example, **proprietary code** functions on only one hardware or software platform. If every company that made transmission media had its own proprietary standard for communicating data, it would be much more difficult to send and receive data, because one company's standards would probably be incompatible with another company's. Using a protocol sets one standard, and everyone benefits by following the rules for that standard.

The protocol used to access the Web is **Hypertext Transfer Protocol**, or **HTTP**. HTTP establishes standards for communications between file servers—the computers that contain or direct information—and **client computers** (clients), which include desktop computers, laptop computers, and netbook computers. Another set of protocols, **Transmission Control Protocol/Internet Protocol** or **TCP/IP**, is used to send small bursts of information called **packets** across communication lines. These two protocols work in tandem. TCP is responsible for ensuring that data is correctly delivered from the client computer to the server. IP moves packets of information from one computer to another.

Using Web Site Addresses

Internet addresses, or IP addresses, are composed of a series of four numbers (from 0 to 255) separated by periods, such as 12.34.222.111. Obviously, it is not easy to remember Web sites based on IP addresses. To make the Web more user friendly, the domain name system was introduced. The **domain name system** refers to Web sites by file server names rather than IP addresses. Initially, only one company was granted permission to create and register domain names. Now, many companies have been granted this right. The domain name is generally a registered trademark or corporate name, such as IBM or CNN. The domain name is followed by a **suffix**, a two- to four-letter abbreviation that groups domain names based on their category, such as .com, .net, .org, .edu, .mil, and .info. A suffix is also called a **top-level domain name**.

A **URL** is the **Uniform Resource Locator**, which is the complete address of the Web site and page you are viewing, such as *http://www.generousdonations.org/charities/index.htm*. When entering a URL in a browser's address bar in Internet Explorer or location bar in Mozilla Firefox, you type forward slashes (/), not backslashes. (The forward slash shares a key with the question mark on most keyboards.) Most Web browsers assume the use of "http" in the URL, so usually you don't have to type it in the address bar or location bar.

Tip

For Web sites that originate in foreign countries, the domain name may include a two-letter country code, such as *uk*, which stands for United Kingdom.

InSight | **Understanding the Parts of a URL**

A URL for a Web page has the following structure:

protocol://service.domainname.suffix/path/filename

For example, the URL *http://www.generousdonations.org/charities/index.htm* has the following components:

- *http* is the protocol
- *www* is the service
- *generousdonations* is the domain name—the name of the domain where the Web server resides
- *.org* is the suffix (the top-level domain name)
- *charities* is the path (a file folder or folders on the server)
- *index.htm* is the name of the Web page you are viewing (the home page for a Web site typically is named index.htm or default.htm)

To transfer a file to or from a server, you can use **FTP** (**File Transfer Protocol**). Depending on the FTP software you use, the URL for an FTP site would contain only the protocol, the domain name, and the suffix, as in *ftp.generousdonations.org*. More commonly, the URL to an FTP site appears with "ftp" followed by a colon, two slashes, and then the domain name, as in *ftp://generousdonations.org*.

You can also use a URL to connect to an e-mail client, such as Microsoft Outlook. Such a URL uses the mailto protocol and the e-mail address, as in *mailto:johndoe@generousdonations.org*.

Creating Links

Allowing readers to quickly find topics of interest is critical to the success of any Web site. Your goal as a Web page author is to get the reader to those places, pages, and sites of interest efficiently. To do this, you need to know how to create links to one of the following four destinations:

- A named section on the same page
- Another page within the same Web site
- A named section on another page within the same Web site
- Another Web site

   To visit each of these destinations, users click a link, which is most often text (called the **link text**), but it can also be an image. You can also use an **image map**, a single image that is divided into clickable areas that each link to a different destination. Links are also used to send e-mail and to access other resources, such as a Microsoft Word or Adobe PDF file stored on a file server.

   You have already created a template file named winter.htm for Travis to work with, so you will begin by showing him how to open the file in his text editor and save the file with a new filename.

Tip

mage for an image
does not have to be a
; it can be any image.

To open the winter.htm file and save it with a new filename:

▶ **1.** In your text editor, open the **winter.htm** file, which is located in the Tutorial.02\ Tutorial folder in your Data Files. Save the file as **winternew.htm** in the same folder.

▶ **2.** Open **winternew.htm** in your browser. Figure 2-1 shows the current appearance of the winternew.htm file.

Figure 2-1 | The original winternew.htm file in the browser

Winter Water

Enjoy the Taste of Winter Water All Year Long

- Cinnamon
- Nutmeg
- Allspice
- Vanilla

What is Winter Water?

For those of you who enjoy the fresh, clean taste of spring water, welcome to the delights of *Winter Water*, a drink you can enjoy throughout the year. *Winter Water* combines natural spring water with a hint of cinnamon, nutmeg, and other flavorful spices. Of course, you can get Winter Water as an unflavored, natural beverage as well. Our spices are known for their freshness.

Either way, you are assured of enjoying one of the most delicious, healthful, and satisfying beverages on the market today. We have more than a hundred years' experience in bottling the purest waters from our natural spring wells, lakes, and streams. You can be sure that you have spent your money on a product you will enjoy throughout the year.

Discover Our Wonderful Flavors

Winter Water was first made available to the residents of our home state of Montana. Everyone from coast to coast now can enjoy the taste of *Winter Water*. All year 'round, we bottle several distinct blends of *Winter Water* that we are sure you will want to buy. Our **Notable Nutmeg** has just the right amount of nutmeg to please the palette. Our **Cinnamon Sensation** blends imported cinnamon into a flavorful beverage that is sure to refresh any day of the year.

We are proud to introduce two new flavors. **Amazing Allspice** has allspice that we import directly from the Caribbean, Mexico, and Central America. If you have not tried this beverage yet, you are in for a real taste treat. **Vastly Vanilla** is one of the tastiest beverages you will ever enjoy. Our vanilla beans are imported from Madagascar and are ground locally here in Montana to guarantee the ultimate in fresh taste.

What Makes Us So Special?

There is nothing artificial in any of our beverages. We do not add sugar, coloring, sodium, preservatives, or anything else that might interfere with your enjoying some of the tastiest beverages on the market today. Our beverages are made from sparkling spring water and natural spices — and that is all. Our Ease Grip bottles make it a delight to carry our beverages around.

The unique shape of our bottle allows you to handle the bottle with ease, no matter what size bottle you purchase and no matter where you take our bottles. Whether you are enjoying our beverages in the comfort of your living room or whether you are sipping our beverages after a long hike up the mountains, our bottle shape will make the pleasure of drinking *Winter Water* even better.

Now is the Time for Winter Water

Stock up on *Winter Water* now while we are having our centennial promotion sale. Check the bottle gripper on our 6-pack, 12-pack, and 24-pack cases. You will find valuable coupons worth up to $3.00 off your next purchase of *Winter Water*. Better still, you can participate in our centennial prize giveaway. You and a traveling companion of your choice can win an all-expenses-paid trip to any of the countries who supply us with the spices we use for our beverages.

You can travel to Mexico, Central America, the Caribbean, Indonesia, or Madagascar. You will stay at a luxury hotel and have an escorted tour of the capital city of the country you visit. Even better still, you can qualify to win a year's supply of *Winter Water*. That's right, you can win a case of your choice of flavors of *Winter Water* every week for an entire year. That certainly is a prize worth winning. Buy *Winter Water* today.

Contact Us:

Now that you have opened and saved the winter.htm file with a new filename, you will show Travis how to type the page title between the <title> tags.

To type the page title:

1. Use the taskbar to switch back to your text editor.

2. Click between the start <title> and end </title> tags. Type the following text, as shown in Figure 2-2.

```
<title>Winter Water</title>
```

Figure 2-2 | The page title

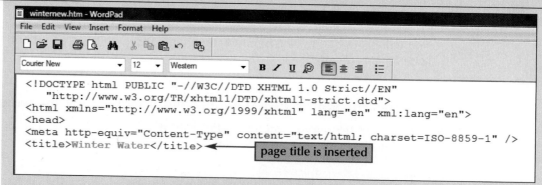

3. Click **File** on the menu bar, and then click **Save**.

It's a good idea to document your work by adding comments to your code as you develop your XHTML document. You'll show Travis how to enter comments next.

To add a comment to the document:

1. Click after the end </title> tag and then press the **Enter** key twice to insert a new blank line in the document.

2. Type the following comment, substituting your name and today's date, as shown in Figure 2-3.

```
<!-- Your First and Last Name
     Tutorial 2
     Today's Date
-->
```

Figure 2-3   Entering a comment in the head section

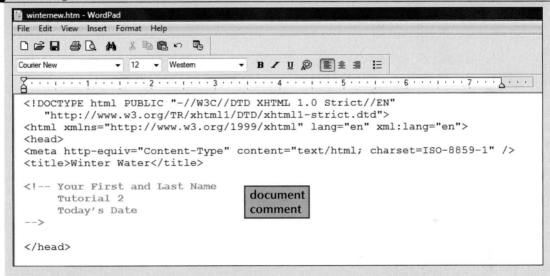

```
<!DOCTYPE html PUBLIC "-//W3C//DTD XHTML 1.0 Strict//EN"
    "http://www.w3.org/TR/xhtml1/DTD/xhtml1-strict.dtd">
<html xmlns="http://www.w3.org/1999/xhtml" lang="en" xml:lang="en">
<head>
<meta http-equiv="Content-Type" content="text/html; charset=ISO-8859-1" />
<title>Winter Water</title>

<!-- Your First and Last Name          document
     Tutorial 2                        comment
     Today's Date
-->

</head>
```

3. Save the file.

A graphic artist in the sales and marketing department has created a logo for the winternew.htm page. Remember that browsers are used to display images, not edit them, so whenever you use an image on a Web page, the image should have the same width and height as the values you specified for the width and height attributes in the image tag code. For example, if the image file had a width of 2000 pixels and a height of 1000 pixels, but you specified a width of 400 pixels and a height of 200 pixels in the image tag code, it would take quite some time for the browser to resize the image. Merely using smaller values for the height and width attributes in the img code has no effect on the image file size, and the image will not download faster. Because you want your images (particularly .jpg files) to download as quickly as possible in the browser, you should use image-editing software such as Adobe Photoshop or Microsoft Expression Web *beforehand* to resize the original image. In addition, it is a good coding practice to always specify a width and height for an image in the image tag code, even though it is not required. The browser uses the information you have supplied for an image's width and height, and it downloads the image (and lays out the page content) faster if you specify these dimensions, especially if you have many images on the Web page. Also, if you want to resize an image later, you conveniently have the image dimensions in the code.

Unfortunately, resizing an image often results in a loss of image clarity; the resized image may appear somewhat blurred or grainy. However, you can use the image-editing software mentioned in the previous paragraph to **resample** an image, which means that you can restore the image to its original clarity after the image has been resized. You will show Travis how to insert the code for the winterlogo image file into his home page.

To insert the code for the winterlogo image:

▶ **1.** Position the insertion point in the <body> section below the comment code for the image.

▶ **2.** Type the following code, as shown in Figure 2-4.

```
<p><img src="winterlogo.gif" alt="Winter Water logo" width="760"
height="200" /></p>
```

Figure 2-4 The code for the winterlogo image

```
</head>

<body>

<!-- Winter Water logo image is below -->

<p><img src="winterlogo.gif" alt="Winter Water logo" width="760" height="200" /></p>

<h1>Winter Water</h1>
<h2>Enjoy the Taste of Winter Water All Year Long</h2>

<ul>
  <li>Cinnamon</li>
  <li>Nutmeg</li>
  <li>Allspice</li>
  <li>Vanilla</li>
</ul>
```

▶ **3.** Save the file.

▶ **4.** Switch to your browser and refresh (or reload) the page, which should look similar to Figure 2-5.

Figure 2-5 The winterlogo image in the browser

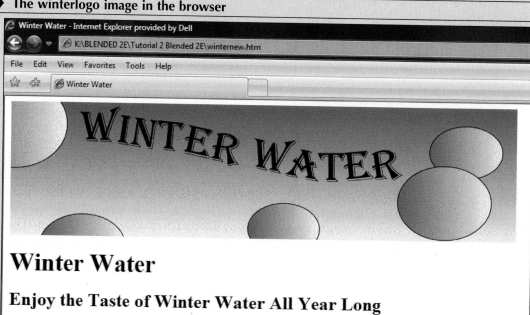

Now that the file has been created and the logo image inserted, you are ready to show Travis how to create links that will make it easier for visitors to navigate the Winter Water home page.

Creating a Link to a Specific Place on the Same Web Page

Ideally, you should catch the reader's attention with the first screen of text on a Web page. If your Web page is longer than one screen, you need to assist your readers to view the remainder of the page quickly and easily. Creating ids is a way to do that. Most visitors to a Web page like to find what they're looking for right away. Forcing your visitors to scroll several screens down the page to find the information they want is a sure way to lose their interest. Allowing visitors to easily find what they are looking for at your Web site is a two-step process. First, you enter code and a value for the **id attribute**, which assigns a unique identifier to an element. Second, you enter code to link to the value of the id attribute. Links to ids are also known as "anchor links" or "bookmark links." The value for the id attribute should be a descriptive name based on the id's location, purpose, or the surrounding text.

If the Web page has several screens of content, make sure you don't strand the reader at the bottom of the page. Depending on which page the reader is viewing, include links back to the top of the page, the next page, the previous page, and the home page.

---

erence Window | Creating an id

- To create an id, use the following code:
  ```
  <element id="idvalue">content</element>
  ```
  where *<element>* is the start tag for a block-level element, *id* is the id attribute, *idvalue* is the value for the id, *content* is the content for the element, and *</element>* is the end tag for a block-level element.

Tip

neral, limit your
page to not more
three screens of
nt.

Because you determine where to insert the code for the ids, you need to plan where this code will be entered. The bottom of the first screen of a Web page is called the **fold**. If your page runs past the fold, you should insert the code for one or more ids past the fold to make it easier for your visitors to locate content below the fold.

It is common to have an id at the top of the page with a value of "top" or "pagetop." Pick a name for this purpose and be consistent throughout your Web site. Enter the code for a pagetop id at the top of the page in whatever element is just below the start <body> tag. Usually, this element is either an image or an h1 or h2 heading. Values for the id attribute must be enclosed by quotes, as shown in the following code:

Tip

d attribute is not
just for links. In later
ials, you will make
isive use of the id
oute.

```
<p id="top">
```

You will show Travis how to enter the code for an id at the top of the page. The first block-level element in the body section is the p element that precedes the code for the winterlogo image. You will give the id attribute a value of "top."

To create the id for the top of the page:

1. Switch back to your text editor.

2. In the <p> tag that precedes the code for the image element, type the following code, as shown in Figure 2-6.

```
<p id="top"><img src="winterlogo.gif" alt="Winter Water logo"
width="760" height="200"/></p>
```

| Figure 2-6 | The code for the id |

```
<!-- Winter Water logo image is below -->

<p id="top"><img src="winterlogo.gif" alt="Winter Water logo" width="760" height="200" /></p>

<h1>Winter Water</h1>
<h2>Enjoy the Taste of Winter Water All Year Long</h2>
```
code for the id named top

Now that you've shown Travis how to create an id, you are ready to show him how to create a link to an id.

Linking to an id on the Same Page

After you have created all the ids, you need links—text or images—that when clicked, display another screen location. The **anchor element** is used for links. The anchor element is an inline element, so the code for the anchor element must be inside the code for a block-level element, such as the paragraph element (<p></p>). In XHTML code, the anchor element is represented by the letter *a*.

Reference Window | **Creating a Link to an id on the Same Page**

- To create a link to an id on the same page, enter the following code:
  ```
  <a id="#idname">linktext</a>
  ```
  where *a* is the start anchor tag, *id* is the id attribute, *#idname* is the name of the id to which you are linking (preceded by the # flag character), *linktext* is the text that the user will click to activate the link, and </a> is the end anchor tag.

To create the link, you enter the code for the start anchor tag, but this time you use the href (hypertext reference) attribute. A **hypertext reference** is a way to access a resource on your computer or on the Internet. The **hypertext reference attribute** is used to access that resource. The value of the hypertext reference attribute identifies the resource. In this instance, the value of the hypertext reference attribute will be "top." Even though the link appears by itself on its own line, the link is included within a paragraph element:

```
<p><a href=
```

Tip

The name attribute, formerly used with the anchor element, is deprecated.

Every Web page should have a link at the bottom of the page that serves as a link (a jump) to the top. In that way, you won't strand the reader at the bottom of the page and force the reader to scroll back to the top. To link to an id, use the id's value as the value for the hypertext reference attribute. However, before the value, you also include a flag character. A **flag character** is a character that has special significance in XHTML code. In this instance, the flag character is the pound symbol (#), as shown in the following code:

Tip

Whenever you refer to a user-defined value, the value is preceded by a # flag character.

```
<p><a href="#top">
```

To complete the link, you need something, such as text, for the user to click. Because this is a link to the top of the page, the words "Back to Top" will be used as the link text.

```
<p><a href="#top">Back to Top
```

The end anchor tag comes last and completes the code for the link:

```
<p><a href="#top">Back to Top</a></p>
```

In the link text, avoid using expressions such as "Click Here." Instead, choose a word or phrase that describes what appears when readers click the link text. If you just use "Click Here" as the link text, the words "Click Here" will be repeated by a screen reader and will appear twice—once as the link text and once as an instruction.

When the winternew.htm page appears in the browser, the words "Back to Top" are underlined and in blue if the link has not been visited. After the link has been clicked, the link text will appear in purple, which identifies the text as a link you have visited. In addition, when the mouse pointer passes over "Back to Top," the pointer changes to an icon of the hand cursor 🖑, indicating that the text is a hypertext reference. You will now show Travis how to enter the code for the link to the anchor named top.

To link to the id named top:

▶ **1.** Below the comment near the bottom of the page, type the following code, as shown in Figure 2-7.

```
<p><a href="#top">Back to Top</a></p>
```

Figure 2-7 ▶ **The code for the link to the id named top**

```
<p>Contact Us:</p>

<!-- e-mail link is below -->


<!-- link to the id named "top" is below -->

<p><a href="#top">Back to Top</a></p>      ◀——  code for the
                                                 link to the id
</body>                                          named top
</html>
```

▶ **2.** Save the file.

▶ **3.** Switch to your browser. Refresh (or reload) the page and compare your document to the one shown in Figure 2-8 to verify that the link to the id named top appears.

Figure 2-8 ▶ **The link to the id named top in the browser**

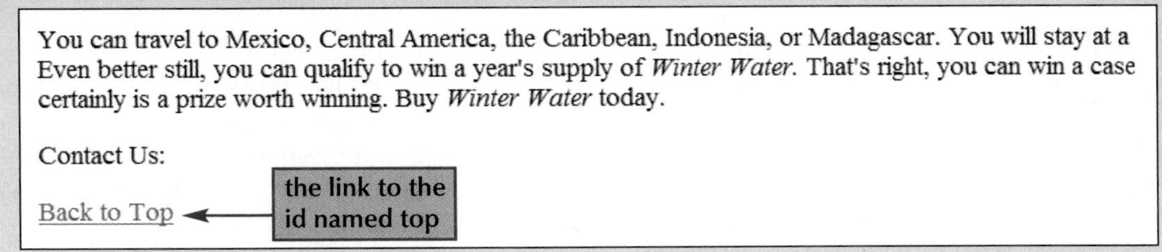

You can travel to Mexico, Central America, the Caribbean, Indonesia, or Madagascar. You will stay at a Even better still, you can qualify to win a year's supply of *Winter Water*. That's right, you can win a case certainly is a prize worth winning. Buy *Winter Water* today.

Contact Us:

Back to Top ◀—— the link to the id named top

▶ **4.** Click the **Back to Top** link text. Verify that the top of the page is displayed on your screen.

Now that you have created a link to a place on the same page, you will show Travis how to create a link to a different Web page.

Linking to a Different Web Page

The code to link to a different page at the same Web site is similar to the link you just created to link to an id on the same page. To link to a different page, make the value of the hypertext reference attribute the name of the page to which you want to link. The page where the link is included is called the **referring page**. The page that appears when the user clicks the link is called the **target page**. To link to a different page, you do not precede the name of the link with the # symbol, as you did when you used a link to an id.

Reference Window	**Creating a Link to a Different Web Page**

- To create a link to a different Web page, use the following code:

  ```
  <a href="filename.htm">linktext</a>
  ```
  where *a* is the start anchor tag, *href* is the hypertext reference attribute, *filename.htm* is the name of the file you are linking to, *linktext* is the text the user clicks to activate the link, and *</a>* is the end anchor tag.

It is common to include several links within the list item tags of an unordered list. The code to link to a different page would be similar to the following example:

```
<li><a href="cinnamon.htm">Cinnamon</a></li>
```

InSight	**Using Placeholders**

During the early stages of Web site development, the home page is developed well before the other pages at the site. In this phase, it is common to dispense with the actual filenames for links on the home page and instead use the pound symbol (#) flag character as a placeholder in a link:

```
<a href="#">Nutmeg</a>
```

Here, the placeholder character serves as a reminder to insert the filename after the page has been created. The link will not work until an actual filename has been provided, but the links can be created as an aid in planning the overall design of the page. The link text will appear to be functioning link text. Of course, the placeholder character should be replaced by the name of the actual target page once the page has been created.

Tip
Web developers often refer to a navigation bar as a "nav bar."

Another common method to place links on a Web page is to create a **navigation bar**, which is a series of links that appear horizontally across most or all of the screen, usually just below the logo or banner section at the top of the page. It is also common to create navigation bars at the bottom of the page in the site footer area. Rather than using an unordered list, navigation bars are easy to construct using the **piping symbol** (|) on your keyboard to separate one link from the next:

HOME | NEW STUDENTS | RETURNING STUDENTS | FINANCIAL AID | DIRECTIONS

In a later tutorial, you will learn how to create a navigation bar using an unordered list. By doing so, you can separate one link from another by using graphics.

The **title attribute** is used to create a ScreenTip for links. Do not confuse the title attribute with the title element, which you use to enter a title for the Web page in the head section of the document. Although the title attribute is not required, its use with links is common for accessibility reasons. The value of the title attribute is read aloud by screen readers, and when a visitor to your Web page passes the mouse pointer over the link in the browser, the ScreenTip appears.

The value of the title attribute is the text that appears in the ScreenTip. If you keep your link text short, you can add more descriptive text as the value for the title attribute. In the following example, you will keep the ScreenTip text short, but Travis can always expand on this text later in the development of the Winter Water Web site. The Web site has four pages already created, but the only fully developed page is cinnamon.htm. Travis will develop the other pages later. You will show Travis how to enter the code for links to the other pages at the Winter Water Web site.

To enter the code to link to other pages:

▶ **1.** Switch back to your text editor.

▶ **2.** In the code for the unordered list, add the following code, as shown in Figure 2-9.

```
<li><a href="cinnamon.htm" title="Delicious Cinnamon
page">Cinnamon</a></li>
<li><a href="nutmeg.htm" title="Spicy Nutmeg
page">Nutmeg</a></li>
<li><a href="allspice.htm" title="Amazing Allspice
page">Allspice</a></li>
<li><a href="vanilla.htm" title="Very Vanilla
page">Vanilla</a></li>
```

Figure 2-9 | **The code for the links to the other pages**

```
<h1>Winter Water</h1>
<h2>Enjoy the Taste of Winter Water All Year Long</h2>

<ul>                                                            links to other pages
    <li><a href="cinnamon.htm" title="Delicious Cinnamon page">Cinnamon</a></li>
    <li><a href="nutmeg.htm" title="Spicy Nutmeg page">Nutmeg</a></li>
    <li><a href="allspice.htm" title="Amazing Allspice page">Allspice</a></li>
    <li><a href="vanilla.htm" title="Very Vanilla page">Vanilla</a></li>
</ul>

<h3>What is Winter Water?</h3>
```

▶ **3.** Save the file.

▶ **4.** Switch to your browser and refresh (or reload) the winternew.htm page. Compare your file with the one shown in Figure 2-10 to verify that the list of links to other Web pages appears in the unordered list.

Figure 2-10 | **The links to the other pages in the browser**

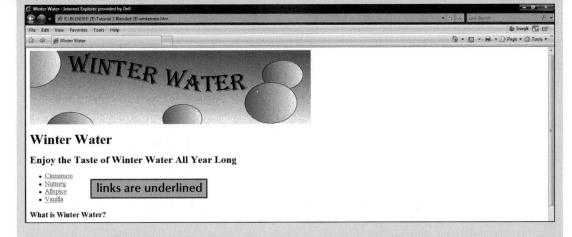

> 5. One by one, pass the mouse pointer over the link text in the links. Observe the text in the ScreenTips.
>
> 6. Click the **Cinnamon** link to verify that the link to the cinnamon.htm page works properly.
>
> 7. Click the **Back** button (or close the appropriate tab) in your browser to return to the winternew.htm page.

Earlier, you created a link to an id on the same page. Now that you have shown Travis how to create links to other Web pages, you are ready to show him how to include a link to an id on a different Web page.

Linking to an id on a Different Page of your Web Site

When you click the link text to view another page, the first screen of that new page is displayed. If your visitors do not find what they want on that first screen, they must scroll through the rest of the page to find the topic of interest. You can eliminate this problem by first linking to a different page and then linking to an id on that page—a double link. Of course, you must enter the code for the ids beforehand in the appropriate places on the target page.

Reference Window	**Creating a Link to an id on Another Page of your Web Site**

- To create a link to an id on another page, enter the following code:
  ```
  <a id="filename.htm#idname">linktext</a>
  ```
  where *a* is the start anchor tag, *id* is the id attribute, *filename* is the name of the file in which the id resides, *#idname* is the name of the id you are linking to (preceded by the # flag character), *linktext* is the text that the user clicks to activate the link, and *</a>* is the end anchor tag.

To link to an id on a different page, make sure the value of the hypertext reference is composed of the following parts:

- The target page
- The flag character
- The id name

Note that the entire value appears together without any spaces, as shown in the following example:

```
<a href="cinnamon.htm#freshness">freshness</a>
```

When the user clicks the word "freshness" in the browser, the first link displays the page named cinnamon.htm, and then the second link displays the screen where the id named freshness is located. You could also link to an id on a page at another Web site, but doing so could be problematic. You have no control over that page, and if the code for the page is revised and the id is moved, renamed, or eliminated, your link to the id on that Web site would no longer work.

An id named *freshness* has already been entered on the cinnamon.htm page in a start <h3> tag. The code on the cinnamon.htm page appears as shown below:

```
<h3 id="freshness">Freshness</h3>
```

You will show Travis how to enter the code on the winternew.htm page that links to the freshness id on the cinnamon Web page.

To link to the freshness id:

▶ **1.** Switch back to your text editor.

▶ **2.** In the last sentence of the first paragraph of the winternew.htm page, precede and follow the word "freshness" with new code, as shown in Figure 2-11.

```
Our spices are known for their
<a href="cinnamon.htm#freshness">freshness</a>.</p>
```

Figure 2-11 ▶ **The code to link to an id on a different page at the same Web site**

```
<p>For those of you who enjoy the fresh, clean taste of spring water, welcome to
the delights of <em>Winter Water</em>, a drink you can enjoy throughout the year.
<em>Winter Water</em> combines natural spring water with a hint of cinnamon, nutmeg,
and other flavorful spices. Of course, you can get Winter Water as an unflavored,
natural beverage as well. Our spices are known for their <a href="cinnamon.htm#freshness">freshness</a>.</p>
```

the link to the id on the cinnamon page

▶ **3.** Save the file.

▶ **4.** Switch to your browser and refresh (or reload) the winternew.htm page. Compare your file with the one shown in Figure 2-12.

Figure 2-12 ▶ **The link to the id on a different page in the browser**

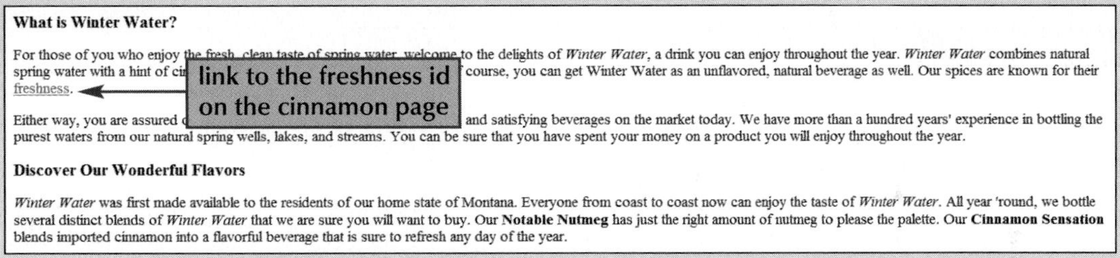

What is Winter Water?

For those of you who enjoy the fresh, clean taste of spring water, welcome to the delights of *Winter Water*, a drink you can enjoy throughout the year. *Winter Water* combines natural spring water with a hint of ci[...] course, you can get Winter Water as an unflavored, natural beverage as well. Our spices are known for their freshness.

link to the freshness id on the cinnamon page

Either way, you are assured [...] and satisfying beverages on the market today. We have more than a hundred years' experience in bottling the purest waters from our natural spring wells, lakes, and streams. You can be sure that you have spent your money on a product you will enjoy throughout the year.

Discover Our Wonderful Flavors

Winter Water was first made available to the residents of our home state of Montana. Everyone from coast to coast now can enjoy the taste of *Winter Water*. All year 'round, we bottle several distinct blends of *Winter Water* that we are sure you will want to buy. Our **Notable Nutmeg** has just the right amount of nutmeg to please the palette. Our **Cinnamon Sensation** blends imported cinnamon into a flavorful beverage that is sure to refresh any day of the year.

▶ **5.** Click the **freshness** link to verify that the link works properly. (You should not have to scroll to view the section on freshness on the cinnamon page.)

▶ **6.** Click the **Back** button (or close the appropriate tab) to return to the winternew.htm page.

Next, you'll show Travis how to link to a page at a different Web site.

Linking to an External Web Site

To create a link to a page at a different (an external) Web site, you must include the complete URL of the site as the value for the href attribute. It is very important that you include the http:// protocol in the value for the href attribute. If you do not include the protocol, the link will not work. For example, to create a link to a page with more information about cinnamon, you would enter the following code:

```
<p><a href="http://en.wikipedia.org/wiki/Cinnamon">Learn More About
Cinnamon</a></p>
```

Reference Window | **Creating a Link to an External Web Site**

- To create a link to an external Web site, use the following format:
  ```
  <a href="http://www.domainname.suffix">linktext</a>
  ```
  where *a* is the start anchor tag, *href* is the hypertext reference attribute, *http://* is the protocol, *www* is the service, *domainname* is the domain name, *suffix* is the top-level domain suffix, *linktext* is the text that the user clicks to activate the link, and *</a>* is the end anchor tag.
- If the Web site does not use "www" for the service, enter the complete URL of the Web site.

Travis thinks that most visitors know what cinnamon, nutmeg, and vanilla are, but he's not so sure that visitors are familiar with allspice. He wants to create a link to a Web site that has more information about allspice. You will show Travis how to include a link to an external Web site, *Wikipedia.org*. This is an example of a site that does not have "www" in its URL.

To create a link to Wikipedia:

▶ **1.** Switch back to your text editor.

▶ **2.** Below the comment about linking to an external Web site about allspice, type the following code, as shown in Figure 2-13.

```
<p><a href="http://en.wikipedia.org/wiki/Allspice">Learn More
About Allspice</a></p>
```

Figure 2-13	The code for the external link

```
<p>We are proud to introduce two new flavors. <strong>Amazing Allspice</strong>
has allspice that we import directly from the Caribbean, Mexico, and Central
America. If you have not tried this beverage yet, you are in for a real taste treat.
<strong>Vastly Vanilla</strong> is one of the tastiest beverages you will ever enjoy.
Our vanilla beans are imported from Madagascar and are ground locally here in Montana
to guarantee the ultimate in fresh taste.</p>
```
link to the wikipedia.org page
```
<!-- link to an external Web site about allspice is below -->

<p><a href="http://en.wikipedia.org/wiki/Allspice">Learn More About Allspice</a></p>

<h3>What Makes Us So Special?</h3>
<p>There is nothing artificial in any of our beverages. We do not add sugar, coloring,
sodium, preservatives, or anything else that might interfere with your enjoying
some of the tastiest beverages on the market today. Our beverages are made from
sparkling spring water and natural spices &mdash; and that is all. Our Ease Grip bottles
make it a delight to carry our beverages around.</p>
```

▶ **3.** Save the file.

▶ **4.** Switch back to your browser and refresh (or reload) the page. Compare your file to the one shown in Figure 2-14.

Figure 2-14	The link to the external Web site in the browser

We are proud to introduce two new flavors. **Amazing Allspice** has allspice that we import directly from the Caribbean, Mexico, and Central America. If you have not tried this beverage yet, you are in for a real taste treat. **Vastly Vanilla** is one of the tastiest beverages you will ever enjoy. Our vanilla beans are imported from Madagascar and are ground locally here in Montana to guarantee the ultimate in fresh taste.

Learn More About Allspice ← link to the external Web site

What Makes Us So Special?

There is nothing artificial in any of our beverages. We do not add sugar, coloring, sodium, preservatives, or anything else that might interfere with your enjoying some of the tastiest beverages on the market today. Our beverages are made from sparkling spring water and natural spices — and that is all. Our Ease Grip bottles make it a delight to carry our beverages around.

The unique shape of our bottle allows you to handle the bottle with ease, no matter what size bottle you purchase and no matter where you take our bottles. Whether you are enjoying our beverages in the comfort of your living room or whether you are sipping our beverages after a long hike up the mountains, our bottle shape will make the pleasure of drinking *Winter Water* even better.

▶ **5.** Click the **Learn More About Allspice** link text. Verify that the link to the *Wikipedia.org* external Web site works.

▶ **6.** Close the Wikipedia Web site window (or close the appropriate tab) in your browser to return to the winternew.htm page.

▶ **7.** If you will not be continuing to the next session, close your text editor and your browser.

In this session, you learned about the different types of links. Each page should have an id at the top of the page and a link at the bottom of the page that links back to the id at the top. You also learned that you can create links to other pages at the same Web site, create a link to an anchor at another page at the same Web site, and create a link to another (an external) Web site. In the next session, you will show Travis how an image can be used with a link. You will also show Travis how to link to other resources.

Review | **Session 2.1 Quick Check**

1. What is a protocol?

2. What protocol is used to access the World Wide Web?

3. What does "URL" stand for?

4. What XHTML element is used for links?

5. What flag character is used when creating a link to an id?

6. What is a navigation bar?

Session 2.2

Using Images with Links

Instead of having your users click text for a link, you can use images. Images such as arrows and pointers are commonly used as navigational icons. A graphic image, such as an upward-pointing or left-pointing arrow, often appears at the bottom of a Web page to serve as a link back to the top of the page, the previous page, or the home page. Later, you will learn how a small image can be used to link to another page that contains a larger instance of the same image. Any text or image code that falls between the start and end anchor tags can be clicked and used as a link in the browser.

Reference Window | **Using an Image as a Link**

- To use an image as a link, use the following code:

```
<a href="filename.htm"><img src="imagename.filetype"
alt="alternatetext" width="widthvalue"
height="heightvalue">linktext</a>
```

where *a* is the start anchor tag, *href* is the hypertext reference attribute, *filename.htm* is the name of the file you are linking to, *img* is the image element, *src* is the source attribute, *imagename* is the filename of the image being used as a link, *filetype* is the type of image file (such as .jpg or .gif), *alt* is the alt attribute, *alternatetext* is the description of the image, *width* is the width attribute, *widthvalue* is the width of the image in pixels, *height* is the height attribute, *heightvalue* is the height of the image in pixels, *linktext* is the text that the user clicks to activate the link, and *</a>* is the end anchor tag.

For example, to create a link using an image that would link from the bottom of the page to the top of a page, you would enter this code:

```
<a href="#top"><img src="arrow.gif" alt="image of up
arrow" width="40" height="40" />Back to Top</a>
```

If you are using an image as a link, it's a good idea to have some link text, just in case the user has set preferences in the browser not to display images or if some other problem occurs that prevents the image from downloading. You will show Travis how to insert an image that links to the top of the page, using alternate link text along with the image.

To use an image as a link:

▶ **1.** If necessary, start your browser, start your text editor, and open the **winternew.htm** file in both applications.

▶ **2.** Switch to your text editor. In the code for the link to the id at the top of the page, position the insertion point to the right of the angle bracket (>) that follows the anchor element code. Type the following code, as shown in Figure 2-15.

```
<p><a href="#top"><img src="arrow.gif" alt="image of up arrow"
width="40" height="40" />Back to Top</a></p>
```

Figure 2-15 | **The code to use an image as a link**

```
<!-- link to the id named "top" is below -->

<p><a href="#top"><img src="arrow.gif" alt="image of up arrow" width="40" height="40" />Back to Top</a></p>

</body>
</html>
```

the link to the id named top using an arrow image

▶ **3.** Save the file.

▶ **4.** Switch to your browser and refresh (or reload) the page. Compare your file to the one shown in Figure 2-16 to verify that the arrow image appears.

Figure 2-16 | **The image link in the browser**

You can travel to Mexico, Central America, the Caribbean, Indonesia, or Madagascar. Even better still, you can qualify to win a year's supply of *Winter Water*. That's right, certainly is a prize worth winning. Buy *Winter Water* today.

Contact Us:

⬆ Back to Top

the arrow image used as a link

▶ **5.** Click the arrow image to verify that the link back to the top of the page works correctly.

Note that the arrow image and the link text have no space between them. Also, it would be better if the image were centered vertically in relation to the link text. By default, the image used as a link also has a purple border around the image. In later tutorials, you will learn how to create space around an image, position an image both horizontally and vertically, wrap text around an image, and change the appearance of (or hide) the image border. In the meantime, you will next show Travis how to use a thumbnail image—a smaller image that can be used as a link to display a larger instance of the same image on its own page.

Creating Thumbnail Links

Because of the potentially large byte size of an image, it's wise not to have too many large images on a page. Also, a page that has little text and several large images is not very informative or interesting; on the contrary, it looks amateurish. If you have many images to display (such as a gallery of images), a useful strategy is to have a smaller image, called a **thumbnail**, on the referring page. The thumbnail serves as a link to a larger instance of the same image on the target page. The code on the referring page would be similar to the following (note that the values for the width and height attributes are an appropriately smaller size):

```
<p><a href="allspice.htm"><img src="allspice_small.jpg"
alt="thumbnail image of allspice seeds" width="100" height="75" />View
Larger Image of Allspice Seeds</a></p>
```

On the page with the full-size image, you should have a link back to the referring page (and the home page) so you don't strand your reader. You will show Travis how to link to a page named allspice.htm, which is a page that Travis can develop later. The allspice.htm page has a larger version of the image of allspice seeds.

To create the thumbnail link:

▶ **1.** Switch back to your text editor.

▶ **2.** Below the comment regarding the thumbnail image link, type the following code, as shown in Figure 2-17. (Press the **Enter** key after you type each line, except the last.)

```
<p><a href="allspice.htm"><img src="allspice_small.jpg"
alt="thumbnail image of allspice seeds" width="100"
height="75" />View Larger Image of Allspice Seeds</a></p>
```

Figure 2-17 | The code for the thumbnail link

```
Water</em> that we are sure you will want to buy. Our <strong>Notable Nutmeg
</strong>has just the right amount of nutmeg to please the palette. Our <strong>
Cinnamon Sensation</strong> blends imported cinnamon into a flavorful beverage that
is sure to refresh any day of the year.</p>

<!-- thumbnail image link is below -->

<p><a href="allspice.htm"><img src="allspice_small.jpg"
alt="thumbnail image of allspice seeds" width="100"
height="75" />View Larger Image of Allspice Seeds</a></p>

<p>We are proud to introduce two new flavors. <strong>Amazing Allspice</strong>
has allspice that we import directly from the Caribbean, Mexico, and Central
America. If you have not tried this beverage yet, you are in for a real taste treat.
<strong>Vastly Vanilla</strong> is one of the tastiest beverages you will ever enjoy.
Our vanilla beans are imported from Madagascar and are ground locally here in Montana
to guarantee the ultimate in fresh taste.</p>

<!-- link to an external Web site about allspice is below -->
```

thumbnail links to larger image (pointing to the `<a href` code line)

3. Save the file.

4. Switch to your browser and refresh (or reload) the page. Compare your file to the one shown in Figure 2-18 to verify that the thumbnail link appears.

Figure 2-18 | The thumbnail link in the browser

Discover Our Wonderful Flavors

Winter Water was first made available to the residents of our home state of Montana. Everyone from several distinct blends of *Winter Water* that we are sure you will want to buy. Our **Notable Nutmeg** blends imported cinnamon into a flavorful beverage that is sure to refresh any day of the year.

thumbnail link in the browser

View Larger Image of Allspice Seeds

text link in addition to the thumbnail

We are proud to introduce two new flavors. **Amazing Allspice** has allspice that we import directly fr yet, you are in for a real taste treat. **Vastly Vanilla** is one of the tastiest beverages you will ever enjoy Montana to guarantee the ultimate in fresh taste.

Learn More About Allspice

What Makes Us So Special?

5. Click the thumbnail image to verify that the link works correctly.

6. Click the **Back** button or the link text (or close the appropriate tab in your browser) to return to the winternew.htm page.

If the information contained in the image is important to the meaning of the page content, then you should provide a longer description of the image than just the value for the alt attribute. The longdesc attribute can be added to the code for an image in addition to the content for the alt attribute. Unfortunately, browser support for the longdesc attribute has been very poor, and so the attribute may become deprecated in HTML 5.0. As a work-around, Web page authors are creating ordinary links (using just the lowercase letter "d" as the link text) beside an image. The letter "d" serves as a link to another page that has a detailed description of the image. Visitors can click the letter "d" to access the link, as they would any other link. Web developers refer to these links as "d links."

For example, if you had an image of a chart that contained information about quarterly sales, it would help your visitors to describe the importance of the data in the chart. You might want to state why sales were higher in one region than another, or how sales are trending overall. Not only are these types of descriptions great for accessibility reasons, d link descriptions are useful to all visitors to your Web site.

Now that you have shown Travis some simple ways to use images as links, you will show him how a single image can be used as a source for several links.

Creating Image Maps

An image map is an image that is divided into sections that each serve as a link. The areas of the image designated to be used as links are called **hotspots**. Any image can be used as the image map—it doesn't have to be an image of a map, although that is commonly true. A graphic artist at Winter Water has provided you with an image file named spices.gif that names the different spices used in Winter Water beverages. You would like to make each of the four words on the image into a link to an appropriate page about that spice. The spices.gif image will be divided into four hotspots, each of which will link to a different page. Your first step is to enter the code for the image. Of course, your Web page usually will have several images, so you need a way to specify that a particular image will have a special purpose; namely, that it will be used as an image map. The **usemap attribute** and its value signal to the browser that an image will be used as an image map and not as a regular image. You can use any value you want as the value for the usemap attribute, but it's a good coding practice for the value to be somewhat descriptive of the image. You have decided to use the value of "spices." In the image code, the value is preceded by a flag character (#), as shown below:

```
<p><img src="spices.gif" alt="image map to spices pages" width="760"
height="150" usemap="#spices" /></p>
```

You will show Travis how to enter the code for the image, the usemap attribute, and its value.

To enter the code for the image:

▶ **1.** Switch back to your text editor.

▶ **2.** Below the comment regarding the image used for an image map, type the following code, as shown in Figure 2-19.

```
<p><img src="spices.gif" alt="image map to spices pages"
width="760" height="150" usemap="#spices" /></p>
```

Figure 2-19 | The code for the map image

```
<h3>Now is the Time for Winter Water</h3>
<p>Stock up on <em>Winter Water</em> now while we are having our centennial promotion
sale. Check the bottle gripper on our 6-pack, 12-pack, and 24-pack cases.
You will find valuable coupons worth up to $3.00 off your next purchase of <em>Winter
Water</em>. Better still, you can participate in our centennial prize giveaway.
You and a traveling companion of your choice can win an all-expenses-paid trip to
any of the countries who supply us with the spices we use for our beverages.</p>
<p>You can travel to Mexico, Central America, the Caribbean, Indonesia, or Madagasc
You will stay at a luxury hotel and have an escorted tour of the capital city of th
country you visit. Even better still, you can qualify to win a year's supply of <em
Water.</em> That's right, you can win a case of your choice of flavors of <em>Winter
Water</em> every week for an entire year. That certainly is a prize worth winning.
Buy <em>Winter Water</em> today.</p>

<!-- the image below will be used for an image map -->

<p><img src="spices.gif" alt="image map to spices pages" width="760" height="150" usemap="#spices" /></p>

<!-- code for an image map is below -->
```

> usemap attribute used with the image code

3. Save the file.

4. Switch to your browser and refresh (or reload) the page. Compare your file to the one shown in Figure 2-20 to verify that the map image appears.

Figure 2-20 | The image to be used for the image map

Now is the Time for Winter Water

Stock up on *Winter Water* now while we are having our centennial promotion sale. Check the bottle gripper on our 6-pack, worth up to $3.00 off your next purchase of *Winter Water*. Better still, you can participate in our centennial prize giveaway. expenses-paid trip to any of the countries who supply us with the spices we use for our beverages.

You can travel to Mexico, Central America, the Caribbean, Indonesia, or Madagascar. You will stay at a luxury hotel and ha Even better still, you can qualify to win a year's supply of *Winter Water*. That's right, you can win a case of your choice of certainly is a prize worth winning. Buy *Winter Water* today.

Vanilla Cinnamon   Allspice Nutmeg

Contact Us:

> the image map

Now that the image code has been entered, you will show Travis how to enter the map code.

Entering Code for an Image Map

Tip

It is good coding practice to place the image map code just below the image code.

The code starts with the **map element**, which is the container for all the code in the image map. The start <map> tag is entered at the start of the map code. The end </map> tag follows all of the code for the map. The map element should itself be within a block-level element, such as the paragraph element.

erence Window | **Creating an Image Map**

- To create an image map, enter the usemap attribute into the image code to be used as a map.

  ```
  <p><img src="imagename.filetype" alt="alternatetext"
   width="widthvalue" height="heightvalue" usemap="#mapname" /></p>
  ```
  where *usemap* is the usemap attribute and *#mapname* is the value assigned to the usemap attribute (preceded by the # flag character).

- Below the code for the image, insert the code for the map element within a block-level element, such as the paragraph element.

  ```
  <p><map id="mapname" name="mapname2">
  </map></p>
  ```
  where *map* is the map element, *id* is the id attribute, *mapname* is the value given the usemap attribute in the image used as a map, *name* is the name attribute, and *mapname2* is the same value as the one used for the id attribute.

- To add hotspots to the map, insert the code for one or more areas between the start and end map tags.

  ```
  <area shape="areashape" coords="coordinates" href="reference"
   alt="alternatetext" />
  ```
  where *area* is the area element, *shape* is the shape attribute, *areashape* is either rect, circle, or poly, *coords* is the coordinates attribute, *coordinates* are the coordinates for the shape, *href* is the hypertext reference attribute, *reference* is the file or location the hotspot is linked to, *alt* is the alt attribute, and *alternatetext* is a description of the file or location to which the hotspot is linked.

The <map> tag identifies the name of the image that will be used as a map. The id attribute is always used with the <map> tag. The value of the id attribute is the value you gave to the usemap attribute, which in this instance is "spices." Although the map name was preceded by a # flag character in the image tag code, the value is not preceded by a # flag character in the start <map> tag:

```
<map id="spices">
```

The name attribute is deprecated, but for the image map to work correctly in the Firefox browser, you must include the name attribute and a value. For the name attribute, use the same value you used for the id attribute, as shown below:

```
<map id="spices" name="spices">
```

An image map is divided into two or more areas. You will next explain to Travis how to divide the image into these different areas.

Using the Area Element

The **area element** is used to create the hotspots that the user clicks as links. You can have as many areas as are feasible given the size of the image. The <area> tag must have the following four attributes: shape, coords, href, and alt. The shape attribute takes one of three values: rect, circle, or poly. Use rect for squares and rectangles, circle for circles and ovals, and poly for any irregular shape (basically, any other shape).

The shapes in Travis' image map are rectangles. To define the shape attribute and its value, you would enter this code:

```
<area shape="rect"
```

The **coordinates attribute** (the "coords" attribute) is used to determine what part of your image will be used as a link. Think of your computer screen as a sheet of transparent graph paper with 1024 columns across and 768 rows down. Each intersection of a column and a row represents a small box on the screen that can be assigned a coordinate value. For example, 45 boxes across and 49 boxes down would be expressed as coordinate values of 45, 49. The four coordinate values for a rectangle indicate the upper-left and lower-right corners of the rectangle.

Three values are used for a circle shape. The first two are coordinate values for the center of the circle. The third value is the circle's radius. For a polygon, each coordinate value pair indicates a point along the shape of the polygon. The more coordinate values you add, the more detail the polygon shape hotspot will have. Unfortunately, you can't determine the coordinates by using XHTML. However, you can use Web authoring programs such as Adobe Dreamweaver or Microsoft Expression Web (or even Microsoft Paint) to determine the coordinates. You have already determined the map coordinates for Travis.

The coordinates for the first hotspot will be that for the vanilla rectangle, which are 62, 23, 386, and 78. All the coordinates that fall between those value pairs will become part of a clickable region of the image. In the <area> tag, you must enclose the coordinates within quotation marks and separate each coordinate value by a comma:

```
<area shape="rect" coords="62, 23, 386, 78"
```

The next attribute for the <area> tag is href. The value of the href attribute identifies the target of the link. In this instance, the link is to the vanilla.htm page:

```
<area shape="rect" coords="62, 23, 386, 78" href="vanilla.htm" />
```

Because each of the areas represents an image, you must use the alt attribute for each area, as shown below:

```
<area shape="rect" coords="62, 23, 386, 78" href="vanilla.htm"
alt="The Vanilla page" />
```

Although the alt attribute is required in the map code, the title attribute is not. However, if you choose not to use the title attribute and a value, the Firefox browser will not display a ScreenTip when you pass the mouse pointer over a hotspot. You can use the same value for the title attribute as the one used for the alt attribute, as shown in the code below:

```
<area shape="rect" coords="62, 23, 386, 78" href="vanilla.htm"
alt="The Vanilla page" title="The Vanilla page" />
```

If there are any more shapes, simply repeat the preceding code, listing the different values for the shape, coords, href, alt, and title attributes. The end </map> tag follows all of the area tags. You are ready to show Travis how to enter the code for the image map.

To create the code for the image map:

▶ **1.** Switch back to your text editor.

▶ **2.** Below the comment to insert the code for the image map, type the following code, as shown in Figure 2-21.

```
<p><map id="spices" name="spices">
  <area shape="rect" coords="62, 23, 386, 78" href="vanilla.htm"
alt="The Vanilla page" title="The Vanilla page" />
  <area shape="rect" coords="63, 80, 385, 139"
href="cinnamon.htm" alt="The Cinnamon page" title="The Cinnamon
page" />
  <area shape="rect" coords="387, 23, 709, 80"
href="allspice.htm" alt="The Allspice page" title="The Allspice
page" />
  <area shape="rect" coords="385, 80, 710, 135" href="nutmeg.htm"
alt="The Nutmeg page" title="The Nutmeg page" />
</map></p>
```

Figure 2-21 ▶ **The code for the image map**

```
<!-- the image below will be used for an image map -->

<p><img src="spices.gif" alt="image map to spices pages" width="760" height="150" usemap="#spices" /></p>

<!-- code for an image map is below -->

<p><map id="spices" name="spices">
    <area shape="rect" coords="62, 23, 386, 78" href="vanilla.htm" alt="The Vanilla page" title="The Vanilla page" />
    <area shape="rect" coords="63, 80, 385, 139" href="cinnamon.htm" alt="The Cinnamon page" title="The Cinnamon page" />
    <area shape="rect" coords="387, 23, 709, 80" href="allspice.htm" alt="The Allspice page" title="The Allspice page" />
    <area shape="rect" coords="385, 80, 710, 135" href="nutmeg.htm" alt="The Nutmeg page" title="The Nutmeg page" />
</map></p>

<p>Contact Us:</p>                      image map code

<!-- e-mail link is below -->
```

▶ **3.** Save the file.

▶ **4.** Switch to your browser and refresh (or reload) the page.

▶ **5.** One by one, click each of the four spice names in the image map. Click the **Back** button (or close the appropriate tab) as necessary in your browser to return to the winternew.htm page.

In your discussion of links, you'd like to spend some time explaining to Travis how he can use folders to organize his files. You also need to explain how to enter the code for a link when files are not in the same folder.

Organizing Files for Your Web Site

So far, the links you have written to other pages are straightforward. The assumption is that the XHTML file and the file to which you are linking both reside in the same folder. This assumption is called relative file addressing. In a **relative file address**, a file is linked in relation to another file at the same Web site and stored in the same folder on the same computer or on the same file server.

However, if the link is to a file on a different file server or at a different Web site, the link must contain an absolute file address, such as *http://www.ford.com/index.html*. An **absolute file address** specifies the entire directory path to a linked file. If you are trying to manage your files for your personal Web page, it's not a problem to store all your files in the root directory on your hard drive or in a single folder on your hard drive or removable disk. But the Internet has sites with thousands or tens of thousands of XHTML, graphics, video, and sound files. If you placed all of those files in the root directory of the hard drive or in one file folder, it would be quite a challenge to locate and manage those files.

Tip

start, place all your
je files in a folder
ed images.

Creating Parent and Child Folders

Your hard drive is divided into the root directory, parent folders, child folders, and sibling folders. A **parent folder** is a folder that is at least one level higher in the directory structure than another folder. A **child folder** is a folder at least one level below a parent folder. **Sibling folders** are two folders on the same level. Figure 2-22 shows a simple file structure involving a parent folder (Cities) and a child folder (Towns).

Figure 2-22 ▶ **File structure with a parent and child folder**

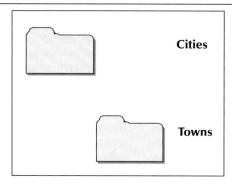

Of course, each folder can also contain some files and other folders. Suppose the parent folder (Cities) contains a file named *miami.htm,* and the child folder (Towns) contains a file named *seaside.htm*. The file structure would be similar to the one shown in Figure 2-23.

Figure 2-23 ▶ **File structure for seaside.htm**

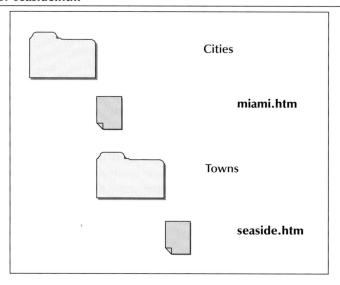

Moving Down One Level in the Directory Structure

Referring to a file that is one level down in the directory structure is fairly simple. For example, suppose that in the file *miami.htm,* you wanted to enter the code for a link to the file named *seaside.htm*. *Seaside.htm* is in the child folder, which is *one folder down* in the directory structure. See Figure 2-24.

Figure 2-24 **Moving down one level in the directory structure**

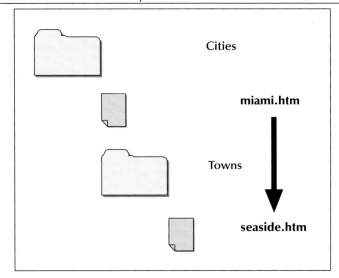

In this instance, you would specify the path as follows: (1) the folder named *Towns*, followed by a slash, and then (2) the file named *seaside.htm*. You would use the following code for the link:

```
<a href="Towns/seaside.htm">A quick tour of Seaside</a>
```

Moving Up One Level in the Directory Structure

Referring to a file that is one level up in the directory structure is also straightforward. Suppose that in the file named *seaside.htm* in the *Towns* folder, you wanted to create a link to the file named *miami.htm* in the *Cities* folder. The file *miami.htm* is in the parent folder—one level above the current folder where *seaside.htm* is stored. See Figure 2-25.

Figure 2-25 **Moving up one level**

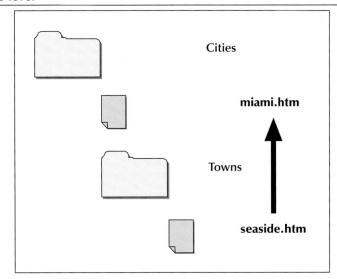

To link to a file that is in a folder one level above the current folder, you have to use the "dot dot" notation (../). You then specify the path to that file. Note the dots and the slashes in the path:

```
<a href="../miami.htm">Let's look at Miami</a>
```

Now take it one step further. Add another folder (Hamlets) and another file (smalltown. htm) to the directory structure, as shown in Figure 2-26.

Figure 2-26 **Adding files to the existing directory structure**

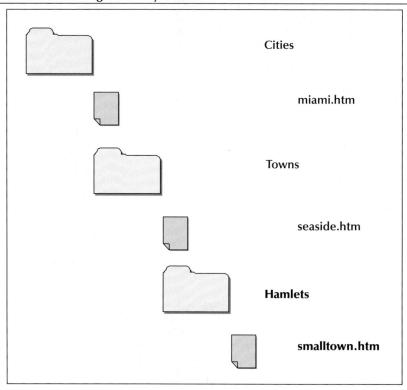

Moving Down Two Levels

Suppose that in the file *miami.htm* in the *Cities* folder, you also want to link to the file named *smalltown.htm* in the *Hamlets* folder. You are linking to a file down two levels in the directory structure, as shown in Figure 2-27.

Figure 2-27 ▷ **Linking to a file down two levels in the folder structure**

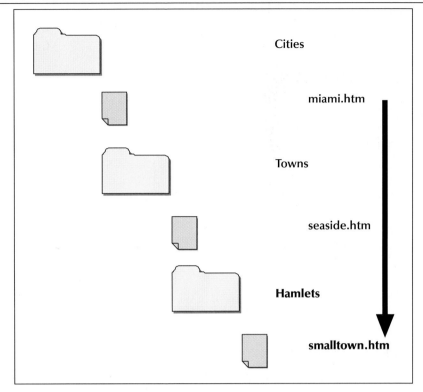

In this instance the path would be put in code, as shown below:

```
<a href="Towns/Hamlets/smalltown.htm">The Smalltown hamlet</a>
```

Moving Up Two Levels

Now suppose that in the file named *smalltown.htm* in the *Hamlets* folder, you want to enter the code for a link to *miami.htm* in the *Cities* folder. As shown in Figure 2-28, you have to go up two levels.

Figure 2-28 ▶ **Moving up two levels in the directory structure**

Tip

To link to a sibling folder, you use the same notation as linking down one folder.

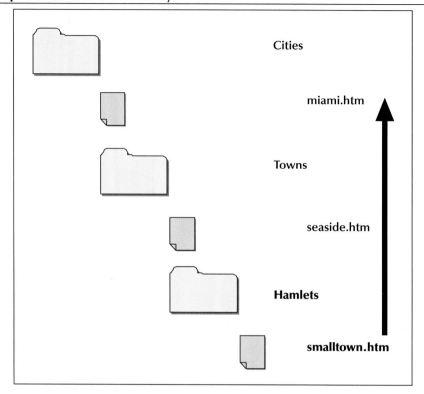

To do so, you enter the double dot notation, and then specify the path as shown below:

```
<a href="../../miami.htm">Visit Miami</a>
```

InSight | **The Target Attribute**

XHTML also has a target attribute, which you should avoid using. It may become deprecated—or at least limited—in HTML 5.0. The target attribute was used with the base element to establish a default window where a file or Web site would open when the user clicked a link. The target attribute was also used to create a pop-up window for links—if the user clicked a link, the new page or Web site would open in a new window, either partially or completely overlaying the original window. Creating new windows in this manner causes problems for users who rely on screen readers because if one window overlays another, it becomes difficult to determine which window to read. The target attribute was also used with framesets. The use of framesets is deprecated in XHTML 1.1 and not supported in HTML 5.0. For all of these reasons, be wary if you use the target attribute.

Now that you have shown Travis how to use images as links, you will show him how to link to resources other than Web pages.

Linking to Other Web Resources

In addition to linking to other Web pages and sites, links are used to access Web resources such as text documents and e-mail. Some documents are stored on the Web as Adobe PDF files. **PDF** is an acronym for **Portable Document Format**, a file format created by Adobe strictly to view and exchange documents. A PDF file stores a file in its original appearance. For example, if you want a visitor to see a Microsoft Excel file, but the visitor does not have Excel installed on his or her computer, the PDF file will open and the contents will appear as they do in Excel. To open a file stored in PDF file format, you need to have the companion viewing software, Adobe Reader, installed on your computer. Adobe Reader is commonly installed on most computers, but if necessary, you can download the free Adobe Reader software at *www.adobe.com*.

Linking to Non-XHTML Files

You can link to any file, such as a Microsoft Word file or an Adobe PDF file. You should always include some text on your page that identifies the file as a non-XHTML file. When visitors click a link, they expect to see another XHTML page, not a page that may require a download or the installation of a plug-in that's necessary to view the page. In the link to a non-XHTML file, include the file extension in the link text so that the visitor knows the link is to a file from another software program, as shown below.

View the Adobe PDF file:
birthday.pdf

The XHTML code for the link would be the same as that for viewing another Web page, except that the link is to the filename instead of to an XHTML file:

```
<p>View the Adobe PDF file:
<br /><a href="birthday.pdf">birthday.pdf</a></p>
```

When the user clicks the link, the File Download dialog box appears, prompting the user to open or save the file.

Creating an E-Mail Link

You probably are familiar with a link at the bottom of a Web page that asks you to contact the Webmaster or to e-mail your comments. An e-mail link does not link to another location on a Web page. Instead, you use an e-mail link to open e-mail messaging software, such as Microsoft Outlook, so that you can compose and send an e-mail message. You create an e-mail link by using the mailto: protocol. When you use the mailto: protocol, you don't include the http:// protocol.

| erence Window | **Creating a Link to an E-Mail Address**

- To create a link to an e-mail address, use the following format:
  `<a href="mailto:addressname@domainname.suffix">linktext</a>`
  where *a* is the start anchor tag, *href* is the hypertext reference attribute, *mailto* is the protocol, *addressname* is the e-mail address of the recipient, *domainname* is the domain name, *suffix* is the suffix, *linktext* is the text that the user will click to activate the link, and *</a>* is the end anchor tag.

E-mail addresses are usually italicized, but they do not have to be. It is important that you not include a space between the colon in the mailto protocol and the e-mail address; if you include a space, the link will not work. The code for a hypertext link to an e-mail address looks like this:

```
<p><a href="mailto:webmaster@winterwaterbrands.com">
<em>Webmaster</em></a></p>
```

Spam is a concern when using an e-mail link. **Spam** is any unsolicited and unwanted e-mail. Some unscrupulous companies use an **e-mail harvester**, software that looks for and collects e-mail addresses for the purpose of sending spam. You can reduce your vulnerability to spam by using an image as a link in the e-mail address instead of link text, like this:

```
<p><a href="mailto:webmaster@winterwaterbrands.com">
<img src="webmaster.gif" alt="webmaster e-mail address image"
width="50" height="20" /></a></p>
```

You can also include a default subject for the e-mail by using the ? character as a flag character after the e-mail address. For example, if the e-mail dealt with customer service, the code for the e-mail link would appear like this:

```
<p><a href="mailto:webmaster@winterwaterbrands.com?
subject=customer service">Contact customer service</a></p>
```

You will show Travis how to create an e-mail link.

To create an e-mail link to Winter Water:

▶ **1.** Switch back to your text editor.

▶ **2.** On a blank line below the words "Contact Us" and the comment regarding e-mail, type the following code, as shown in Figure 2-29.

```
<p><a href="mailto:webmaster@winterwaterbrands.com?
subject=customer service">Contact customer service</a></p>
```

Figure 2-29	The code for the e-mail link

```
<p>Contact Us:</p>                                       code for the e-mail link

<!-- e-mail link is below -->

<p><a href="mailto:webmaster@winterwaterbrands.com?
subject=customer service">Contact customer service</a></p>

<!-- link to the id named "top" is below -->

<p><a href="#top"><img src="arrow.gif" alt="image of up arrow" width="40"
height="40" />Back to Top</a></p>
```

▶ **3.** Save the file.

▶ **4.** Switch to your browser and refresh (or reload) the page. Compare your file to the one shown in Figure 2-30.

Figure 2-30	The e-mail link in the browser

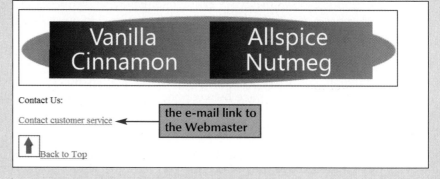

Contact Us:

Contact customer service ◀ the e-mail link to the Webmaster

Back to Top

▶ **5.** If e-mail software is installed on your computer, click the e-mail link. When your e-mail program opens and displays a new message window, close the e-mail program without sending a message.

▶ **6.** Submit the results of the **winternew.htm** file to your instructor, either in printed or electronic form, as requested.

▶ **7.** If you will not be completing the Review Assignments or the Case Problems, close your text editor and your browser.

In this session, you learned how to use an image as a link, and you learned that it's possible to use a smaller image, called a thumbnail, to link to a page that has a larger version of the same image. You created an image map, in which a single image is the source for several links. You also learned that you can link to other resources, such as Adobe PDF or Microsoft Word files. Finally, you learned how to create an e-mail link.

Review | Session 2.2 Quick Check

1. If you are using an image as a link, what else should you include in case users have a browser that doesn't support images or have turned off images in their User Preferences?

2. What is a thumbnail link?

3. How do you determine what the coordinates are for an image map?

4. If the shape of the area you want to define as a hotspot is a square, which value would you use for the shape attribute?

5. If the shape of the area you want to define as a hotspot is irregular, which value would you use for the shape attribute?

6. If the shape of the area you want to define as a hotspot is oval, which value would you use for the shape attribute?

Review | Tutorial Summary

The anchor element is used with links. You can link to an id on the same page, link to a different page, link to an id on a different page, link to a different Web site, or create a link to an e-mail client. The href attribute and its value specifies the target of a link. The referring page is the page with links to another page. The target page is the page that appears when the user clicks a link in the referring page. If you are linking to another Web site, you must include the complete URL of that Web site as the value for the href attribute. A thumbnail is a small version of a larger image. A hotspot is an area of an image that is used as a link in an image map. The usemap attribute is used to declare an image for use as a map. The map element contains the code for the image map. The area element defines the general area of an image that can be used for links. The shape attribute takes one of three values: rect, circle, or poly. The coords attribute and its values specify the exact coordinates for the link. The coordinate values cannot be obtained within XHTML; they must be obtained from graphics software or from Web page authoring software. You can also link to resources other than Web pages, such as documents and multimedia files. Use the mailto: protocol to establish an e-mail link.

Key Terms

absolute file address	Hypertext Transfer Protocol	relative file address
anchor element	id attribute	resample
area element	image map	sibling folders
child folder	Internet Protocol	spam
client computers	link	suffix
coordinates attribute	link text	target page
domain name system	map element	TCP/IP
e-mail harvester	navigation bar	thumbnail
File Transfer Protocol	packets	title attribute
flag character	parent folder	top-level domain name
fold	PDF	Transmission Control Protoco
FTP	piping symbol	Uniform Resource Locator
hotspots	Portable Document Format	URL
HTTP	proprietary code	usemap attribute
hypertext reference	protocol	
hypertext reference attribute	referring page	

Practice | Review Assignments

time to practice kills you learned e tutorial using ame case ario.

Data Files needed for the Review Assignments: cinnamon.htm, cinnamon.jpg, cinnamonlogo.gif, and contest.pdf

Travis has asked for your help in developing the cinnamon.htm page at the Winter Water Web site. He wants to have some links to help users navigate the page more efficiently. A preview of the Web page appears in Figure 2-31.

Figure 2-31

Winter Water Cinnamon Flavor

It's Always Cinnamon Season!

Enter Our Contest

Varities of Cinnamon

- Cinnamomum dubium
- Cinnamomum ovalifolium
- Cinnamomum litseafolium
- Cinnamomum citriodorum
- Cinnamomum rivulorum
- Cinnamomum sinharajense
- Cinnamomum capparu-corende

Some Recently Published Books About Cinnamon

Applebest, Roger
    The Story of Cinnamon. Purple Press, ©2010.
Turencic, Adele
    Cinnamon Wonders. Hearthland Publishers ©2011.
Xeppfts, Boris
    Cinnamon Uses Across the World. Distinct, Inc. ©2012.
Zapamater, Ursula
    My Years with Cinnamon. Hartlett and Bynes ©2012.

Freshness

Our cinnamon is imported in bulk and is ground right here in our bottling facility in the United States. We never use cinnamon that has been ground by a third-party supplier. All of the ingredients that are used in our bottled products are prepared locally on site and under our direct supervision. We always want to ensure the freshness and purity of our products. We don't outsource anything.

Open the Adobe PDF file: contest.pdf

Home

Top

Complete the following:

1. Use your text editor to open the file named **cinnamon.htm,** which is provided in your Data Files in the Tutorial.02\Review folder. Save the file as **cinnamonnew.htm** in the same folder. Between the <title> </title> tags, type **Cinnamon Page**.

2. In the <head> section and below the page title, create a three-line comment with the following information, substituting your name and the date where indicated:
   Your First and Last Name
   Tutorial 2, Review Assignment
   Today's Date

3. In the start <p> tag before the code for the cinnamonlogo.gif image, insert the code for an id named pagetop.

4. At the bottom of the page, use the word "Top" as the link text and create a link to the id named pagetop.

5. Near the bottom of the page and in the start <p> tag before the text that begins "Open the PDF file ...", insert the code for an id named contest. Also, using "contest.pdf" as the link text, create a link to the non-XHTML file, contest.pdf.

6. Near the top of the page in the h2 heading, use the words "Enter Our Contest" as the link text and create a link to the id named contest.

7. Near the bottom of the page, use the word "Home" as the link text and create a link to ../tutorial/winternew.htm.

8. Save your **cinnamonnew.htm** file, and then open the file in your browser.

9. Test all of the links.

10. Submit the results of the preceding steps to your instructor, either in printed or electronic form, as requested.

11. If you are not completing the next assignment, close your text editor and your browser. Close all open documents.

| Apply | **Case Problem 1** |

Use the skills you learned in the tutorial to create a Web page for a baking company.

Data Files needed for this Case Problem: barker.htm, barkerlogo.gif, leftarrow.gif, week.htm, week.jpg, and week_small.jpg

Barker Bread and Roll   Barker Bread and Roll is a Cleveland, Ohio, bakery renowned for its fresh bread and pastry products. Hannah Barker, the owner, describes her company's success in one word: freshness. Barker Bread and Roll is a chain of 12 small retail outlets in the Cleveland area and surrounding suburbs. All of the bread is baked on the premises and in limited quantities all day long. Because of the frequency of baking and high turnaround, products generally stay on the shelves for only a short time each day. Hannah has approached you about designing a Web page for her company. A preview of the Web page appears in Figure 2-32.

Figure 2-32

Barker Bread and Roll
Barker is Better

Make Barker Your Baker

Fresh Baked Goods All Day Long

What makes Barker better? We never take a break when it comes to giving you the freshest products on the market. We bake our products on demand. You will never purchase anything that has been sitting on the shelves for days or even for a few hours. We know our customers and we know precisely how to meet demand. All our ordering and scheduling is computerized, and we use those computer models to predict demand based upon the day of the week and the time of the year. We even factor the day's weather into our computerized modeling. If the forecast is for heavy snow or rain, we know not to bake as many of our products on that day. If there's a holiday approaching, we use our historical data to project sales for each product based on past performance. When we receive special orders, we factor in those sales figures as well so that we can always meet our customers' regular demand.

Fresh, Fresh, Fresh!

In real estate, they say the top three rules are location, location, and location. At Barker Bread and Roll, we feel that it's freshness, freshness, and freshness. We want our customers to be satisfied whenever they make a purchase at any of our stores. We never sell anything that isn't fresh. You always walk out of one of our stores with warm bread products that will make your mouth water for more.

Let Them Eat Cake

We carry over our business principles to our pastry products as well. We bake only on demand, and we rely on orders from our customers to determine that demand. We can craft a specialty cake of any kind for you. If you need a birthday or anniversary cake, we can bake a cake that you will be proud to serve. If you need a large sheet cake with specialty decorations, please sit down with one of our cake designers so that we can design just the right cake for your occasion. We are experts at pleasing our customers with our specialty cake designs. Do not worry about freshness here, too. We will bake your specialty cake only several hours before the scheduled pick up time. We do not bake our specialty cakes a day or two in advance. We wait until we are ready to meet your needs, not ours.

Let Them Eat Croissants

Okay, it's not the easiest word to pronounce, but it's one of our tastiest new products. Our croissants are full of buttery, flaky goodness. Eat them plain or with cream cheese or fruit, but eat them! You might know croissants as crescent rolls, but they are delicious no matter what you call them. For those new to this treat, croissants are a puff pastry with layers of dough rolled to perfection. Around lunch time, we also make croissants filled with American or Swiss cheese, ham, pepperoni, and other cold cuts. Check out our picture of the **croissant of the week** below.

The Croissant of the Week

Complete the following:

1. Use your text editor to open the file named **barker.htm,** which is provided in your Data Files in the Tutorial.02\Case1 folder. Save the file as **barkernew.htm** in the same folder. Between the <title> </title> tags, type **Barker Bread and Roll**.

2. In the <head> section and below the page title, create a three-line comment with the following information, substituting your name and the date where indicated:
   Your First and Last Name
   Tutorial 2, Case Problem 1
   Today's Date

3. In the body section and between the <p></p> tags, enter the code for the barkerlogo.gif image. Use "Barker logo image" as the alternate text. The image has a width of 760 pixels and a height of 150 pixels.

4. Below the comment to insert a thumbnail link, insert the code to use the week_small.jpg image as a thumbnail link to a file named **weeknew.htm**. Use "thumbnail of croissant image" as the alternate text. The thumbnail image has a width of 100 pixels and a height of 75 pixels.

5. Below the thumbnail link that uses the week_small.jpg image, create a text link to **weeknew.htm**. Use "The Croissant of the Week" as the link text.

6. Save your **barkernew.htm** file, and then open the file in your browser.

7. Open the **week.htm** page in your text editor.

8. In the <head> section and below the page title, create a four-line comment with the following information, substituting your name and the date where indicated:

   Your First and Last Name
   Tutorial 2, Case Problem 1
   weeknew.htm
   Today's Date

9. Use the **leftarrow.gif** image to create a link to the barkernew.htm page.

10. Use the words "Back to Home Page" to create a text link to the barkernew.htm page.

11. Save the file as **weeknew.htm**, and then open the file in your browser.

12. Test all of the links in both the barkernew.htm and weeknew.htm files.

13. Submit the results of the preceding steps to your instructor, either in printed or electronic form, as requested.

14. If you are not completing the next assignment, close your text editor and your browser.

| Apply | **Case Problem 2** |

Use what you've learned, and expand your skills, to create a Web page for a college business club.

Data Files needed for this Case Problem: club.htm and clublogo.gif

Byron Pond College Business Club Professor Sandra Gomez, advisor to the Byron Pond College Business Club in Summit Landing, West Virginia, is preparing a list of Web sites that she has been researching. She wants your assistance in creating a Web page that links to several external Web sites that would be of interest to the club members. She has provided you with the Web site URLs, but she needs your help in creating the Web page, which will be posted on the campus Web site that will publish her research. A preview of the Web page appears in Figure 2-33.

Figure 2-33

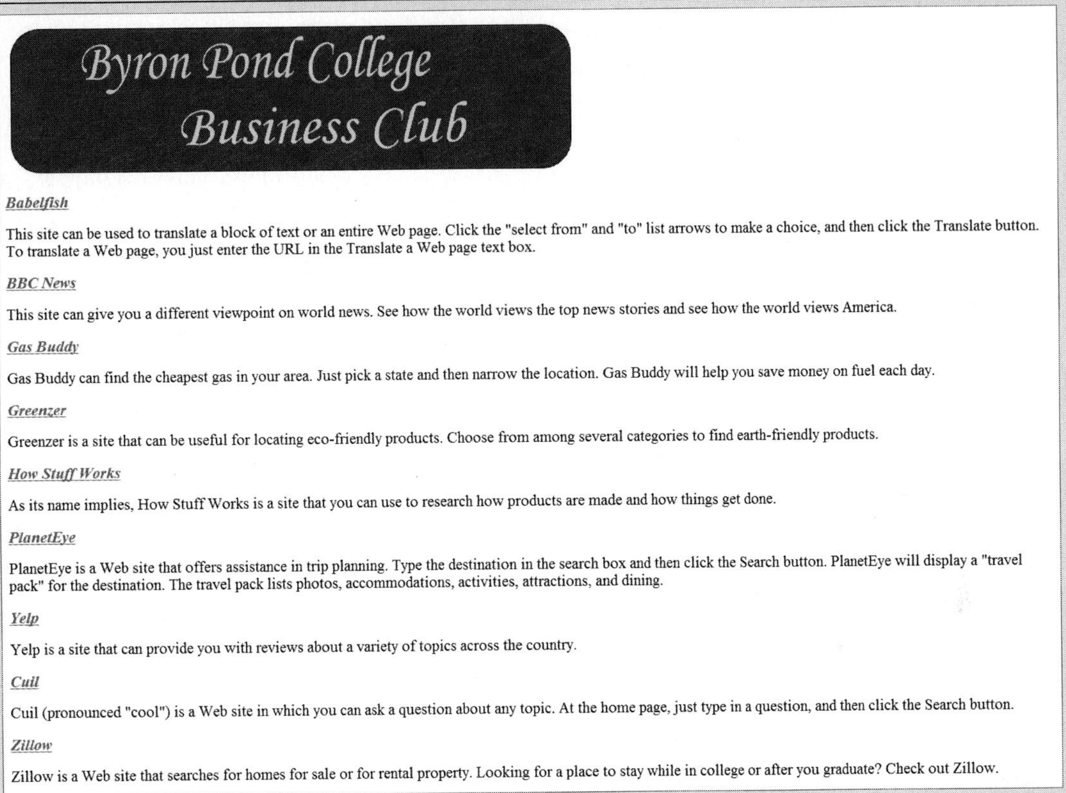

Byron Pond College Business Club

Babelfish

This site can be used to translate a block of text or an entire Web page. Click the "select from" and "to" list arrows to make a choice, and then click the Translate button. To translate a Web page, you just enter the URL in the Translate a Web page text box.

BBC News

This site can give you a different viewpoint on world news. See how the world views the top news stories and see how the world views America.

Gas Buddy

Gas Buddy can find the cheapest gas in your area. Just pick a state and then narrow the location. Gas Buddy will help you save money on fuel each day.

Greenzer

Greenzer is a site that can be useful for locating eco-friendly products. Choose from among several categories to find earth-friendly products.

How Stuff Works

As its name implies, How Stuff Works is a site that you can use to research how products are made and how things get done.

PlanetEye

PlanetEye is a Web site that offers assistance in trip planning. Type the destination in the search box and then click the Search button. PlanetEye will display a "travel pack" for the destination. The travel pack lists photos, accommodations, activities, attractions, and dining.

Yelp

Yelp is a site that can provide you with reviews about a variety of topics across the country.

Cuil

Cuil (pronounced "cool") is a Web site in which you can ask a question about any topic. At the home page, just type in a question, and then click the Search button.

Zillow

Zillow is a Web site that searches for homes for sale or for rental property. Looking for a place to stay while in college or after you graduate? Check out Zillow.

Complete the following:

1. Use your text editor to open the file named **club.htm**, which is provided in your Data Files in the Tutorial.02\Case2 folder. Save the file as **clubnew.htm** in the same folder. Between the <title> </title> tags, type **Business Web Sites**.

2. In the <head> section and below the page title, create a three-line comment with the following information, substituting your name and the date where indicated:
   Your First and Last Name
   Tutorial 2, Case Problem 2
   Today's Date

3. Use the commented text as the source of the URLs to create external links to each of the sites listed. Copy and paste the URL from the comment into the code you will create for the link.

4. Save your **clubnew.htm** file, and then open the file in your browser.

5. Test each of the links on the Web page.

6. Submit the results of the preceding steps to your instructor, either in printed or electronic form, as requested.

7. If you are not completing the next assignment, close your text editor and your browser.

Challenge | Case Problem 3

Use the skills you learned in the tutorial to create a Web page for a national men's clothier.

Data Files needed for this Case Problem: clothing.htm, clothinglogo.gif, home.gif, piechart.gif, and regions.htm

Bremerson Clothiers Bremerson Clothiers is a national retailer of men's wear. With its headquarters in Dallas, Texas, Bremerson Clothiers has aggressively expanded its stores across the United States over the past five years. The expansion is paying off, as sales have increased by more than $10 million this year over the same period last year. Bremerson thinks that it might be able to expand into Canada or Mexico in the near future. Salvatore Davies, the national sales manager, has asked for your help in creating a Web page that provides information about sales performance for all four regions in which the company operates. You will work with several files in this case problem. A preview of the Web page with the image map you will create appears in Figure 2-34.

Figure 2-34

Bremerson Clothiers First Quarter Results

Total Market Share by Region

Click a map section to see detailed results for each region

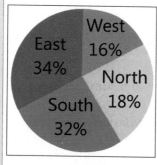

Complete the following:

1. Use your text editor to open the file named **clothing.htm**, which is provided in your Data Files in the Tutorial.02\Case3 folder. Save the file as **clothingnew.htm** in the same folder. Between the <title> </title> tags, type **Bremerson Clothiers**.

2. In the <head> section and below the page title, create a four-line comment with the following information, substituting your name and the date where indicated:
   Your First and Last Name
   Tutorial 2, Case Problem 3
   clothingnew.htm
   Today's Date

3. Do not close the clothingnew.htm file. Open your text editor again so that you have two windows open.

4. In the new window of your text editor, open the file named **regions.htm**, which is provided in your Data Files in the Tutorial.02\Case3 folder. Save the file as **regionsnew.htm** in the same folder. Between the <title> tags, type **Bremerson Clothiers Results by Region**.

5. In the <head> section and below the page title, create a four-line comment with the following information, substituting your name and the date where indicated:

    Your First and Last Name

    Tutorial 2, Case Problem 3

    regionsnew.htm

    Today's Date

6. In the start <p> tag before the Bremerson logo image code, insert the code for an id named top.

7. Using the comments as your guide, insert the appropriate ids in the start <h2> tags for each of the four regions: Eastern, Western, Northern, and Southern.

⊕ EXPLORE

8. Near the bottom of the page, between the <p></p> tags, insert a link to the following external Web site: *www.businessweek.com*. Use "More Business News" as the link text. Create a ScreenTip for this link so that the following text appears when the user passes the mouse pointer over the link: "Visit Businessweek.com".

9. Below the external link, and between the <p></p> tags, enter the code for a link to the id named top. Use "Back to Top of Page" as the link text.

10. Below the code for the link to the id named top, and between the <p></p> tags, enter the code to use the **home.gif** image as a link to the clothingnew.htm page.

11. Below the image used as a link and between the <p></p> tags, enter the code for a text link to the clothingnew.htm page. Use the word "Home" as the link text.

12. Save the **regionsnew.htm** file.

13. Switch to your browser and open the **regionsnew.htm** file. On the regionsnew.htm page, test the links to *www.businessweek.com*, the id named top, and the links to the home page (clothingnew.htm). Use the browser's Back button, close tabs, or close windows as necessary to return to the regionsnew.htm file.

14. Use your taskbar to switch back to the **clothingnew.htm** file in your text editor.

15. Below the appropriate comment and between the <p></p> tags, insert the code for the **piechart.gif** image, which will be used as an image for an image map. Use "pie chart of first quarter results by region" as the alternate text. The image has a width of 400 pixels and a height of 400 pixels. In the image code for the piechart.gif image, use "piechart" as the value for the usemap attribute.

⊕ EXPLORE

16. Below the appropriate comment and between the <p></p> tags, insert the code to create an image map using the piechart.gif image. The map has four polygon shapes. Refer to the following chart to enter values for the coords, href, alt, and title attributes.

coords	href	Values for the alt and title Attributes
13, 10, 199, 4, 196, 189, 5, 281	regionsnew.htm#eastern	eastern region results
205, 9, 203, 187, 399, 87, 399, 0	regionsnew.htm#western	western region results
202, 194, 399, 91, 397, 356, 310, 357	regionsnew.htm#northern	northern region results
198, 195, 5, 284, 6, 395, 304, 391, 303, 353, 201, 195	regionsnew.htm#southern	southern region results

17. Save the **clothingnew.htm** file.

18. Open the **clothingnew.htm** file in the browser. One by one, test each of the four image map links to the ids in regionsnew.htm.

19. Submit the results of the preceding steps to your instructor, either in printed or electronic form, as requested.

20. If you are not completing the next assignment, close your text editor and your browser. Close all open files.

| Create | **Case Problem 4** |

Create a Web page about Web sites that you think would interest college students.

Data File needed for this Case Problem: college.htm

College Student Web Sites   Create a Web page that lists Web sites you think would interest college students. You might want to include Web sites that have information about financial aid or scholarships, internships, job-hunting tips, resume writing, interview strategies, travel abroad, sports, hobbies, health and fitness, diet and exercise, proper food and nutrition, volunteering to work for a charity organization, social networking, and careers. For each Web site you list, create paragraph text and write several sentences explaining why you think the site would benefit college students.

Complete the following:

1. Use your text editor to open the file named **college.htm**, which is provided in your Data Files in the Tutorial.02\Case4 folder. Save the file as **collegenew.htm** in the same folder. Within the <title> </title> tags, type **Web Sites for College Students**.

2. In the <head> section and below the page title, create a three-line comment with the following information, substituting your name and the date where indicated:
   Your First and Last Name
   Tutorial 2, Case Problem 4
   Today's Date

3. In the body section, create examples of the following:
   • At least five links to external Web sites (use the title attribute in the code for each external link)
   • An id
   • A link to an id
   • An image used as a link (Include an image you have obtained from the Web or another source. In the image code, use alternate text and state the image width and height.)
   • A thumbnail link

4. Save your **collegenew.htm** file, and then open the file in your browser.

5. Browse to the *http://validator.w3.org* site. Validate the collegenew.htm file by using the Validate by File Upload method. Correct any errors noted by the validation.

6. Submit the results of the preceding steps to your instructor, either in printed or electronic form, as requested.

7. Close your text editor and your browser.

| Review | **Quick Check Answers** |

Session 2.1

1. a standard for sending and receiving data over phone lines, cable, or by satellite
2. http
3. Uniform Resource Locator
4. the anchor element
5. the # character
6. a list of links that runs horizontally across the screen

Session 2.2

1. some link text
2. a smaller image that links to a page with a larger version of the same image
3. You need to use third-party software such as Adobe Dreamweaver or Microsoft Expression Web.
4. rect
5. poly
6. circle

Ending Data Files

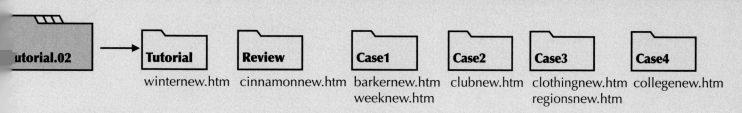

Tutorial.02 → Tutorial   Review   Case1   Case2   Case3   Case4

winternew.htm   cinnamonnew.htm   barkernew.htm   clubnew.htm   clothingnew.htm   collegenew.htm
                                      weeknew.htm   regionsnew.htm

Introducing Cascading Style Sheets

Using CSS Element Selectors to Format Web Pages

Case | Tanner Taxi

Tanner Taxi serves the city of Bennings, which is located about 30 miles northeast of Mobile, Alabama. With the completion of a new automobile manufacturing facility and the relocation of the corporate headquarters of one of the country's largest retailers, Bennings has enjoyed unprecedented growth during a time of economic downturn. Tanner Taxi has expanded its fleet to well over 30 vehicles, which includes a mix of small and mid-sized automobiles, vans, limousines, and SUVs. Tanner Taxi prides itself on being an environmentally friendly company, as all of the company's vehicles are powered by hybrid engine technology. Also, the company has just purchased six new all-electric vehicles. Kim Lee, the owner of Tanner Taxi, has asked for your assistance in creating a new home page for the company Web site. You will create the site and then use Cascading Style Sheets to format it.

Starting Data Files

Tutorial.03 →

Tutorial
taxi.htm
taxilogo.gif

Review
service.htm
servicelogo.gif

Case1
meyer.htm
meyerlogo.gif

Case2
record.htm
recordlogo.gif

Case3
contact.htm
gild.htm
gildlogo.gif

Case4
slake.htm

Session 3.1

Introducing Cascading Style Sheets

In Tutorial 1, you entered XHTML elements and content on your Web page. The purpose of XHTML is to create structure for the page content. Cascading Style Sheets (CSS) is used for the presentation—the formatting of your Web pages. CSS provides a way to easily and efficiently format an unlimited number of Web pages so they have the same appearance. CSS offers many advantages over using XHTML alone, including the following:

- **Greater consistency in your Web site**. You can apply styles you create in one document to some or all of the other pages in your Web site.
- **Easily modified code**. When you modify code to change the style of one page, all of the pages in your Web site can change, which helps you maintain a consistent design.
- **More flexible formatting**. You can format and position text in ways that you cannot with XHTML.
- **Greater functionality**. Many features of word-processing programs, such as tab indents, line spacing, and margins—none of which are available in XHTML—are available in CSS.

Using the feedback you received at a prior meeting with Kim, you have already created an XHTML document for the Tanner Taxi Web page and named the page taxi.htm. You have composed some promotional copy for the page, and you have created a banner image named taxilogo.gif for the Web page as well. You will show Kim how to open the taxi.htm file and save it with a new filename.

To open the taxi.htm file and save it with a new filename:

▶ 1. In your text editor, open the **taxi.htm** file, which is located in the Tutorial.03\ Tutorial folder included with your Data Files. Enter your name and today's date in the comment section where noted.

▶ 2. Save the file as **taxinew.htm** in the same folder.

▶ 3. Open **taxinew.htm** in your browser. Figure 3-1 shows the current appearance of the taxinew.htm file.

Figure 3-1   **The taxinew.htm file in the browser**

Tanner Taxi

We Have the Greenest Yellow Cabs

Make *Tanner Taxi* your one stop for your transportation needs in and around the Bennings area. Not only do we offer car service in the Bennings area, we also have **regularly scheduled** van service to Mobile each day. We also have scheduled service to Mobile *on Friday and Saturday evenings.* We offer limousine service to and from Mobile as well. We also offer car service to all the major golf courses in the area.

Our Modern Fleet

All our vehicles are either hybrid or electric vehicles. When you ride with us, you are doing yourself and the environment a favor. We have recently added six new all-electric vehicles for short trips here in Bennings. Need a larger vehicle than a passenger car? Call for our SUV, van, or limousine service. We have vans that comfortably fit up to 16 passengers, and there is ample space for luggage as well. If you need special service or if you just want to travel in a more luxurious manner, we have limousine service within Bennings and also to and from Mobile.

Corporate Accounts

You can charge your car service through your corporate account and receive a monthly statement. There is no easier way to keep track of your expenses. We also offer an annual statement billing that summarizes all of the services provided to your company for the entire year. Use this statement for your accounting or tax purposes. The annual statement also makes it easy to audit the services provided to eliminate employee fraud or abuse.

We Never Close

Our services are available all day and all night, seven days a week and 365 days a year. We are always here when you need us. There are no extra charges or surtaxes for holiday service or for off-hour and nightly service. We charge one flat rate for all services. You pay a fair fare at all times. Our drivers are experienced, professional, and courteous. You will not only enjoy your ride, enjoy paying a reasonable rate for services, but you will also appreciate traveling with drivers who know the area, have excellent driving records, and who are deeply concerned about customer satisfaction. We also offer emergency service if you need a designated driver. We do our best to keep the Bennings area roads safe at night. Let us be your designated driver.

You Also Might Want to Know:

- In a taxicab, several people ride for the price of one
- 100% of our vehicles are "clean air" vehicles
- We use state-of-the-art GPS computer dispatching
- We have safe, clean, air conditioned vehicles
- We accept credit card and debit card payments
- We have ten all-wheel-drive SUVs to meet your travel needs during severe weather

Call Us at 423 567-TAXI

Next, you'll show Kim how to insert the banner image you have created for the Web page. The banner image file is named taxilogo.gif, and it is stored with the Tutorial 3 Data Files.

To insert the code for the banner image:

▶ **1.** In your text editor, click a blank line below the <body> tag.

▶ **2.** Type the following code, as shown in Figure 3-2.

```
<p><img src="taxilogo.gif" alt="Tanner Taxi banner image"
width="780" height="180" /></p>
```

Figure 3-2   **The code for the banner image**

image tag code is inserted

```
<p><img src="taxilogo.gif" alt="Tanner Taxi banner image" width="780" height="180" /></p>

<h1>Tanner Taxi</h1>
<h2>We Have the Greenest Yellow Cabs</h2>

<p>Make <strong><em>Tanner Taxi</em></strong> your one stop for your transportation needs in and around
the Bennings area. Not only do we offer car service in the Bennings area, we also
have <strong>regularly scheduled</strong> van service to Mobile each day. We also have scheduled service
to Mobile <em>on Friday and Saturday evenings.</em> We offer limousine service to and from
Mobile as well. We also offer car service to all the major golf courses in the area.</p>

<h3>Our Modern Fleet</h3>

<p>All our vehicles are either hybrid or electric vehicles. When you ride with us,
you are doing yourself and the environment a favor. We have recently added six new
all-electric vehicles for short trips here in Bennings. Need a larger vehicle
```

▶ **3.** Save the file.

▶ **4.** Switch to your browser and refresh or reload the **taxinew.htm** file, as shown in Figure 3-3.

Figure 3-3 | **The banner image in the browser**

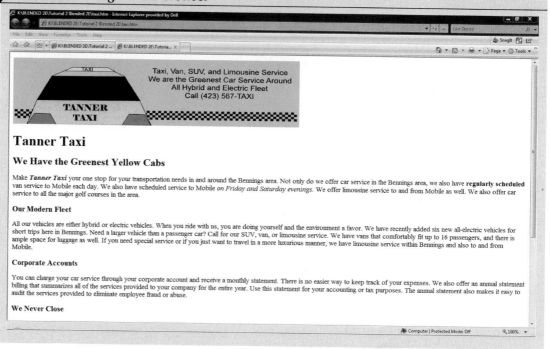

Like HTML and XHTML, CSS has been through several versions. The current version of CSS is 2.1. Ideally, all browsers would display all of the CSS properties and values, and they would display them in the same way. When a CSS feature appears in all browsers without any differences, the feature is said to have **cross-browser support**. However, no contemporary browser supports all the features of CSS, nor do these browsers support CSS in a consistent manner. So, it's a good idea to test your Web pages in at least the current and prior versions of the four major browsers, which, as of this writing, are Mozilla Firefox, Microsoft Internet Explorer, Google Chrome, and Apple Safari. Next, you will show Kim how to create CSS styles.

Understanding How Styles Are Written

Using CSS, you can change how an XHTML element appears in the browser. For example, the XHTML strong element makes text appear as bold, but the strong element does not change the font, size, or color of the text. Using CSS, you can create a *style* for the strong element so that whenever you use it, *you* control how that text appears in the browser. For example, you could create a style to format any strong text in your Web page to appear in the Arial font, in a larger type size, and in red.

You are familiar with styles of dress and styles of music. A **style** is a consistent, recognizable pattern. A **CSS style** is a collection of one or more rules, and a **style sheet** is a collection of styles. A style sheet can be written within an XHTML document or as a separate file. A **rule** is the combination of a selector, a property, and a value. The **selector** identifies the element to which you are applying a style.

CSS has several kinds of selectors, but the three most common are element selectors, class selectors, and id selectors. **Element selectors**, also known as **type selectors**, are used to format XHTML elements. **Class selectors** are used to select a specific XHTML element or format one or more elements on a Web page. **Id selectors** are used to uniquely format a single element on a Web page. In this tutorial, you will only work with element selectors. In later tutorials, you will work with class and id selectors.

In Tutorial 1, you worked with attributes and values. Recall, for example, that the img element used the alt attribute and that you gave the alt attribute a value. CSS properties and values are similar to XHTML attributes and values. In CSS, the **property** describes how the selector will be modified. The value indicates the manner or extent to which the property will be modified. In the following example, *color* is the property and *white* is the value:

```
color: white;
```

Recall that XHTML code has syntax—specific rules for how the XHTML code should be entered. CSS also has its own syntax, and you must follow it; otherwise, the CSS code will not function properly. In writing CSS code, the selector comes first. For example, if the h1 element were the selector, the code to style the h1 element selector would begin with h1.

Reference Window | Creating a CSS Rule

- In a text document, type the selector followed by a left brace, as in the following code, and then press the Enter key.
  ```
  selector {
  ```
- Type the declarations (each indented by two or three spaces), separating a property from a value with a colon. Type a semicolon after each declaration, and then press the Enter key, as in the following code.
  ```
  property: value;
  ```
- Type a right brace on its own line (but not indented) below the declaration list. The following code shows the complete syntax for a rule:
  ```
  selector {
      property: value;
      property: value;
  }
  ```

Each property and value pair (for example, `color: white`) is called a **declaration**. The declarations are preceded by a start (left-facing) brace, like this:

```
h1 {
```

A colon follows the property. There should be only one space after the colon. A semicolon follows the value. The declaration should be indented two or three spaces to make the code easier to read.

```
h1 {
  color: white;
```

If there is more than one declaration, type each declaration on a separate line and indent the code for each.

```
h1 {
  color: white;
  background-color: teal;
```

Type an end (right-facing) brace to close the **declaration list**, the group of all the declarations. Type the end brace on a separate line, but do not indent the end brace.

```
h1 {
  color: white;
  background-color: teal;
}
```

InSight | **Writing CSS Rules**

When writing CSS rules, make sure you include the following parts of the code:

- A selector
- A left-facing brace before the declaration list
- A colon between each property and its value
- A semicolon at the end of each declaration
- A right-facing brace at the end of the declaration list

In your CSS code, it's the punctuation that matters—the braces, the colons, and the semicolons. What doesn't matter is the spacing, indentation, line returns, or the position of the braces. If you are creating Web pages for personal use, pick a format for your CSS code and stick to it. In the workplace, use your company's best practices (the prescribed manner) for writing XHTML and CSS code. Although you can omit the semicolon after the last declaration, it's good coding practice to include it. If you later decide to add more declarations, the correct punctuation will already be in place.

Because you will frequently mention these CSS terms to Kim, you have composed a CSS quick glossary for her reference, as shown in Figure 3-4.

Figure 3-4 | **The CSS terminology quick glossary**

CSS Terminology Quick Glossary	
CSS style	A collection of one or more rules
style sheet	A collection of styles
rule	The combination of a selector and one or more properties and values
selector	What is being styled
property	How the selector will be modified
value	The manner or extent to which the property will be modified
declaration	A property and value pair
declaration list	All the declarations for the same selector

Figure 3-5 shows the components of a CSS style.

Figure 3-5 | **The components of a CSS style**

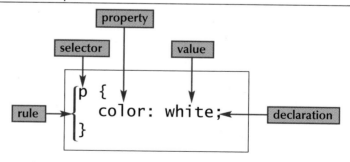

The W3C does not have a particular preference for how to indent and space CSS code, but you should avoid using paragraph format for writing your code. **Paragraph format** places all the CSS code on one or more lines as wrapping text, like this:

```
h1 {color: white; background-color: navy; font-size: 1em; font-weight:
bold; font-family: Arial, Helvetica, sans-serif; }
```

Code written in paragraph format is not easy to read or debug. In addition, most CSS editing software, such as Adobe Dreamweaver and Microsoft Expression Web, creates code with the same formatting as you have been showing Kim. The selector and the starting brace are written on a separate line. Each declaration is written on a separate line and indented two spaces so that the declarations stand out from the selector. The end closing brace is placed on a separate line, indicating the end of the style code for the selector, as shown in the following example:

```
h2 {
  color: white;
  background-color: navy;
}
```

Although it is not required, it is a good coding practice to always end the declaration list with a semicolon. If the declaration list is revised and more declarations are added, you won't have to remember to type the semicolon after the last declaration. You also will avoid a potential syntax error. Next, you will explain to Kim how to enter the code for the first two CSS properties she will work with: the color property and the background-color property.

Working with Color

Kim thinks the heading at the top of the page would get more attention if the text had both a color and a background color. The **color property** is used to change the foreground (the text) color of an element. The **background-color property** changes the background color of an element.

Whenever you change either the foreground color or the background color, it is important to have sufficient contrast between the two colors. Be mindful, too, that some visitors to your Web site might have some form of color blindness. To assist those visitors, it's best to avoid green-on-red or red-on-green combinations.

Color is actually a combination of three colors: red, green, and blue. Mixing these three colors and varying their strength (their intensity) is what produces the color palette you see in the world around you. Computer monitors vary the intensity (in voltage) of red, green, and blue. In CSS code, colors are most commonly entered in three ways: (1) by name, (2) by their RGB triplet, or (3) by a hexadecimal value.

Referring to a color by its name is easy. Some Web color names, such as white, red, and navy, are familiar to you. Other CSS named colors, such as *moccasin* or *peachpuff*, are probably not so familiar. There are 216 named colors, which is not a large number, but not all of them may be supported by all browsers. If you are just learning XHTML and CSS, it is easier to use a named color in the CSS code so you have a better idea of whether you have entered your code correctly.

Most Web page designers use hexadecimal values for color because there are several million color values from which to choose, which offers you great variety. Obviously, you cannot remember all these values, but you should know how hexadecimal values are derived. The more familiar decimal system is based on the number 10, and uses the numbers 0-9. The **hexadecimal system** is based on the number 16, and uses the numbers 0-15. The numbers 0-9 are also used in hexadecimal, but after the number 9, the letters A through F represent the numbers 10 through 15, as shown in Figure 3-6.

Figure 3-6 ▸ **Comparison of decimal and hexadecimal numbers**

Decimal	0–9	10	11	12	13	14	15
Hexadecimal	(Same)	A	B	C	D	E	F

When entering hexadecimal color values in CSS code, you precede each value with a flag character, the # symbol. A flag character has special significance in XHTML or CSS code. In this instance, the # flag character indicates that the numbers after it should be treated as code, not as numbers. After the flag character, you enter three pairs of hexadecimal numbers or letters, each representing the intensity of red, green, and blue, respectively. In the hexadecimal system, 00 is the lowest intensity and FF is the highest. For example, the hexadecimal notation for the color navy is #000080, and the notation for yellow is #FFFF00.

Most Web developers refer to hexadecimal numbers simply as **hex code**. Repeating values can be entered into code using a shorthand notation called short hex. In **short hex**, you use just the first number or letter to enter each pair, but only if the pairs have repeating characters. For example, the color yellow has three repeating pairs of letters and numbers: FF, FF, and 00. So, instead of entering the code for yellow as #FFFF00, some Web developers will use the short hex notation of #FF0 instead.

If you've ever shopped for a television set, you know that not all televisions display the same picture in the same manner. The same is true of computer monitors; they can display colors differently. The color values in the following list are often called the **Web-safe colors** because all computer monitors should be able to display them correctly. CSS version 2.1 has 17 Web-safe colors.

Figure 3-7 lists the Web-safe colors by their name, RGB value, and hexadecimal value.

> **Tip**
>
> In CSS 2.1, orange was added as the 17th Web-safe color.

Figure 3-7 ▸ **The Web-safe colors**

Name	RGB Triplet	Hexadecimal Value
Aqua	(0,255,255)	#00FFFF
Black	(0,0,0)	#000000
Blue	(0,0,255)	#0000FF
Fuchsia	(255,0,255)	#FF00FF
Gray	(128,128,128)	#808080
Green	(0,128,0)	#008000
Lime	(0,255,0)	#00FF00
Maroon	(128,0,0)	#800000
Navy	(0,0,128)	#000080
Olive	(128,128,0)	#808000
Orange	(255,165,0)	#FFA500
Purple	(128,0,128)	#800080
Red	(255,0,0)	#FF0000
Silver	(192,192,192)	#C0C0C0
Teal	(0,128,128)	#008080
White	(255,255,255)	#FFFFFF
Yellow	(255,255,0)	#FFFF00

Later in this tutorial, you will validate your CSS code by using a Web-based service run by the World Wide Web Consortium. If you use named colors in your Web code as values for the color property, the CSS validation software will flag as an error any named color other than the 17 Web-safe colors. To avoid generating errors or warnings during validation, it's a good idea to use hexadecimal or RGB values for colors other than the 17 named colors. It's also a good coding practice to type the hex code value using lower-case letters, so that you can tell the difference between the number 0 and the capital let-ter O, and between the number 1 and the letter l. Lowercase letters appear smaller in the code than numbers, so you can differentiate them more easily. Kim would like to make the text color white and the background color teal. Both colors are Web-safe colors, so you will use named colors for these two declarations. You will show Kim how to enter the code for declaring the color and background color properties.

Creating an Embedded Style Sheet

An **embedded style sheet** is one in which the CSS code is written in the <head> section of an XHTML document. The primary advantage to creating an embedded style sheet is that the XHTML code and CSS code are on the same page, which makes it easy to enter and modify the CSS code while you are developing the Web page. Once the Web page is finalized and you are satisfied with the CSS code, you can move the CSS code to an external style sheet, a separate document where you can store and easily revise your styles.

Tip

ed styles are also
d internal styles.

The **style element** in XHTML is a special element that serves as a container for all the style code. The **type attribute**, with a value of text/css, is always entered within the start <style> tag. The code for the start <style> tag looks like this:

```
<style type="text/css">
```

---

erence Window | Creating an Embedded Style Sheet

- On a blank line in the <head> section of an XHTML document, type:
  ```
  <style type="text/css">
  ```
- Press the Enter key four times.
- Type the end `</style>` tag.
- Position the insertion point on the blank line between the start `<style>` and end `</style>` tags.
- Type the CSS code.
- The following code shows the syntax for an embedded style sheet:
  ```
  <style type="text/css">

  . . . CSS code is typed here . . .

  </style>
  ```

You are ready to show Kim how to style the h1 heading to have white text on a teal background.

To create the style for the h1 heading:

1. Switch back to your text editor.
2. Click just above the </head> tag.
3. Press the **Enter** key twice.
4. Press the **Up arrow** key.

5. On a blank line in the head section, type the following code, as shown in Figure 3-8.

```
<style type="text/css">

h1 {
   color: white;
   background-color: teal;
}

</style>
```

Figure 3-8 | **The h1 heading style**

```
<!--
Tutorial 3
Your Name:
Today's Date:
Filename: taxinew.htm
-->

<style type="text/css">

h1 {
   color: white;
   background-color: teal;
}
```

6. Save the file.

7. Switch to your browser and refresh or reload the **taxinew.htm** page. Your document should be similar to the one shown in Figure 3-9.

Figure 3-9 | **The h1 heading style shown in the browser**

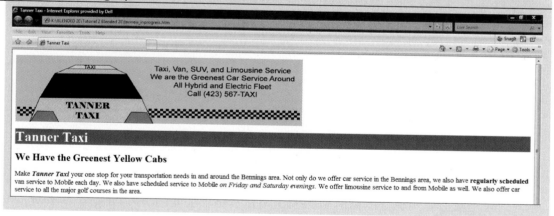

Kim sees that the background color extends from the left edge of the screen to the right edge, which isn't what she wants. She wants only the text to have a background color. You tell her that she can use the CSS **display property** to change whether the background color extends the full screen width. The display property determines how an element will be displayed. The display property has 17 values, but the two most commonly used are block and inline. Block is the default value, which extends the color across the screen. Assigning the display property a value of inline will place a background color behind the text only. You will show Kim how to use this property and value to correct the problem with the h1 heading.

To change the appearance of the background color:

▶ **1.** Switch back to your text editor.

▶ **2.** Click to the right of the semicolon that follows "teal" in the value for the background-color property.

▶ **3.** Press the **Enter** key.

▶ **4.** Press the **Spacebar** twice. Type the following code, as shown in Figure 3-10.

```
display: inline;
```

Figure 3-10	The code for the display property

```
h1 {
    color: white;
    background-color: teal;
    display: inline;
}
```

▶ **5.** Save the file.

▶ **6.** Switch to your browser and refresh or reload the **taxinew.htm** page. Your document should be similar to the one shown in Figure 3-11.

Figure 3-11	The revised h1 heading style shown in the browser

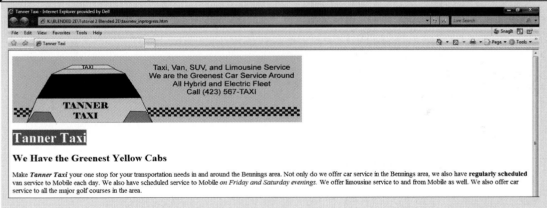

Next, you will show Kim how to group selectors, which is a way to apply a style to more than one selector at a time.

Grouping Element Selectors

If you want to apply the same style to more than one element so they have the same appearance, you can group several selectors together. **Grouped selectors** are selectors with the same declarations grouped into a comma-separated list. Without grouping, if you wanted text in both the paragraph element and list item element to appear in navy, you would enter the following code in your style sheet:

```
p {
    color: navy;
}

li {
    color: navy;
}
```

However, it is not necessary to create a separate style for each selector if the selectors will have the same declarations. To group selectors, type each element selector separated by commas, like this:

```
p, li {
   color: navy;
}
```

You will show Kim how to style the paragraph element and list item element as grouped selectors.

To style both the paragraph and list item elements:

▶ **1.** Switch back to your text editor.

▶ **2.** In the head area, click below the ending brace for the h1 style.

▶ **3.** Press the **Enter** key.

▶ **4.** On a blank line, type the following code, as shown in Figure 3-12.

```
p, li {
   color: navy;
}
```

Figure 3-12 ▶ **The code for the grouped element selectors**

```
<style type="text/css">

h1 {
   color: white;
   background-color: teal;
   display: inline;
}

p, li {
   color: navy;
}

</style>
```

▶ **5.** Press the **Enter** key.

▶ **6.** Save the file.

▶ **7.** Switch to your browser and refresh or reload the **taxinew.htm** page. Your document should be similar to the one shown in Figure 3-13. If necessary, scroll down to view the unordered list.

Figure 3-13 The grouped selector styles shown in the browser

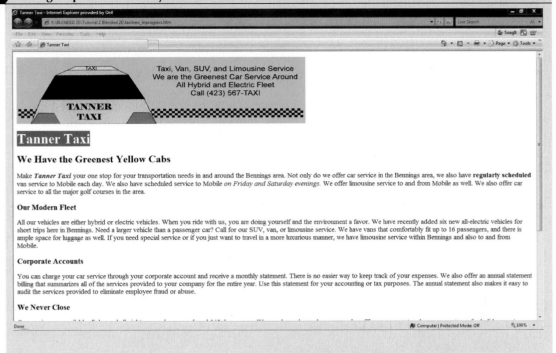

CSS **inheritance** is the method whereby a **child element** inherits characteristics from the **parent element**. A block-level element, such as p, is very often the parent element to an inline element, such as strong. For example, let's say you applied the color green to the p element. By default, any of the child elements of the p element, such as strong, will also have text appear in green. Because the child (the strong element) inherits the green color from its parent (the p element), you don't have to create a separate style for the strong element to have that text appear in green. Note that if you do not want a child element to inherit the style of the parent element, you can apply a different style to the child.

The body element is the parent element to many elements on a Web page. Because of these parent-child relationships, you can apply a style to the body element to affect other styles of the entire Web page, such as the page margins, font, foreground color, and background color. For example, if you style the body element to have text appear in green, all of its child elements (such as the p, em, strong, ul, ol, and heading elements) will also appear in green, unless you have specifically styled those element selectors otherwise.

Next, you will show Kim how to nest element selectors, just as you did when you worked with XHTML in an earlier tutorial.

Using Descendant Selectors

In XHTML, you can nest tags to apply multiple formatting features to the same text. For example, if you want text to appear as both bold and italic, you nest tags as in the following XHTML code:

```
<strong><em>some text here</em></strong>
```

With this code, the text "some text here" will appear in both bold and italics.

Tip

Descendant selectors are also referred to as contextual selectors.

A **descendant selector** is a selector nested within another selector. For example, suppose that you want bold and italic text to appear as maroon. To achieve this effect, you would create the following style:

```
strong em {
   color: maroon;
}
```

This descendant selector specifies that whenever the code for an em element is nested within the strong element, the text will appear in maroon. In all other instances where the em element is used by itself, the em text will continue to appear only in italics, as it normally would, unless you create a different style for the em element. Similarly, strong text by itself will continue to appear only as bold text, but not in maroon.

Note that in the first paragraph of the taxinew.htm document, the text is sometimes bold and italic, sometimes bold, and sometimes italic. Kim would like the bold and italic text to appear in maroon. You will show her how to enter the code for the descendant selector.

To create descendant selectors:

▶ **1.** Switch back to your text editor.

▶ **2.** In the head area, click below the ending brace for the grouped (p, li) selector.

▶ **3.** Press the **Enter** key.

▶ **4.** On the blank line, type the following code, as shown in Figure 3-14.

```
strong em {
   color: maroon;
}
```

Figure 3-14 ▶ **The code for the descendant selectors**

```
p, li {
   color: navy;
}

strong em {
   color: maroon;
}
```

▶ **5.** Press the **Enter** key.

▶ **6.** Save the file.

▶ **7.** Switch to your browser and refresh or reload the **taxinew.htm** page. Your document should be similar to the one shown in Figure 3-15.

The descendant selector styles shown in the browser

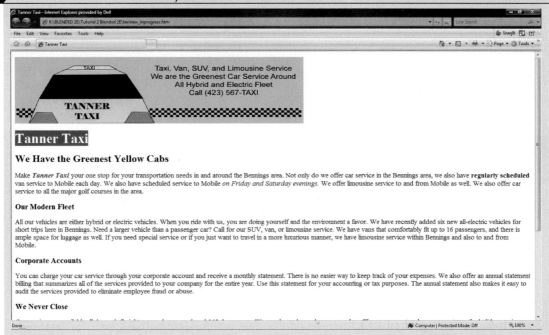

8. If you will not be completing the next session, close your text editor and your browser.

Kim is impressed by the effects of using the color and background color properties, but she would like to know how she can add more visual interest to the text. In the next session, you will show Kim how to change the appearance of text by using the font properties.

Review | **Session 3.1 Quick Check**

1. What is a style?

2. What is a selector?

3. Name the three components of a CSS rule.

4. Which two components of a CSS rule make up the declaration?

5. What precedes the first declaration in a declaration list?

6. What follows the last declaration in a declaration list?

7. What punctuation mark separates a property from its value? What punctuation mark follows each rule?

8. What is an embedded style? Specifically, where must the style code be written for an embedded style?

Session 3.2

Using the Font Properties

In the preceding session, you learned about the color properties. Another commonly used group of properties is the **font properties**, which include bold and italic, text capitalization (referred to as the "case" of text), text size, and the typeface. Figure 3-16 describes the font properties.

Figure 3-16 ▶ **The font properties**

Font Property	Description
font-style	Sets the appearance of text as italic, oblique, or normal
font-weight	Sets the weight of text as lighter, bold, bolder, or normal
font-variant	Displays text in small caps or normal
font-size	Sets the size of text
font-family	Sets the typeface, such as serif or sans-serif
font	Sets all the font properties using one declaration

Changing the Font Style and Font Weight

The **font-style property** has three possible values: italic, oblique, and normal. Italic text is usually a separate font face, with small changes made to each character to slant them at approximately a 12-degree angle. Italic text also has **finishing strokes**, hooks and tails that add more visual detail to the characters. Oblique text, on the other hand, is simply a slanted version of normal, upright text. Currently, browsers do not support oblique text. If you specify a value of oblique, the text will appear in italics. Normal text is neither italic nor oblique. Use the value of normal to remove italics from text that normally would appear in italics, such as the text between <em> </em> tags.

The **font-weight property** uses one of four keywords to change the weight or thickness of text. A **keyword** is a value that has a specific meaning for a property in CSS. The four keywords for the font-weight property are lighter, bold, bolder, and normal. The keyword "bold" makes text appear as bold text, "bolder" and "lighter" darken or lighten the text in relation to the surrounding text, and "normal" removes the bold.

You can also use numeric values for the font-weight property. The values range from 100 to 900 in increments of 100. Typically, a font-weight value of 100 to 500 will give text normal weight, a value of 600 to 800 will make text bold, and a value of 900 will make the text as bold as possible. You specify keyword and numeric font-weight values as in the following examples:

```
h2 {
   font-weight: bolder;
}

h4 {
   font-weight: 900;
}
```

Because of poor browser support for the numeric and keyword font property values, it's unlikely you will notice any difference in using the keywords or numeric values for the font-weight property.

Kim would like the h2 heading to appear as italic text, but not as bold text. She would also like the h2 text to appear in green. You will show Kim how to use the font-style and font-weight properties to change the appearance of the h2 heading.

To change the appearance of the h2 heading:

1. If necessary, open your browser and open your text editor. If necessary, open the taxinew.htm file in your text editor.

2. In the head area, click below the ending brace for the descendant (strong em) style.

3. Press the **Enter** key.

4. On a blank line, type the following code, as shown in Figure 3-17.

```
h2 {
   font-style: italic;
   font-weight: normal;
   color: green;
}
```

| Figure 3-17 | The code for font-style and font-weight |

```
strong em {
   color: maroon;
}

h2 {
   font-style: italic;
   font-weight: normal;
   color: green;
}
```

5. Save the file.

6. Switch to your browser. Open the **taxinew.htm** page, or refresh or reload it. Your document should be similar to the one shown in Figure 3-18.

| Figure 3-18 | The h2 element styled in the browser |

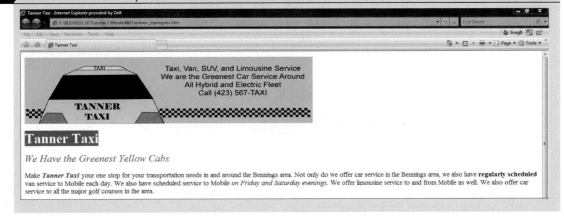

Kim would like to make the contact information stand out at the bottom of the page. You will next show Kim how to make text appear in small capital letters.

Making Text Appear in Small Capital Letters

The **font-variant property** makes text appear in small caps. **Small caps** refers to text that has a slightly smaller point size than regular text (usually 2 points smaller) and is in all capital letters. To indicate a capital letter in small caps, the first letter of a word is about 2 points larger than the other letters in the word. The font-variant property has only two values: normal and small-caps. You specify the value of small-caps as shown in the following example:

```
h4 {
    font-variant: small-caps;
}
```

Tip

To see the font-variant effect on text, you may have to increase the font size from the default value.

XHTML does not have an element that is equivalent to font-variant, underscoring the major benefit of CSS—you can format text in CSS in ways that you cannot by using XHTML. Kim would like the h4 heading at the bottom of the page to stand out, so you will show her how to use the font-variant property to have that text appear in small capitals.

To change the appearance of the h4 heading:

▶ 1. Switch back to your text editor.

▶ 2. In the head area, click below the ending brace for the h2 heading style.

▶ 3. Press the **Enter** key.

▶ 4. On a blank line, type the following code, as shown in Figure 3-19.

```
h4 {
    font-variant: small-caps;
    color: orange;
    background-color: black;
    display: inline;
}
```

Figure 3-19 ▶ **The code for the h4 element**

```
h2 {
    font-style: italic;
    font-weight: normal;
    color: green;
}

h4 {
    font-variant: small-caps;
    color: orange;
    background-color: black;
    display: inline;
}
```

▶ 5. Save the file.

▶ 6. Switch to your browser. Refresh or reload the **taxinew.htm** page. If necessary, scroll down to view the h4 text. Your document should be similar to the one shown in Figure 3-20.

Figure 3-20 ▶ **The h4 element styled in the browser**

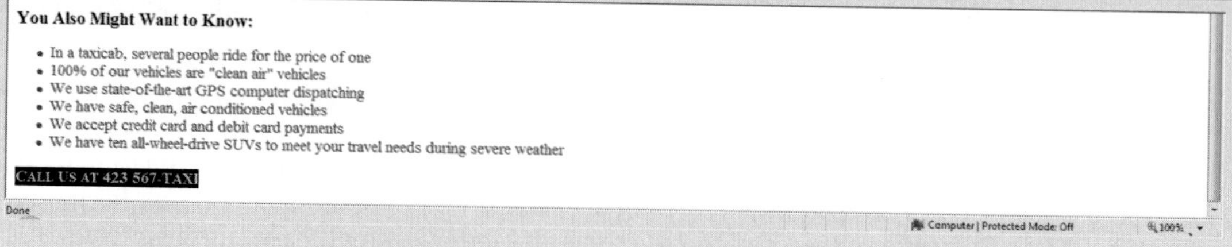

You Also Might Want to Know:

- In a taxicab, several people ride for the price of one
- 100% of our vehicles are "clean air" vehicles
- We use state-of-the-art GPS computer dispatching
- We have safe, clean, air conditioned vehicles
- We accept credit card and debit card payments
- We have ten all-wheel-drive SUVs to meet your travel needs during severe weather

CALL US AT 423 567-TAXI

Done | Computer | Protected Mode: Off | 100%

The next property you will show Kim how to use is the font-size property, which changes the size of type.

Changing the Font Size

The **font-size property** is used to change the font size. When you change the font size, you are telling the browser how tall you want the characters to be. Recall that when you used the XHTML heading elements, you changed the font size, but you had only six font sizes from which to choose. Using CSS, you can specify any font size you want.

You can express font size in CSS code in several ways. CSS supports the following units of measurement:

- Centimeters (cm)
- Inches (in)
- Millimeters (mm)
- Points (pt), equal to 1/72 of one inch
- Picas (pc), equal to 1/6 of one inch
- Pixels (px)
- x-Height (ex)
- em
- Percentage

Because you have probably worked with one or more of the programs in the Microsoft Office suite, you might be most familiar with expressing the font size in point values, such as 14pt and 24pt. Because point sizes are used primarily in typography, it's best to express the font size in points only if you are creating a style sheet designed to print a Web page. You will create such a style sheet in a later tutorial.

In CSS code, it is much more common to express font size as an em value (not to be confused with the em element), as a percent, or as a keyword. An **em unit** equals the width of an uppercase letter M in the browser's default font size, which is usually a font size of 12 points (16 pixels). For example, a font size of 2em would be twice the browser's default font size. In addition to the CSS units of measurement, seven keywords can be used to express the font size.

Figure 3-21 shows how the XHTML headings can be expressed in point sizes and keywords when used as values for the font-size property.

Tip

using pixel sizes for
ize values; browsers
ally have trouble
ng pixel values.

Figure 3-21 **Heading, point, and keyword sizes**

XHTML Heading Size	Point Size	Keyword
n/a	36	xx-large
h1	24	x-large
h2	18	large
h3	14	medium
h4	12	small
h5	10	x-small
h6	8	xx-small

When writing code, be careful not to insert a space between the number and the type of measurement. For example, "2 em" would be invalid because of the space between 2 and em—the font size will remain unchanged.

Em units and percents are examples of a **relative value**, a value that increases or decreases in size in relation to its parent element, which usually is the body element. Point values are an **absolute value**, a fixed value that will not increase or decrease in size in relation to its parent element. Because contemporary browsers allow the user to make the text size larger or smaller, it's important to use relative values for your font sizes. For example, in Internet Explorer, you can click View on the menu bar, point to Text Size, and then select from a number of text sizes, such as Smallest (to decrease the text size on the Web page) to Largest (to increase the text size). In Internet Explorer, if you use relative values for your font sizes, the text will adjust accordingly in the browser regardless of the View size, which is what you and the viewer want. However, if you use an absolute value such as points for your font sizes, the text will remain fixed at that point size in some browsers and not scale appropriately, which is undesirable for accessibility reasons. To make text larger in the Firefox browser, press the Ctrl and plus (+) keys. To make text smaller, press the Ctrl and minus (–) keys. Firefox will scale *all* measurement units and keywords proportionately—even absolute values, such as points. For your Web pages to appear correctly in Internet Explorer, currently you must use em units and percentages as values for the font-size property. Use point values when creating a style sheet to print the Web page.

Kim would like the h3 headings to be larger. You will show her how to use an em unit value to change the size of the h3 headings.

To change the font size of the h3 headings:

▶ **1.** Switch back to your text editor.

▶ **2.** In the head area, click below the ending brace for the h4 heading style.

▶ **3.** Press the **Enter** key.

▶ **4.** On a blank line, type the following code, as shown in Figure 3-22.

```
h3 {
   font-size: 1.4em;
   color: olive;
}
```

| **Figure 3-22** | **The code for the h3 element** |

```
h4 {
   font-variant: small-caps;
   color: orange;
   background-color: black;
   display: inline;
}

h3 {
   font-size: 1.4em;
   color: olive;
}
```

▶ **5.** Save the file.

▶ **6.** Switch to your browser and refresh or reload the **taxinew.htm** page. Your document should be similar to the one shown in Figure 3-23.

Figure 3-23 ▶ **The h3 element styled in the browser**

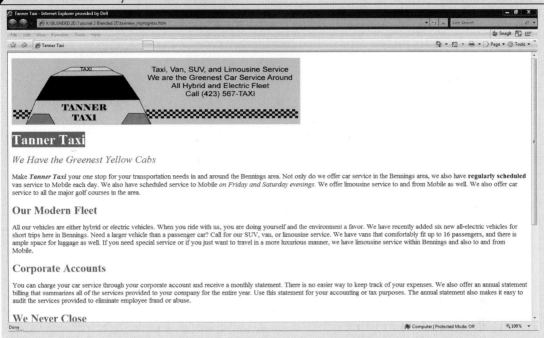

The last property you will show Kim how to use is the font-family property, which involves several considerations.

Changing the Font Family

The **font-family property** is used to change the typeface of text. People sometimes confuse a font with a font family. A **font** is the recognizable, distinct design of a collection of characters in a particular typeface, such as Arial. A **font family** is a set of fonts that have similar characteristics, such as Arial, Arial Narrow, and Arial Black, and are designed to be used together. Although thousands of fonts are available for printed text, only certain fonts are commonly used on Web pages. The fonts you see on Web pages depends on the **platform**—the type of computer and operating system—that you are using. The platform, which is what installs fonts on your computer, typically installs several dozen fonts, far fewer than the number of fonts available.

Because it is quite a challenge to install and use all of the available fonts, a group of nonspecific, generic fonts are used on the Web. A **generic font** attempts to duplicate as many features of a specific font as possible. On the Web, a generic font is designed to be the default option if none of the specified fonts are installed on the user's computer.

Five generic fonts are used on the Web: serif, sans-serif, monospace, cursive, and fantasy. These five fonts are designed to be **cross-platform**, meaning that they are fonts that will be displayed on any computer regardless of the platform. The letters in a **serif font** have finishing strokes—hooks and tails. Because of their detail, serif fonts are very easy to read. For example, Century Schoolbook, a font used in primary-grade reading books, is a familiar serif font. A **sans-serif font**, such as Arial, lacks finishing strokes. Sans-serif fonts are considered to have a more contemporary appearance. A **monospace font** has a fixed-letter width, meaning that every letter takes up the same amount of space. For example, in a monospace font, the letter "i" takes up as much space as the letter "w." Computer programming code is often illustrated in a monospace font such as Courier or Courier New. A **fantasy font**, such as Broadway, is an example of a font that is artistic and decorative. **Cursive fonts**, such as Lucida Calligraphy or Edwardian Script, are examples of fonts that are designed to resemble handwritten letters or handwritten script. The five generic font families are shown in Figure 3-24.

Figure 3-24	The generic fonts

Generic Font	Description	Example
serif	Letters have finishing serifs (hooks and tails) at the top or bottom	Times New Roman
sans-serif	Letters do not have finishing strokes	Arial or Helvetica
monospace	Letters have a fixed width	Courier Courier New
fantasy	Letters are decorative and artistic	**Broadway**
cursive	Letters are designed to look like handwriting or script	*Lucida Calligraphy* *Edwardian Script*

Besides using the five generic fonts as values for the font-family property, you can use any other font name, such as Optima, Bookman, or Helvetica. However, use caution if you specify a font other than the generic fonts, because users must have the font installed on their computer. If the font is not installed on the user's computer, the browser displays its default font, which usually is Times New Roman. Although serif, sans-serif, and mono-space fonts are commonly installed on most computers, fantasy and cursive fonts are not. Different computers interpret fantasy and cursive fonts differently, so in general you should limit the use of these fonts on your Web pages. A common workaround for this problem is to create text with cursive or fantasy fonts in a design program, such as Adobe Illustrator or Microsoft Expression Design, save that text as an image file, and then use the image file on your Web page.

Sometimes PC and Apple computers refer to the same font by different names. For example, the default sans-serif font on many Windows computers is Arial, which on an Apple Mac computer is called Helvetica or Swiss. The default serif font on many Windows computers is Times New Roman, while on Apple computers, it is called Times or Dutch. These variations in font names can lead to trouble when you try to make your Web pages appear uniformly in all browsers. Because you don't know what fonts users have installed on their computers, it's a good coding practice to list several fonts as values for the font-family property, including at least one generic font at the end of the list. For example, if you want to specify the Arial font, include "sans-serif" at the end of the **font list**, the list of fonts in which you would like the text to appear in the browser. The browser will use this generic sans-serif font in case the other specific options in the font list are not installed. In the font list, type a comma between each font name, like this:

```
h1 {
    font-family: Arial, Helvetica, sans-serif;
}
```

In the preceding example, the browser would interpret the instruction to style the h1 element like this: Use the Arial font, and if you can't find Arial, use Helvetica; otherwise, use the default sans-serif font that is installed on the computer.

If the font-family value is more than one word, such as "Times New Roman," you must enclose the value in single or double quotation marks, as shown in the following example; otherwise, the browser will interpret each word in the font name as a separate font:

```
h2 {
    font-family: "Times New Roman", serif;
}
```

Kim would like to change the font family for the entire page to a sans-serif font. You will show Kim how to change the font to Arial for the taxinew.htm Web page. Because this change will affect the entire Web page, you will show Kim how to style the body

Tip

You don't have to capitalize font names in your CSS code, but it's a good coding practice.

Tip

Fonts commonly installed on Apple computers include Swiss, Dutch, Times, Geneva, Helvetica, and Courier.

Tip

In the declaration, you do not have to include spaces after commas in the font list, but it is a good coding practice to do so.

element. It's a good coding practice to enter the code for the body element style at the top of the style sheet.

To change the font family for the body element:

▶ **1.** Switch back to your text editor.

▶ **2.** In the head area, click after the right-facing angle bracket in the start <style> tag.

▶ **3.** Press the **Enter** key twice.

▶ **4.** Type the following code, as shown in Figure 3-25.

```
body {
    font-family: Arial, Helvetica, sans-serif;
}
```

Figure 3-25	The code for the body element

```
body {
    font-family: Arial, Helvetica, sans-serif;
}

h1 {
    color: white;
    background-color: teal;
    display: inline;
}
```

▶ **5.** Save the file.

▶ **6.** Switch to your browser and refresh or reload the **taxinew.htm** page. Your document should be similar to the one shown in Figure 3-26.

Figure 3-26	The body element styled in the browser

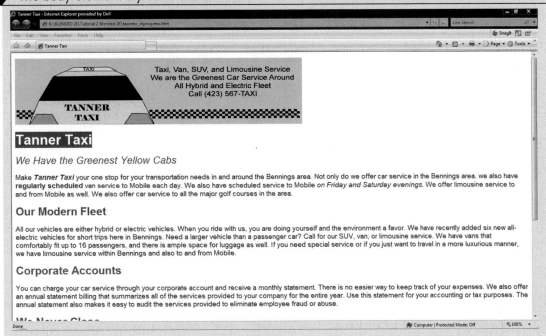

Next, you will show Kim how to use the font shorthand property to reduce the number of declarations to be typed when creating a style using several font properties.

Using the Font Shorthand Property

The font property is one of several CSS shorthand properties. A **shorthand property** is used to set a related group of properties in one declaration. Some Web developers refer to a shorthand property as a **shortcut property**. In this instance, you can set some or all of the font properties in one declaration. For example, it would be acceptable to use the following code to style the h3 element with a particular font style, weight, size, and family:

```
h3 {
  font-style: italic;
  font-weight: normal;
  font-size: 1.2em;
  font-family: Arial, Helvetica, sans-serif;
}
```

Reference Window | Using the Font Shorthand Property

- Following the selector and the left-facing bracket, type `font:` on its own line, as shown in the following code:
  ```
  h2 {
     font:
  ```
- Type values for the font's style, weight, variant, size, and family as applicable.
- Enter spaces between the values for the font properties.
- Enter commas between values for the font family.
- The following code shows the syntax for a completed rule:
  ```
  h2 {
     font: normal bold 1.4em Verdana, Helvetica, sans-serif;
  }
  ```

Compare the preceding code to the code below, which uses the font shorthand property to achieve the same result, but by using far less code:

```
h3 {
  font: italic normal 1.2em Arial, Helvetica, sans-serif;
}
```

Here's how the font shorthand property works. You begin by using an element as a selector, as you normally would. For the declarations, however, you type the word "font" followed by a colon. Next, you type only the values for the font-style, font-weight, font-variant, font-size, and font-family properties. You can list as few (or as many) values for the font properties as you want. Property values are separated by spaces; font list properties are separated by commas. By using the font shorthand property, you can write a single declaration, which lets you type substantially less code.

Although you do not have to list values for all five font properties, if you use the font shorthand property, you *must* specify values for both the font-size and font-family properties. You also must list the values for the font properties in the following order:
font-style
font-weight
font-variant
font-size
font-family

For example, to specify that an h3 element should have only a different font style and font weight, you still would have to enter values for the font size and font family—those values are required. To change just the font style and font weight, you would enter the following code (entering four values, not two):

```
h3 {
   font: italic bold 1em Courier, monospace;
}
```

InSight	**Creating Inline Styles**

Inline styles are used to apply a style to a section of text within the document body. To create an inline style, you place the style code within the tag in the XHTML document where you want the style to take effect. Within the start tag, type the word "style" followed by the equal sign, with no space around the equal sign. The code looks like this:

```
<p><em style=
```

You must place quotation marks before and after the style code. A semicolon separates each declaration, and a semicolon should follow the last declaration (again, just as a good coding practice), as in the following example:

```
<p><em style="color: blue; background-color: orange;">Text for
the inline style here.</em></p>
```

It's a good coding practice to type both quotation marks first, and then type the styles code between the quotes. If you follow this practice, you won't have to remind yourself to type the closing quotation mark after the inline style code. The quotation marks are important; if you omit either one, the style will not take effect. In general, avoid using inline styles and instead use either embedded or external style sheets, both of which make it easier to locate and revise your CSS styles code.

Kim would like users to notice the list items near the bottom of the Web page, so you will show her how to use the font shorthand property to format the list item element. The items are in an unordered list, so you will use a descendant selector for the style.

To use the font shorthand property:

1. Switch back to your text editor.

2. In the head area, click after the h3 style.

3. Press the **Enter** key.

4. On a blank line, type the following code, as shown in Figure 3-27.

```
ul li {
   font: italic bold 1em Arial, Helvetica, sans-serif;
}
```

Figure 3-27	**The code for the unordered list item style**

```
h3 {
   font-size: 1.4em;
   color: olive;
}

ul li {
   font: italic bold 1em Arial, Helvetica, sans-serif;
}
```

5. Save the file.

6. Switch to your browser and refresh or reload the **taxinew.htm** page. Your document should be similar to the one shown in Figure 3-28.

Figure 3-28   **The unordered list in the browser**

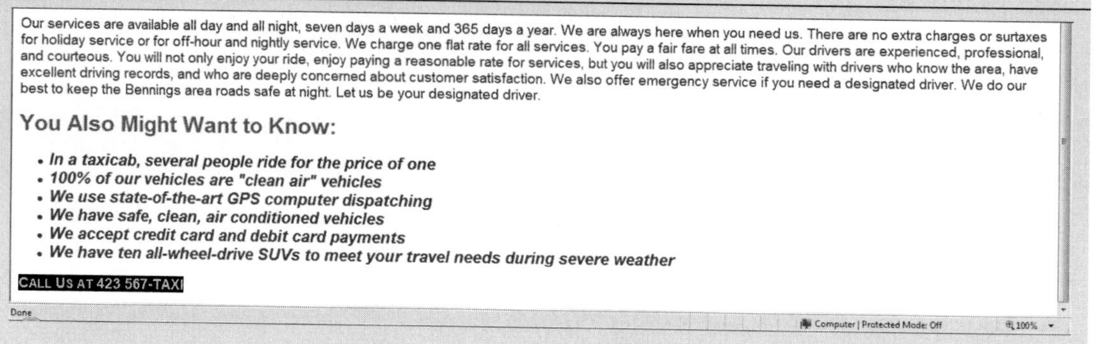

Our services are available all day and all night, seven days a week and 365 days a year. We are always here when you need us. There are no extra charges or surtaxes for holiday service or for off-hour and nightly service. We charge one flat rate for all services. You pay a fair fare at all times. Our drivers are experienced, professional, and courteous. You will not only enjoy your ride, enjoy paying a reasonable rate for services, but you will also appreciate traveling with drivers who know the area, have excellent driving records, and who are deeply concerned about customer satisfaction. We also offer emergency service if you need a designated driver. We do our best to keep the Bennings area roads safe at night. Let us be your designated driver.

You Also Might Want to Know:

- *In a taxicab, several people ride for the price of one*
- *100% of our vehicles are "clean air" vehicles*
- *We use state-of-the-art GPS computer dispatching*
- *We have safe, clean, air conditioned vehicles*
- *We accept credit card and debit card payments*
- *We have ten all-wheel-drive SUVs to meet your travel needs during severe weather*

CALL US AT 423 567-TAXI

Done   Computer | Protected Mode: Off   100%

Validating the CSS Code for the Completed File

In a prior tutorial, you validated a document to check the correctness of the XHTML code. You can also validate a document to check the correctness of the CSS code. Validating the CSS code does not check for spelling, typographical, or grammar errors; it checks only to see if the code complies with the CSS 2.1 standard. Validating a file for CSS code is optional, but because this is Kim's first attempt at creating a Web page, you want to show her how to check her CSS code when you are no longer there to assist her. The validating service to check the CSS code is not the same one used to check the XHTML code. The W3C maintains a site that has a free CSS code validator service: *http://jigsaw.w3.org/css-validator*.

Reference Window | **Validating a File for CSS Code**

- To validate a file to see if the CSS code meets the standard:
  - Open your browser and navigate to *http://jigsaw.w3.org/css-validator*.
  - If necessary, click the By file upload tab.
  - Click the Browse button. Navigate to the storage location of the file to be validated.
  - Double-click the filename to enter it in the Local CSS file text box.
  - Click the Check button.

At the W3C CSS validation page, you will see two methods for validating a document that has not been posted to a Web server: "By file upload" and "By direct input." When you choose By file upload, navigate to the storage location of the file you want to validate, and then click the Check button. If you choose By direct input, you have to copy and paste (or type) the code into the text box on the validation page, and then click the Check button. The By direct input method is generally used when you want to check just a few lines of code (often called a **code snippet**) rather than the entire document. You will now show Kim how to validate the taxinew.htm file by using the By file upload method.

To validate the taxinew.htm file:

▶   1. Open your browser and navigate to *http://jigsaw.w3.org/css-validator*.

The W3C CSS Validation Service site opens, as shown in Figure 3-29.

Figure 3-29 | **The W3C CSS Validation Service Web site**

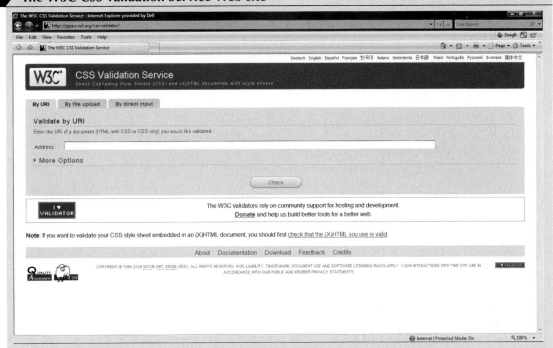

2. If necessary, click the By file upload tab.

3. Click the **Browse** button.

4. Navigate to the storage location of your taxinew.htm file.

5. Double-click the **taxinew.htm** filename to insert it in the Local CSS file text box.

6. Click the **Check** button. The document validates, as shown in Figure 3-30.

Figure 3-30 | The result of the validation

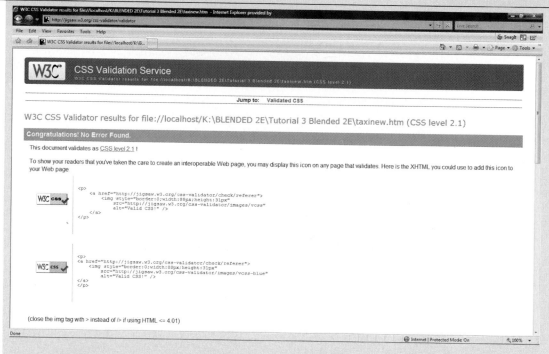

> **Trouble?** If the document does not pass validation, note the errors and debug your document accordingly.

7. Submit the results of the taxinew.htm file to your instructor, either in printed or electronic form, as requested.

8. If you will not be completing the Review Assignments or the Case Problems, close your text editor and your browser.

In this session, you learned about the font properties. Using the font-style and font-weight properties, you can make text appear in italic or bold. The font-variant property makes text appear in small capital letters. The font-size property sets the size of text. Use em values or percentage values for the font-size property. The font-family property is used to change the font. The font shorthand property is used to combine several declarations for the font properties into one statement. To finish the session, you validated a document to check the accuracy of your CSS code.

Review | **Session 3.2 Quick Check**

1. What are the six font properties?
2. What property is used to have text appear in italics?
3. What property is used to have text appear in bold?
4. What property is used to have text appear in all capital letters in a slightly smaller text size?
5. What property is used to change the size of type?
6. How does a font differ from a font family?
7. What will be the type size if you specify a value of "18 pt"?
8. What are the five font families?

In this tutorial, you learned that XHTML works together with CSS to create Web pages. In the first session, you learned that CSS allows for easier coding, greater consistency in your code, and more flexible formatting than XHTML permits. You learned about styles, rules, and declarations. An embedded style sheet is written within the <head> section of an XHTML document. Styles can also be written in a separate document called an external style sheet. In the second session, you learned about the font properties, which change the appearance of text. You learned that not all fonts are installed on all browsers. Use a font list to ensure that your text appears in the browser as you intended.

Key Terms

absolute value	font	parent element
background-color property	font family	platform
child element	font list	property
class selectors	font properties	relative value
code snippet	font-family property	rule
color property	font-size property	sans-serif font
cross-browser support	font-style property	selector
cross-platform	font-variant property	serif font
CSS style	font-weight property	short hex
cursive fonts	generic font	shortcut property
declaration	grouped selectors	shorthand property
declaration list	hex code	small-caps
descendant selector	hexadecimal system	style
display property	id selectors	style element
element selectors	inheritance	style sheet
em unit	keyword	type attribute
embedded style sheet	monospace font	type selectors
fantasy font	paragraph format	Web-safe colors
finishing strokes		

Practice | Review Assignments

Take time to practice the skills you learned in the tutorial using the same case scenario.

Data Files needed for the Review Assignments: service.htm and servicelogo.gif

Kim has asked you to make another page for her Web site. Tanner Taxi has been aggressively marketing its expanding travel services, and Kim would like you to create a page that describes the features of these services. A preview of the Web page appears in Figure 3-31.

Figure 3-31

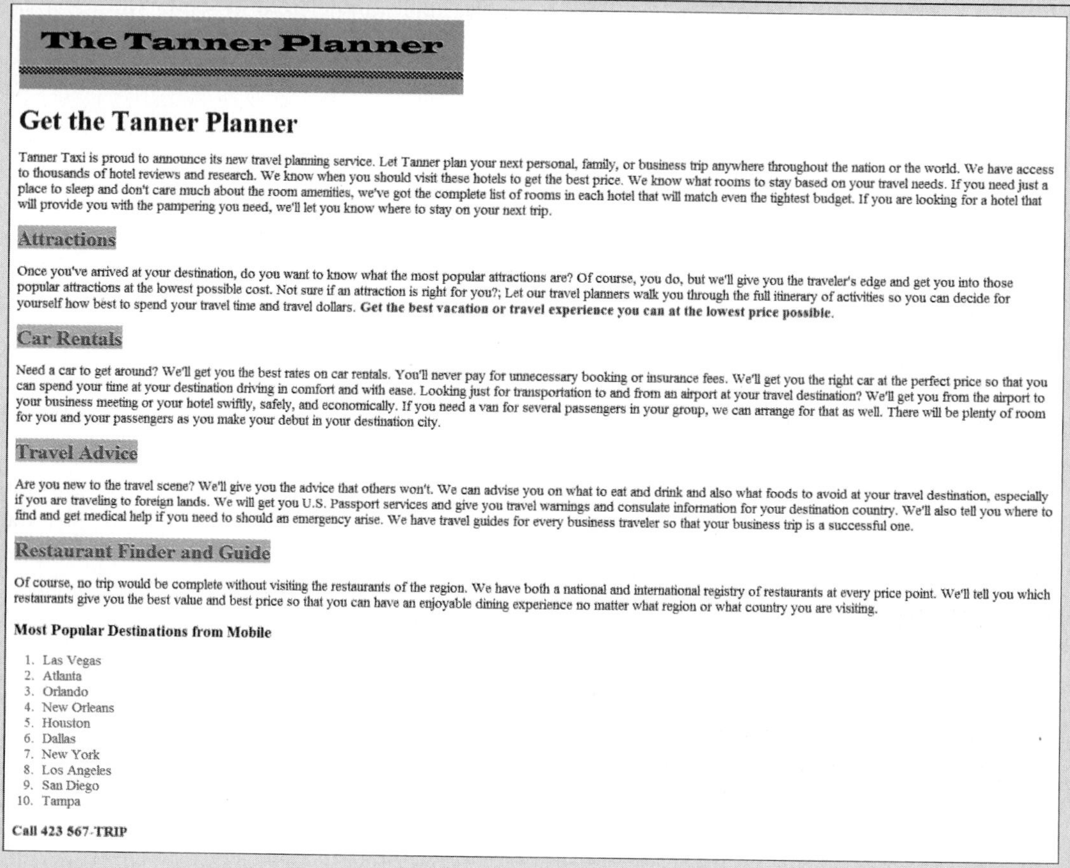

The Tanner Planner

Get the Tanner Planner

Tanner Taxi is proud to announce its new travel planning service. Let Tanner plan your next personal, family, or business trip anywhere throughout the nation or the world. We have access to thousands of hotel reviews and research. We know when you should visit these hotels to get the best price. We know what rooms to stay based on your travel needs. If you need just a place to sleep and don't care much about the room amenities, we've got the complete list of rooms in each hotel that will match even the tightest budget. If you are looking for a hotel that will provide you with the pampering you need, we'll let you know where to stay on your next trip.

Attractions

Once you've arrived at your destination, do you want to know what the most popular attractions are? Of course, you do, but we'll give you the traveler's edge and get you into those popular attractions at the lowest possible cost. Not sure if an attraction is right for you?; Let our travel planners walk you through the full itinerary of activities so you can decide for yourself how best to spend your travel time and travel dollars. **Get the best vacation or travel experience you can at the lowest price possible.**

Car Rentals

Need a car to get around? We'll get you the best rates on car rentals. You'll never pay for unnecessary booking or insurance fees. We'll get you the right car at the perfect price so that you can spend your time at your destination driving in comfort and with ease. Looking just for transportation to and from an airport at your travel destination? We'll get you from the airport to your business meeting or your hotel swiftly, safely, and economically. If you need a van for several passengers in your group, we can arrange for that as well. There will be plenty of room for you and your passengers as you make your debut in your destination city.

Travel Advice

Are you new to the travel scene? We'll give you the advice that others won't. We can advise you on what to eat and drink and also what foods to avoid at your travel destination, especially if you are traveling to foreign lands. We will get you U.S. Passport services and give you travel warnings and consulate information for your destination country. We'll also tell you where to find and get medical help if you need to should an emergency arise. We have travel guides for every business traveler so that your business trip is a successful one.

Restaurant Finder and Guide

Of course, no trip would be complete without visiting the restaurants of the region. We have both a national and international registry of restaurants at every price point. We'll tell you which restaurants give you the best value and best price so that you can have an enjoyable dining experience no matter what region or what country you are visiting.

Most Popular Destinations from Mobile

1. Las Vegas
2. Atlanta
3. Orlando
4. New Orleans
5. Houston
6. Dallas
7. New York
8. Los Angeles
9. San Diego
10. Tampa

Call 423 567-TRIP

Although you will not be instructed to do so after each step, you should do the following whenever you enter code to create a style in your text editor: Save the file, switch to your browser, refresh or reload the page, verify that you entered the style code correctly, and then switch back to your text editor to continue with the next step.

Complete the following:

1. Use your text editor to open the file named **service.htm**, which is provided in your Data Files in the Tutorial.03\Review folder. Save the file as **servicenew.htm** in the same folder.
2. Between the <title></title> tags, type **Tanner Planner**.
3. In the head section and below the page title, enter your name and today's date in the comment section where noted.
4. In the <head> section and below the comment, enter the code for the start style tag, its attribute, and its value.
5. In the <head> section and below the start style tag, type the end style tag.
6. Between the start style and end style tags, press the Enter key three times to create some white space.

7. In the embedded style sheet code, create a style for the h1 element so that h1 text appears in navy.

8. Style the h2 element so that the foreground color (the text) is teal and the background color is orange. Use the display property and the appropriate value so that only the text has a background color.

9. Specify a style so the ol element text will appear in green.

10. Specify a style so the strong element text will appear in maroon.

11. In the body section and between the <p></p> tags, insert the code for the servicelogo.gif image. Use "Tanner planner logo image" as the alternate text. The image has a width of 600 pixels and a height of 100 pixels.

12. Save your **servicenew.htm** file, and then open the file in your browser.

13. Submit the results of the preceding steps to your instructor, either in printed or electronic form, as requested.

14. If you are not completing the next assignment, close your text editor and your browser.

| Apply | **| Case Problem 1** |

*he skills you
ed in the tutorial
ate a Web page
:ompany that
vireless devices.*

Data Files needed for this Case Problem: meyer.htm and meyerlogo.gif

Meyer Wireless Meyer Wireless is a small startup company near Dearborn, Michigan. You will create a Web page that introduces their new line of personal communication devices. You will create a document with an embedded style sheet to simplify formatting of the Web page. A preview of the Web page appears in Figure 3-32.

Figure 3-32

Meyer Wireless for Your Office

Meyer Wireless is your best place for your wireless needs. Need a wireless network installed in your home or business? We can do that. Need a GPS system for a fleet of company cars or just need one for your own personal automobile? We can do that, too. Meyer Wireless *offers the lowest prices* of *anyone* in the Dearborn area. We won't be beat.

Meyer Wireless for Your Home

Meyer Wireless specializes in residential Personal Area Networks. We'll take care of all your wireless connections, including choosing the best *Bluetooth products* for your home office. We will keep you connected and we will do so at the lowest cost in town.

Get a Video Phone for Near or Far

Meyer Wireless will install a video phone in your home or office. Talk to your family, friends, and business contacts over the phone. See the person you are talking to! Video phone is a great tool to see family members across the continent or across town. Need to check up on a sick relative? You can do so if you both have a video phone. Want to conduct important business but don't want to go through the trouble of setting up a video conference? Your video phone will get you connected for a fraction of the cost of videoconferencing hardware and software.

There's no need to waste time sitting in traffic on the way to the airport or dealing with all the other inconveniences and expenses of business travel. Equip your business contacts with video phones, and you can conduct business face to face at any time. Say goodbye to the airport and all the expenses that go along with business travel. Ask us about installing video phones for your family or your business.

CONTACT US RIGHT NOW
1-800 233-WIRE

Although you will not be instructed to do so after each step, you should do the following whenever you enter code to create a style in your text editor: Save the file, switch to your browser, refresh or reload the page, verify that you entered the style code correctly, and then switch back to your text editor to continue with the next step.

Complete the following:

1. Use your text editor to open the file named **meyer.htm**, which is provided in your Data Files in the Tutorial.03\Case1 folder. Save the file as **meyernew.htm** in the same folder.

2. Between the <title></title> tags, type **Meyer Wireless**.

3. In the head section and below the page title, enter your name and today's date in the comment section where noted.

4. In the <head> section and below the comment, enter the code to create an embedded style sheet.

5. Create a style for the body element so that text on the Web page appears in a font size of 1.2em and in Arial, which is a sans-serif font. Also format the body element to have a background color of #e6e6fa.

6. Add a style to make emphasized text appear in green.

7. Add a style to make h3 headings to appear in maroon, with small capital letters, a font size of 1.3em, and in the Verdana font, which is a sans-serif font.

8. In the body section and between the <p></p> tags, enter the code for the meyerlogo.gif image. Use "Meyer Wireless logo image" as the alternate text. The image has a width of 600 pixels and a height of 212 pixels.

9. Save your **meyernew.htm** file, and then open the file in your browser.

10. Submit the results of the preceding steps to your instructor, either in printed or electronic form, as requested.

11. If you are not completing the next assignment, close your text editor and your browser.

| Apply | **Case Problem 2** |

Use the skills you learned in the tutorial to create a Web page for a record company.

Data Files needed for this Case Problem: record.htm and recordlogo.gif

Bremtone Vinyl Records   Bremtone Vinyl Records is a Duluth, Minnesota company that is capitalizing on the resurgence of the popularity of vinyl records. With tens of thousands of vinyl records in stock, Bremtone has a wide variety of titles to offer its customers. Bremtone also sells phonographs, record needles, speakers, and other vinyl-record accessories. You have been asked to design a Web page for Bremtone records. A preview of the Web page appears in Figure 3-33.

Figure 3-33

Welcome to Bremtone Records

Your One Stop for All Things Vinyl

Bremtone is your one stop if you are seeking the pure, true sound of recordings etched on vinyl. There's nothing like the experience of hearing your favorite artists perform in their authentic sound. If you like the sound of music the way it was and the way it can be today, we urge you to contact us today.

Popular Formats We Stock

12" (30 cm) / 33 1/3 rpm LP
7" (17.5 cm) / 45 rpm EP or Single
10" (25 cm)/ 45 rpm LP and 12" (30 cm) / 33 1/3 rpm LP
12" (30 cm) / 33 or 45 rpm Maxi Single

Genres We Stock

We have many formats for you to choose from.[*]

- Blues
- Big Band
- Classical
- Country
- Rap
- Dance
- Techno
- Eurosynth
- R&B (especially from the 1950's and 60's)
- Pop (dating back to the 1940's to the present date)

Accessories

We have all types of accessories for you to purchase to enhance your listening experience. We carry a full line of turntables, speakers, woofers, and tweeters. We have every type of cable you will need. We also have an exhaustive collection of turntable cartridges and needles. We carry a full line of protective sleeve jackets and vertical racks so that you can properly store your recordings. We also have an extensive selection of books and magazines about the vinyl listening experience. We also service and repair turntables.

Handling

You'll get the most enjoyment from your vinyl recordings if you use the proper care. Avoid touching the playing surface of any record. Handle the record on its side edges only. Don't leave your records in a horizontal position. When you are not playing a record, store the record in a vertical position in a record rack in its protective sleeve. Don't use a plastic or metal rack to store your records unless you have placed the record first in its protective sleeve.

Cleaning

Clean your disks frequently, particularly after you have played a recording. You want to ensure there is no damage from dust and static, and you want to make sure that you will be storing your disks safely as well. We stock a wide variety of cleaning materials and cloths for eliminating dust and static from your records. Above all, do not use tap water, which might contain harmful minerals and chemicals, to clean your records. Use either spring water or a water-based solution that contains not more than 20% isopropyl alcohol. Cleaning solutions are very effective at removing dust, dirt, and other contaminants that the record may have encountered, especially during the handling process. Clean the disk in the direction of the grooves, never against the direction of the grooves, which might cause tiny particles from the cleaning cloth to collect on the recording surface.

Storage

You want to get the longest life from your records, so the proper storage of your records is key to maintaining the enjoyment of your records for years to come. Consider the temperature and humidity of the room where you will be storing your records. Store your records in an environment that will be heated in winter and cooled during the summer. Don't store your records in an attic or a garage, where temperature extremes might cause warping or other damage to the record. An environment of 60-70 degrees is best, and humidity in the range of 33-50%. You don't want your records being damaged by heat or humidity. Never store your records where there is any exposure to sunlight. Also be mindful of other room factors that might affect the heat level next to the disks, such as heaters, vents, air conditioners, and lighting. Avoid dusty environments such as an attic or basement. Keep your recordings (vertically) in an airtight container, a cabinet with doors, or a sealable box. If your home or apartment has an open-floor layout, be mindful that smoke and cooking greases from the kitchen or outdoor barbeques can affect your records as well.

Special Artists in Vinyl This Month

1964
The Four Seasons, the Beach Boys, the Four Tops, the Supremes, the Beatles, the Rolling Stones, Gerry and the Pacemakers, the Searchers, Little Anthony and the Imperials, Martha and the Vandellas, Dusty Springfield, the Animals, Herman's Hermits, Manfred Mann, and Neil Diamond.
1967
The Doors, Sly and the Family Stone, the Beatles, the Rolling Stones, the Lovin' Spoonful, the Young Rascals, Jefferson Airplane, Pink Floyd, the Who, Chicago, the Jimi Hendrix Experience, the Monkees, the Mommas and the Poppas, Nancy Sinatra, the Turtles, Mitch Ryder and the Detroit Wheels, Sonny and Cher, the Spencer Davis Group, and Donovan.

[*]This represents only a partial list of genres.

Back to Top

Although you will not be instructed to do so after each step, you should do the following whenever you enter code to create a style in your text editor: Save the file, switch to your browser, refresh or reload the page, verify that you entered the style code correctly, and then switch back to your text editor to continue with the next step.

Complete the following:

1. Use your text editor to open the file named **record.htm**, which is provided in your Data Files in the Tutorial.03\Case2 folder. Save the file as **recordnew.htm** in the same folder.

2. Between the <title></title> tags, type **Bremtone Vinyl Records**.

3. In the head section and below the page title, enter your name and today's date in the comment section where noted.

4. In the <head> section and below the comment, enter the code to create an embedded style sheet.

5. Create a style for the body element so that text on the Web page appears in Verdana, which is a sans-serif font. Also format the body element to have a background color of #c0e59b.

6. Add a style to make the dt element appear in bold, navy text.

7. Add a style to make the dd element appear in italic text.

8. Below the start <body> tag and in the start <p> tag, enter the code for an id named "top."

9. Above the </body> tag and between the <p></p> tags, enter the code for a link to the id named "top." Use "Back to Top" as the link text.

10. Below the code for the id named "top" and between the <p></p> tags, enter the code for the recordlogo.gif image. Use "Bremtone logo image" as the alternate text. The image has a width of 780 pixels and a height of 200 pixels.

⊕ **EXPLORE**　　11. Convert the items in the Genres We Stock section to an unordered list.

⊕ **EXPLORE**　　12. Convert the items in the "Special Artists in Vinyl This Month" section to a definition list. Make 1964 and 1967 the defined terms and make the recording artists after each defined term the definition data.

13. In the Genres We Stock section, after the words "We have many formats for you to choose from," insert a dagger special character. Also make the dagger character appear as a superscript.

14. Insert a dagger special character before the word "This" in the last sentence at the bottom of the page. Also make the dagger character appear as a superscript.

15. Save your **recordnew.htm** file, and then open the file in your browser. In the browser, test the link to the id named top to ensure that the link works properly.

16. Submit the results of the preceding steps to your instructor, either in printed or electronic form, as requested.

17. If you are not completing the next assignment, close your text editor and your browser.

| Challenge | **Case Problem 3** |

Use what you've learned, and expand your skills, to create a Web site for a global shipping company.

Data Files needed for this Case Problem: contact.htm, gild.htm, and gildlogo.gif

Gild Shipping　　Gild Shipping is one of the world's largest container freight shipping companies. With its corporate headquarters in San Diego, California, Gild Shipping transports container freight to every country in the Pacific Rim region. Gild Shipping does much of its business with companies in India and along the east coast of Africa. Phillip Green, the marketing director, has approached you to redesign the Gild Shipping home page. Phillip wants a simple page that will download quickly and explain what Gild Shipping can do for its customers. A preview of the Web page appears in Figure 3-34.

Figure 3-34

Although you will not be instructed to do so after each step, you should do the following whenever you enter code to create a style in your text editor: Save the file, switch to your browser, refresh or reload the page, verify that you entered the style code correctly, and then switch back to your text editor to continue with the next step.

Complete the following:

1. Use your text editor to open the file named **gild.htm**, which is provided in your Data Files in the Tutorial.03\Case3 folder. Save the file as **gildnew.htm** in the same folder.

2. Between the <title></title> tags, type **Gild Global Shipping**.

3. In the head section and below the page title, enter your name and today's date in the comment section where noted.

4. In the <head> section and below the comment, enter the code to create an embedded style sheet.

5. Style the body element so that text on the Web page appears in a font size of 1.1em and in Arial (Helvetica on Apple platforms), which is a sans-serif font. Also format the body element to have a background color of #c19b76.

⊕ EXPLORE 6. Use the font shorthand property to create a style for the h1 element so that h1 text appears in italic, does not appear in bold, has a font size of 150%, and is in Cooper Black, which is a serif font.

EXPLORE

7. Use a grouped selector to style both the h2 and h3 heading text to appear in white with a background color of teal. Use the display property and the appropriate value so that only the text has a background color.

8. Style the h4 element so that text appears in small capital letters and has a size of 1.2em.

EXPLORE

9. Use a descendant selector to style the em element so that whenever it appears nested within the strong element, the text will appear in green and as bold as possible (use a numeric value). The em text should not appear in italics.

10. In the body section and between the <p></p> tags, enter the code for the gildlogo.gif image. Use "Gild Shipping logo image" as the alternate text. The image has a width of 760 pixels and a height of 200 pixels.

11. In the <h2> heading, replace each of the forward slash (/) characters with a large bullet special character. Use a named reference for the special character.

12. In the We Keep You Afloat section, insert the code for the registered trademark special character after the word "GildPak." Use a named reference for the special character.

13. In the same section, insert the code for the abbr element to create a ScreenTip for the abbreviation "RFID." Use "Radio-Frequency Identification" as the text for the ScreenTip.

14. At the bottom of the page and between the <p></p> tags, create a link to the Web page **contact.htm**, which is provided in your Data Files in the Tutorial.03\Case3 folder.

15. Save your **gildnew.htm** file, and then open the file in your browser.

16. Pass your mouse pointer over the RFID abbreviation in the We Keep You Afloat section to verify that the ScreenTip works as intended.

17. Browse to the *http://validator.w3.org* Web site. Validate the gildnew.htm file to check that the XHTML code is correct. If necessary, click the Validate by File Upload tab.

18. Browse to the *http://jigsaw.w3.org/css-validator* Web site. Validate the gildnew.htm file to check that the CSS code is correct. If necessary, click the By file upload tab.

19. Submit the **gildnew.htm** file to your instructor, either in printed or electronic form, as requested.

20. If you are not completing the next assignment, close your text editor and your browser.

| Create | **Case Problem 4** |

Create a file for a campus library that will be a center for international education.

Data File needed for this Case Problem: slake.htm

Slake College Library of International Education   Slake College is located near Chicago, Illinois, a city that has always prided itself as being culturally diverse. Slake College wants to construct a new campus library of international education that celebrates the ethnic mosaic that exists in Chicago. Slake College has been gathering ideas from its student body about what type of building to construct and what the library should offer its students and the city in general. Write at least five paragraphs about what books, DVDs, computers, and periodicals you think the library should have. What types of multimedia should the library have? What types of events should be held in the library? What sort of dining facilities or shops should it have? Should it have special rooms such as classrooms, a concert hall, a theatre, lecture halls, a conference center, or a ballroom? Complete the following:

1. Use your text editor to open the file named **slake.htm**, which is provided in your Data Files in the Tutorial.03\Case4 folder. Save the file as **slakenew.htm** in the same folder.

2. Within the title tags, type **Slake College Library of International Education**.

3. In the head section and below the page title, enter your name and today's date in the comment section where noted.

4. In the <head> section, enter the code to create an embedded style sheet.

Figure 3-35 lists the properties and values that you learned about in this tutorial:

Figure 3-35

Property	Values Normally Expressed As
font-style	italic, normal
font-weight	lighter, bold, bolder
font-variant	small-caps, normal
font-size	em units or as a percentage
font-family	(create a font list)
font	(you must specify a font size and a font family)
color	any named color or hexadecimal value
background-color	any named color or hexadecimal value
display	inline, block

5. Using an embedded style sheet, create styles for each of the following elements:
   - p (use the font shorthand property to style this element)
   - h1, h2, and h3
   - em
   - strong
   - ul li

6. In the body section, make sure you enter the code for the following:
   - A comment
   - The h1, h2, and h3 headings (change the color and background color for at least one of the headings)
   - An image (obtained from the Web or another source; use alternate text and include the image width and height)
   - Five paragraphs of content
   - At least one special character
   - The em element
   - The strong element
   - An unordered or ordered list
   - A superscript or subscript
   - An abbreviation (create a ScreenTip for this abbreviation)
   - A link to an external Web site that has information about studying abroad

7. Save your **slakenew.htm** file, and then open the file in your browser.

8. Browse to *http://validator.w3.org*. If necessary, click the Validate by File Upload tab. Validate the file to check the accuracy of the XHTML code. If necessary, correct any errors listed by the validation.

9. Browse to *http://jigsaw.w3.org/css-validator*. If necessary, click the By file upload tab. Validate the file to check the accuracy of the CSS code. If necessary, correct any errors listed by the validation.

10. Submit the **slakenew.htm** file to your instructor, either in printed or electronic form, as requested.

11. Close your text editor and your browser.

Review | **Quick Check Answers**

Session 3.1

1. A rule or collection of rules that change how the contents of an XHTML selector will appear
2. The XHTML element whose characteristics you want to modify
3. The selector, the property, and the value
4. The property and the value
5. Left brace
6. Right brace
7. Colon; semicolon
8. A style written in an XHTML page itself; the style code must be written in the <head> section

Session 3.2

1. font-style, font-weight, font-variant, font-size, font-family, and font
2. font-style
3. font-weight
4. font-variant
5. font-size
6. A font is a particular font; a font family is a set of fonts with distinctly similar characteristics.
7. The default font size; there must not be any space between the value and the unit of measurement.
8. Serif, sans-serif, monospace, fantasy, and cursive

Ending Data Files

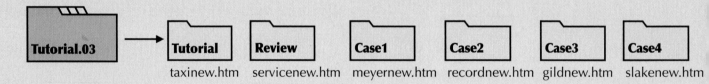

Tutorial.03 → Tutorial   Review   Case1   Case2   Case3   Case4

taxinew.htm servicenew.htm meyernew.htm recordnew.htm gildnew.htm slakenew.htm

Formatting Text

Working with Class Selectors

Case | Jupiter Gorge College Career Fair

Jupiter Gorge College, located in San Morillo, Texas, is preparing for its annual career fair. The career fair is one of the most important events of the year for graduating seniors. More than 100 prospective employers will participate this year, representing the fields of accounting, law, business, information systems, retail, and manufacturing. Prior to the event, the college offers seminars for graduating seniors on interviewing techniques, professional etiquette, business ethics, and writing an effective cover letter and resume. Richard Chen, the event coordinator, has asked for your help in creating and formatting Web pages to advertise the career fair. Richard would like the Web pages to have a consistent appearance. He has already created several Web pages for the career fair. You will show Richard how to use the text properties and classes to enhance the formatting of the site.

tarting Data Files

Tutorial.04 →

Tutorial

career.htm
careerlogo.gif
cover.htm

Review

cover.htm

Case1

berger.htm
bergerlogo.gif

Case2

web.htm

Case3

diamond.gif
power.htm
solar.jpg

Case4

donate.htm

Session 4.1

Using CSS to Format Text

While XHTML provides structure to a document, the function of CSS is to provide formatting for a document. Even basic formatting tasks, such as setting the line spacing, indenting text to create a tab indent, and setting margins, do not exist in XHTML. In an earlier tutorial, you used the CSS font properties to change the appearance of text. In this tutorial, you will learn about the CSS text properties, another group of properties that format text. You'll also see how CSS classes can be used to format the same element in different ways.

Before you begin working with Richard to create styles for his document, you'd like to look at the career.htm Web page he has created and edit a comment to identify the file.

To view Richard's document:

▶ **1.** In your text editor, open the **career.htm** file, which is located in the Tutorial.04\ Tutorial folder included with your Data Files. In the head section and below the page title, enter your name and today's date in the comment section where noted (see Figure 4-1).

Figure 4-1 Adding a comment to the head section

document comment

```
<!--
Tutorial 4
Your Name:
Today's Date:
Filename: careernew.htm
-->
```

▶ **2.** Save the file as **careernew.htm** in the same folder.

▶ **3.** Open the **careernew.htm** file in your browser. The file is shown in Figure 4-2.

Figure 4-2 The original careernew.htm file

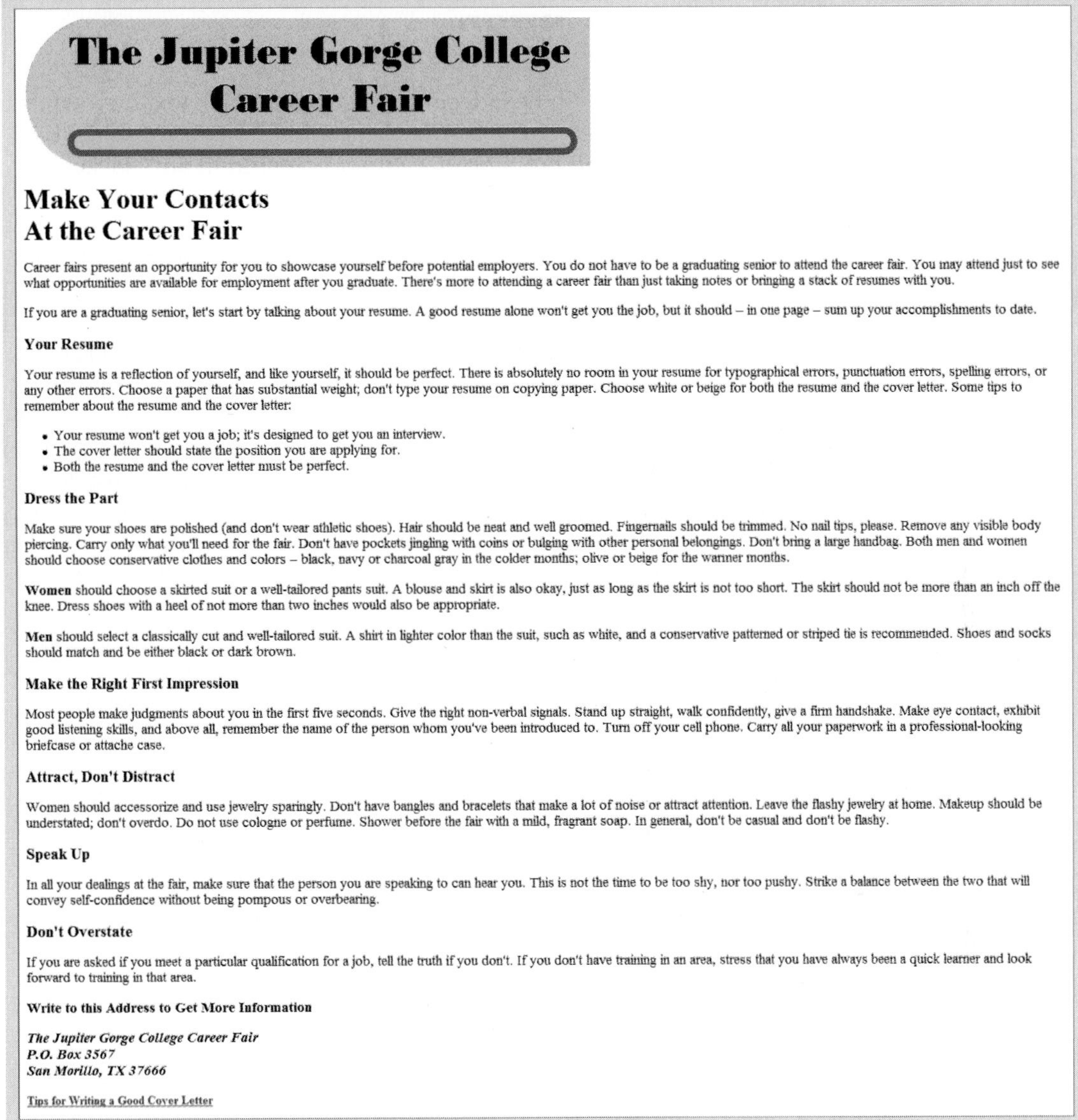

The Jupiter Gorge College Career Fair

Make Your Contacts
At the Career Fair

Career fairs present an opportunity for you to showcase yourself before potential employers. You do not have to be a graduating senior to attend the career fair. You may attend just to see what opportunities are available for employment after you graduate. There's more to attending a career fair than just taking notes or bringing a stack of resumes with you.

If you are a graduating senior, let's start by talking about your resume. A good resume alone won't get you the job, but it should – in one page – sum up your accomplishments to date.

Your Resume

Your resume is a reflection of yourself, and like yourself, it should be perfect. There is absolutely no room in your resume for typographical errors, punctuation errors, spelling errors, or any other errors. Choose a paper that has substantial weight; don't type your resume on copying paper. Choose white or beige for both the resume and the cover letter. Some tips to remember about the resume and the cover letter:

- Your resume won't get you a job; it's designed to get you an interview.
- The cover letter should state the position you are applying for.
- Both the resume and the cover letter must be perfect.

Dress the Part

Make sure your shoes are polished (and don't wear athletic shoes). Hair should be neat and well groomed. Fingernails should be trimmed. No nail tips, please. Remove any visible body piercing. Carry only what you'll need for the fair. Don't have pockets jingling with coins or bulging with other personal belongings. Don't bring a large handbag. Both men and women should choose conservative clothes and colors – black, navy or charcoal gray in the colder months; olive or beige for the warmer months.

Women should choose a skirted suit or a well-tailored pants suit. A blouse and skirt is also okay, just as long as the skirt is not too short. The skirt should not be more than an inch off the knee. Dress shoes with a heel of not more than two inches would also be appropriate.

Men should select a classically cut and well-tailored suit. A shirt in lighter color than the suit, such as white, and a conservative patterned or striped tie is recommended. Shoes and socks should match and be either black or dark brown.

Make the Right First Impression

Most people make judgments about you in the first five seconds. Give the right non-verbal signals. Stand up straight, walk confidently, give a firm handshake. Make eye contact, exhibit good listening skills, and above all, remember the name of the person whom you've been introduced to. Turn off your cell phone. Carry all your paperwork in a professional-looking briefcase or attache case.

Attract, Don't Distract

Women should accessorize and use jewelry sparingly. Don't have bangles and bracelets that make a lot of noise or attract attention. Leave the flashy jewelry at home. Makeup should be understated; don't overdo. Do not use cologne or perfume. Shower before the fair with a mild, fragrant soap. In general, don't be casual and don't be flashy.

Speak Up

In all your dealings at the fair, make sure that the person you are speaking to can hear you. This is not the time to be too shy, nor too pushy. Strike a balance between the two that will convey self-confidence without being pompous or overbearing.

Don't Overstate

If you are asked if you meet a particular qualification for a job, tell the truth if you don't. If you don't have training in an area, stress that you have always been a quick learner and look forward to training in that area.

Write to this Address to Get More Information

The Jupiter Gorge College Career Fair
P.O. Box 3567
San Morillo, TX 37666

Tips for Writing a Good Cover Letter

In looking at the careernew.htm file, you notice that the default font face is not attractive. You suggest to Richard that he change the font face for the document. The body element can be styled to change the appearance of the entire Web page, so you will begin by showing Richard how to style the body element.

Styling the Body Element

Each browser has default settings for the font, font size, margins, color, and background color, as well as for other settings. Declaring your own values in the body element over-rides any browser default values, which means that your pages will be displayed more consistently, regardless of the browser. The following example shows some properties and values that are frequently used when styling the body element.

```
body {
  font-size: 1.1em;
  font-family: Arial, Helvetica, sans-serif;
  color: #000000;
  background-color: #FFFFFF;
}
```

The colors chosen here (in hexadecimal values) are black text on a white background. It might seem redundant to create a style to have black text on a white background, but you can't assume that all browsers have these foreground and background colors by default.

InSight	**Using the CSS Properties in Web Design Software**

You have already learned about properties that affect text color and background color, and you have learned about the font properties. In this tutorial, you learn about the text properties. In later tutorials, you will learn about other groups of CSS properties, such as the box properties. After you complete your study of XHTML and CSS, you might want to further your knowledge of Web page design by learning how to use advanced XHTML and CSS Web design software such as Adobe Dreamweaver or Microsoft Expression Web. These software programs refer to styles created for the body element as setting the "page properties." They also refer to the Web page as "the canvas." Both terms are contrived; neither "page properties" nor "canvas" is specified in XHTML or CSS. However, HTML 5.0 will have a canvas element, which will be used to render dynamic bitmap graphics on the fly, such as for graphs or games. These software programs sometimes take liberties in regrouping (or creating groups for) the CSS properties. For example, in Microsoft Expression Web, the CSS text properties are called the "block properties." In CSS, however, the block properties do not exist. When using these software programs for the first time, you may be thrown off a bit because the software does not strictly follow the CSS standard for grouping and naming the CSS properties.

You will show Richard how to style the body element selector to create declarations for the font size, font family, color, and background color.

To style the body element selector:

1. Make sure the careernew.htm file is open in your text editor.

2. On a blank line after the comment code, type the following code to create an embedded style sheet and to style the body element selector, as shown in Figure 4-3.

```
<style type="text/css">

body {
  font-size: 1.1em;
  font-family: Arial, Helvetica, sans-serif;
  color: black;
  background-color: #ffe4c4;
}

</style>
```

Figure 4-3 ▶ The body element style

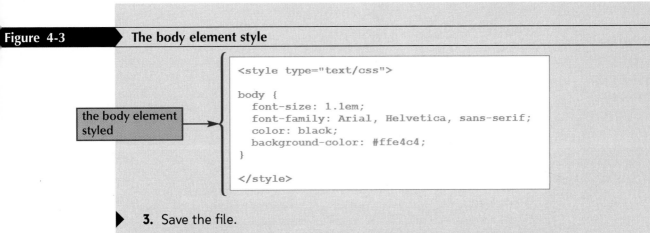

the body element styled

```
<style type="text/css">

body {
    font-size: 1.1em;
    font-family: Arial, Helvetica, sans-serif;
    color: black;
    background-color: #ffe4c4;
}

</style>
```

▶ **3.** Save the file.

▶ **4.** Switch to your browser, refresh or reload the **careernew.htm** page, and then compare your file to Figure 4-4 to confirm that the body element has been styled correctly.

Figure 4-4 ▶ The body element styled in the browser

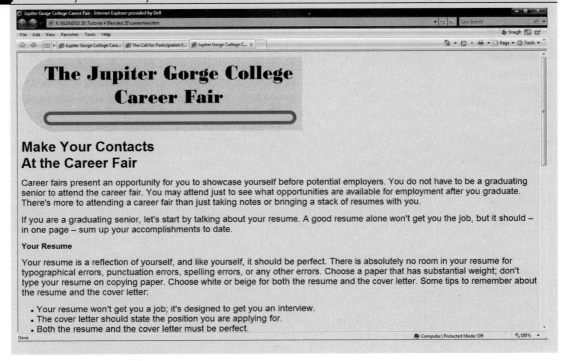

The page already looks better than Richard's original. Richard is familiar with using the font properties to change the appearance of text. The careernew.htm page has a considerable amount of text, so you will introduce Richard to the text properties, which will create interesting text effects for the document.

Using the Text Properties

The text properties add several word-processing capabilities to your Web documents, such as controlling the amount of white space between words and letters, aligning text, establishing tab indents, changing the case of text, and controlling the line spacing. Two text properties that are generally used together are the letter-spacing and word-spacing properties. You will use these two properties to show Richard how to create a special effect for the h1 heading at the top of the page.

Creating a Spread Heading

The **letter-spacing property** controls the amount of white space between letters. Similarly, the **word-spacing property** controls the amount of white space between words. Letter spacing is also known as **kerning**. Letter spacing and word spacing are commonly used together to create a **spread heading**, in which the letters of one word or several words are spaced apart.

Reference Window | **Creating a Spread Heading**

- To create a style for a spread heading, use the following syntax:

```
selector {
    letter-spacing: letter_spacing_value;
    word-spacing: word_spacing_value;
}
```
where *selector* is an element, a class, or an id, *letter-spacing* is the letter-spacing property, *letter_spacing_value* is a value expressed as an em value or a percentage, *word-spacing* is the word-spacing property, and *word_spacing_value* is a value expressed as an em value or a percentage.

Tip

When specifying letter spacing and word spacing, less is more. Keep your text readable—don't place too much white space between letters or words.

Browsers are not consistent in the amount of letter spacing and word spacing that is rendered. For example, the same values produce substantially more space in the Firefox browser than in the Internet Explorer 7 browser. Always preview your Web pages in the most recent version of several contemporary browsers to see how your letter spacing and word spacing is rendered. For example, if a one-line heading spans two lines in the browser as the result of letter or word spacing, reduce the amount of spacing between letters or words. Internet Explorer 8 and the Firefox browser render letter spacing and word spacing more consistently. Also, for better consistency in how letter and word spacing is rendered among browsers, use points or pixels as the unit of measurement, not em values.

Richard thinks that adding letter spacing and word spacing to the h1 heading would help grab the attention of visitors to the Web site. In this instance, you will use letter spacing and word spacing values of less than 1em. Because the period character might be overlooked, it's a good coding practice to enter a zero in the code before any value of less than 1. You will show Richard how to enter the code to create a spread heading at the top of the page.

To create the spread heading:

1. Switch back to your text editor.

2. On a blank line after the body element style code, type the following code to create the spread heading, as shown in Figure 4-5.

```
h1 {
    letter-spacing: 10px;
    word-spacing: 10px;
}
```

Figure 4-5 ▶ **The code for the spread heading**

letter spacing and word spacing create the spread heading →

```
h1 {
    letter-spacing: 10px;
    word-spacing: 10px;
}
```

3. Save the file.

▶ **4.** Switch to your browser, refresh or reload the **careernew.htm** page, and then compare your file to Figure 4-6 to verify that the h1 heading is now a spread heading.

Figure 4-6 ▶ **The spread heading in the browser**

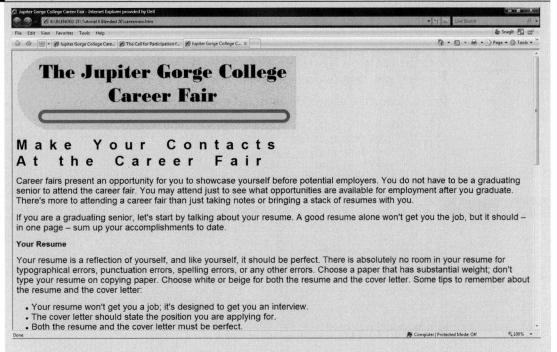

Trouble? If the amount of space between letters and words in your file does not match that of Figure 4-6, do not be concerned. Browsers can differ significantly in the amount of space assigned to letter and word spacing.

You will next show Richard one of the basic formatting features of the text properties: aligning text horizontally on a Web page.

Aligning Text

Richard would like the spread heading to be centered horizontally on the page. You tell him that the **text-align property** is used to align text horizontally. The text-align property takes the following values:

- left (the default)
- center
- right
- justify

The value of "left" is the default and creates an uneven right margin, as it would if you were typing a word-processing document. Left-justified text is said to have a "ragged right" margin. The value of "center" is used to center text. The value of "right" aligns text at the right edge of the browser window. The value of "justify" aligns text on both the left and the right, and each line of text fills the entire width of the document window. Justified text is commonly used in newspapers and magazines to create perfectly even ("blocked") margins on both the left and right sides.

Richard definitely wants the spread heading to be centered, so you will show him how to add another rule to the h1 style you created earlier.

To center the h1 spread heading:

► **1.** Switch back to your text editor.

► **2.** In the h1 style, position the insertion point after the semicolon in the word-spacing declaration.

► **3.** Press the **Enter** key to create a new line.

► **4.** Press the **Spacebar** twice.

► **5.** Type `text-align: center;`.

► **6.** Compare your code with that shown in Figure 4-7.

```
h1 {
    letter-spacing: 10px;
    word-spacing: 10px;
    text-align: center;
}
```

Figure 4-7   **The code for the text-align property**

the text-align property with a value of center →

```
h1 {
    letter-spacing: 10px;
    word-spacing: 10px;
    text-align: center;
}
```

► **7.** Save the file.

► **8.** Switch to your browser, refresh or reload the **careernew.htm** page, and then compare your file to Figure 4-8 to verify that the h1 spread heading text is now centered.

Figure 4-8   **The h1 spread heading centered in the browser**

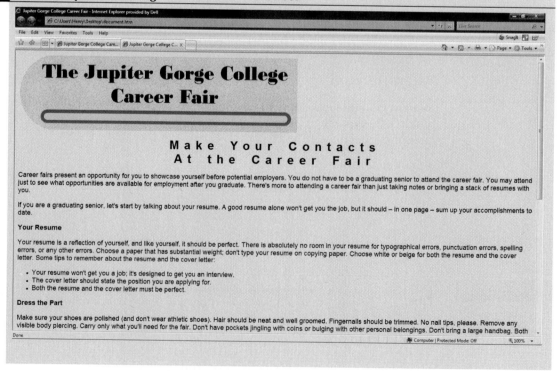

Not all browsers display Web pages the same way. Each browser has its own default ("built-in") styles that control the page margins, the font size, the background color, and the font family. Although the styles are fairly consistent from browser to browser, it's still a good idea to view your Web pages in the current and previous version of each of the contemporary browsers to see how your pages appear. A good strategy is to create a style for the body element to ensure that, regardless of the browser, your Web page will appear with *your* choices for the font size, the font and font color, the background color, and the page margins. Always style the body element to have declarations for the color and the background color, even if your choices are black text on a white background.

Next, you'll show Richard how CSS can create tab indents using the text-indent property.

Indenting Text

You can use the **text-indent property** to indent the first line of paragraph text, similar to pressing the Tab key on a keyboard. The value for the text-indent property can be stated in em values, in pixels, or as a percentage. Indenting the first line of a paragraph is most useful if your paragraphs do not have single line spacing, because the tab indent makes it easier to see where one paragraph begins and another ends. The **line-height property** is used to change the line spacing—for example, from single spacing to double spacing.

Because the careernew.htm Web page contains a considerable amount of text, you suggest to Richard that he increase the line spacing so that the text has more white space between the lines, which will make the text easier to read. A line-height value of 2.0 would change the text to double spacing, but Richard prefers less of an increase. You will instead use a line-height value of 1.5, which will be interpreted by the browser as the instruction to multiply the default line spacing by 1.5. The line-height property is one of the few properties in which a measurement (such as pixels, percents, ems, or points) does not have to be stated for the value. You can use measurements if you want, of course. For example, expressing the line height as 2em or 150% is valid. You will show Richard how to create a style for the paragraph element that indents paragraphs and changes their line spacing as well.

To indent paragraphs and change the line spacing:

▶ **1.** Switch back to your text editor.

▶ **2.** On a blank line after the h1 style, type the following code, as shown in Figure 4-9.

```
p {
   text-indent: 2em;
   line-height: 1.5;
}
```

Figure 4-9 | **The code for the paragraph style**

the paragraph style to change line height and create a text indent ⟶

```
p {
   text-indent: 2em;
   line-height: 1.5;
}
```

▶ **3.** Save the file.

▶ **4.** Switch to your browser, refresh or reload the **careernew.htm** page, and then compare your file to Figure 4-10 to verify that the paragraphs are indented and have a line height of 1.5.

Figure 4-10 | **The indented paragraphs and the increased line height**

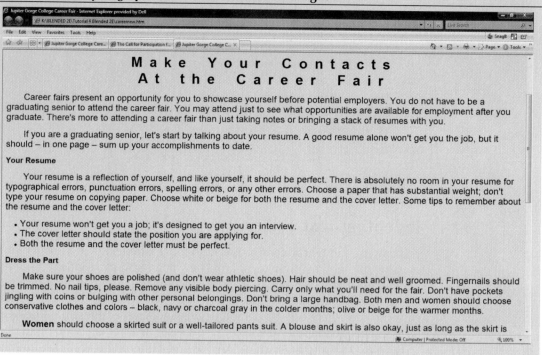

You will now show Richard a text property that he can use to change the case of text.

Changing the Case of Text

As you learned in an earlier tutorial, the font-variant property formats text in small capitals and makes the first letter of each word slightly larger. The **text-transform property**, however, has several other ways of changing the case of text. The text-transform property takes the following values:

- uppercase (TEXT APPEARS IN ALL CAPS)
- capitalize (Text Appears With The First Letter Of Each Word Capitalized)
- lowercase (text appears in lowercase)
- none (removes any of the preceding values)

The careernew.htm file has several h3 headings, and Richard has decided he wants to display all of them in uppercase. In addition, he wants to change the font size and color of h3 heading text. You will show him how to style the h3 headings to make the changes he wants.

To style the h3 headings:

▶ **1.** Switch back to your text editor.

▶ **2.** On a blank line after the code for the paragraph style, type the following code, as shown in Figure 4-11.

```
h3 {
    font-size: 1.3em;
    color: #00008b;
    text-transform: uppercase;
}
```

Figure 4-11 | **The code for the h3 heading style**

```
p {
    text-indent: 2em;
    line-height: 1.5;
}

h3 {
    font-size: 1.3em;
    color: #00008b;
    text-transform: uppercase;
}

</style>

</head>
```

the h3 element with the text-transform property and a value of uppercase

3. Save the file.

4. Switch to your browser, refresh or reload the **careernew.htm** page, and then compare your file to the one shown in Figure 4-12. If necessary, scroll down the page to verify that the h3 headings are in uppercase, are navy, and have a font size of 1.3em.

Figure 4-12 | **The h3 headings styled in the browser**

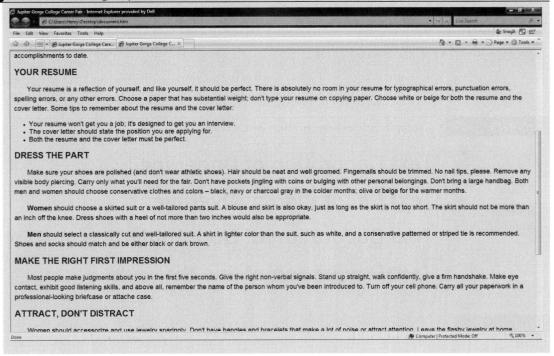

You'll now show Richard a very useful, if perhaps misnamed, property—the text-decoration property. It doesn't "decorate" text as you might expect.

Using the text-decoration Property

The **text-decoration property** is used to insert a line above, through, or under text. The most common use of the text-decoration property is to either create or remove the underline for link text. You'll also show Richard how the text-decoration property can be used to create a ruled line both above and below a line of text, such as a heading. The text-decoration property takes the following values:

- underline
- overline
- line-through
- blink
- none

Reference Window | **Creating a Heading Rule**

- To create a heading rule, use the following syntax:
  ```
  hn {
     text-decoration: underline overline;
  }
  ```
  where hn is a heading element, text-decoration is the text-decoration property, and underline overline is the value for the text-decoration property.

The text-decoration value of "underline" does just that—it underlines text; however, you should not underline text in your Web pages, because it might be confused with link text. The text-decoration value of "overline" displays a line above the text, as you might see in math equations. The value of "line-through" places a horizontal line through the text, but you should avoid using this value because elements that place a line through text are deprecated in HTML 5.0. The value of "blink" makes text flash on and off. Do not use this value, as it is considered amateurish and distracting. The value of "none" removes any of the preceding values. You'll often see the declaration text-decoration: none; used to eliminate the underline in visited links. Figure 4-13 illustrates the use of the text-decoration property.

Figure 4-13 **Examples of text-decoration properties**

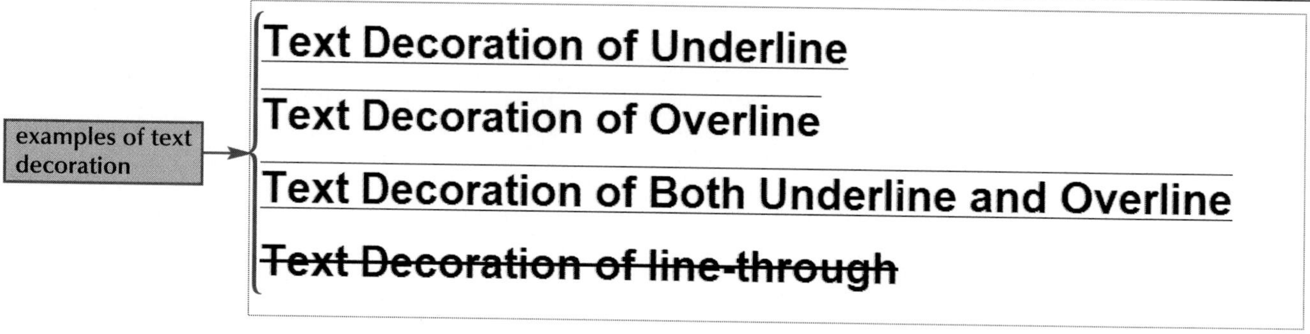

examples of text decoration →

Text Decoration of Underline

Text Decoration of Overline

Text Decoration of Both Underline and Overline

~~**Text Decoration of line-through**~~

Tip

The value of 0 does not need a unit measurement (such as em, pt, or a percent) following it.

Keep in mind that the value of none and the value 0 are not the same. If you want to have a text-decoration value of none, you must use that value, not the number 0.

Although it is not a shorthand property, you can use more than one value with the text-decoration property. You can assign the value of "underline overline" to create a **heading rule**, a ruled line above and below a heading. Heading rules can be especially useful to draw attention to smaller headings, such as h3 and h4. The declaration would be entered this way:

```
h4 {
   text-decoration: underline overline;
}
```

Leave a space, not a comma, between the values underline and overline. It is okay to switch the values around, so the following declaration would also be correct:

```
h4 {
   text-decoration: overline underline;
}
```

In the browser, the underline and overline are displayed in the same color as the text. In a later tutorial, you will use the border properties to create both horizontal and vertical ruled lines. Using the border properties, you can also change the color and style of the ruled line. For now, Richard would like to format the contact information at the bottom of the page to have a heading rule, so you will show him how to enter the code to style the h4 element with a text decoration of underline and overline. You will also change the color of the h4 heading text.

To style the h4 heading:

1. Switch back to your text editor.

2. On a blank line after the code for the h3 style, type the following code, as shown in Figure 4-14.

```
h4 {
   text-decoration: underline overline;
   color: maroon;
}
```

| Figure 4-14 | The code for the h4 heading style |

```
h3 {
   font-size: 1.3em;
   color: #00008b;
   text-transform: uppercase;
}

h4 {
   text-decoration: underline overline;
   color: maroon;
}

</style>
```

the h4 element styled for underline and overline

3. Save the file.

4. Switch to your browser, refresh or reload the **careernew.htm** page, and then compare your file to the one shown in Figure 4-15. If necessary, scroll down the page to verify that the h4 heading now appears in maroon and has a text decoration of underline and overline.

| Figure 4-15 | The h4 heading styled in the browser |

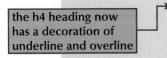

Write to this Address to Get More Information

the h4 heading now has a decoration of underline and overline

The Jupiter Gorge College Career Fair
P.O. Box 3567
San Morillo, TX 37666

5. If you will not be completing the next session, close all files, and exit your text editor and browser.

In this session, you learned about the text properties and how to use them to change the appearance and alignment of text. You changed the case of text and used the letter-spacing and word-spacing properties together to create a spread heading. You worked with text decoration to create an effect for a heading. In the next session, you will show Richard how to create styles that can format more than one element.

Review | **Session 4.1 Quick Check**

1. What property would you use to create or remove underlining?
2. What property would you use to indent text for a paragraph?
3. What property would you use to center text?
4. What effect do the letter-spacing and word-spacing properties usually create?
5. How does the text-transform property differ from the font-variant property?
6. What text-decoration value would create a heading rule?

Session 4.2

Creating and Using Classes

While Richard worked on the career fair Web page, he was faced with a common XHTML design problem. What do you do if you want to style an element selector more than one way? For example, what if you want to single-space some paragraphs and double-space others? You only have *one* paragraph element selector to style.

The solution is to use CSS class selectors. Class selectors format several instances of one or more elements. Using class selectors, you can modify the appearance of any XHTML element in a virtually unlimited number of ways. However, unlike element selectors, once you create a style for a class selector, you must *apply a class* to the start tag of one or more elements on a Web page. Classes can either be dependent or independent. A **dependent class** styles a particular element, such as the p or em element. An **independent class** styles any element. You will begin your work with classes by showing Richard how to enter the code for a dependent class.

Creating and Applying a Dependent Class

In the careernew.htm Web page, Richard has already used the strong and em elements to make text bold and italic and draw the reader's attention to it. However, Richard also wants to call the reader's attention to important information, such as who qualifies for counseling. You tell him that the solution is to create a dependent class. To begin creating a dependent class, you give the class a name. Class names can contain only alphabetic or numeric characters, must be one word, and should describe the purpose of the class. Do not start the class name with a number because not all browsers will recognize it. For example, you suggest to Richard that he could name his new class "crucial." In the style sheet, you would declare the selector for this dependent class as follows:

```
em.crucial {
```

Note that a period serves as a flag character and separates the element selector (em) from the name of the dependent class (crucial). Next, you enter the declarations as you normally would. For example, Richard wanted to increase the font size of the em selector, but he does not want the text to appear in italics. However, he does want the text to have a more attention-getting orange text on a black background. The code for the crucial dependent class for the em element would look like this:

```
em.crucial {
   font-size: 1.2em;
   font-style: normal;
   color: orange;
   background-color: black;
}
```

Richard can use the crucial class whenever he has text on a Web page that he wants to make sure the reader doesn't miss.

After you enter the code for a class in a style sheet, there's still more work to do. You have to enter code in the body section to specify what element will use the class. Using the class in the body section is called "applying a class." You apply the class in the start tag of an element—in this instance, the <em> tag. In the start tag, you enter the code for the class attribute, an equal sign, and the value for the class attribute, which is the name of the class you want to apply. The code to apply the crucial class would look like this:

```
<p>Here are some rules regarding appliance repair. First, be sure
to <em class="crucial">unplug the appliance</em>  before making
any repairs.</p>
```

You will next show Richard how to apply a dependent class named "navyback" to the paragraph element that precedes the code for the careerlogo.gif image code. You will give this paragraph a background color of navy.

To create and apply the navyback dependent class:

1. If necessary, open your browser and your text editor.

2. In your text editor, on a blank line after the code for the h4 style, type the following code, as shown in Figure 4-16.

```
p.navyback {
   background-color: navy;
}
```

Figure 4-16 ▶ **The code for the navyback dependent class**

```
h4 {
   text-decoration: underline overline;
   color: maroon;
}

p.navyback {
   background-color: navy;
}

</style>
```

the navyback style will give the logo image a navy background

3. Position the insertion point in the start <p> tag that precedes the code for the careerlogo.gif image. Press the **Spacebar** once.

4. Type `class="navyback"`

5. Compare your code with that shown in Figure 4-17.

Figure 4-17 ▸ The navyback class applied

applying the navyback class →

```
</head>

<body>

<p class="navyback"><img src="careerlogo.gif" alt="career fair logo
image" width="760" height="200" /></p>

<h1>Make Your Contacts
<br />At the Career Fair</h1>
```

▸ **6.** Save the file.

▸ **7.** Switch to your browser, refresh or reload the **careernew.htm** page, and then compare your file to the one shown in Figure 4-18. Verify that the navyback class has been applied and a blue background now appears behind the careerlogo.gif image.

Figure 4-18 ▸ The navyback style in the browser

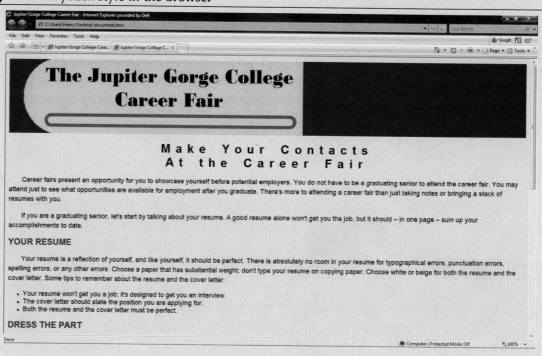

Next, you will show Richard how to create and apply an independent class, a class that can be used to format any element.

Creating and Applying an Independent Class

You might want to use a particular style to format several XHTML element selectors in the same way. For example, you may want to center several blocks of text in your document. Independent classes can format any element. An independent class selector is preceded by the period flag character, like this:

```
.center {
```

You then enter the code for the declarations, just as you would for any other style:

```
.center {
    text-align: center;
}
```

Next, you enter the class name in the start tag for the element tag, just as you did before for dependent classes:

```
<p class="center">Jupiter Gorge College</p>
```

Richard would like to center some text in both the h4 heading and the h5 heading at the bottom of the page. This is a good opportunity to show him how to create and apply an independent class.

Tip

ose meaningful names
class selectors rather
class1, class2, and
orth.

To create and apply the center independent class:

1. Switch back to your text editor.

2. On a blank line after the code for the p.navyback dependent class, type the following code, as shown in Figure 4-19.

```
.center {
   text-align: center;
}
```

Figure 4-19   The code for the .center independent class

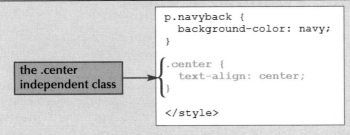

the .center
independent class

```
p.navyback {
   background-color: navy;
}

.center {
   text-align: center;
}

</style>
```

3. In the body section, position the insertion point after the number "4" in the start <h4> tag near the bottom of the page, in the line that begins with the words "Write to this Address... ."

4. Press the **Spacebar** once.

5. Type `class="center"`

6. Position the insertion point after the number "5" in the start <h5> tag that formats the three-line address at the bottom of the page.

7. Press the **Spacebar** once.

8. Type `class="center"`

9. Compare your code with that shown in Figure 4-20.

Figure 4-20   The code to apply the .center independent class

he code to apply the
center independent
class

```
<h4 class="center">Write to this Address to Get More Information</h4>

<h5 class="center"><strong><em>The Jupiter Gorge College Career Fair
<br />P.O. Box 3567
<br />San Morillo, TX 37666</em></strong></h5>

<h6><a href="cover.htm">Tips for Writing a Good Cover Letter</a></h6>
```

10. Save the file.

11. Switch to your browser, refresh or reload the **careernew.htm** page, scroll down the page if necessary, and then compare your file to the one shown in Figure 4-21. Verify that the .center independent class has been applied to both the h4 heading and the h5 heading.

| Figure 4-21 | The center class style in the browser |

DON'T OVERSTATE

If you are asked if you meet a particular qualification for a job, tell the truth if you don't. If you don't have training in an area, stress that you have always been a quick learner and look forward to training in that area.

<u>Write to this Address to Get More Information</u>

The Jupiter Gorge College Career Fair
P.O. Box 3567
San Morillo, TX 37666

<u>Tips for Writing a Good Cover Letter</u>

Although they are not part of the text properties, you know of two other ways to format text that you think Richard would be interested in learning. Both involve creating pseudo-elements.

Creating Pseudo-Elements

In addition to using the text properties, you can use pseudo-elements to format a single character or an entire line of text. The word *pseudo* means "not genuine." You might be familiar with the term *pseudonym*, which is an alias. For example, the famous author Samuel Clemens used the pseudonym of Mark Twain. A **pseudo-element** formats a part of text that does not directly relate to an XHTML element selector. In XHTML, the **:first-letter pseudo-element** is used to style the first letter of a word. The **:first-line pseudo-element** is used to style the first line of a block of text.

Although there are several CSS pseudo-elements, you will show Richard only the :first-letter and :first-line pseudo-elements. Currently, the other pseudo-elements have limited browser support. The colon before the element name is required and is part of the pseudo-element name. You can use the :first-letter and :first-line pseudo-elements either separately or together. Both of these pseudo-elements work only with block-level elements.

Tip
The term "pseudo-element" is always hyphenated.

Using the :first-letter Pseudo-Element

The :first-letter pseudo-element is commonly used to create a **drop cap**, in which the first letter of a word appears in a decorative font and a larger point size. In typography, it's common to use a drop cap for the first letter to signal the start of a new chapter. Richard wants to create a drop cap that makes the first letter of a word three times larger than normal, in orange and with a black background. The code to create Richard's drop cap using the :first-letter pseudo-element would look like this:

```
.dropcap:first-letter {
  font-size: 3em;
  color: orange;
  background-color: black;
}
```

The colon before :first-letter and :first-line is required. If you omit the colon, the property will not take effect. Don't add a space before or after the colon in the pseudo-element; if you do, the style will not work. For example, the drop cap will appear as normal text if you enter either of the following lines of code for the :first-letter pseudo-element:

```
.dropcap :first-letter {
.dropcap: first-letter {
```

The position of the drop cap and the shading behind the drop cap letter are markedly different in each browser. The Firefox browser, for example, tends to have a larger shaded area behind the drop cap than the same area in Internet Explorer. You should open the file in several browsers to see if the drop cap looks acceptable to you. You might want to increase or decrease the font size or change other properties and values that affect the appearance of the drop cap.

Richard would like to use the :first-letter pseudo-element to style the first letter of the first h3 heading. You will show him how to use the :first-letter pseudo-element with an independent class named "dropcap."

To create and apply the dropcap class:

1. Switch back to your text editor.

2. On a blank line after the code for the .center independent style, type the following code, as shown in Figure 4-22.

```
.dropcap:first-letter {
  font-size: 3em;
  color: orange;
  background-color: black;
}
```

Figure 4-22 ▶ **The code for the :first-letter pseudo-element**

the dropcap style →
```
.dropcap:first-letter {
  font-size: 3em;
  color: orange;
  background-color: black;
}
```

3. Position the insertion point after the number "3" in the start <h3> tag before the "Your Resume" h3 heading.

4. Press the **Spacebar** once.

5. Type `class="dropcap"`

6. Compare your code with that shown in Figure 4-23.

Figure 4-23 ▶ **The code to apply the dropcap dependent class**

applying the dropcap style
```
<p>If you are a graduating senior, let's start by talking about your
resume. A good resume alone won't get you the job, but it should &ndash;
in one page &ndash; sum up your accomplishments to date.</p>

<h3 class="dropcap">Your Resume</h3>
<p>Your resume is a reflection of yourself, and like yourself, it should
be perfect. There is absolutely no room in your resume for typographical
errors, punctuation errors, spelling errors, or any other errors. Choose a
paper that has substantial weight; don't type your resume on copying
paper. Choose white or beige for both the resume and the cover letter.
Some tips to remember about the resume and the cover letter:</p>
```

7. Save the file.

▶ 8. Switch to your browser, refresh or reload the **careernew.htm** page, and then compare your file to the one shown in Figure 4-24 to verify that the .dropcap class has been applied.

Figure 4-24 ▶ The dropcap class in the browser

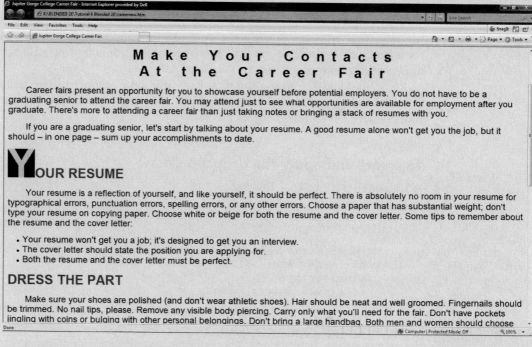

Trouble? The drop cap looks different in Firefox than in Internet Explorer, which is shown in Figure 4-24.

Reference Window	**Styling Pseudo-Elements**

- To apply a style to the first letter of an element, use the following syntax:
  ```
  selector.class:first-letter
  ```
  where `selector` is an element in the document and `class` is a dependent class.
- To apply a style to the first line of an element, use the following syntax:
  ```
  selector.class:first-line
  ```
  where `selector` is an element in the document and `class` is a dependent class.

Next, you will show Richard how to use the :first-line pseudo-element to format the first line of a block of text.

Now that you have worked with several groups of properties, such as the font properties and text properties, you should try to group these declarations together whenever you enter the code in your style sheets. In the following example, note that the color, font, and text properties are mixed together rather than grouped. This is an example of how code should *not* be written:

```
h2 {
    font-family: Arial, Helvetica, sans-serif;
    color: white;
    font-weight: bold;
    background-color: teal;
    font-style: italic;
    text-transform: uppercase;
    font-size: 2em;
}
```

You should list the properties and values by their groups so that other Web developers, who may also have to work with your code, will easily understand your code. Also, remember that certain properties, such as the font properties, must be written in a particular order (font style, weight, variant, size, and family). As you compose your CSS code, pick a grouping order for your declarations and be consistent. The following declaration list, grouped by function, is much more understandable than the previous one. The font properties (in the correct order) are listed first, followed by the color and background color properties. A text property ends the list.

```
h2 {
    font-style: italic;
    font-weight: bold;
    font-size: 2em;
    font-family: Arial, Helvetica, sans-serif;
    color: white;
    background-color: teal;
    text-transform: uppercase;
}
```

Using the :first-line Pseudo-Element

The :first-line pseudo-element formats just the first line of a block of text, usually a paragraph. Note that the colon before :first-line is part of the pseudo-element name. Again, in typography, it's common to format the first line of a paragraph in a chapter in a different font style or font size. The :first-line pseudo-element nearly always occurs as a dependent style within the <p> element selector, as shown in the following example:

```
p.opening:first-line {
  font-size: 1.2em;
  color: maroon;
}
```

To apply the style, you do not include the term ":first-line". You use the name of the style (which in this example is "opening"), just as you would when applying any dependent or independent style.

```
<p class="opening">If you are a graduating senior, let's start by
 talking about your resume. A good resume alone won't get you the
 job, but it should &ndash; in one page &ndash; sum up your
 accomplishments to date.</p>
```

Richard would like to use the :first-line pseudo-element in the paragraph that begins, "If you are a graduating senior...". You will show him how to create and apply the opening style.

To create and apply the opening class:

▶ **1.** Switch back to your text editor.

▶ **2.** On a blank line after the code for the .dropcap style, type the following code, as shown in Figure 4-25.

```
p.opening:first-line {
   font-size: 1.2em;
   color: maroon;
}
```

Figure 4-25	The code for the p.opening dependent class

```
.dropcap:first-letter {
   font-size: 3em;
   color: orange;
   background-color: black;
}

p.opening:first-line {
   font-size: 1.2em;
   color: maroon;
}

</style>
```

the opening dependent class

▶ **3.** Position the insertion point after the letter "p" in the start <p> tag before the words "If you are a graduating senior …".

▶ **4.** Type `class="opening"`

▶ **5.** Compare your code with that shown in Figure 4-26.

Figure 4-26	The code to apply the opening dependent class

applying the opening dependent class

```
<p class="opening">If you are a graduating senior, let's start by talking
about your resume. A good resume alone won't get you the job, but it
should &ndash; in one page &ndash; sum up your accomplishments to date.
</p>
```

▶ **6.** Save the file.

▶ **7.** Switch to your browser, refresh or reload the **careernew.htm** page, and then compare your file to the one shown in Figure 4-27 to verify that the opening dependent class has been applied.

Figure 4-27 **The opening dependent class in the browser**

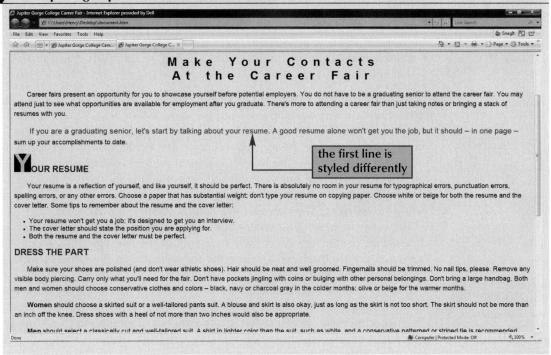

You can combine the :first-letter and :first-line pseudo-elements by styling the selector twice—once to style the :first-letter pseudo-element and once to style the :first-line pseudo-element. The following example styles the :first-letter and :first-line pseudo-elements for their color and font-size properties as a dependent class for the paragraph element.

```
p.opening:first-letter {
   font-size: 3em;
   color: brown;
}


p.opening:first-line {
   font-size: 1.5em;
   color: navy;
}
```

In addition to the pseudo-element selectors, you can use pseudo-class selectors, which is what you will show Richard next.

Using Pseudo-Class Selectors

In an earlier tutorial, you created links. When testing your links, you knew that if the link text was blue, you had not yet clicked the link. Similarly, if the link text was purple, you knew you had clicked the link. The **link pseudo-class selectors** expand on the concept that visitors to your Web site benefit from visual cues about the **link state** (whether the link has been clicked or not). By using the link pseudo-class selectors, you can style links based on the following four states: link, visited, hover, and active. These selectors are described in the following list. Note the colon between the "a" element and the pseudo-class selector, and note that the colon does not have spaces before or after it.

- **a:link** is the selector for normal links (links that haven't been clicked)
- **a:visited** is the selector for visited links (links that have been clicked)
- **a:hover** is the selector for the hover state (when the mouse pointer passes over the link)
- **a:active** is the selector for active links (when a user holds down the mouse button to click a link)

By using the a:link pseudo-class selector, you can assign a color to style your normal (unvisited) link text to stand out from the surrounding text. Visited links, in contrast, should not stand out; they should have a more subdued color. For the hover state, you might want to change the foreground color and background color of the link text to draw the visitor's attention to the link; this helps the user confirm which link is selected. For the brief moment that links are clicked, you might want to style the a:active link pseudo-class selector to have the link text appear in an attention-getting color, such as orange or yellow, to verify for the user that the link has been clicked.

The order in which you enter code for the link pseudo-class selectors in your style sheets does matter. You don't have to use all of the pseudo-class selectors in your code, but if you do use them, you must enter the selectors in this order: a:link, a:visited, a:hover, and a:active.

Use the anchor element selector to style links to ids. If you style the anchor element but do not style the :link pseudo-class selector as well, all links will appear as you styled the anchor element. If you style both the anchor element and the a:link pseudo-class selector, your links to ids will appear different from all other links on the Web page. For example, in the following code, link text to ids will appear in orange, but all other link text on the page will appear in green:

```
a {
   color: orange;
}


a:link {
   color: green;
}
```

Richard has decided to create a link from the careernew.htm page to another page he has been working on, cover.htm. He would like to use several of the pseudo-class selectors. You will show Richard how to enter the code for three of the link pseudo-class selectors. The link code is currently inside an h6 element, so you will also show him how to style the h6 element to increase its font size as well.

To enter the code for the pseudo-class selectors:

1. Switch back to your text editor.

2. On a blank line below the code that styles the opening :first-line pseudo-element, type the following code, as shown in Figure 4-28.

```
a:link {
   color: yellow;
   background-color: #8b0000;
   font-weight: bold;
}


a:visited {
   color: gray;
   text-decoration: none;
}
```

Tip

Use a mnemonic device to remember the correct order of the link pseudo-class selectors, such as "little Victor hates asparagus" for "link, visited, hover, and active."

```
a:hover {
   color: #8b0000;
   background-color: white;
}


h6 {
 font-size: 1em;
}
```

Figure 4-28   **The code for the pseudo-classes**

the code for the :link,
:visited, and :hover
pseudo-classes

```
a:link {
   color: yellow;
   background-color: #8b0000;
   font-weight: bold;
}

a:visited {
   color: gray;
   text-decoration: none;
}

a:hover {
   color: #8b0000;
   background-color: white;
}

h6 {
 font-size: 1em;
}
```

▶ **3.** Save the file.

▶ **4.** Switch to your browser and refresh or reload the **careernew.htm** page. Note the color of the link. Pass your mouse pointer over the link and note what happens when you do. Click the link. When the cover.htm page appears in the browser, click the browser's Back button or close the appropriate tab in your browser to return to the careernew.htm page. Note the color of the link now indicates that you have visited the cover.htm page, as shown in Figure 4-29.

Figure 4-29   **The visited link in the browser**

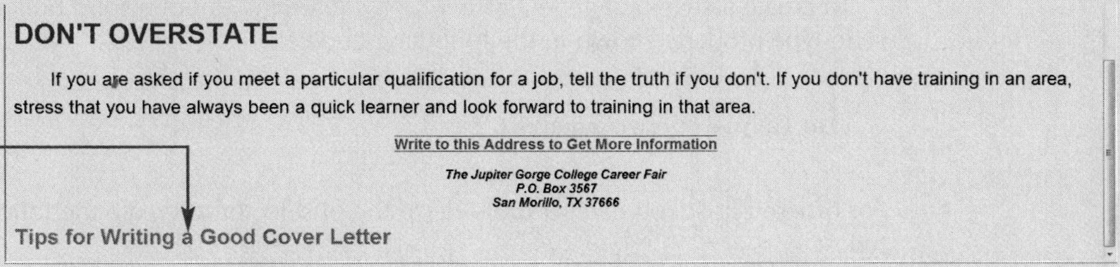

DON'T OVERSTATE

If you are asked if you meet a particular qualification for a job, tell the truth if you don't. If you don't have training in an area, stress that you have always been a quick learner and look forward to training in that area.

Write to this Address to Get More Information

The Jupiter Gorge College Career Fair
P.O. Box 3567
San Morillo, TX 37666

visited link is no
ger underlined
d appears in gray

Tips for Writing a Good Cover Letter

Tip

erm "pseudo-class"
ays hyphenated.

Richard is pleased with the changes to the careernew.htm Web page. However, he would like to make sure that visitors to the Web page don't overlook the important information in the unordered list. Next, you will show Richard how to change the appearance of ordered and unordered lists.

Changing the Appearance of Lists

Richard wants to know if there is any way to style lists to make them stand out. He thinks that the important points in the "Your Resume" section might go unnoticed. You tell him that he can use the list style properties to change the appearance of lists. You can change the list style type and the list style position.

Reference Window | **Setting List Properties**

- To specify the format of a list, enter the following code where you want the list to appear:
  ```
  ul {
  list-style-property: value;
  ```
- Use the following properties to set the appearance of the list:
  - list-style-type—Use this to change the bullet type, the numbering, or the lettering for a list. Values are disc, circle, square, decimal, lower-roman, upper-roman, lower-alpha, upper-alpha, and none.
  - list-style-image—Use this to insert an image as a marker instead of one of the list style types. Specify a value in the format *url(imagename)*. Do not enclose the filename in quotes.
  - list-style-position—Use this to position the bullet either inside or outside the indented text for the list item. Values are inside or outside (the default).
  - list-style—This shorthand property specifies the type, the image, and the position; list the values for each property in the order shown.

Lists can also be enhanced by graphics and images, using the list-style-type, list-style-position, and list-style-image properties.

Using the list-style-type Property

You use the **list-style-type property** to change the appearance of the default solid bullet for unordered lists. Unordered lists can use only one of three list-style-type values:

- disc (the default)
- circle (a hollow circle)
- square (a square)

To create a style that generates an open square instead of a solid bullet, use the list-style-type property shown in the following code:

```
ul {
  list-style-type: square;
}
```

For ordered lists, you can set the style of the ol selector to create the following list-style types:

- decimal (the default Arabic numbers)
- lower-roman (i, ii, iii, and so forth)
- upper-roman (I, II, III, and so forth)
- lower-alpha (a, b, c, and so forth)
- upper-alpha (A, B, C, and so forth)

For example, to create a style that numbers a list using lowercase Roman numerals, use code similar to the following:

```
ol {
   list-style-type: lower-roman;
}
```

Figure 4-30 illustrates the use of the list-style-type property.

Figure 4-30 ▶ **The list-style-type property in the browser**

examples of list styles for both unordered and ordered lists →

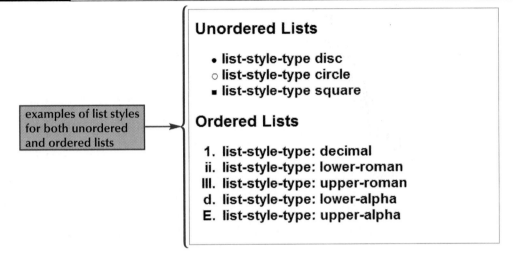

Using the list-style-position Property

You use the **list-style-position property** to change the position of the bullet included with a list. You can have unordered lists with bullets inside the element, such as a paragraph indent, or outside the element, which is the default. The following example shows a bullet with a list style type of square and a list style position of inside:

■ **This is some text for the bulleted item. As you can see, this bulleted item has the appearance of a paragraph indent.**

To style the list that contains the preceding bullet, you would enter the following code:

```
ul {
   list-style-type: square;
   list-style-position: inside;
}
```

Using the list-style-image Property

Use the **list-style-image property** to change the bullet to a graphic image. For example, to use an image named star.gif as the bullets, type the following code. Do not enclose the filename in quotes.

```
ul {
   list-style-image: url(star.gif);
}
```

Tip

ou use an image as a
et, save the image and
XHTML file in the
e storage location;
erwise, specify the
h to the image.

Using the list-style Shorthand Property

The **list-style property** is the shorthand property for list styles. You use this property to set the list-style-type, the list-style-image (if you are using one), and the list-style-position. You need to specify the position only if you want to position bullets inside the element (outside is the default value). Examples include:

```
ul {
   list-style: square inside;
}

ul {
   list-style: url(bubbles.gif);
}

ol {
   list-style: upper-roman inside;
}
```

You would also use the list-style property if you do not want to have bullets. To do so, change the list-style value to none:

```
ul {
   list-style: none;
}
```

You will show Richard how to enter the code to create a style for unordered list items. You will change the list style type and increase the line height to make the list items stand out. To eliminate any potential conflicts in case an ordered list is added later to the careernew.htm Web page, you will create a style for the list item as a descendant selector.

To enter the code for the list item style:

1. Switch back to your text editor.

2. On a blank line below the code to style the h6 element selector, type the following code, as shown in Figure 4-31.

```
ul li {
   font-weight: bold;
   color: maroon;
   list-style-type: square;
   line-height: 2.0;
}
```

Figure 4-31 **The code for the list item**

the list item
descendant selector →

```
ul li {
   font-weight: bold;
   color: maroon;
   list-style-type: square;
   line-height: 2.0;
}
```

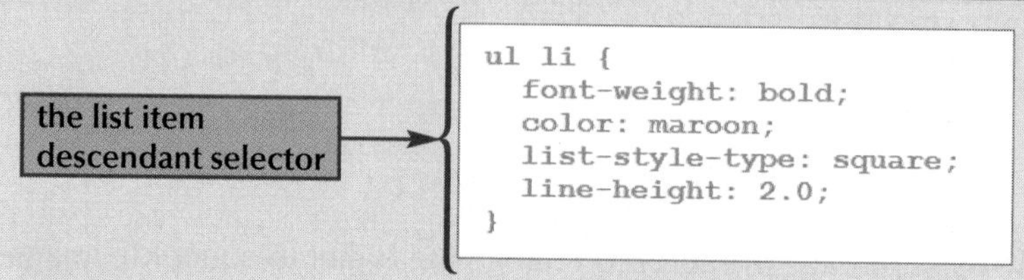

3. Save the file.

4. Switch to your browser, refresh or reload the **careernew.htm** page, and compare your file to the one shown in Figure 4-32 to verify that the list items have been styled.

Figure 4-32 The list items styled in the browser

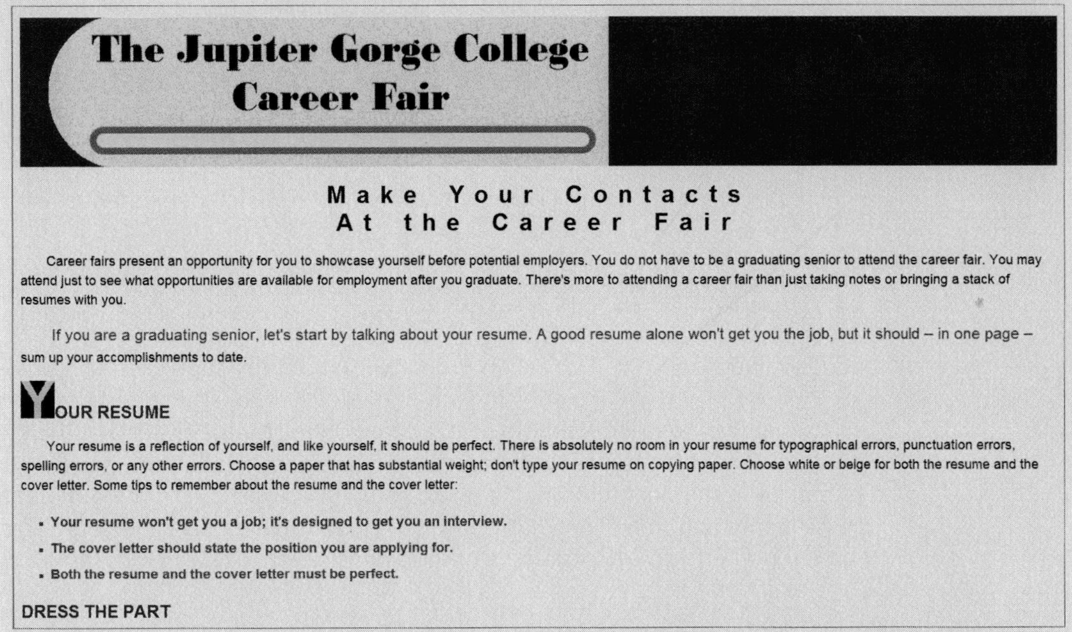

5. If you will not be completing the Review Assignments or the Case Problems, close your browser and text editor.

A **marker** appears to the left of the list item text. Examples of markers include an image, a bullet, a number, or a letter. Figure 4-33 shows the values for each of the properties that change the list style.

Figure 4-33 Properties that change the list marker

List-style-type	circle I disc I square I armenian I decimal I decimal-leading-zero I georgian I lower-alpha I lower-greek I lower-latin I lower-roman I upper-alpha I upper-latin I upper-roman I none I inherit
List-style-position	inside I outside I inherit
List-style-image	url (name of file) I none I inherit
List-style (shorthand property)	list-style-type list-style-position list-style-image I inherit

Using the vertical-align Property

When you have an image with one line of text beside it, you often need to align the image with the text. You can use the vertical-align property to position images and other elements vertically with text. The vertical-align property has several values, but the following are the most common:

- top—The top of the image is aligned with the text.
- middle—The image is aligned to be vertically centered with the text.
- bottom—The bottom of the image is aligned with the text.

If you want to align an image with a single line of text, enter the code for the dependent class in the CSS style sheet based on what type of alignment you want for the image, like so:

```
img.middle {
    vertical-align: middle;
}
```

Next, in the body of the document, apply the "middle" dependent class in the image tag code:

```
<p><img src="bottom.gif" alt="bottom image" width="100"
height="100" class="middle" />This is vertical align middle</p>
```

The values for the vertical-align property are not fully supported by contemporary browsers, so you may have to substitute a different value to achieve the result you want. In Internet Explorer, for example, use the text-bottom value instead of the bottom value. In addition, you cannot use the vertical-align property to align an image used as a list marker. In the next tutorial, however, you will use several of the box properties to precisely align an image used as a list marker. Figure 4-34 lists the values for the vertical-align property and descriptions of their effects.

Figure 4-34 | **Values for the vertical-align property**

baseline	The default value. The element is placed on the baseline (the bottom) of the parent element.
top	The top of the element is aligned with the top of the tallest element on the line.
text-top	The top of the element is aligned with the top of the parent element's font.
middle	The element is placed in the middle of the parent element.
bottom	The bottom of the element is aligned with the lowest element on the line.
text-bottom	The bottom of the element is aligned with the bottom of the parent element's font.
sub	Aligns the element as a subscript.
super	Aligns the element as a superscript.

Figure 4-35 illustrates the use of the vertical-align property with an image and a single line of text.

Figure 4-35 ▶ **The vertical-align property used to align an image**

images aligned by top, middle, and bottom →

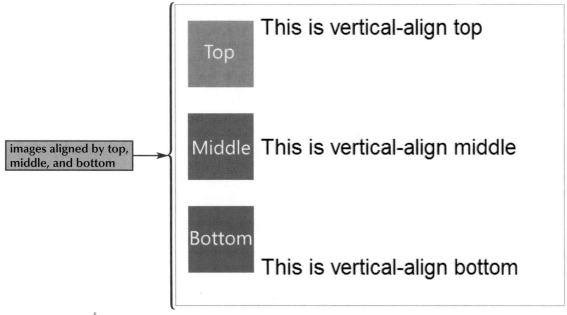

Figure 4-36 summarizes the properties and pseudo-elements that affect the appearance or positioning of text.

Figure 4-36 ▶ **Summary of properties that affect text appearance and position**

Property or Pseudo-Element	Purpose
font-family	Sets the font family
font-size	Sets the font size
font-style	Sets the font style to italic or oblique
font-variant	Formats text to appear in small capitals
font	Shorthand property
letter-spacing	Increases or decreases space between characters
word-spacing	Increases or decreases space between words
line-height	Sets the line height
text-align	Sets horizontal alignment
text-decoration	Places or removes a line above or under text
text-indent	Sets indent of first line
text-transform	Determines capitalization of text
vertical-align	Controls vertical alignment
:first-letter	Formats first letter of a word
:first-line	Formats first line of a paragraph

In this session, you worked with two pseudo-elements, :first-line and :first-letter, to change the appearance of a single letter or a single line. You worked with pseudo-elements to create link styles, and you worked with list styles to change the appearance of lists.

Review | **Session 4.2 Quick Check**

1. What are the two types of classes?
2. After you enter the code for the class, what must you also do in the body section of the document to have the class take effect?
3. What is a drop cap?
4. What is a marker?
5. Which pseudo-class can be used to style links the visitor has not yet clicked?
6. Which pseudo-class can be used to style links the visitor has clicked?

Review | **Tutorial Summary**

In this tutorial, you learned that classes are used to extend the number of selectors that are available to style. Classes can be dependent, which means they will only work with a particular XHTML element selector. Classes can also be independent, which means they will work with any XHTML element selector. To apply either an independent or a dependent class, use the word *class* within the XHTML element selector you want to style. You also learned about the following text properties: letter-spacing, word-spacing, text-align, text-indent, text-transform, and text-decoration. Pseudo-elements can be used to style the first letter of a word or the first line of a paragraph. Pseudo-classes are often used to create styles for links. Finally, you learned about the vertical-align property.

Key Terms

a:active	independent class	list-style-type property
a:hover	kerning	marker
a:link	letter-spacing property	pseudo-element
a:visited	line-height property	spread heading
dependent class	link pseudo-class selectors	text-align property
drop cap	link state	text-decoration property
:first-letter pseudo-element	list-style property	text-indent property
:first-line pseudo-element	list-style-image property	text-transform property
heading rule	list-style-position property	word-spacing property

Practice | **Review Assignments**

Data File needed for the Review Assignments: cover.htm

Richard is satisfied with the career fair Web page. He now needs your help in creating a Web page that will help students prepare for an interview by writing an effective cover letter. Richard knows that a great cover letter is as important as having an attractive resume. Richard has already created the XHTML file, which he named cover.htm. He would like your help in formatting it.

Although you will not be instructed to do so after each step, you should do the following whenever you enter code to create a style in your text editor: Save the file, switch to your browser, refresh or reload the page, verify that you entered the style code correctly, switch back to your text editor, and then complete the next step. A preview of the Web page you will format appears in Figure 4-37.

Figure 4-37

The Cover Letter

THE MECHANICS OF THE LETTER

It may go without saying, but the cover letter must be perfect. The cover letter is not intended to get you the job, it's intended to get your foot in the door. You can eliminate yourself from being considered for a job if your cover letter isn't perfect. Proofread the letter at least three times. Have someone else proofread the letter, too. A second set of eyes can find mistakes that you might miss. Grammar and punctuation must be 100% correct. No typos, please. Don't rely on just the spell check feature of a word processor alone. *Proofread for meaning*.

Paper – The paper must be at least 20lb. paper, preferably a 100% cotton fiber. A more substantial paper weight of 24lb. would be better. Choose bright white or off-white (beige). Don't choose a color such as red or bright yellow that will actually put off a potential employer. A white or a neutral color works best.

Font – Don't choose a font face that is hard to read, such as a fantasy font or a script font. Choose Arial or Times New Roman. Arial is a more modern typeface. Times New Roman is a more conservative type face. If you are applying for a position with a more conservative company, choose a serif font, like Times New Roman.

EXPLAIN WHY YOU ARE WRITING TO THIS EMPLOYER

Identify your skills and accomplishments. Don't embellish. State the truth in simple facts. If you started a newsletter, participated in charity events, were the president or an officer of one or more clubs, or was the quarterback of the football team – just state what you did and why it mattered to you. All of these activities give you experience in leadership and working as part of a team.

TELL THE EMPLOYER WHY YOU WANT TO WORK FOR THE COMPANY

Do some research. What makes this company so special? Is it that they are a start-up company and you have a special talent that will help them get off the ground? Is it an established company whose reputation and stability are the attraction? Tell the employer that you want to be part of that organization and that it really matters to you that you get the job. Don't tell them that you need a job – tell them how *their company* will benefit from hiring you.

WRAP IT UP

Thank the reader for his or her time, and invite him or her to contact you. Give them your phone number(s) and e-mail address. Invite the reader to contact you so that you may better explain in greater detail why you are qualified for the position you are seeking. *Your gain is their gain*.

The Career Fair
P. O. Box 35657A
San Morillo, TX 37888

Complete the following:

1. Use your text editor to open the **cover.htm** file, which is provided in your Data Files in the Tutorial.04\Review folder.
2. Save the file as **covernew.htm** in the same folder. Open the file in your browser and observe the appearance of the original file.
3. Switch back to your text editor. In the head section, enter **Composing the Cover Letter** as the page title.
4. In the head section and below the page title, enter your name and today's date in the comment section where noted.
5. Below the comment and in the head section, insert the start and end tags necessary to create an embedded style sheet.
6. Within the tags for the embedded style sheet, style the body element to have text appear in a font size of 1.1em and in the Verdana font (a sans-serif font), with a text color of black and a background color of #eee8aa.

7. Save the **covernew.htm** file. Open the file in the browser. Verify that the body element style appears correctly in your file.

8. Switch back to your text editor. In the embedded style sheet and below the body style, style the p element to have a text indent of 2em and a line height of 1.2em.

9. Create a style for the h1 element to have text appear in blue.

10. Create a style for the h3 element to have text appear in teal and in uppercase. (Use a text property to change the case—do not retype the h3 headings in uppercase.)

11. Create a style for the em element to have text appear in bold and maroon.

12. Save the **covernew.htm** file. Switch to your browser and refresh or reload the page. Compare your file to the preview file in Figure 4-37 to verify that your file is correct.

13. Submit the results of the preceding steps to your instructor, either in printed or electronic form, as requested.

14. If you are not completing the next assignment, close your text editor and your browser.

Apply | Case Problem 1

Use the skills you learned in the tutorial to create a Web page for a popular restaurant.

Data Files needed for this Case Problem: berger.htm and bergerlogo.gif

The Berger Street Grille   The town of Chesapeake Haven, Maryland, is home to a local landmark restaurant, the Berger Street Grille. The restaurant offers casual dining in a spacious waterfront setting and serves several hundred diners on any given evening. Although the restaurant is famous for its grilled meat dishes, its location near the Chesapeake River and the Atlantic Ocean make the restaurant a favorite for seafood lovers as well. Ben O'Brien, the owner of the restaurant, has asked for your assistance in creating a Web page for the Berger Street Grille.

Although you will not be instructed to do so after each step, you should do the following whenever you enter code to create a style in your text editor: Save the file, switch to your browser, refresh or reload the page, verify that you entered the style code correctly, and then switch back to your text editor and complete the next step. A preview of the Web page appears in Figure 4-38.

Review | Quick Check Answers

Session 4.1

1. text-decoration
2. text-indent
3. text-align
4. A spread effect
5. The text-transform property will display text in all capitals, all lowercase, or in initial capitals. The font-variant property displays text in small capitals.
6. underline overline

Session 4.2

1. Dependent and independent
2. Apply the class
3. A special appearance given to the first letter of a word
4. What appears to the left of the list item text
5. a:link
6. a:visited

Ending Data Files

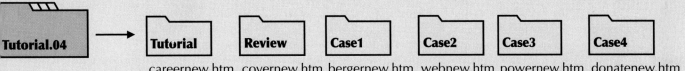

Tutorial.04 → Tutorial   Review   Case1   Case2   Case3   Case4

careernew.htm   covernew.htm   bergernew.htm   webnew.htm   powernew.htm   donatenew.htm

Working with the Box Model

Working with the Margin, Padding, and Border Properties

Case | SmallPaper Solutions

The concept of the paperless office was devised in the last century, but today, many businesses still rely on paper as the lifeblood of their day-to-day operations. SmallPaper Solutions is a Richfield, Kentucky, firm that specializes in designing, installing, and implementing paperless office hardware and software. SmallPaper Solutions knows that there are limits to how much paper can reasonably be eliminated from an office environment, particularly in the fields of insurance, law, finance, and accounting, so the company works with businesses to reduce—not necessarily eliminate—the use of paper in the office. The cost savings in converting to digital systems can be substantial. Printers and copying machines are costly to purchase, repair, and maintain. Filing cabinets and storage rooms consume valuable area that could be converted to useful office space. The environmental payback from reducing deforestation is also a driving force in using less paper in the office. Tahira Jones, the head of the marketing department, seeks your assistance in creating a Web page that will highlight the company's services.

tarting Data Files

utorial.05 → **Tutorial**

arrow.gif
list.gif
paper.htm
paperlogo.gif
stacks.jpg

Review

consult.htm
paperlogo.gif

Case1

planet.htm
planetlogo.gif
planets.gif

Case2

event.htm
track.gif

Case3

back.gif
bio.gif
books.htm
bookstyles.css
pointer.gif
sand.gif
science.gif
travel.gif

Case4

hope.css
hope.htm

Session 5.1

Understanding the Box Model

The CSS **box model** describes the boxes that are formed around elements in a Web page. In XHTML, every element is treated as though it were a box. The box model consists of four parts: a content area, padding, borders, and margins. Because the elements you have created so far haven't had a border, you haven't seen the boxes—but they have been there. The **content area** is the area that contains the box content, such as text or an image. By default, the content just barely fits into the box; there is no white space surrounding the content. The **box properties** are used to add white space and a border around the content. The three most commonly used CSS box properties are padding, border, and margin. Two other box properties you have already used are width and height. The padding, border, and margin properties further affect the width and height of an element.

    Padding is white space that surrounds the box content. A **border**, a solid or decorative ruled line, can be placed around the padding. Borders are useful because they can separate the content of one box from another or call attention to a box. Optionally, you can change the border's color, style, and width. The **margin** is white space outside the border. The margin creates **breathing room**—separation among the boxes so they aren't crowded on the page. To some extent, you have already seen margin space around block-level elements, such as headings. For example, you have seen that headings are preceded and followed by what appears to be a blank line. However, the browser is actually using its own default settings to create the top and bottom margins for the heading. The relationship among the padding, the border, and the margins are shown in Figure 5-1.

Figure 5-1	The box model

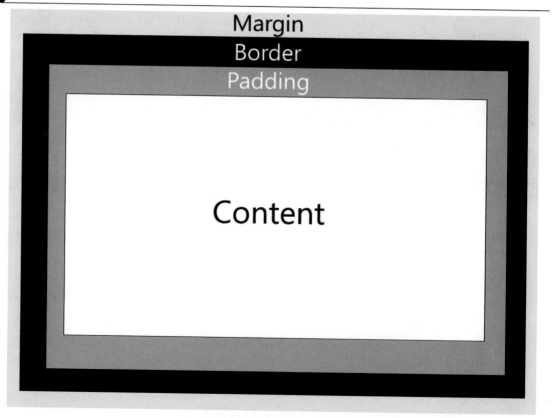

You don't have to use all three of these box properties at the same time. For example, you may want to have padding and margin space around the contents of an element, but not a border. Tahira has begun work on a Web page, paper.htm, for the SmallPaper Solutions Web site. Before you begin working with her to further develop her Web page, you'd like to take a look at the page she has created. You'll save the file with a new filename and create a comment in the head section.

To view Tahira's Web page:

▶ **1.** In your text editor, open the **paper.htm** file, which is located in the Tutorial.05\ Tutorial folder included with your Data Files. In the head section and below the page title, enter your name and today's date in the comment section where noted.

▶ **2.** Save the file as **papernew.htm** in the same folder.

▶ **3.** Open **papernew.htm** in your browser. Figure 5-2 shows the current appearance of the papernew.htm file.

Figure 5-2 ▶ The initial SmallPaper Solutions page

Meeting Your Business Needs

Creating the Paper *Less* Office

Our Business Rationale

Many offices are stocked with printers, reams of paper, filing cabinets, folders and shelving – all of which take up considerable floor space, cost money to purchase and resupply. For more than 20 years, we've been helping businesses like yours migrate from the 20th century to the 21st century by providing them with the business office solutions they need to achieve greater productivity, increase efficiency, and reduce costs. We make your workers comfortable with change and follow a slow immersion strategy. You don't have to throw out every sheet of paper in your office. We'll help you pick a launch date, whereby you can work forward to enter just your present documents into a digital system. Older documents can later be scanned or destroyed if no longer needed.

The Cost Justification

Most businesses today want to go paperless. That's fantasy, of course. The reality is that your company can use far less paper than it does now. Most businesses also know that going paperless is the environmentally responsible thing to do – using less paper results in greater efficiencies, reduces costs, and helps the environment. Think also about other indirect costs such as shipping paper across the nation, disposing of paper, shredding paper, and storing paper. Think again about the deforestation across the globe and the effects that it is having on our planet. We can help you get on the right track towards using less paper. If you are looking for justification for your return on investment, think about all the costs that are involved in consuming, using, storing, and distributing paper. Paper costs money, and on the average, paper prices have increased by 10% over the last 12 months alone. It costs money to purchase printers, maintain and service printers, and buy and replace toner cartridges. Converting storage rooms or "document libraries" into usable office space yields big savings each month. Think of all the filing cabinets in your office that store paper. Not only do you have to purchase office equipment to store that paper, the square footage taken up by filing cabinets quickly adds up. Here at SmallPaper Solutions, we'll get you started on the path to paper freedom and reducing or eliminating all of these costs.

What We Provide

We will provide you with assistance in three areas – hardware, software, and consulting

Hardware

- Servers for document management and storage
- High-speed scanners to scan very large volumes of paper
- Wide-format scanners to scan engineering or oversize drawings
- Photo scanners to digitize small and large photos
- Book copiers to digitize large in-house manuscripts and manuals
- Network printers with audit device controls to monitor who is printing what
- Document management software to aggregate all documents for easy search, retrieval, archiving and deletion
- Electronic storage and backup
- Audit tracking hardware so that all printing and copying is client billable

Software

- Collaboration software to help manage multiple versions of document edits
- Fax to PDF conversion software to eliminate the need to print faxes
- Client and Case Management software for e-mail, calendaring, and scheduling
- Human Resources software for forms creation and management
- Process Approval software to keep track of project status and approval
- Requisition management software to eliminate the need for paper forms for requistions

Consulting

1. Proposal specifications
2. Return on Investment Analysis
3. On-site supervision of hardware
4. Software installation
5. Training
6. Federal and state government compliance for record retention

When you combine the cost savings of using digital records with other benefits such as improved security, risk management protection, and the environmental benefits, it makes good sense to speak to one of our agents. Call us today, won't you, to get started on your way to lower costs and greater efficiencies. Get SmallPaper today.

SmallPaper Solutions • 120 Trent Highway • Richfield, KY 24579

Back to Top

You will begin by showing Tahira how to style the body element selector to create declarations for the font size, font family, color, and background color.

To style the body element selector:

▶ **1.** Switch back to your text editor. On a blank line below the comment code, type the following code to create an embedded style sheet and to style the body element selector, as shown in Figure 5-3.

```
<style type="text/css">

body {
  font-size: 1.1em;
  font-family: Verdana, sans-serif;
  color: white;
  background-color: #6d6f58;
}

</style>
```

Figure 5-3 ▶ **The body element style**

```
Filename: papernew.htm
-->

<style type="text/css">

body {
  font-size: 1.1em;
  font-family: Verdana, sans-serif;
  color: white;
  background-color: #6d6f58;
}

</style>

</head>
```

the body
element styled →

2. Save the file.

3. Switch to your browser, refresh or reload the **papernew.htm** page, and then compare your file to Figure 5-4 to confirm that the body element has been styled correctly.

Figure 5-4 ▶ **The body element styled in the browser**

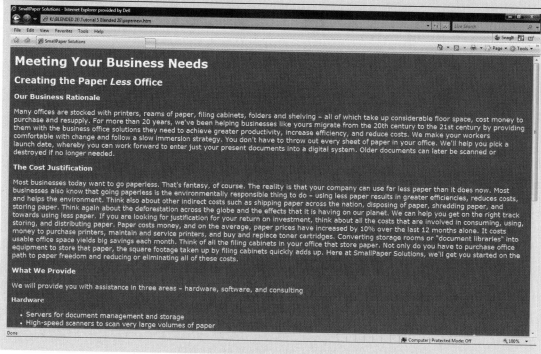

You have also created an image named paperlogo.gif that you can use for Tahira's Web page. The paperlogo.gif file has the same background color as the Web page, so the image will blend in seamlessly to the page background for the papernew.htm page. You will show Tahira how to insert the paperlogo.gif file.

To insert the paperlogo.gif file:

▶ **1.** Switch back to your text editor.

▶ **2.** On a blank line below the comment code regarding the paperlogo.gif image in the <body> area, type the following code to insert the paperlogo.gif image, as shown in Figure 5-5.

```
<p><img src="paperlogo.gif" alt="SmallPaper Solutions logo"
width="500" height="188" /></p>
```

Figure 5-5	The code for the paperlogo.gif image

code for the perlogo.gif image ⟶

```
<body>

<!-- insert the code for the paperlogo.gif image below -->

<p><img src="paperlogo.gif" alt="SmallPaper Solutions logo" width="500"
height="188" /></p>

<h1 id="top">Meeting Your Business Needs</h1>

<h2>Creating the Paper <em>Less</em> Office</h2>
```

▶ **3.** Save the file.

▶ **4.** Switch to your browser, refresh or reload the **papernew.htm** page, and then compare your file to Figure 5-6 to confirm that the image appears in the document.

Figure 5-6	The paperlogo.gif image in the browser

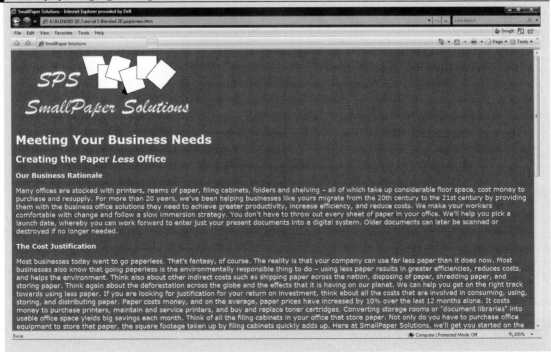

The page already looks much better than Tahira's original. She is familiar with using the font properties and text properties to change the appearance of text. She has noticed that text sometimes appears too close to an image and that images often have too much space around them. You will explain to Tahira how the CSS box properties can be used to solve these problems.

Understanding the Padding and Margin Properties

As explained earlier, padding is the internal white space that surrounds the contents of an element; the **padding properties** control this internal white space. By default, the content of an element does not have padding. The values for both the padding and the margin properties can be expressed by using several different measurements:

- em (em values)
- px (pixels)
- mm (millimeters)
- cm (centimeters)
- in (inches)
- % (as a percentage of the container element)

Reference Window | **Setting Padding**

- To set the padding within an element, use:
  padding: *width*;
  where *width* is the size of the padding using one of the CSS units of measure.

You can set the padding for each side individually by using the following four properties:

- padding-top:
- padding-right:
- padding-bottom:
- padding-left:

For example, to set the padding on the left for an image using em values, you would use the following code:

```
img {
    padding-left: 1em;
}
```

The **margin properties** control the external white space, which is the white space outside the border. The margin properties are often used to create white space around images. By default, there's only one pixel of space above, below, and to the left and right of an image. One pixel is very little white space, which means that images will appear too close to their surrounding text.

Following are the margin properties:

- margin-top:
- margin-right:
- margin-bottom:
- margin-left:

Tip

Although the margin properties are often used with images, the padding properties are not.

Reference Window | **Setting Margins**

- To set the margin space around an element, use:
  margin: *width*;
  where *width* is the size of the margin using one of the CSS units of measure.

Using the Padding and Margin Shorthand Properties

It would be acceptable to create declarations for the top, right, bottom, and left margins, as shown in the following code:

```
img {
    margin-top: 4px;
    margin-right: 0;
    margin-bottom: 4px;
    margin-left: 0;
}
```

However, you can take advantage of shorthand properties for padding and margins. The **padding property** is a shorthand property that sets the padding on all four sides. The following code would create the same amount of padding on all four sides of an h1 element:

```
h1 {
    padding: 4px;
}
```

Similarly, the **margin property** is a shorthand property that sets the margin on all four sides. The following code would create the same amount of margin space on all four sides of an h2 element:

```
h2 {
    margin: 1em;
}
```

You can also use the padding and margin properties to be more specific than declaring the same value for all four sides at once. Here's how these shorthand properties work:

- If one value is listed, the value is used for all four sides equally.
- If two values are listed, the first value is applied to the top and bottom sides equally, and the second value is applied to the left and right sides equally.
- If three values are listed, the first value is applied to the top side, the second value is applied to the left and right sides equally, and the third value is applied to the bottom side.
- If four values are listed, the values are applied in this order: top, right, bottom, and left.

Tip

developers seldom
e a unit measurement
r the value of 0. Zero
ny measurement is 0.

Every value, except for 0, must have an accompanying measurement, with no space between the value and the measurement—in other words, 1em, not 1 em. For values that are less than 1, it's a good coding practice to precede the value with a leading zero (for example, 0.2em), so that anyone reading your code will know that the value is less than 1.

Figure 5-7 summarizes how to set values for the padding and margin shorthand properties.

Figure 5-7 ▷ **Setting values for the padding and margin shorthand properties**

Values	Applies to these sides, in this order	Example
1	All sides equally	padding: 4px;
2	Top and bottom equally, left and right equally	margin: 10px 4px;
3	Top, left and right equally, bottom	padding: 4px 10px 4px;
4	Top, right, bottom, left	margin: 0 0 0 4px;

| InSight | | **Understanding How Margins Collapse** |

When designing a Web page, you could have two adjacent vertical boxes on the page. For example, it's quite common to place an image above or below another image to create an image gallery. In such a case, it can be difficult to determine the top and bottom of the images because of **margin collapse**, which occurs when two adjoining top and bottom margins combine to form a single margin. The browser renders the greater of the two margins, not the sum of both the top and bottom margins. For example, let's say that you had two images on your Web page, with one image positioned directly below the other. If the top image had a bottom margin of 25px and the bottom image had a top margin of 20px, you would expect the distance between the top image and bottom image to be 45px because 25 + 20 = 45. However, the actual distance would be 25px, which is the larger of the two margins. Margin collapse only occurs when two vertical margins come in contact. Two images that are side by side will not have their margins collapse. In the tutorials on CSS layouts, you will learn how to correct margin collapse problems.

Tahira would like to style both the h1 and h2 headings. You will show her how to use the margin and padding properties to style these elements.

To style the h1 and h2 elements:

▶ **1.** Switch back to your text editor.

▶ **2.** On a blank line below the body style, type the following code to style the h1 and h2 elements, as shown in Figure 5-8.

```
h1 {
   background-color: black;
   padding: 4px;
   margin: 0 0 0 10px;
   text-align: center;
}

h2 {
   background-color: gray;
   padding: 4px;
   margin: 10px 0 0 10px;
   text-align: center;
}
```

| Figure 5-8 | ▶ | **The code to style the h1 and h2 elements** |

```
h1 {
   background-color: black;
   padding: 4px;
   margin: 0 0 0 10px;
   text-align: center;
}

h2 {
   background-color: gray;
   padding: 4px;
   margin: 10px 0 0 10px;
   text-align: center;
}

</style>

</head>
```

the h1 and h2 elements styled

▶ **3.** Save the file.

▶ **4.** Switch to your browser, refresh or reload the **papernew.htm** page, and then compare your file to Figure 5-9 to confirm that the h1 and h2 elements have been styled correctly.

Figure 5-9 ▶ The h1 and h2 elements styled in the browser

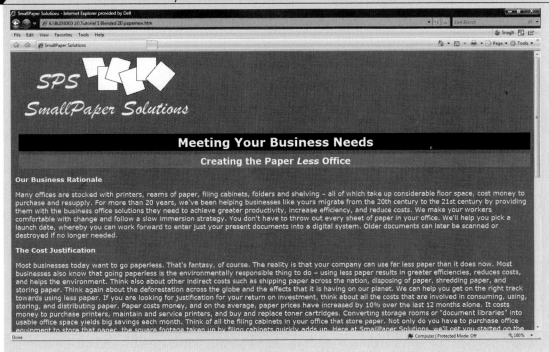

Next, you will show Tahira another set of box properties, the border properties.

Using the Border Properties

You use the **border properties** to place a decorative border around the contents of an element. Recall that in the box model, the border is between the padding and the margin. You can change the border's style, color, and width. The border value can be any one of the following:

- solid
- double
- dotted
- dashed
- groove
- ridge
- inset
- outset
- none (the default; there is no border)

Border styles, unfortunately, can look different in each browser. Figure 5-10 illustrates the border styles as they appear in Internet Explorer.

Figure 5-10 | **Border styles**

There are five border-style properties:

- border-top-style:
- border-right-style:
- border-bottom-style:
- border-left-style:
- border-style:

The **border-style property** is the shorthand property you can use to set the values for all four border styles with one declaration.

Reference Window | **Setting the Appearance of all Four Borders at Once**

- To set the border width, use:
  ```
  border-width: width;
  ```
  where *width* is one of the CSS units of measure.
- To set the border color, use:
  ```
  border-color: value;
  ```
  where *value* is a named color, RGB color, or hexadecimal color value.
- To set the border style, use:
  ```
  border-style: style;
  ```
  where *style* is either none, solid, double, dotted, dashed, outset, inset, groove, or ridge.
- To use the border shorthand property, enter:
  ```
  border: style color width;
  ```
  where *style* is the border style, *color* is the border color, and *width* is the border width. Although not all three values need to be specified, and values can be entered in any order, you must specify a border style.

The border width can be expressed by the keywords thin, medium, and thick or as a pixel, em, or percentage value. Browsers display the thicknesses of the keyword values slightly differently, but in general, a thin border is 1px wide, a medium border is 3px or 4px wide, and a thick border is 4px (or more) wide. In general, Internet Explorer adds greater thickness to the keyword values than the Firefox browser. When creating page layouts in which elements have borders, it's best to avoid these browser discrepancies, so instead of using keywords, rely on pixel values to express the border thickness. Figure 5-11 illustrates the various border widths.

Figure 5-11   **Border widths**

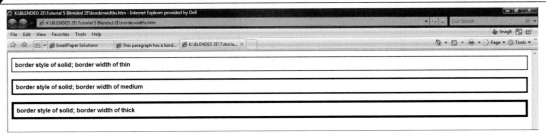

There are five border-width properties:

- border-top-width:
- border-right-width:
- border-bottom-width:
- border-left-width:
- border-width:

The **border-width property** is the shorthand property you can use to set the width values for all four borders at once.

The border color can be a named color or a hex value. There are five border-color properties:

- border-top-color:
- border-right-color:
- border-bottom-color:
- border-left-color:
- border-color:

The **border-color property** is the shorthand property you can use to set the color values for all four borders at once. Figure 5-12 illustrates the border colors.

Figure 5-12   **Border colors**

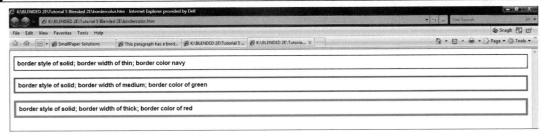

Using the Border Shorthand Properties

There are eight border shorthand properties. As you saw in the previous section, the following three properties change the border style, width, or color for all four borders:

- border-color:
- border-style:
- border-width:

The following four properties change the border style, width, and color for an individual border:

- border-top:
- border-right:
- border-bottom:
- border-left:

Finally, the following property changes the border style, width, and color for all four borders:

- border:

The **border property** is the most commonly used border shorthand property. You must specify a border style when you use the border shorthand property. Use spaces, not commas, to separate the values when using the border shorthand properties.

The following border shorthand property sets the border color for all sides to maroon:

```
h1 {
    border-color: maroon;
}
```

The following code sets the top border to be solid, thin, and red:

```
h2 {
    border-top: solid thin red;
}
```

The following code sets all borders to be inset, thick, and orange:

```
h3 {
    border: inset thick orange;
}
```

You can list the border style, thickness, and color in any order, and you do not have to specify three values, but you must specify a border style if you use two values. If you omit a value for color, the border appears in the same color as the element's color. For example, to use the border shorthand property to change the borders to appear in navy, you would enter the following code (note that a border style—in this instance, dotted—also must be specified):

```
h1 {
    border: dotted navy;
}
```

The border property is clearly favored over the use of the XHTML horizontal rule (the <hr/>) element, which draws a horizontal line across the screen. Screen readers have trouble interpreting the horizontal rule element, so for accessibility reasons, always substitute the border property in place of the horizontal rule element. Another advantage of using the CSS border properties is that you can create vertical ruled lines by changing the border on the left or right. You cannot create vertical ruled lines by using XHTML code.

You will show Tahira how to use the border-bottom shorthand property for the h3 elements on her Web page. She wants a solid orange bottom border only. You will also use the padding property to create some white space between the bottom border and the h3 heading text.

To create a bottom border for the h3 elements:

▶ **1.** Switch back to your text editor.

▶ **2.** On a blank line below the style for the h2 element, type the following code to style the h3 element, as shown in Figure 5-13.

```
h3 {
   border-bottom: solid thick orange;
   padding-bottom: 0.5em;
}
```

Figure 5-13 | **The code to style the h3 element**

```
h2 {
   background-color: gray;
   padding: 4px;
   margin: 10px 0 0 10px;
   text-align: center;
}

h3 {
   border-bottom: solid thick orange;
   padding-bottom: 0.5em;
}

</style>

</head>
```

the h3 element styled

▶ **3.** Save the file.

▶ **4.** Switch to your browser, refresh or reload the **papernew.htm** page, and then compare your file to Figure 5-14 to confirm that the h3 element has been styled correctly.

Figure 5-14 | **The h3 element styled in the browser**

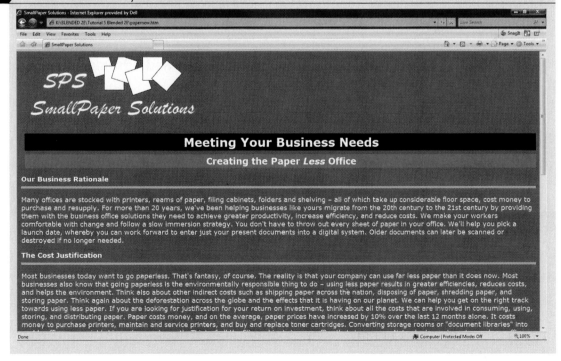

Next, you will show Tahira how to wrap text around an image by using the float property.

Using the Float Property

The CSS **classification properties** allow you to control how to display and position an element, and how to control the visibility of an element. Two commonly used classification properties, especially in Web page layout, are the float property and the clear property. The **float property** is used to position boxes on the page and to wrap content, such as text, around a box. The **clear property** is used to reposition an element below another element on the page.

Tahira has noticed a great deal of white space to the right of the paperlogo.gif image. She wonders if she can make the text wrap to the right of the image. You mention to Tahira that the float property is used to position an element (and its contents) either at the left or right edge of the screen. If the float property has a value of left, the element appears at the left edge of the browser window, and the text wraps to the right of the element. If the float property has a value of right, the element appears at the right edge of the browser window and the text wraps to the left of the element.

Reference Window | **Using the Float Property**

- To float an element, use the style:
  ```
  float: position;
  ```
  where *position* is left, right, or none.

Any element can be floated, but two elements are floated most commonly: the image element, which is an inline element; and the div element, which is a block-level element commonly used to create page layout. You will learn about the div element in the next tutorial. It is very important to remember that any floated element must have a width. When you float an image, the width is stated in the image tag code.

Because the paperlogo.gif image is the only image on the page, you will show Tahira how to create a style for the img element to float left. You will also give the image some margin space to its right and below it.

Tip

The float property does not have a value of center.

To float the paperlogo.gif image left and add margin space:

1. Switch back to your text editor.

2. On a blank line below the style for the h3 element, type the following code to style the img element, as shown in Figure 5-15.

   ```
   img {
      float: left;
      margin: 0 10px 10px 0;
   }
   ```

Figure 5-15 ▶ **The code to style the img element**

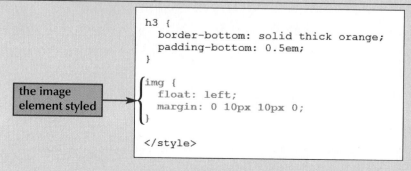

```
h3 {
   border-bottom: solid thick orange;
   padding-bottom: 0.5em;
}

img {
   float: left;
   margin: 0 10px 10px 0;
}

</style>
```

the image element styled

3. Save the file.

4. Switch to your browser, refresh or reload the **papernew.htm** page, and then compare your file to Figure 5-16 to confirm that the image element now has text that wraps to its right. The h3 heading "Our Business Rationale" also wraps around the image, which is an issue you will address with Tahira shortly.

Figure 5-16 | **The image element floated left**

To emphasize the benefits of working with SmallPaper Solutions, Tahira has provided you with a JPEG file named stacks.jpg. The image shows an inbox and an outbox overflowing with stacks of paper. She would like to place the image to the right of the paragraph below the h3 heading "The Cost Justification." There is one problem, however. You have already styled the img element to float left, and Tahira wants this image to float right. You can't style the same element two different ways, but Tahira can create a dependent class for the img element. The dependent class will be named "right" and will float an image right. She also wants to use the margin property to create white space on the top, bottom, and left side of the image. Finally, she wants to use the border property to give the image a border. She should insert the code for the image (including the code to apply the class) in the paragraph below the Cost Justification h3 heading.

To create and apply the dependent class:

1. Switch back to your text editor.

2. On a blank line below the style for the img element, type the following code to create the dependent class, as shown in Figure 5-17.

```
img.right {
  float: right;
  margin: 10px 0 10px 10px;
  border: double thick black;
}
```

Figure 5-17 > **The code for the dependent class**

the image right dependent class →

```
img {
  float: left;
  margin: 0 10px 10px 0;
}

img.right {
  float: right;
  margin: 10px 0 10px 10px;
  border: double thick black;
}

</style>
```

▶ **3.** In the body text below the Cost Justification h3 heading and the comment, type the following code to insert the stacks.jpg image and apply the "right" dependent class, as shown in Figure 5-18.

```
<p><img src="stacks.jpg" alt="photo of in box and out box
overflowing with stacks of paper" width="400" height="300"
class="right" /></p>
```

Figure 5-18 > **The code for the stacks.jpg image**

the stacks.jpg image code →

```
<h3>The Cost Justification</h3>

<!-- insert the code for the stacks.jpg image below -->

<p><img src="stacks.jpg" alt="photo of in box and out box overflowing with
stacks of paper" width="400" height="300" class="right" /></p>

<p>Most businesses today want to go paperless. That's fantasy, of course.
```

▶ **4.** Save the file.

▶ **5.** Switch to your browser, refresh or reload the **papernew.htm** page, and then compare your file to Figure 5-19 to confirm that the stacks.jpg image element floats right and that text wraps to its left.

Figure 5-19 ▷ **The stacks.jpg image element floated right**

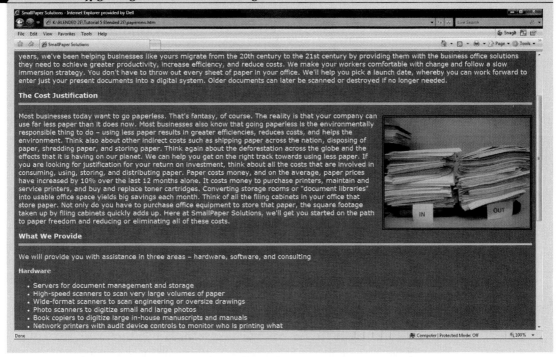

Tahira has noticed a problem near the top of the page. The h3 heading "Our Business Rationale" should begin below the paperlogo.gif image, not beside it. Next, you will show Tahira how to use the clear property to solve this problem.

Using the Clear Property

Use the clear property to make the contents of an element appear below an element that has been floated. This is also called "clearing past" an element. The clear property takes the following values:

Tip

're not sure which property value to se the value of both.

- left (text begins below an element floated left)
- right (text begins below an element floated right)
- both (text begins below an element floated either left or right)

---

erence Window | **Using the Clear Property**

- To clear past an element, use the following style:
    ```
    clear: position;
    ```
  where *position* is left, right, or both.

Because other elements on the page might have to use the clear property, you tell Tahira it's better to create an independent class, one that can work with all the elements, rather than create a dependent class that would work only with the h3 element. You will show Tahira how to create and apply an independent class named "clear."

To create and apply the clear independent class:

1. Switch back to your text editor.

2. On a blank line below the style for the img.right dependent class, type the following code to create the "clear" independent class, as shown in Figure 5-20.

```
.clear {
  clear: both;
}
```

Figure 5-20 | The code for the "clear" independent class

```
img.right {
  float: right;
  margin: 10px 0 10px 10px;
  border: double thick black;
}

.clear {
  clear: both;
}

</style>
```

the "clear" independent class

3. In the start h3 tag for the Our Business Rationale h3 element, insert the following code to apply the "clear" independent class, as shown in Figure 5-21.

```
<h3 class="clear">Our Business Rationale</h3>
```

Figure 5-21 | The code to apply the "clear" independent class

```
<!-- insert the code for the paperlogo.gif image below -->

<p><img src="paperlogo.gif" alt="SmallPaper Solutions logo" width="500"
height="188" /></p>

<h1 id="top">Meeting Your Business Needs</h1>

<h2>Creating the Paper <em>Less</em> Office</h2>

<h3 class="clear">Our Business Rationale</h3>
<p>Many offices are stocked with printers, reams of paper, filing
cabinets, folders and shelving &ndash; all of which take up considerable
floor space, cost money to purchase and resupply. For more than 20 years,
we've been helping businesses like yours migrate from the 20th  century to
```

the "clear" class applied

4. Save the file.

5. Switch to your browser, refresh or reload the **papernew.htm** page, and then compare your file to Figure 5-22 to confirm that the Our Business Rationale h3 heading now appears below the paperlogo.gif image.

| Figure 5-22 | The h3 heading cleared |

6. If you will not be completing the next session now, close the papernew.htm file. Exit your text editor and your browser.

Now that you've fine-tuned the position of images on the papernew.htm Web page, you're ready to show Tahira how to use another group of properties—the background properties.

Review | **Session 5.1 Quick Check**

1. What is the box model?
2. What is padding?
3. What is the margin?
4. When using the border shorthand property, what value must always be specified?
5. What are the values for the float property?
6. What are the values for the clear property?

Session 5.2

Understanding the Background Properties

The **background properties** set the background effects for an element. You have already worked with the background-color property to set the background color for an element. To create greater visual interest, you can also use the **background-image property** to use an image as the background for an element. You can use the **background-repeat property** to repeat an image vertically, horizontally, or both. To position a background image within an element, use the **background-position property**. You can also use the **background-attachment property** to set a fixed or scrolling background image. Finally, you can use the **background property** to set all of the background image properties in one declaration.

Reference Window | **Setting Background Properties**

Use the following properties to set the appearance of the background:
- background-image—Place an image behind the contents of an element. The image can be any GIF, PNG, or JPEG image, but the syntax must be in the form *url(imagename.gif)*.
- background-color—Place a color behind an element's contents.
- background-position—Position an image within an element. Use keywords or pixel, em, or percentage values.
- background-repeat—Repeat an image horizontally or vertically (or both) to fill the contents of an element.
- background-attachment—Have a background image scroll with the cursor.
- background—Use this shorthand property to change all of the background properties. Values (if used) must be listed in this order: image value, color value, position value, repeat value, and attachment value.

Using the background-image Property

The background-image property is used to fill the background of an element with an image. To create the image, you can use image-editing software such as Adobe Photoshop, or you can use image creation software such as Adobe Illustrator or Microsoft Expression Design. First, you select an appropriate image for the background. Make sure that the text is readable against the image. The background image should contrast with the text rather than compete with it. The value for the background-image property begins with the letters "url". Although it is not incorrect to enclose the filename for the background image with either single or double quotation marks, most Web developers omit the quotes. The name of the image file is then specified in parentheses, as shown in the following code.

```
body {
   background-image: url(tile.jpg);
}
```

Tip

The url value is the name and location of the image file. Store the image file and the XHTML file in the same folder or specify the path to the image in the url value.

If the background-image property is used with the body element as a selector, and if the image is repeated both horizontally and vertically, then the background image will occupy the entire screen.

It's a good coding practice to always use the background-color property when you use the background-image property. Select a complementary background color to your background image. That way, if the background image is not displayed, at least the foreground and background colors will still be readable. When a browser has a problem displaying an image, some browsers (such as Internet Explorer) will show a placeholder icon instead of the image to alert you to the problem. However, if the background-image code contains an error, an image placeholder icon is not displayed. If you specify a background color, the element's contents will still appear against the background color even if there is an error in the image code. Also, specifying a background-color property overrides any default setting in the browser for background color, which usually is white. If you are using a background image for the body element, make sure your body text has a contrasting color, not a competing color.

Setting the background-position Property

The background-position property allows you to position an image in different locations within its container element, such as a div element. If the container element is the body element, you are positioning the element on the page. The values for the background-position property can be expressed by using keywords, percent values, or any other CSS measurement units, such as pixels or ems. The keywords are used together to position the image in nine regions behind the element, as shown in Figure 5-23. The default value for the background-position property is "top left."

Figure 5-23 | Keywords that describe the position of the background image

top left	top center	top right
center left	center center	center right
bottom left	bottom center	bottom right

Tip

...only specify one ...rd, the second value ...e "center."

You can also use percentage pairs instead of keywords. The first percentage describes the horizontal position, and the second percentage describes the vertical position. Figure 5-24 shows values expressed in percentages instead of keywords. The top left corner is 0% 0%, and the bottom right corner is 100% 100%. Enter a space, not a comma, between the values.

Figure 5-24 | Percentage values that describe the position of the background image

0% 0%	50% 0%	100% 0%
0% 50%	50% 50%	100% 50%
0% 100%	50% 100%	100% 100%

You don't have to use the percentages of 0, 50, and 100%. You can specify any percentage from 0 to 100 for the horizontal and vertical positions, such as 5% 98%. If only one percentage is given, it is assumed to be the horizontal position; the other percentage is assumed to be the vertical position of 50%. Although they are less commonly used, you can also use pixel and em values to precisely position the contents of an element within its containing block.

Using the background-repeat Property

You use the background-repeat property to have copies of an image appear behind an element horizontally, vertically, or in both orientations. Repeating an image is also known as **tiling** an image. The background-repeat property takes the four values shown in Figure 5-25.

Figure 5-25	Values for the background-repeat property

Tip

The background-repeat property is often used to create a background for the entire Web page.

Property	What it does
repeat	The image is repeated (tiled) to the right and down to fill the element's contents; this is the default value
repeat-x	The image is repeated only horizontally
repeat-y	The image is repeated only vertically
no-repeat	The image is displayed once in the upper-left corner of the element and is not repeated

InSight | **Using the background-attachment Property**

The background-attachment property allows you to make an image scroll down the page along with the cursor. This property takes two values: scroll, in which the image scrolls down the page along with the insertion point; and fixed, in which the image stays in place and text overlays the image as the user scrolls down the page. This value would be useful, for example, to ensure that a corporate logo always appears at the top of the page, even as the user scrolls down. The value of "scroll" is not used often on Web pages, probably because some visitors find it distracting to have an image travel with the cursor, so be judicious in your use of this value.

Using the background Shorthand Property

The background property is the shorthand property that specifies any or all of the background properties. You can use as few or as many of the properties as you want, but you must specify the properties and their values in the following order:

- background-image
- background-color
- background-position
- background-repeat
- background-attachment

Use spaces, not commas, to separate the values, as shown below.

```
body {
    background: url(flowers.jpg) yellow top left repeat-y;
}
```

Tahira wants to use a background image to emphasize the h4 headings that precede the unordered lists, and to emphasize the h5 heading at the bottom of the page. Tahira has an image named list.gif, which will create a textured background for the h4 and h5 elements. As a good coding practice, you'll enter the code for the h4 and h5 heading selectors after the h3 heading selector code.

To style the h4 and h5 selectors:

▶ **1.** If necessary, open the papernew.htm file in both your browser and your text editor.

▶ **2.** In your text editor, position the insertion point to the right of the closing brace for the h3 style.

▶ **3.** Press the **Enter** key twice.

▶ **4.** Type the following code to style the h4 and h5 elements, as shown in Figure 5-26.

```
h4 {
   background-image: url(list.gif);
   background-color: yellow;
   display: inline;
   padding: 4px;
   color: black;
}

h5 {
   background-image: url(list.gif);
   background-color: yellow;
   color: black;
   padding: 4px;
   text-align: center;
   font-size: 1.1em;
}
```

Figure 5-26 **The code for the h4 and h5 elements**

```
      border-bottom: solid thick orange;
      padding-bottom: 0.5em;
   }

   h4 {
      background-image: url(list.gif);
      background-color: yellow;
      display: inline;
      padding: 4px;
      color: black;
   }

   h5 {
      background-image: url(list.gif);
      background-color: yellow;
      color: black;
      padding: 4px;
      text-align: center;
      font-size: 1.1em;
   }

   img {
      float: left;
      margin: 0 10px 10px 0;
   }
```

the h4 and h5 elements styled

▶ **5.** Save the file.

▶ **6.** Switch to your browser, refresh or reload the **papernew.htm** page. Scroll down if necessary, and then compare your file to Figure 5-27 to confirm that the h4 and h5 elements have been styled correctly.

Figure 5-27 The h4 and h5 elements styled in the browser

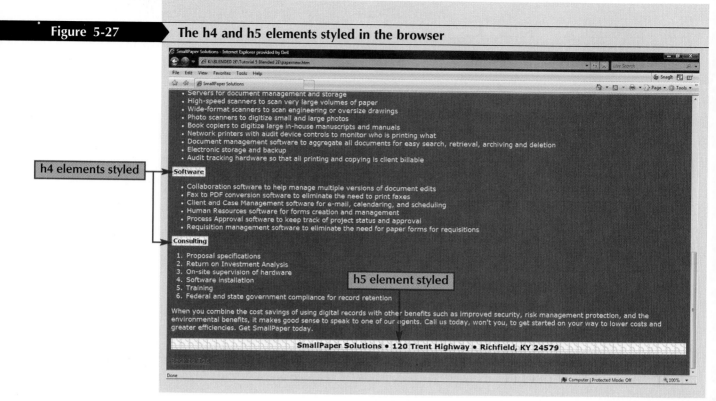

Next, you'll show Tahira how to add a background image to a list item and use the margin and padding properties to position the background image.

Using a Background Image for List Items

Although you can use CSS to change the list style type from solid round bullets to squares or hollow circles, CSS does not provide any control over the positioning of list style markers, particularly images used as bullets. Depending on the image used as a marker, the bullet might be either too high or too low in relation to the text to its right in the list item. Unfortunately, the CSS vertical-align property cannot be used to position bullets in a list. However, you can control the appearance of images used as list markers by using the background-image property to style the list item element.

The position of the list marker and the padding will vary depending on the font size and the size of the image used as a list marker. To accommodate the size of the bullet you choose, you might also have to style the ul element to create more (or less) line spacing between the list items. By default, an XHTML bullet in an unordered list is about 15px square. If you create an image to be used as a list marker that is larger than 15px, you should also increase the line height to adjust for the size of the image.

Tahira would like to highlight the items in the Consulting list by changing the bullet to a bright yellow arrow. To do this, you first have to remove any list style type, and then you must change the line height to accommodate the image. You next specify the padding and a left margin. XHTML lists have a certain amount of indentation, but browsers differ on how to create the indent. Some browsers use padding, while others use margins. To compensate for browser differences in the way they render lists, you will eliminate the padding and set the left margin. With this approach, you determine the dimensions of the indent yourself, without relying on the browser default setting. The code for the ol element would be entered as shown below.

```
ol {
    line-height: 1.4;
    list-style-type: none;
    padding: 0;
    margin-left: 1em;
}
```

Next, you must set the properties and values for the list item element. In addition to using the arrow figure for the bullet, you can provide a background color to highlight the list items. This color will not apply to the image; rather, it will provide a background color for the list item element. Because you want to affect only the appearance of list items within ordered lists, you need to create a descendant selector for the ordered list element. You don't want the list marker image to repeat, so the value for the background-repeat property will be no-repeat. The code for the list item would begin as shown.

```
ol li {
  background-image: url(arrow.gif);
  background-color: black;
  background-repeat: no-repeat;
}
```

The next step is to position the image marker. You will need to create a margin on the left and some padding between the margin and the image marker, and you will need to position the marker in relation to the list item text to its right. In this instance, the background-position property positions the image marker 0.3em from the left. The complete code for the list item element is shown below.

```
ol li {
  background-image: url(arrow.gif);
  background-color: black;
  background-repeat: no-repeat;
  padding-left: 30px;
  background-position: 0.3em;
}
```

Tahira is ready to create a style to use the arrow.gif image as a list item marker for the items in the Consulting list. You will have Tahira use the background shorthand property, rather than enter separate declarations for the background.

To create the style for the arrow.gif list item marker:

1. Switch back to your text editor.

2. On a blank line below the "clear" style, type the following code, as shown in Figure 5-28.

```
ol {
  line-height: 1.4;
  list-style-type: none;
  padding: 0;
  margin-left: 1em;
}

ol li {
  background: url(arrow.gif) black 0.3em no-repeat;
  padding-left: 30px;
}
```

Figure 5-28 — The code for the ordered list and list item marker

```
.clear {
   clear: both;
}

ol {
   line-height: 1.4;
   list-style-type: none;
   padding: 0;
   margin-left: 1em;
}

ol li {
   background: url(arrow.gif) black 0.3em no-repeat;
   padding-left: 30px;
}

</style>

</head>
```

the ordered list and list items for the ordered list styled

▶ **3.** Save the file.

▶ **4.** Switch to your browser, refresh or reload the **papernew.htm** page, and then compare your file to Figure 5-29. Confirm that arrow.gif is used as a background image to create a list marker for the Consulting section.

Figure 5-29 — The list items with image markers in the browser

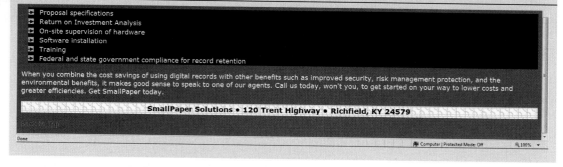

Figure 5-30 summarizes the background properties.

Figure 5-30   **The background properties**

Property	What it does	Values
background-image	Places an image behind an element's content	Any GIF, JPEG, or PNG file; for example, *url(imagename.gif)*
background-color	Places a color behind an element's content	Any named color, RGB, or hexadecimal value
background-position	Positions an image within an element's content	Use keywords, percentages, pixel, or em values
background-repeat	Repeats an image within an element's content	repeat (the default; the image is copied to the right and down to fill the element) no-repeat (the image appears once in the upper-left corner of the element) repeat-x (the image is repeated horizontally across the element) repeat-y (the image is repeated vertically down the element)
background-attachment	Determines whether an image scrolls with the cursor	fixed scroll
background	The shorthand property used to change all (or some) of the background properties	Not all values must be stated, but if used, they must be stated in this order: image, color, position, repeat, and attachment

Recall that pseudo-class selectors can be used to change the appearance of links. The :link pseudo-class selector styles unvisited links, the :visited pseudo-class selector styles visited links, and the :hover pseudo-class selector creates a hover effect when the mouse pointer passes over a link. The :active pseudo-class selector creates a style for the moment when the user clicks a link. The bottom of the papernew.htm Web page contains a link back to the page top. Tahira would like to ensure that the link does not go unnoticed, so you will show her how to create several styles for the :link, :hover, and :visited pseudo-class selectors.

To create styles for the link to the page top:

▶ **1.** Switch back to your text editor.

▶ **2.** On a blank line below the ol li descendant selector, type the following code, as shown in Figure 5-31.

```
a:link {
   color: orange;
}

a:hover {
   color: blue;
   background-color: yellow;
}

a:visited {
 color: maroon;
}
```

Figure 5-31 | **The code for the pseudo-class selectors**

styles for the :link, :hover, and :visited pseudo-class selectors

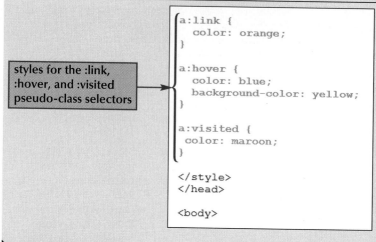

```
a:link {
   color: orange;
}

a:hover {
   color: blue;
   background-color: yellow;
}

a:visited {
 color: maroon;
}

</style>
</head>

<body>
```

▶ **3.** Save the file.

▶ **4.** Switch to your browser and refresh or reload the **papernew.htm** page. Compare your file to Figure 5-32 to confirm that the link color has changed to orange.

Figure 5-32 | **The link color changed in the browser**

When you combine the cost savings of using digital records with other benefits such as improved security, risk management protection, and the environmental benefits, it makes good sense to speak to one of our agents. Call us today, won't you, to get started on your way to lower costs and greater efficiencies. Get SmallPaper today.

link color changed to orange

SmallPaper Solutions • 120 Trent Highway • Richfield, KY 24579

Back to Top

Computer | Protected Mode: Off   100%

▶ **5.** Pass the mouse pointer over the link and click the link. Scroll to the bottom of the page and confirm that the link color has changed to maroon, the visited link color.

Now that the document is complete, you want to show Tahira how to move the styles to an external style sheet. First you need to explain to her how styles cascade.

Resolving Style Conflicts

So far, you have worked solely with embedded style sheets—your styles have all been inserted directly into your XHTML files. In the next section, you will be introduced to another source of styles—external style sheets. You have to be careful when using external style sheets, however, because you might inadvertently apply different styles to the same element, placing one style in your embedded style sheet and the other in an external style sheet. Which style would the browser use? The term **cascade** in Cascading Style Sheets refers to the methods used to determine which style rules apply if more than one rule styles the same element.

Style precedence determines the order of the cascade, and is one of the methods used to resolve style conflicts. There are five sources for styles. Their order of precedence (from highest to lowest) is as follows:

1. User-defined styles
2. Inline styles
3. Embedded style sheet styles
4. External style sheet styles
5. The browser's style sheet (the browser's default styles)

As this list shows, user styles have precedence over all other styles. **User-defined styles** are set by the reader in the browser, usually to improve Web accessibility; for example, the text size can be increased to compensate for a visual impairment. To change the user styles in the Firefox browser, for example, click Tools on the menu bar, and then click Options. In the Options dialog box, click the Content icon, as shown in Figure 5-33. The resulting dialog box allows the user to change several of the font and color properties.

Figure 5-33 **The Content Options dialog box in the Firefox browser**

As a Web page author, you control the next three types of styles after user-defined styles: inline, embedded, and external. Inline styles are written in the document body, and are the next highest in style precedence; therefore, they override all styles other than user styles. The use of inline styles is actually discouraged, because they can become buried in the body of the document. You are familiar with embedded style sheets, but you haven't yet worked with external style sheets. An **external style sheet** contains the CSS style code in a separate file, which you then apply to several files or all the files at your Web site.

Always create either embedded or external style sheets for your styles so that the styles can be easily located and edited. If you do create an inline style, remember that it will take precedence over any embedded or external styles for that element. The browser's default styles have the lowest style precedence. This means that the browser's styles are applied only when you have not specified a style of your own.

You have seen how style conflicts are resolved based on their source, but style conflicts can also arise in the same location. What happens if you mistakenly style the same element two different ways in the same embedded or external style sheet? When conflicts occur between two styles in the same location, the style that is lower in the styles list usually takes precedence. For example, in the following embedded style sheet, what font size will h2 text have?

```
<style type="text/css">

h2 {
  font-size: 1em;
}
```

```
. . . (other styles here). . .

h2 {
   font-size: 2em;
}

</style>
```

The style written last in the style list has the greater precedence, so in this instance, h2 text will appear in a font size of 2em. In a later tutorial, you will learn about specificity, another means of resolving conflicts between two styles.

Tahira wants to know what would happen if the first style had other declarations in addition to the font size. For example, what if the first h2 style also had a declaration for the background color, but the second style did not? This example is shown in the following code:

```
h2 {
   font-size: 1em;
   background-color: yellow;
}

h2 {
   font-size: 2em;
}
```

In the second h2 style, your intent is to style the h2 heading so that the text *only* appears in a font size of 2em. However, because the first style for the h2 heading also has a background color of yellow, all h2 headings will appear in the browser with a background color of yellow. The cascade only resolves style conflicts. Any rules that don't conflict still take effect. Because the second style does not specify a background color, the background color from the first style takes effect. The result will be the same as if you had entered the following code:

```
h2 {
   font-size: 2em;
   background-color: yellow;
}
```

Now that you have seen how the cascade and style precedence resolve conflicts, you are ready to show Tahira how to create an external style sheet.

Understanding External Style Sheets

Many contemporary Web sites consist of hundreds or thousands of pages. If you used embedded style sheets on all of your Web pages and later decided to change a style or two, you would have to open each file, revise the embedded styles code, and save the file. Imagine doing that a thousand times! When you use an external style sheet, you can make a change to a style simply by editing the external style sheet file. Those edits would automatically be reflected in each of the Web documents that use that style sheet—an enormous time-saver.

You can type CSS code directly into an external style sheet, but a better method is to begin with an embedded style sheet, as you have with the papernew.htm file. It's easier to work with an embedded style sheet while you are developing the file because you don't have to keep switching between the XHTML file and the CSS file. Once you finish the XHTML file, you can cut the code from the XHTML file and paste it into an external style sheet. External style sheet documents follow the same naming conventions as any other file, but external style sheet files must end with the filename extension of .css.

erence Window | **Creating and Applying an External Style Sheet**

- Create a new file for the external style sheet, and include a CSS comment at the top of the page to document the author name and the creation date. Do not enter any XHTML code in this file.
- Switch to the XHTML file. In the embedded style sheet, delete the start and end style tags.
- In the XHTML file, cut the CSS code from the embedded style sheet and paste the code into the CSS file.
- Save the CSS file with a .css filename extension and close it.
- In the <head> section of the XHTML file, enter the following code to link to the external CSS file:

  ```
  <link rel="stylesheet" href="filename.css" type="text/css" />
  ```
  where *filename.css* is the name of the external style sheet file.

External style sheets separate formatting from content. All of the style codes are stored in a separate file that contains *only* CSS code. The code for an external style sheet would look like the following example (though it would have many more styles):

```
/* Created by Tahira Jones
 All files for this Web site link to this style sheet */

body {
  font-size: 1.1em;
  font-family: Arial, Helvetica, sans-serif;
  color: white;
  background-color: #6d6f58;
}
```

Note that the style sheet began with a CSS comment. The code for a CSS comment is slightly different from the code for an XHTML comment. A CSS comment begins with a forward slash and an asterisk, and then the comment text follows. The comment ends with an asterisk and a forward slash.

Creating an External Style Sheet

To create an external style sheet, you type the CSS code in a separate document and save it with a .css extension. An external style sheet document does not have any XHTML code. Do not enter the code for a document type declaration or any other XHTML code.

Because Tahira is responsible for maintaining the style sheet, you will show her how to create a comment that identifies her as the Web developer who created the style sheet. If other Web developers have questions about the style sheet, they will know whom to contact. External style sheets usually begin with a comment that identifies the style sheet, such as its purpose, the author, the last revision date, and so forth. Like an XHTML comment, a CSS comment can have as few or as many lines as you want.

Tip

code to begin and
a CSS comment is
referred to as "slash
' and "star slash,"
ectively.

Tip

't use an XHTML com-
t in a CSS file.

To create an external style sheet and add a CSS comment:

▶ **1.** Switch back to your text editor. Do not close the **papernew.htm** document.

▶ **2.** Open a second instance of your text editor and create a new document.

▶ **3.** In the new document, type the comment code on two lines, as shown in Figure 5-34. Use today's date in the first line of the comment.

```
/* Created by Tahira Jones on Today's Date
All files for this Web site link to this style sheet */
```

Figure 5-34 ▸ **The CSS comment code**

the CSS comment code

```
/* Created by Tahira Jones on Today's Date
All files for this Web site link to this style sheet */
```

▸ **4.** Press the **Enter** key twice.

▸ **5.** Save the file as **paper.css** in the Tutorial.05\Tutorial folder included with your Data Files.

Now that the comment has been created, you will show Tahira how to cut the CSS code from the embedded style sheet in the papernew.htm file and paste it into the paper.css file.

To cut and paste the CSS code:

▸ **1.** Switch back to the **papernew.htm** file in your text editor. Do not close the **paper.css** file.

▸ **2.** In the embedded style sheet of the **papernew.htm** file, delete the start `<style type="text/css">` tag and the end `</style>` tag.

▸ **3.** Position the insertion point before the letter "b" in the body element style code.

▸ **4.** Click and drag through the ending brace for the a:visited style to select all of the style code (do not select any XHTML code).

▸ **5.** Press the **Ctrl+X** keys to cut the CSS code.

▸ **6.** Switch back to the **paper.css** document. Do not close the **papernew.htm** file.

▸ **7.** In the **paper.css** document, position the insertion point on a blank line below the comment.

▸ **8.** Press the **Ctrl+V** keys to paste the code, as shown in Figure 5-35 (not all of the code is shown).

Figure 5-35 ▸ **The CSS code pasted into the paper.css file**

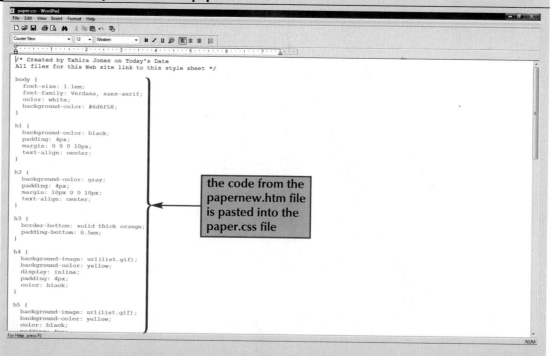

the code from the papernew.htm file is pasted into the paper.css file

> **9.** Save and close the **paper.css** file.

> **10.** Switch to your browser and refresh or reload the **papernew.htm** file. Verify that the style code has been removed, as shown in Figure 5-36.

Figure 5-36 **The style code removed from the papernew.htm file**

Meeting Your Business Needs

Creating the Paper *Less* Office

Our Business Rationale

Many offices are stocked with printers, reams of paper, filing cabinets, folders and shelving – all of which take up considerable floor space, cost money to purchase and resupply. For more than 20 years, we've been helping businesses like yours migrate from the 20th century to the 21st century by providing them with the business office solutions they need to achieve greater productivity, increase efficiency, and reduce costs. We make your workers comfortable with change and follow a slow immersion strategy. You don't have to throw out every sheet of paper in your office. We'll help you pick a launch date, whereby you can work forward to enter just your present documents into a digital system. Older documents can later be scanned or destroyed if no longer needed.

The Cost Justification

Most businesses today want to go paperless. That's fantasy, of course. The reality is that your company can use far less paper than it does now. Most businesses also know that going paperless is the environmentally responsible thing to do – using less paper results in greater efficiencies, reduces costs, and helps the environment. Think also about other indirect costs such as shipping paper across the nation, disposing of paper, shredding paper, and storing paper. Think again about the deforestation across the globe and the effects that it is having on our planet. We can help you get on the right track towards using less paper. If you are looking for justification for your return on investment, think about all the costs that are involved in consuming, using, storing, and distributing paper. Paper costs money, and on the average, paper prices have increased by 10% over the last 12 months alone. It costs money to purchase printers, maintain and service printers, and buy and replace toner cartridges. Converting storage rooms or "document libraries" into usable office space yields big savings each month. Think of all the filing cabinets in your office that store paper. Not only do you have to purchase office equipment to store that paper, the square footage taken up by filing cabinets quickly adds up. Here at SmallPaper Solutions, we'll get you started on the path to paper freedom and reducing or eliminating all of these costs.

What We Provide

We will provide you with assistance in three areas – hardware, software, and consulting

Hardware

- Servers for document management and storage
- High-speed scanners to scan very large volumes of paper
- Wide-format scanners to scan engineering or oversize drawings
- Photo scanners to digitize small and large photos
- Book copiers to digitize large in-house manuscripts and manuals
- Network printers with audit device controls to monitor who is printing what
- Document management software to aggregate all documents for easy search, retrieval, archiving and deletion
- Electronic storage and backup
- Audit tracking hardware so that all printing and copying is client billable

Software

- Collaboration software to help manage multiple versions of document edits
- Fax to PDF conversion software to eliminate the need to print faxes
- Client and Case Management software for e-mail, calendaring, and scheduling
- Human Resources software for forms creation and management
- Process Approval software to keep track of project status and approval
- Requisition management software to eliminate the need for paper forms for requisitions

Consulting

1. Proposal specifications
2. Return on Investment Analysis
3. On-site supervision of hardware
4. Software installation
5. Training
6. Federal and state government compliance for record retention

When you combine the cost savings of using digital records with other benefits such as improved security, risk management protection, and the environmental benefits, it makes good sense to speak to one of our agents. Call us today, won't you, to get started on your way to lower costs and greater efficiencies. Get SmallPaper today.

SmallPaper Solutions • 120 Trent Highway • Richfield, KY 24579

Back to Top

The CSS file now has all of the CSS code, but there's still more work to do before the style sheet will work. The XHTML file and the CSS file have to be linked. The code to create the link is entered in the head section of the XHTML file. Next, you will show Tahira how to create a link between the papernew.htm file and paper.css file.

Linking an XHTML File to an External Style Sheet

The true power of CSS lies in the ability to use an external style sheet to determine the appearance of as many documents as you want. The **link element** is used to link an XHTML file to another file, such as a CSS file. An unlimited number of XHTML files can link to the same external style sheet file. You enter the code for the link element in the <head> section for each document you want to link to the external style sheet file. The following code is an example of how to link an XHTML file to an external style sheet file:

```
<link rel="stylesheet" href="paper.css" type="text/css" />
```

Tip

The link element is an empty element, and must end with the space-slash (/) combination.

The link element takes several attributes such as rel, href, and type. "Rel" stands for "relationship"; the rel attribute value is always "stylesheet". "Href" stands for "hypertext reference." The href attribute value is the name of the CSS file to which you are linking, which in this instance is paper.css. The type attribute value is always text/css.

Reference Window | **Creating a Link to a CSS File**

- To create a link to a CSS file, enter the following code between the <head> </head> tags in an XHTML document:
  ```
  <link rel="stylesheet" href="document.css" type="text/css">
  ```
  where the *rel* attribute and its value specify the link to a style sheet file, the *href* attribute and its value identify the CSS file that is the source of the style code, and the *type* attribute and its value identify a text file.

You are ready to show Tahira how to create the link to the external style sheet file, paper.css.

To link papernew.htm to the paper.css file:

▶ 1. Switch back to the **papernew.htm** file in your text editor.

▶ 2. Position the insertion point after the end </title> tag.

▶ 3. Press the **Enter** key twice.

▶ 4. On a blank line, type the following code, as shown in Figure 5-37.

```
<link rel="stylesheet" href="paper.css" type="text/css" />
```

| Figure 5-37 | The link code |

```
<meta http-equiv="Content-Type" content="text/html; charset=ISO-8859-1" />
<title>SmallPaper Solutions</title>

<link rel="stylesheet" href="paper.css" type="text/css" />

<!-- Your First and Last Name
     Tutorial 5
     Today's Date
-->
```

the link code to establish a link to paper.css

▶ 5. Save the file.

▶ 6. Switch to your browser. Refresh or reload the **papernew.htm** page. Verify that your file looks similar to the one shown in Figure 5-38.

| Figure 5-38 | The result of the link to the external CSS file |

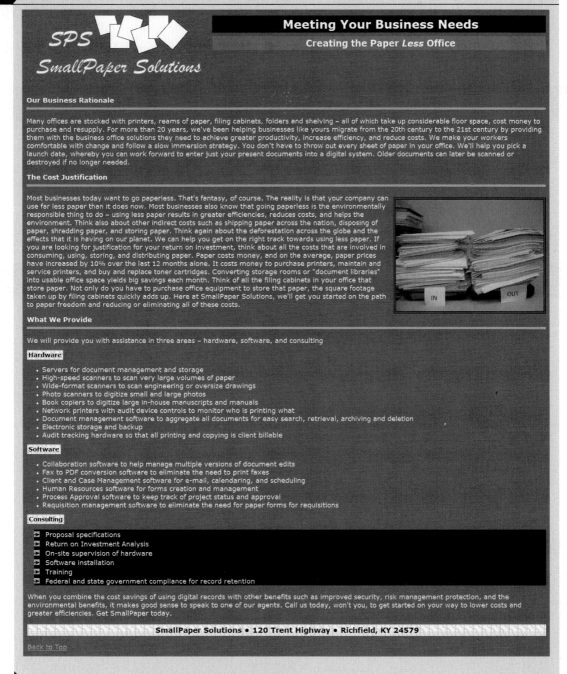

7. Submit the results of the **papernew.htm** and **paper.css** files to your instructor, either in printed or electronic form, as requested.

8. If you will not be completing the Review Assignments or Case Problems, close your text editor and your browser.

When validating documents that contain a link to an external style sheet, validate the XHTML file (the parent file) only for the accuracy of the XHTML code. Validate the CSS file for the accuracy of the CSS code. Do not validate the parent XHTML file for the accuracy of the CSS code, as you would if the document contained an embedded style sheet. If you do, you will receive an error message: "No style sheet found."

In this session, you worked with the background properties to set the background for an element. You learned that you can change the background image, color, and position. You learned that you can repeat an image horizontally, vertically, or both. You used an image as a list item marker. You learned about cascading order, you created an external style sheet, and you learned how to link an XHTML file to a CSS file.

Review | **Session 5.2 Quick Check**

1. What are the values for the background-repeat property?
2. If you use the background shorthand property, in what order must you list the values?
3. Can you use the vertical-align property to align an image used as a list marker?
4. What code should be at the beginning of every CSS style sheet?
5. What XHTML code should be entered in a CSS style sheet?
6. What element is used to access a CSS style sheet?

Review | **Tutorial Summary**

In this tutorial, you learned about the box model. All elements have a transparent padding, margin, and border by default. Borders can be given a style, color, and width. The float property is used to "float" an element to the left or the right. Use the clear property with a value of left, right, or both to reposition an element below another element on the page. The background properties are used to provide a background for an element. The background properties include background-image, background-color, and background-repeat. The term "cascade" in Cascading Style Sheets refers to how you determine which style rules apply if more than one rule styles the same element. Style precedence determines the order of the cascade, and is one of the methods used to resolve style conflicts. External style sheets are used to format more than one XHTML document. An external style sheet file must have the .css filename extension. The link tag is used to link an XHTML file to a CSS file.

Key Terms

background properties	border-style property	link element
background property	border-width property	margin
background-attachment property	box model	margin collapse
background-image property	box properties	margin properties
background-position property	breathing room	margin property
background-repeat property	cascade	padding
border	classification properties	padding properties
border properties	clear property	padding property
border property	content area	style precedence
border-color property	external style sheet	tiling
	float property	user-defined styles

Practice | **Review Assignments**

time to practice
kills you learned
e tutorial using
ame case
ario.

Data Files needed for the Review Assignments: consult.htm, paperlogo.gif

Tahira likes the emphasis you helped her place on the consulting services that SmallPaper Solutions provides to its customers. Tahira has a new Web page named consult.htm, and she would like your assistance in developing this new page to have a more attractive appearance. She could format the page by simply linking the consult.htm file to her paper.css style sheet, but she has decided to create a unique appearance for the three subfiles she'll eventually create (one on hardware, one on software, and this one on consulting). After you help her establish the appearance of her consult.htm file, she'll create an external style sheet that she can apply to all three subfiles. Although you will not be instructed to do so after each step, you should do the following after entering the code to create a style in your text editor: Save the file, switch to your browser, refresh or reload the page, verify that you entered the style code correctly, and then switch back to your text editor and complete the next step. A preview of the Web page you will create appears in Figure 5-39.

Figure 5-39

Consulting

We Can Assist You in All of These Areas

PROPOSAL SPECIFICATIONS

We can help you with your proposal specifications. You need to justify your Return on Investment, and we can provide you with the facts and figures on how we can establish cost savings for your firm. We specify not just the hard numbers, the savings on hardware and supplies that you no longer have to purchase, but we also factor in the soft savings, such as increased productivity and efficiency. We can give you a payback schedule on your return on investment that will give you the cost justification you are seeking to employ a paperless office solution.

RETURN ON INVESTMENT ANALYSIS

We've got the facts and the figures you need to send to upper management to back your ideas with cost-saving facts. We'll give you not just the numbers, but the charts and the database data you need to support your argument to upper management that a paperless office is the way to go.

ON-SITE SUPERVISION OF HARDWARE

Once you have purchased a hardware or a software solution from us, we won't leave you hanging. We are there to literally stand behind you as you work towards the implementation of a plan to reduce costs in your office. We will work with your to set up a timetable for conversion, and we will have staffing on site when you decide to move towards a new hardware or software solution. Whether you decide to implement on a department-by-department basis or whether you have a move-forward cutoff date established for your entire company, we will be there to ensure that the transition goes smoothly and seamlessly.

SOFTWARE INSTALLATION

We know that our customers are not computer experts and may not have the IT staff to implement a software migration. We will be there to install and debug software. Once we are there, we are in no hurry to leave. We won't leave you with a hit-and-run solution, where software is installed and any problems that might occur are left for you to resolve. We will be on site to install and ensure that the installation of all new software works as planned.

TRAINING

It doesn't take much training not to use less paper or shred fewer documents, but if you are stepping up to a more global, system-wide solution, we can provide your IT staff with the business intelligence to maximize the features of any new software solution that we propose for your business. We can arrange for small or large classes. You can come to one of our training sites, or we can come to your site to conduct on-site training classes. We have full documentation for all software that we implement.

FEDERAL AND STATE GOVERNMENT COMPLIANCE

We can help you with these important regulatory issues:

- Records Retention laws
- Sarbanes-Oxley
- Freedom of Information Act

SmallPaper Solutions • 120 Trent Highway • Richfield, KY 24579

Back to Top

Complete the following:

1. Use your text editor to open the **consult.htm** file, which is provided in your Data Files in the Tutorial.05\Review folder. In the head section and below the page title, enter your name and today's date in the comment section where noted.

2. Save the file as **consultnew.htm** in the same folder. Open the file in your browser and observe the appearance of the original file.

3. Switch back to your text editor. Below the comment and in the head section, insert the start and end tags necessary to create an embedded style sheet.

4. Within the tags for the embedded style sheet, style the body element to have text appear with a line height of 1.5em, in a font size of 1.1em, and in the Georgia (serif) font.

5. Save the **consultnew.htm** file. Switch to your browser and refresh or reload the page. Verify that the body element style appears correctly in your file.

6. Switch back to your text editor. Create a style for the h1 element to have text appear in navy, have a bottom border that is solid, thin, and teal, and have a padding of 15px on the bottom.

7. Create a style for the h3 element to have text appear in teal and in uppercase. (Use a text property to change the case; do not retype the h3 headings in uppercase.)

8. Create a style for the h4 element so that the text is centered, appears in navy, and has a text decoration of both overline and underline.

9. Create a style for the img element to float the image right. Use the margin shorthand property to set margins for the image of 0 on the top and right and 10px on the bottom and left.

10. Create a style for the list item element so that the list style uses a square marker, not a round bullet.

11. Save the **consultnew.htm** file. Switch to your browser and refresh or reload the page. Compare your file to Figure 5-39 to verify that your file is correct.

12. Submit the results of the preceding steps to your instructor, either in printed or electronic form, as requested.

13. If you are not completing the next assignment, close your text editor and your browser.

| Apply | **Case Problem 1** |

Use the skills you learned in the tutorial to create a Web page for a planetarium.

Data Files needed for this Case Problem: planet.htm, planets.gif, planetlogo.gif

Shore River Planetarium When it is completed next month, the Shore River Planetarium will be one of the largest planetariums in the South. Located in East Landing, about 20 miles northeast of Charleston, South Carolina, this state-of-the-art facility will house a space museum in addition to the planetarium. Edward Ortiz, the director of the facility, has asked you to create a Web page that describes the attractions at the Shore River Planetarium. After you complete a step to create a style (or a set of steps to create and apply a class), verify in your browser that the style code has been entered correctly, and then switch back to your text editor. A preview of the Web page you will create appears in Figure 5-40.

Figure 5-40

The Shore River Planetarium

WHAT IS A PLANETARIUM?

A planetarium is a building with a domed ceiling that uses special projection equipment to reproduce images of the night sky. A planetarium offers the visitor a theatre-like experience in that the room itself is dark, and the "show" is narrated usually by a famous actor or actress.

Each season, the planetarium offers different shows based upon the night sky of that particular season. Shows run for a period of about three months and are not repeated after that. If you've been to the planetarium more than three months ago, there's a new, never-been-seen show waiting for you. Of course, there's no harm in seeing the same show more than once, as many people do. Most shows are about 42 minutes long, which allows time for exit and entry between shows. Shows start on the hour every hour the planetarium is open. The planetarium is not only a place to enjoy a show about the stars, but it's also a place to experience what the stars are about. A visit to the planetarium is interesting, educational, and fun.

Group Rates and Admission

Regular admission is $10 for adults and $7 for children under 12. There are discounted admission plans for public and private schools and colleges. Discounted admission is for groups of 20 or more for shows Monday through Thursday. Reservations must be made at least 60 days in advance. Group rates do not apply on weekends. In addition, there are some dates when group rates do not apply, such as all federal and state holidays. There is a separate admission charge for both the IMAX theatre, and for the StarTours virtual reality ride. Admission to those events is discounted for students only and only for shows during the hours of 9 a.m. to 3 p.m. You must be 12 or older to take the StarTours virtual reality ride.

Chaperone Policy

The planetarium requires a chaperone ratio of 1:5 for grades 1-8 and 1:10 for grades 9-12. Chaperones (including teachers) receive free museum admission. Chaperones must accompany students at all times. We have separate bathroom facilities for school groups. We also have separate dining facilities for school groups. Educators may visit the planetarium Monday through Thursday and speak with a planning representative, who will give you detailed information about how to plan your trip to the planetarium. There is no admission charge or fees of any kind for these planning visits.

Special Note for School Field Trips

Teachers and chaperones should follow these rules for field trips:

- Disembark in the designated arrival area.
- Conduct a head count on arrival.
- Wait for the guide to greet you and escort you into the facility.

The Planetarium for Adults

The planetarium is not just a learning experience for children. Adults will enjoy many of the other features we have at the Shore River Planetarium. Our *Moonbeam Restaurant* is open from 6 p.m. till 12 midnight. The Moonbeam offers the best of fine dining. The *Galaxy Coffee Bar* is located above the Moonbeam Restaurant. The Galaxy serves coffee, tea, juice, salads, and our universally-famous desserts. The *Comet's Tail Food Court* is open at all times while the Planetarium is open.

The *StarStruck Nightclub* is open for dancing from 9:30 p.m. till 2 a.m. on Friday and Saturday nights. There is a separate admission to the StarStruck Nightclub. The *Comet Theatre* shows first-run movies on a 3-story tall movie screen. There is a separate admission charge for the Comet Theatre. Adults can purchase a *Night on the Stars* package, which includes a one-price discounted admission to all ticketed events: the planetarium show, the StarTours virtual reality ride, the StarStruck Nightclub, and the Comet Theatre.

The Shore River Planetarium • 45 River Drive • East Landing, SC

Complete the following:

1. Use your text editor to open the **planet.htm** file, which is provided in your Data Files in the Tutorial.05\Case1 folder. In the head section and below the page title, enter your name and today's date in the comment section where noted.
2. Save the file as **planetnew.htm** in the same folder. Open the file in your browser and observe the appearance of the original file.
3. Switch back to your text editor. In the code for the embedded style sheet, style the body element to have text appear in 1.2em and in Arial, a sans-serif font. The text should appear as white text on a black background.
4. Save the **planetnew.htm** file. Switch to your browser and refresh or reload the page. Verify that the body element style appears correctly in your file.
5. Switch back to your text editor. In the embedded style sheet and below the body style, create the following styles for the h1 element:
   - Have the text appear in uppercase.
   - Create a text decoration of underline and overline.
   - Center the h1 text.
   - Set the color to #ebdb56.
6. Style the h3 element to also appear in the hexadecimal color #ebdb56.
7. Create the following styles for the h4 element:
   - Set the top border so that it appears solid, thick, and with a color value of #ebdb56.
   - Add padding of 10px on the top.

- Center the h4 text.
- Set the color to orange.

8. For the image element, create a dependent class named "left" that floats images left. Use the margin shorthand property to set margins of 0 on the top, 15px on the right, 10px on the bottom, and 0 on the left.

9. In the image code for the planetlogo.gif image, apply the left dependent class to the right of the code for the height property and value.

10. For the image element, create a dependent class named "right" that floats images right and has margins of 10px on the top, 0 on the right, 10px on the bottom, and 10px on the left.

11. In the image code for the planets.gif image, apply the "right" dependent class to the right of the code for the height property and value.

12. Create an independent class named "clear" that clears an element on both the left and the right.

13. Apply the "clear" independent class to the start <p> tag for the second paragraph of the document. This paragraph begins with the words "Each season ...".

14. Save the **planetnew.htm** file. Switch to your browser and refresh or reload the page. Compare your file to Figure 5-40 to verify that your file is correct.

15. Submit the results of the preceding steps to your instructor, either in printed or electronic form, as requested.

16. If you are not completing the next assignment, close your text editor and your browser.

| Apply | **Case Problem 2** |

Use the skills you learned in the tutorial to create and style a Web page about corporate event planning.

Data Files needed for this Case Problem: event.htm, track.gif

Corporate Event Planning   Corporate event planning is a multifaceted field that is attracting many people. Event planning can occur on many levels, from planning a simple dinner party for a few people to arranging the details for a convention that may be attended by thousands of people. You have been asked to format a Web page that describes this interesting and growing field. After you complete a step to create a style (or a set of steps to create and apply a class), verify in your browser that the style code has been entered correctly, and then switch back to your text editor. A preview of the Web page you will create appears in Figure 5-41.

Figure 5-41

Corporate Event Planner

What is a Corporate Event Planner?

Almost everyone has had some experience at planning an event. It may have been planning a birthday party, a high school or college reunion or even a wedding. You may not have realized it at the time, but even just going out on a date involves the logistics of where to go, when to arrive and depart, what to do, how much to spend, what to wear, and how to get there. If you've ever gone out on a prom date, you are quite familiar with the planning it took to get you and your date ready for your big night. It was a lot of fun, but it also involved a great deal of preparation on the part of many individuals.

What Does a Planner Do?

Corporate event planners are needed to plan for a ceremony, such as an awards ceremony, a luncheon or dinner party, or a convention. Of course, on the corporate level, the stakes are higher. You are planning an event for dozens or even hundreds of people in attendance. How the event fares has a great deal to do with how the company is perceived. Even though the company may not have planned the event, if the event does not turn out to be an enjoyable one, certainly the company will appear to be the one to be blamed. Mismanaged events have a way of inferring the company itself is mismanaged, so every corporate event has a lot riding on it. The event may be just for employees only, but then, again, there may be hundreds of clients — or potential clients — in attendance. Your goal as a corporate event planner is to cast the company in the most favorable light.

Event planning involves a great many business skills. Certainly the accounting side of budgeting is an important one. You won't be given an unlimited amount of cash to stage the event; you will be expected to match or come under budget. You also can't pick dates at random. You have to choose a date (and perhaps an alternate date), interview people, inspect the event site, and coordinate transportation and parking for those in attendance, in particular the executives of the company you are planning the event for. Project management skills, and a knowledge of project management software, are a must. You have to establish a timeline of events — and determine how each of those events impact the other. You have to determine the critical path — the timeline of key tasks that will impact the most on the event should a problem occur with that task over the course of staging the event.

What's Expected of You?

Event planners may also be asked to develop a theme for the event, plan for the decoration of the hall or outdoor area, arrange for speakers to appear, and arrange for their transportation to and from the event. If the event is outdoors, there are a number of critical issues to be confronted that you would not have to worry about if the event will be held indoors. You have to arrange for electricity, heating or cooling, tables, chairs, flowers, tablecloths, a band or DJ, security, portable toilets, signage, and cleanup of the area once the event is over. Event planners also need to know how to delegate work. Most corporate planners delegate the smaller, but still important details, such as the food, drinks, guest list, advertising and marketing, and decorations. There is a great deal of preparation in planning the event, and if you try to do too much yourself, you will not do a good job at either the larger aspects of the event nor the smaller ones. You need to know whom to trust with both the large and small details of the event. Over time, you will develop a relationship with your staff, so you will know whom to entrust with a particular planning event.

You need a particular disposition to be an event planner. Because there's so much to do, you have to be a take-charge person who likes the challenge of acting on a great many details perhaps without a great deal of time. You have to respond well to pressure, work efficiently, and be diplomatic. You will be interfacing with a great many people, and you need the cooperation and support of these people. Your appearance does matter. You need to be appropriately dressed to engage in a professional manner with executives and clients. Of course, you will need excellent written and verbal skills. Above all, you have to gain the confidence of others because you will be directing a great many other people in the successful planning of the event. Whether you are coordinating a conference, planning a convention, arranging for a special event, or coordinating and managing a meeting, you need to be your professional, competent, and energetic self at all times. You also have to throw away the clock because many events occur during the evening and on weekends. Corporate event planning is a relatively new field, but it can be a lucrative one for the person with the right organizational, management, and communication skills.

The Basics

Corporate event planning involves the following areas:

- Scheduling
- Facility Management
- Budgeting
- Logistics
- Marketing
- Travel and Lodging
- Project management
- Exhibitor management

Top

Complete the following:

1. Use your text editor to open the **event.htm** file, which is provided in your Data Files in the Tutorial.05\Case2 folder. In the head section and below the page title, enter your name and today's date in the comment section where noted.

2. Save the file as **eventnew.htm** in the same folder. Open the file in your browser and observe the appearance of the original file.

3. Switch back to your text editor. Within the tags for the embedded style sheet, create the following styles for the body element:
   - Set the font size to 1.2em.
   - Set the font to Verdana (a sans-serif font).

- Set the line height to 1.25em.
- Add a background color with the value of #e8f2f3.

4. Save the **eventnew.htm** file. Switch to your browser and refresh or reload the page. Verify that the body element style appears correctly in your file.

5. Switch back to your text editor. Below the body style, create a style for the image element so that images are floated left. Use the margin shorthand property to create margins of 0 on top, 10px on the right, 10px on the bottom, and 0 on the left.

6. Create an independent class named "clear" that clears an element on both the left and the right. Apply the "clear" independent class to the start h3 heading for "What is a Corporate Event Planner?"

7. Create the following styles for the h1 element:
   - Set the letter spacing to 0.2em.
   - Set the word spacing to 0.2em.
   - Center the text.
   - Add 1.5em padding on the top.

8. Style the h3 element to appear with a bottom border that is solid, thick, and teal. Also style the h3 element to have 0.5em padding on the bottom.

9. Style the list item element to display the list marker as a circle.

10. In the start <p> tag before the code for the track.gif image, create an id named top.

11. At the bottom of the page, use the word "Top" to create a link to the id named top.

12. Save the **eventnew.htm** file. Switch to your browser and refresh or reload the page. Compare your file to Figure 5-41 to verify that your file is correct. Depending on your browser and browser version you may see different letter spacing and word spacing than that shown in Figure 5-41. Test your link to the id named top.

13. Submit the results of the preceding steps to your instructor, either in printed or electronic form, as requested.

14. If you are not completing the next assignment, close your text editor and your browser.

Challenge | Case Problem 3

Use what you've learned and expand your skills to create and style a Web page for a book retailer.

Data Files needed for this Case Problem: back.gif, bio.gif, books.htm, bookstyles.css, pointer.gif, sand.gif, science.gif, travel.gif

Wordpendium Books   Wordpendium Books, a regional book retailer in Kanihilo, Hawaii, has always relied on print media to promote its new book listings. Wordpendium would like to open an online store so it can market its books in other states. You have been asked to create a Web page that will highlight some of Wordpendium's books. After you complete a step to create a style (or a set of steps to create and apply a class), verify in your browser that the style code has been entered correctly, and then switch back to your text editor. A preview of the Web page you will create appears in Figure 5-42.

Figure 5-42

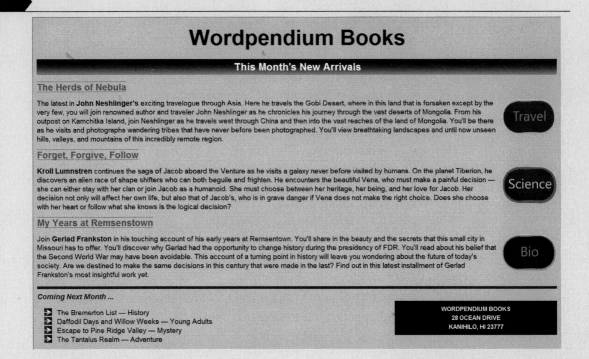

Complete the following:

1. Use your text editor to open the **books.htm** file, which is provided in your Data Files in the Tutorial.05\Case3 folder. In the head section and below the page title, enter your name and today's date in the comment section where noted.

2. Save the file as **booksnew.htm** in the same folder. Open the file in your browser and observe the appearance of the original file.

3. Switch back to your text editor. Within the tags for the embedded style sheet, style the body element to use an image named sand.gif as the background. Repeat the image both horizontally and vertically. In addition, create the following styles for the body element:
   • Set the font size to 1.2em.
   • Set the font to Arial (a sans-serif font).
   • Set the line height to 1.25em.

4. Save the **booksnew.htm** file. Switch to your browser and refresh or reload the page. Verify that the body element style appears correctly in your file.

5. Switch back to your text editor. In the code for the embedded style sheet and below the body element style, style the img element to float right. Using the margin shorthand property, set margins of 0 on the top and right and 10px on the bottom and left.

6. Create the following styles for the h1 element:
   • Set the top margin to 0.5em.
   • Center the h1 text.
   • Set the font size to 3em.
   • Add 25px of padding on the bottom.

7. Style the h2 element to use a background image named back.gif. The image should repeat horizontally. In addition, create the following styles for the h2 element:
   • Center the h2 text.
   • Set the color to white.

- Set the font size to 1.4em.
- Add 10px of padding on all sides (use the padding shorthand property).

8. Create the following styles for the h3 element:
   - Set the color to teal.
   - Set the font size to 1.3em.
   - Add a text decoration of overline and underline.

9. Create the following styles for the h4 element:
   - Center the h4 text.
   - Set the color to white.
   - Add a background color of black.
   - Float the h4 text "right."
   - Set the width to 30%.
   - Add padding of 10px on all sides (using the padding shorthand property).
   - Display text in all capital letters (use a text property for this declaration).

EXPLORE
10. Create a dependent class for the p element selector named "border." Create the following styles for the class:
    - Add a top border that is solid and navy, with a thickness of 0.4em.
    - Add padding on the top of 0.4em.
    - Set the font weight to bold.
    - Set the font style to italic.
    - Set the color to #26301a.
    - Set the bottom margin to 0.

11. Apply the border class to the start <p> in the last paragraph (which begins "Coming Next Month ...").

EXPLORE
12. Create the following styles for the unordered list element:
    - Float the element "left."
    - Set the width to 40%.
    - Set the list style type to none.
    - Add padding of 0 on all four sides.
    - Add a top margin of 1em.
    - Add a left margin of 1em.

EXPLORE
13. Create the following styles for the list item element:
    - Use the pointer.gif file as a background image. Do not repeat the image.
    - Add padding on the left of 1.75em.

14. Save the **booksnew.htm** file. Switch to your browser and refresh or reload the page. Compare your file to Figure 5-42 to verify that your file is correct.

15. Switch back to your text editor. In the embedded style sheet, delete all of the code for the start <style> tag. Delete the end </style> tag. Select all of the remaining CSS code for the embedded style sheet. Press the Ctrl+X keys to cut the CSS code.

16. In the head section and on a blank line below the page title, enter the code to link to a CSS file named **bookstylesnew.css**.

17. Save and then close the **booksnew.htm** file.

18. In your text editor, open the **bookstyles.css** file, which is provided in your Data Files in the Tutorial.05\Case3 folder. Enter your name and today's date in the comment section where noted.

19. On a blank line below the comment code, paste the CSS code that you cut from booksnew.htm.

20. Save the file as **bookstylesnew.css** in the same folder.

21. Switch to your browser and refresh or reload the page for the **booksnew.htm** file. Observe the result; the file should look similar to the preview file in Figure 5-42.

22. In your browser, go to *http://validator.w3.org* to open the W3C validator. Validate the **booksnew.htm** file by using the Validate by File Upload method. Note any errors and correct them in your file if necessary.

23. In your browser, navigate to *http://jigsaw.w3.org/css-validator*. Validate the **bookstylesnew.css** file by using the By file upload method. Note any errors and correct them in your file if necessary.

24. Submit the results of the **booksnew.htm** and **bookstylesnew.css** files to your instructor, either in printed or electronic form, as requested.

25. If you are not completing the next assignment, close your text editor and your browser.

| Create | | **Case Problem 4** |

a Web page for vernance of a lanet.

Data Files needed for this Case Problem: hope.css, hope.htm

Planet Hope   Astronomers have discovered a new planet, which they have tentatively named planet Hope. The planet is similar to Earth in size, land, sea mass, and atmosphere. Assuming you were in charge of colonizing this planet, how would you do it? What government would you choose for its residents? Would you create cities or use the planet for agriculture? What would you do if you learned that the planet had enormous mineral and energy riches, but extracting them would substantially damage the environment? Create a Web page that outlines how you intend to govern the planet and how you will use its land and sea resources.

Complete the following:

1. Use your text editor to open the **hope.htm** file, which is provided in your Data Files in the Tutorial.05\Case4 folder. In the head section, give your page an appropriate title. Below the page title, enter your name and today's date in the comment section where noted.

2. Save the file as **hopenew.htm** in the same folder.

3. Within the tags for the embedded style sheet, format the body element with the text size, font, color, and background color of your choice. Ensure that the text is readable and attractive.

4. Include at least one image that illustrates what life would be like on the new planet. Use the float property to style the image and float the image either left or right.

5. In the styles you create for the hopenew.htm document, create examples of the following properties:
   margin
   padding
   border
   background
   float
   clear

6. In the body section, enter text for at least five paragraphs that describe how you plan to govern the planet. Use at least two examples of h1, h2, h3, or h4 headings.

7. Save the **hopenew.htm** file. Switch to your browser and refresh or reload the page. Verify that all styles work correctly.

8. Switch back to your text editor. Open the **hope.css** file, which is provided in your Data Files in the Tutorial.05\Case4 folder. Enter your name and today's date in the comment section where noted.

9. Save the file as **hopenew.css**.

10. Without closing the hopenew.css file, switch back to the hopenew.htm file. In the head section, use the link element to create a link to the hopenew.css file.

11. In the **hopenew.htm** file, delete the start and end style tags in the embedded style sheet.

12. Cut and paste the remaining embedded style sheet code from the hopenew.htm file into the hopenew.css external style sheet.

13. Save the **hopenew.css** file and the **hopenew.htm** file.

14. Open your browser and go to *http://validator.w3.org*. Use the Validate by File Upload method to check the **hopenew.htm** document and ensure that the XHTML code is correct. If necessary, correct any errors detected by the validation.

15. In your browser, go to *http://jigsaw.w3.org/css-validator*. Use the By file upload method to check the **hopenew.css** file and ensure that the CSS code is correct. If necessary, correct any errors detected by the validation.

16. Submit the results of the **hopenew.htm** and **hopenew.css** files to your instructor, either in printed or electronic form, as requested.

17. Close your text editor and your browser. Close all open windows.

Review | Quick Check Answers

Session 5.1

1. The box model describes the boxes that are formed around elements in a Web page.
2. the internal white space
3. the external white space
4. the border style
5. left and right
6. left, right, and both

Session 5.2

1. no-repeat, repeat, repeat-x, repeat-y
2. image, color, position, repeat, and attachment
3. no
4. a CSS comment
5. none
6. the link element

nding Data Files

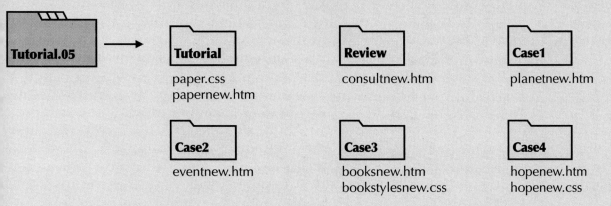

Objectives

Creating Fixed-Width Layouts

Using Pixel Values for Layouts

Case | The Anne Billings Art Gallery

The Anne Billings Art Gallery is one of the leading art galleries in Seattle, Washington. The gallery has recently been featuring the work of Pierre Henri Bernard, a Parisian artist who recently moved to Seattle. His abstract box paintings have won him rave reviews both in France and the United States. Critics point to the simplicity and use of color in his "box art" designs, comparing him favorably with famous abstract artists of the twentieth century. Not only is Pierre a winning artist, he is also computer-savvy and is familiar with basic Web page design. He has been working on a draft of a Web page to promote his next showing with the Anne Billings Art Gallery. You will work with Pierre to design a layout for this promotional page on the gallery's Web site.

Starting Data Files

Tutorial.06

Tutorial
art.htm
artlogo.gif
dawn.gif
fixed.htm
navfooter.css
wrapper.gif

Review
artlogo.gif
direct.htm

Case1
biz.htm
bizlogo.gif
cloth.gif

Case2
back.gif
griff.htm
grifflogo.gif
links.css

Case3
footer.css
greenback.gif
ziller.htm
zillerstyles.css

Case4
rounded.png
travel.css
travel.htm
triangle.gif

Session 6.1

Understanding Web Page Layouts

At present, neither XHTML nor CSS has a standard method for creating Web page layouts. This is because there are many ways to create a Web page layout; each Web developer eventually settles on a preferred method. Each method involves tradeoffs—there are advantages and disadvantages to each, which you will discuss with Pierre in this session and the next one. Some designers like to use negative margins or the CSS positioning properties to create page layout, while others shun these methods.

Layouts take planning, and as you design and test your layouts, it's common to encounter problems. The term **broken layout** is used to describe layouts that don't appear on the screen as planned. For example, a column that was intended to appear beside another column may inexplicably appear below that column instead. This problem, called **column drop**, occurs when there isn't enough horizontal space to display all of the columns in your layout. An example of column drop is shown in Figure 6-1.

Figure 6-1 — **An example of column drop**

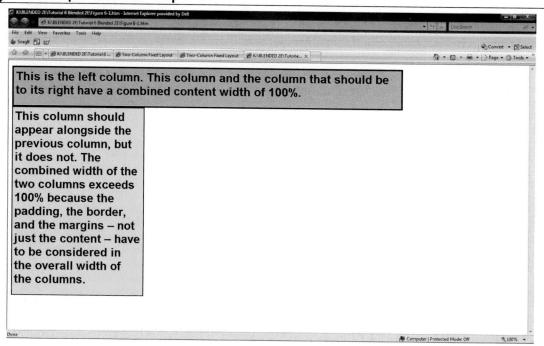

A major goal of all the methods for laying out a Web page is to ensure that users can view the page without having to scroll horizontally—something most people find tedious and annoying. Generally, Web page layouts fall into two major categories: fixed width or fluid. In a **fixed-width layout**, the page and columns are set to a certain width using pixel values. Fixed-width layouts are the most common on the Web today. In contrast, a **fluid layout** expands and contracts so that the content fills the entire screen width. You will learn about fluid layouts in the next tutorial. In a fixed-width layout, the Web page designer chooses how wide the page content should appear in the document window, which is the content area for the Web page. The **viewport** is another name for the document window.

In the past, the most common screen resolution was 800 by 600 pixels, but with today's larger monitors, it is at least 1024 by 768 pixels. When you design a Web page using a fixed-width layout, you are making an educated guess about the viewport size your visitors will use to view your Web page. Note that even if you design your Web page for a width of 1024 pixels, you must actually create a design that is somewhat narrower. Some browsers have a 1- or 2-pixel frame on both the left and right sides of the viewport. Also, some browsers always display a vertical scroll bar (usually about 19 pixels wide), regardless of whether the scroll bar is needed.

Designing Web pages for the maximum screen width can be difficult. For example, some users do not view Web pages with the browser screen maximized. Other viewers may have **widget sidebars**—software add-ons used to enhance a particular browser—that appear vertically on either side of the viewport, reducing the viewing area. Also, several methods can be used to change the appearance of Web page content, such as pressing the Ctrl and plus (+) keys to enlarge the content or the Ctrl and minus (–) keys to shrink the content. If you have a wheel mouse, you can zoom in to the current location of the mouse pointer by holding down the Ctrl key and scrolling the mouse wheel forward. To zoom out from the current location of the mouse pointer, hold down the Ctrl key and scroll the mouse wheel backward.

Before you work with Pierre on the Web page that promotes his work at the Anne Billings Gallery, you'd first like to work with him on a practice document so that Pierre can better grasp the principles of fixed-width layout design. After Pierre understands these principles, you will work with him in the next session to design his Web page. You'll begin by showing Pierre how to open the fixed.htm practice document, create a comment, and then save the file with a new filename.

Tip

Internet Explorer
ser always displays a
cal scroll bar; the
ox browser displays
only if the page con-
exceeds one screen.

To open the fixed.htm file and save it with a new filename:

▶ **1.** In your text editor, open the **fixed.htm** file, which is located in the Tutorial.06\ Tutorial folder included with your Data Files. In the head section and below the page title, enter your name and today's date in the comment section where noted.

▶ **2.** Save the file as **fixednew.htm** in the same folder.

In this session, you will work with Pierre on a two-column fixed-width layout. In the next session, you will work with him to create a three-column fixed-width layout. You'll start by explaining to Pierre how Web pages commonly divide their content.

Creating a Two-Column Fixed Layout

Web page designers typically use layouts that include one or more of the following design components:

- A horizontal **header** row at the top of the page that usually includes a corporate logo or banner advertising
- A horizontal **navbar** (a navigation bar for links), which is a row usually placed just below the header
- A **sidebar**, which is a narrow column used to display a list of links or content of secondary importance
- A **main content area,** a wide column used to display the primary page content
- A **footer**, a horizontal row at the bottom of the page that usually displays contact information for the Web site and links to other Web pages at the site

Figure 6-2 shows a preview of the document layout you will create for Pierre.

Figure 6-2 **The proposed layout for the fixednew.htm Web page**

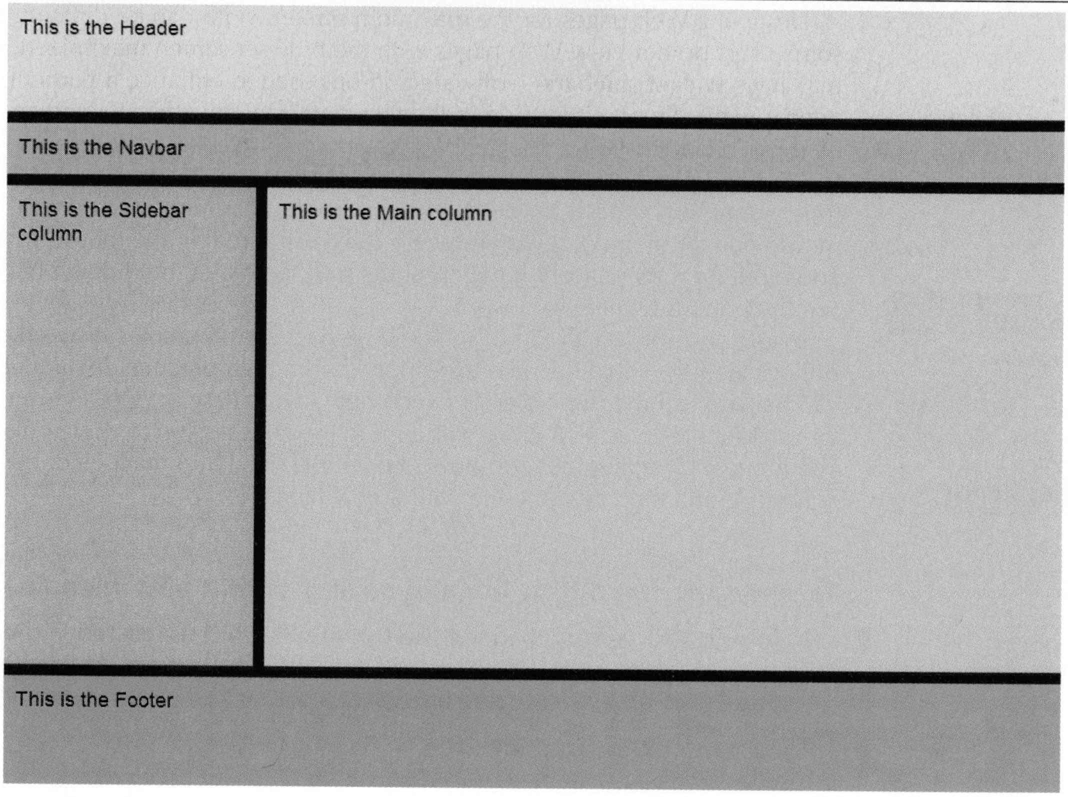
This is the Header
This is the Navbar
This is the Sidebar column
This is the Main column
This is the Footer

You tell Pierre that creating a Web page layout is similar to creating one of his box paintings. The **div element** defines a division in an XHTML document. It is a block-level element with no formatting of its own; it merely serves as a content container. You tell Pierre to think of the div element as an empty box in which he can place any sort of content.

> **Tip**
> Web page designers refer to the div element as "a div," which is short for "division."

An id selector is used to select a single element on a page. In the CSS style sheet code, an id selector name is preceded by the # flag character, as shown in the following code:

```
#header {
  width: 930px;
  background-color: #6e8953;
  margin-bottom: 10px;
}
```

You then apply the id attribute to the element you want to select, as shown in the following code:

```
<div id="header">
```

Unlike class selectors, which can be used to format several elements, id selectors are used to select only one instance of a particular element. Two elements on the same page cannot have the same id attribute. Do not confuse the id selector with the id attribute, which was used in an earlier tutorial to create a link to an id, and will be used in a later tutorial for other purposes.

Of course, Pierre also needs a canvas on which to paint. Later, you will show Pierre how to create a **container div**, a page division that can enclose all of the div boxes on the Web page. Figure 6-3 compares Pierre's painting tools with the tools used to create Web page layouts.

Figure 6-3   Pierre's painting tools and Web page layout tools

Pierre's Tools	Web Page Layout Tools
A box shape that he paints on the canvas	A div element
A palette with oils	A style sheet with id selectors
A brush	Applying an id selector
A canvas	A container div element that encloses all the other div elements

Each browser has its own styles for determining the margins and padding for the viewport, as well as other elements on the Web page. To ensure that your Web pages appear as consistently as possible in all browsers, it's a good coding practice to **zero out** (cancel) any margins and padding that the browser might add to the Web page by default. Later, you will create styles that selectively add margins and padding to elements. Bear in mind that despite your best efforts, the appearance of your Web pages will vary in different browsers. It's always a good idea to preview your work in the latest and prior versions of each of the contemporary browsers to check the appearance of your Web pages across all browser platforms.

The **universal selector** is used to select all of the elements on the Web page. In CSS code, the universal selector is represented by an asterisk. For example, the following code would make all text on the Web page appear in navy.

```
* {
  color: navy;
}
```

If you enter the following lines of code at the start of your style sheet, you will remove the default browser margins and padding from every element.

```
* {
  margin: 0;
  padding: 0;
}
```

You remind Pierre that 0 is one of the few values in CSS code that does not need a unit measurement because 0 of any measurement is 0. All other measurements in the layout will be expressed in pixel values. You want to emphasize that understanding the box properties is key to planning a Web page layout, so you want to give Pierre a brief refresher about the margin and padding shorthand properties. When only one value is used for these shorthand properties, the value is applied to all four sides. When two values are used, the first value is applied to the top and bottom sides equally and the second value is applied to the left and right sides equally. When four values are used, they are applied individually to each side in this order: top, right, bottom, and left. You will now show Pierre how to enter the code to style the universal selector.

To create a style for the universal selector:

1. In your text editor, position the insertion point on a blank line below the start <style> tag in the embedded style sheet code. Type the following code, as shown in Figure 6-4.

```
* {
  padding: 0;
  margin: 0;
}
```

Tip

g out the value for a
rty is also referred to
tializing" the value.

Figure 6-4 | **The universal selector code**

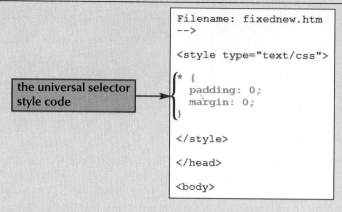

the universal selector style code

```
Filename: fixednew.htm
-->

<style type="text/css">

* {
    padding: 0;
    margin: 0;
}

</style>

</head>

<body>
```

▶ **2.** Save the file.

In the layout you're creating for Pierre, the background color of the body element will fill the entire screen. You also decide that each div will have its own background color to make it easy to tell one div from another.

You will show Pierre how to style the body element to create styles for the font size and font family. The body will also have a background color of gray.

To style the body element:

▶ **1.** In your text editor, position the insertion point below the style for the universal selector. On a blank line, type the following code, as shown in Figure 6-5.

```
body {
    font-size: 1.1em;
    font-family: Arial, Helvetica, sans-serif;
    background-color: gray;
}
```

Figure 6-5 | **The body element style code**

```
* {
    padding: 0;
    margin: 0;
}

body {
    font-size: 1.1em;
    font-family: Arial, Helvetica, sans-serif;
    background-color: gray;
}

</style>
```

the body element style code

▶ **2.** Save the file.

▶ **3.** Open **fixednew.htm** in your browser. Verify that the background for the body element now appears in gray, as shown in Figure 6-6.

Figure 6-6 | **The body element style in the browser**

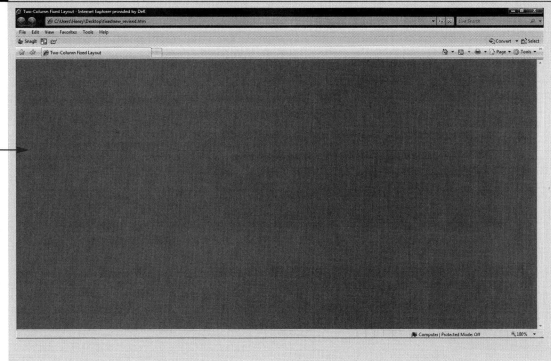

body area has been styled for a gray background

All of the div elements that have content will themselves be contained in a large container div. You will next show Pierre the advantages of creating a container div.

Creating the Container Div

A container div serves as a large box in which you can place all the other boxes (the smaller content divs). Using a container div offers several advantages and serves several important functions:

- It determines the width of the page layout.
- It can be used to center the layout horizontally.
- It can have a border applied around it, which serves to unify the page content.
- It can be used to apply a background color or image to contrast the background color or image of the body element.

Tip

oper" is another
non term used to
ibe a container div.

Id selectors are used to style the divs on the Web page. The id selector name is preceded by the # flag character. For a screen width of 1024 pixels, most Web designers today create their layouts to have a width of 900 to 960 pixels. As stated earlier, you don't have the full screen width available for your layout, so the container div cannot be 1024 pixels wide. You must account for each browser's frame (borders) on the left and right, scroll bars, and other inconsistencies among browsers.

erence Window | Creating an id Selector

- To create an id selector, use the declaration:
  ```
  #id {
     property: value;
  }
  ```
  where #id is the id selector, property is any one of the CSS properties, and value is any one of the applicable values for that property.

Pierre would like the layout to be centered horizontally. To center the layout, you need to apply "auto" as the value for the left and right margins. The "auto" value will make the left and right margins expand or contract to fit the container width. You will use the margin shorthand property to set the top and bottom margins to 0 and the margins on the left and right to "auto." You decide that the layout will have a width of 930 pixels. A border width of 1px will be added so that the document will center correctly in the Firefox browser if the user selects the zoom function to make the content larger. Finally, you will give the container a background color of navy, which will contrast against the background color of gray you set for the body element. You will now show Pierre how to enter the style for the container id selector.

To style the container id selector:

1. In your text editor, position the insertion point below the body element style. On a blank line, type the following code, as shown in Figure 6-7.

```
#container {
    width: 930px;
    border-width: 1px;
    margin: 0 auto;
    background-color: navy;
}
```

Figure 6-7   **The container id selector code**

```
body {
    font-size: 1.1em;
    font-family: Arial, Helvetica, sans-serif;
    background-color: gray;
}

#container {
    width: 930px;
    border-width: 1px;
    margin: 0 auto;
    background-color: navy;
}

</style>
```

the container id selector code

2. Save the file.

Now that the container id selector has been created, you need some content to which you can apply the id style. You create boxes on a Web page by entering a series of <div> </div> tags in the body section, as shown in the following code. In this instance, a set of div tags is created for the header div.

```
<body>

<div id="header">
<p>This is the Header</p>
</div>
```

The container div (as well as other wrapper divs) surrounds other divs. The id selector is applied to the appropriate start div tag, so identifying where a div starts is not a problem. The end div tags pose a problem. Because a Web page can have quite a few divs, it's a good coding practice to enter comments that identify each end div tag. Rather than having a baffling section of end </div> tags at the bottom of your page that looks like this:

```
</div>
</div>
</div>
```

You should instead have well-documented code that looks like this:

```
</div> <!-- section ends here -->
</div> <!-- wrapper ends here -->
</div> <!-- container ends here -->
```

You will now show Pierre how to create the container div and apply the container id style that you created earlier.

To enter the code for the container div:

▶ **1.** In your text editor, position the insertion point below the start <body> tag. On a blank line, type the following code, and then press the **Enter** key four times after you type the start <div> tag, as shown in Figure 6-8.

```
<div>



</div> <!-- container ends here -->
```

Figure 6-8	The container div code

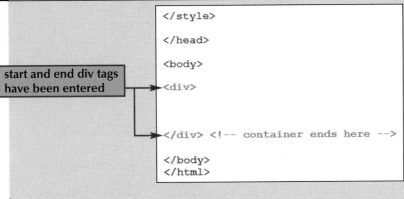

```
</style>

</head>

<body>

<div>



</div> <!-- container ends here -->

</body>
</html>
```

start and end div tags have been entered

▶ **2.** Save the file.

| InSight | **Creating Boxes with Rounded Corners** |

CSS offers several methods to create boxes with rounded corners. Unfortunately, they all require quite a bit of CSS code—up to eight additional div tags are needed to achieve the rounded corner effect. These divs are added to enhance presentation, not structure. Recall that the goal of CSS is to separate structure from presentation, so adding extra divs solely for presentation is not recommended.

To create boxes with rounded corners, you need to use design software to create four or more images for the corner effects. The methods for creating rounded corners vary, but the technique generally involves creating a box and then superimposing the corner images using the CSS background properties, as shown in the following code.

```
.corner_left{
  background: url(topleft.gif) no-repeat top left;
}
.corner_right {
  background: url(topright.gif) no-repeat top right;
}
.corner_bottomleft {
  background: url(bottomleft.gif) no-repeat bottom left;
}
.corner_bottomright {
  background: url(bottomright.gif) no-repeat bottom right;
}
```

Using this method requires some expertise in CSS, the design software to create the rounded images, and the knowledge of how to export these images for use on the Web.

Some designers, especially those who are not expert in CSS code, use several workarounds to create boxes with rounded corners. These designers use a design tool such as Adobe Illustrator or Microsoft Expression Design to create a single image of a box with rounded corners, a task that takes just a few seconds. You then type the text that will appear in the box and layer (place the text on top of) the image. Finally, you export the image from the design program as a GIF or PNG file for use (along with its layered text) on the Web page. While this single-image technique makes it far easier to create a box with text and rounded corners, it does require some maintenance; if the text needs to be revised, you must use the design program, not your text editor, to make the revisions and perhaps also resize the box. If you use the single-image method, you also should provide detailed alternate text to make the box accessible for screen reader software.

Another method to create boxes with rounded corners is to create a tab or rounded box in design software and use that image as a background image for a div, such as a sidebar. Using this method, you enter the text for the box directly in the XHTML code, so there is no need for ongoing maintenance if the text must be revised later.

In CSS 2.1, you can use the -moz-border-radius property to create boxes with rounded corners, but the property is proprietary and only supported by the Firefox browser. At some point in the future, CSS 2.1 will be replaced by the next version, which is CSS 3. In CSS 3, the border-radius properties can be used to create rounded corners easily, so the process will be simpler and standardized in the future. Currently, CSS 3 has poor browser support, so you'll have to wait until it's fully supported to use the border-radius properties.

Boxes with rounded corners are often used to draw attention to a "pull quote," which is also known as a "callout." A **pull quote** is a quotation or excerpt from an article in a newspaper or on your Web page. The pull quote usually appears in a larger font size to highlight an important point from the article. It might resemble the following example, a quote from Thomas Paine's *Common Sense*, written in 1776.

"Time makes more converts than reason."

You apply id styles in the same way you apply styles for classes, except that you use "id" instead of "class." You will apply the container id style to the appropriate div element, which in this instance is the container div.

To apply the container id style:

▶ **1.** In your text editor, position the insertion point at the end of the word "div" in the start <div> tag for the container div.

▶ **2.** Press the **Spacebar** once.

▶ **3.** Type the following code, as shown in Figure 6-9.

```
<div id="container">
```

| Figure 6-9 | The container style applied |

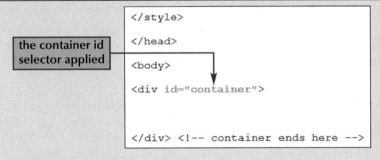

the container id selector applied

```
</style>

</head>

<body>

<div id="container">



</div> <!-- container ends here -->
```

Tip

an apply both an id
tor and a class selec-
the same element.

▶ **4.** Save the file.

Now that the container div has been established, you are ready to show Pierre how to calculate the width of the columns in the page layout.

Determining the Content and Column Widths

Recall that you set the container div to have a width of 930px, which means no div that spans the entire page, such as the header or footer div, can have a width greater than 930px. Similarly, no group of side-by-side columns, such as the sidebar and main column, can have a combined width greater than 930px; otherwise, the layout will break.

erence Window | Determining the Content Width

- To determine the value for the width property of a div element to be used for column content:
  - If a div such as a header or footer div spans the entire row, subtract the sum of the left and right margins, the border, and the padding values from the width of its parent container to determine the content width.
  - For side-by-side columns, choose an appropriate content width for each column. Columns of secondary importance, such as sidebar and section columns, should be narrow. The column of primary importance, such as the main column, should be the widest.

You ask Pierre how he would determine the value for the width property of the header div, which will span the entire screen width. Pierre thinks this is a trick question, because if the header div spans the entire screen, the width of the header div should be 930px, the same as the container div. However, that assumption is wrong.

Divs are boxes, and they make full use of the box properties, such as margins, borders, and padding—all of which take up space on the screen. When you enter the value for the width property of an id selector, you need to enter the value for the content width. You explain to Pierre that several terms are used to describe widths in layouts, as shown in Figure 6-10.

Figure 6-10 | **Different types of widths**

Width Type	Definition
Parent container width	The size of the containing box. The container div is the parent for divs that span the full width of the screen, such as the header, the navigation bar, and the footer.
Content width	The width of only the box content, which might be text, an image, a table, or any other type of content. The content width is the value for the id selector used for layout.
Column width	The sum of the content and its left and right margins, borders, and padding. For side-by-side columns, the sum of the column widths must not exceed the parent container width.

You'll start by calculating the content width for the header div. The header will not have a left or a right margin, nor will it have a border. The header will have some text, so you have decided to add padding of 10px on all sides to create some white space. Add the sum of the padding widths, the border widths, and the margin widths used in the header div, as shown in Figure 6-11.

Figure 6-11 | **Sum of the margin, border, and padding widths**

Pixels	Used For
0	Left margin width
0	Left border width
10	Padding width on the left
10	Padding width on the right
0	Right border width
0	Right margin width
20	Total number of pixels in the margin, border, and padding

The parent div for the header is the container div, which has a width of 930px. If you subtract the padding (20px) from the width of the parent container div (930px), the result is 910px. In other words, 910px is the content width; you will enter this value for the width property when you enter the code for the header id selector.

When you create a style for the id selectors, it's a good coding practice to list the properties in this order: width, margin, border, and padding. If you group the properties in this order, it will help you to locate the pixel values you need to determine the content width. Also, in fixed-width layouts, use a pixel value rather than a keyword for the border width. Browsers interpret keyword values slightly differently and will assign more (or less) thickness to a keyword value. Miscalculating by even one or two pixels could break your layout. For the remaining style declarations, group the color property with the background-color property (and background-image property if used). Group the font properties, listing them in the specific order required, and list all of the other properties and values for the id selector in alphabetic order.

You will use the height property with the header id selector declarations as well. While you are developing a Web page layout, it's a good idea to give your divs a height so that you can better see how the layout appears on a Web page. After you finish creating and debugging the layout, you should then delete the height declarations. As you will explain to Pierre later, do not give your divs a height when you are creating your final layout. You will now show Pierre how to style the header id selector.

To style the header id selector:

1. In your text editor, position the insertion point in the embedded style sheet below the container id style. On a blank line, type the following code, as shown in Figure 6-12.

```
#header {
  width: 910px;
  margin: 0 0 10px 0;
  padding: 10px;
  background-color: yellow;
  height: 75px;
}
```

Figure 6-12 ▶ **The header id selector code**

```
#container {
  width: 930px;
  border-width: 1px;
  margin: 0 auto;
  background-color: navy;
}

#header {
  width: 910px;
  margin: 0 0 10px 0;
  padding: 10px;
  background-color: yellow;
  height: 75px;
}
```

the header id selector code

2. Save the file.

During the development process, you don't want to use the actual content of the Web page. To focus on whether the layout is correct, you enter placeholder text into each of the divs. **Placeholder text** is text used solely to demonstrate the typography or layout in a document. The placeholder text can be any word or short phrase—even the words "placeholder text." After the layout has been finalized, you can globally delete the placeholder text and then enter the actual content.

Now that the header id selector has been created, you will show Pierre how to enter the code for the header div and apply the header id style as well. You will also enter some placeholder text for the header div.

To create the header div code:

▶ **1.** In your text editor and in the document body, position the insertion point below the start <div> tag for the container div code. On a blank line, type the following code, as shown in Figure 6-13.

```
<div id="header">
<p>This is the Header</p>
</div> <!-- header ends here -->
```

Figure 6-13	The header div code

```
<body>

<div id="container">

<div id="header">
<p>This is the Header</p>
</div> <!-- header ends here -->

</div> <!-- container ends here -->

</body>
```

the content for
the header div

▶ **2.** Save the file.

▶ **3.** Switch to your browser, refresh or reload the **fixednew.htm** page, and then compare your file to Figure 6-14 to confirm that the header has been styled correctly. Because of cross-browser incompatibility, you may not see the blue bottom margin in your browser, depending on your browser and browser version.

Figure 6-14	The header div in the browser

This is the Header

The navbar will also span the entire screen width and will be placed below the header. You will now show Pierre how to create a style for the navbar.

Creating a Style for the Navbar

A navbar (sometimes called a "text-links bar") typically is placed below the header. If the Web page has a sidebar column that contains links, usually the navbar will contain only important links such as those to other content areas on the Web site. In your practice file, the navbar will contain only placeholder text. The navbar will have 10px of padding on all sides, so the value for the width property of the navbar id selector will be the same as that for the header id—910px. You'll also give the navbar a background color and a height of 25px.

To style the navbar id selector:

▶ **1.** In your text editor and in the embedded style sheet, position the insertion point below the header id style. On a blank line, type the following code, as shown in Figure 6-15.

```
#navbar {
   width: 910px;
   margin: 0 0 10px 0;
   padding: 10px;
   background-color: silver;
   height: 25px;
}
```

▶ **2.** Save the file.

Figure 6-15 ▶ The navbar id selector code

```
#header {
   width: 910px;
   margin: 0 0 10px 0;
   padding: 10px;
   background-color: yellow;
   height: 75px;
}

#navbar {
   width: 910px;
   margin: 0 0 10px 0;
   padding: 10px;
   background-color: silver;
   height: 25px;
}

</style>

</head>
```

the code for the navbar id selector

Now that the navbar id selector has been created, you will show Pierre how to enter the code for the navbar div and apply the navbar id as well. You will also enter some placeholder text for the navbar div.

To create the navbar div code:

▶ **1.** In your text editor, and in the document body, position the insertion point below the end </div> code for the header div. On a blank line, type the following code, as shown in Figure 6-16.

```
<div id="navbar">
<p>This is the Navbar</p>
</div> <!-- navbar ends here -->
```

Figure 6-16 ▶ The navbar div code

```
<div id="header">
<p>This is the Header</p>
</div> <!-- header ends here -->

<div id="navbar">
<p>This is the Navbar</p>
</div> <!-- navbar ends here -->

</div> <!-- container ends here -->
```

the navbar div code

▶ **2.** Save the file.

3. Switch to your browser, refresh or reload the **fixednew.htm** page, and then compare your file to Figure 6-17 to confirm that the navbar has been styled correctly. Depending on your browser and browser version, you may not see the blue bottom margin in your browser.

Figure 6-17

The navbar styled in the browser

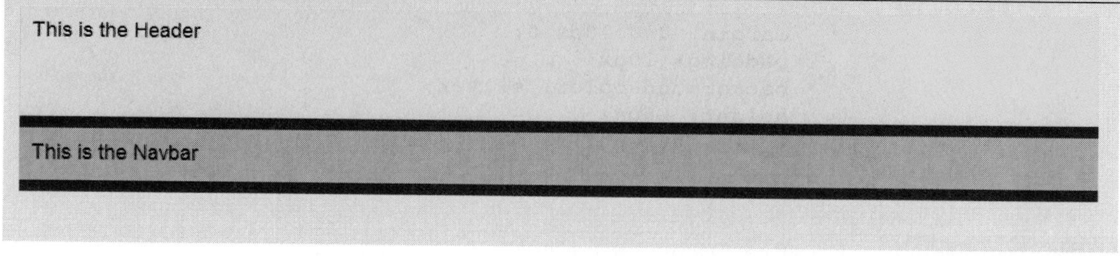

This is the Header

This is the Navbar

Now that the navbar div has been established, you will next show Pierre how to style the sidebar column.

Creating a Style for the Sidebar

The body will have two side-by-side columns—a narrow sidebar column on the left and a larger main column to its right. Recall that the container div, which will be the parent div to the side-by-side columns, has a width of 930px. The content of the sidebar column and the main column, as well as all their margins, borders, and padding, cannot exceed a total of 930px. One of the two side-by-side columns will need a margin to create a **gutter** (white space between columns). You can create a right margin for the sidebar column or create a left margin for the main column—the choice is up to you. In this instance, you have chosen to give the sidebar column a right margin of 10px.

Because a sidebar column should be narrow, you suggest to Pierre that 200px would be a good width. To allow some internal white space, the sidebar column will also have 10px of padding on all sides. The sidebar column will not have a border. With this information, you can now determine the column width of the sidebar column. Jot down this figure because you will need it later to calculate the width of the main column. The width of the sidebar column will be 230px, as shown in Figure 6-18.

Figure 6-18

Determining the column width for the sidebar column

Left Margin Width	Left Border Width	Left Padding Width	Content Width	Right Padding Width	Right Border Width	Right Margin Width	Column Width
0	0	10	200	10	0	10	**230**

The top and bottom margins for a div do not figure into the calculation for the column width or the content width, but those margin values are important. The bottom margin for the sidebar column will be 10px, which will create some white space below the sidebar column. To make the bottom margins even for the sidebar column and the main column, both columns will need to have the same bottom margin of 10px.

In a previous tutorial, you learned about the float property and used it to float an image left or right. The float property is used extensively in page layouts to position div elements left or right. In Pierre's layout, you will float the sidebar column left. To see the layout better, you'll also assign a background color and a height to the sidebar column. You will now show Pierre how to enter the code for the sidebar id selector.

To style the sidebar id selector:

► **1.** Switch back to your text editor. In the embedded style sheet, position the insertion point below the navbar id style. On a blank line, type the following code, as shown in Figure 6-19.

```
#sidebar {
    width: 200px;
    margin: 0 10px 10px 0;
    padding: 10px;
    background-color: orange;
    float: left;
    height: 400px;
}
```

► **2.** Save the file.

Figure 6-19 The sidebar id selector code

```
#navbar {
    width: 910px;
    margin: 0 0 10px 0;
    padding: 10px;
    background-color: silver;
    height: 25px;
}

#sidebar {
    width: 200px;
    margin: 0 10px 10px 0;
    padding: 10px;
    background-color: orange;
    float: left;
    height: 400px;
}

</style>
```

the sidebar id selector code →

Now that the sidebar id selector has been created, you can show Pierre how to enter the code for the sidebar div and apply the sidebar id to it.

To create the sidebar div code:

► **1.** In your text editor, and in the document body, position the insertion point below the end </div> code for the navbar div. On a blank line, type the following code, as shown in Figure 6-20.

```
<div id="sidebar">
<p>This is the Sidebar column</p>
</div> <!-- sidebar column ends here -->
```

► **2.** Save the file.

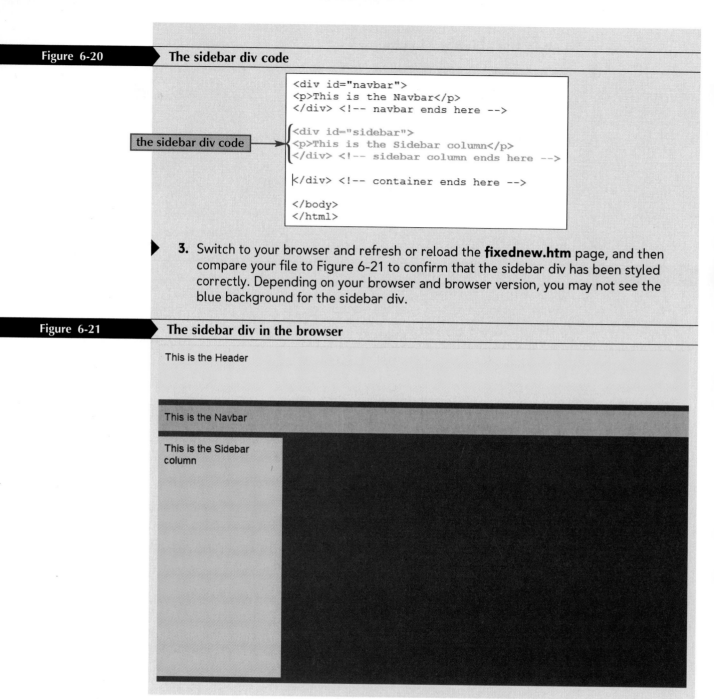

Figure 6-20 | The sidebar div code

```
<div id="navbar">
<p>This is the Navbar</p>
</div> <!-- navbar ends here -->

<div id="sidebar">
<p>This is the Sidebar column</p>
</div> <!-- sidebar column ends here -->

</div> <!-- container ends here -->

</body>
</html>
```

the sidebar div code

3. Switch to your browser and refresh or reload the **fixednew.htm** page, and then compare your file to Figure 6-21 to confirm that the sidebar div has been styled correctly. Depending on your browser and browser version, you may not see the blue background for the sidebar div.

Figure 6-21 | The sidebar div in the browser

This is the Header

This is the Navbar

This is the Sidebar column

Next, you will show Pierre how to determine the width of the main column.

Creating a Style for the Main Column

Now that the sidebar column has been established, you need to calculate the width of the main column. Recall that the container div is 930px wide. The sidebar column has a width of 230px, so the column width of the main column will be 700px (930 – 230 = 700). The main column for this layout will not have margins or a border, but it will have padding of 10px on all sides. You now have all the data you need to determine the content width for the main column, as shown in Figure 6-22:

Figure 6-22 **Determining the content width of the main column**

700px	The width of the main column
20px	The margins, borders, and padding (10px of padding on both the left and right)
680px	The content width of the main column (700 – 20)

InSight | **Using Dependent id Selectors**

Recall that classes can be dependent, meaning that the class can only be applied to a particular element, or they can be independent (the class can be applied to any element). You can also make id selectors dependent on an element as well. You have already seen examples in which id selectors have been created by entering the # flag character followed by the id selector name. Some Web designers like to make the id selectors used for layout dependent on the div element, like this:

```
div#header
```

When you create dependent id selectors, the principle is the same as that for creating dependent classes. In the previous example, the header id can be applied only to a div element. The following code:

```
#header {
   background-color: teal;
}
```

when used for layouts, has the same effect as entering this code:

```
div#header {
   background-color: teal;
}
```

Be consistent in how you enter the code for your div id selectors when you create page layout. The div#header id selector can be applied only to the div element, but the #header id selector can be applied to any element.

You have calculated 680px as the value to use for the width property of the main id selector. Now that you have determined the content width for the main div, you will show Pierre how to enter the code to style the main id selector.

To style the main id selector:

▶ **1.** Switch back to your text editor. In the embedded style sheet code, position the insertion point below the sidebar id style. On a blank line, type the following code, as shown in Figure 6-23.

```
#main {
   width: 680px;
   margin: 0 0 10px 0;
   padding: 10px;
   background-color: aqua;
   float: right;
   height: 400px;
}
```

▶ **2.** Save the file.

Figure 6-23 | **The main id selector code**

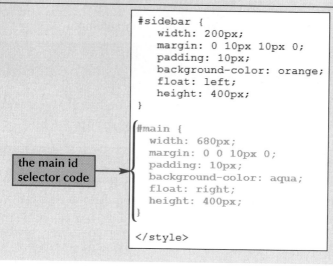

the main id selector code

```
#sidebar {
    width: 200px;
    margin: 0 10px 10px 0;
    padding: 10px;
    background-color: orange;
    float: left;
    height: 400px;
}

#main {
    width: 680px;
    margin: 0 0 10px 0;
    padding: 10px;
    background-color: aqua;
    float: right;
    height: 400px;
}

</style>
```

Now that the code for the main id selector has been entered, you can type the code for the main div and apply the main id to it.

To create the main div code:

1. In your text editor, and in the document body, position the insertion point below the end </div> code for the sidebar div. On a blank line, type the following code, as shown in Figure 6-24.

```
<div id="main">
<p>This is the Main column</p>
</div> <!-- main column ends here -->
```

2. Save the file.

Figure 6-24 | **The main div code**

```
<div id="sidebar">
<p>This is the Sidebar column</p>
</div> <!-- sidebar column ends here -->

<div id="main">
<p>This is the Main column</p>
</div> <!-- main column ends here -->

</div> <!-- container ends here -->
```

the main div code

3. Switch to your browser, refresh or reload the **fixednew.htm** page, and then compare your file to Figure 6-25 to confirm that the main div has been styled correctly. Depending on your browser and browser version, you may not see the blue border around several of the div boxes.

Figure 6-25 **The main div in the browser**

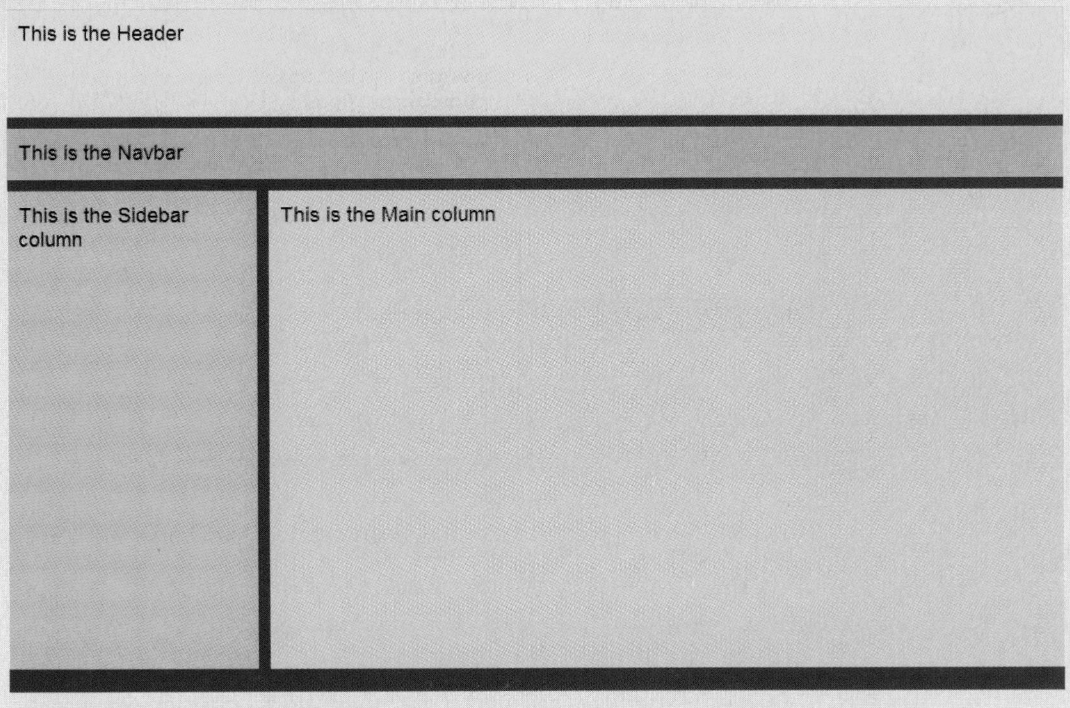

Tip

he value of "both"
r than "left" or
t" for the clear
erty. This way, you
have to change the
property value
d the sidebar later
ated right instead
t.

This is the Header

This is the Navbar

This is the Sidebar
column

This is the Main column

Next, you need to show Pierre how to create a style for the footer id selector.

Creating a Style for the Footer

Pierre wants the footer to appear below the sidebar and main columns. The footer style will be similar to the header id and navbar id styles you created earlier. The footer will not have margins or a border, but it will have 10px of padding on all sides. The width will be 910px, the same as the header and navbar. However, you will also use the clear property to clear past both the sidebar and the main columns. You will now show Pierre how to style the footer id selector.

To style the footer id selector:

1. Switch back to your text editor. In the embedded style sheet code, position the insertion point below the main id style. On a blank line, type the following code, as shown in Figure 6-26.

```
#footer {
   width: 910px;
   padding: 10px;
   background-color: lime;
   clear: both;
   height: 75px;
}
```

2. Save the file.

Figure 6-26 ▸ **The footer id selector code**

```
#main {
  width: 680px;
  margin: 0 0 10px 0;
  padding: 10px;
  background-color: aqua;
  float: right;
  height: 400px;
}

#footer {
  width: 910px;
  padding: 10px;
  background-color: lime;
  clear: both;
  height: 75px;
}

</style>
```

the footer id code

Now that the footer id selector has been created, you can enter the code for the footer div and apply the footer id to it.

To create the footer div code:

▸ **1.** In your text editor, and in the document body, position the insertion point below the end </div> code for the main div. On a blank line, type the following code, as shown in Figure 6-27.

```
<div id="footer">
<p>This is the Footer</p>
</div> <!-- footer ends here -->
```

▸ **2.** Save the file.

Figure 6-27 ▸ **The footer div code**

```
<div id="main">
<p>This is the Main column</p>
</div> <!-- main column ends here -->

<div id="footer">
<p>This is the Footer</p>
</div> <!-- footer ends here -->

</div> <!-- container ends here -->

</body>
</html>
```

the footer div code

▸ **3.** Switch to your browser, refresh or reload the **fixednew.htm** page, and then compare your file to Figure 6-28 to confirm that the footer div has been styled correctly.

Figure 6-28 | **The footer div in the browser**

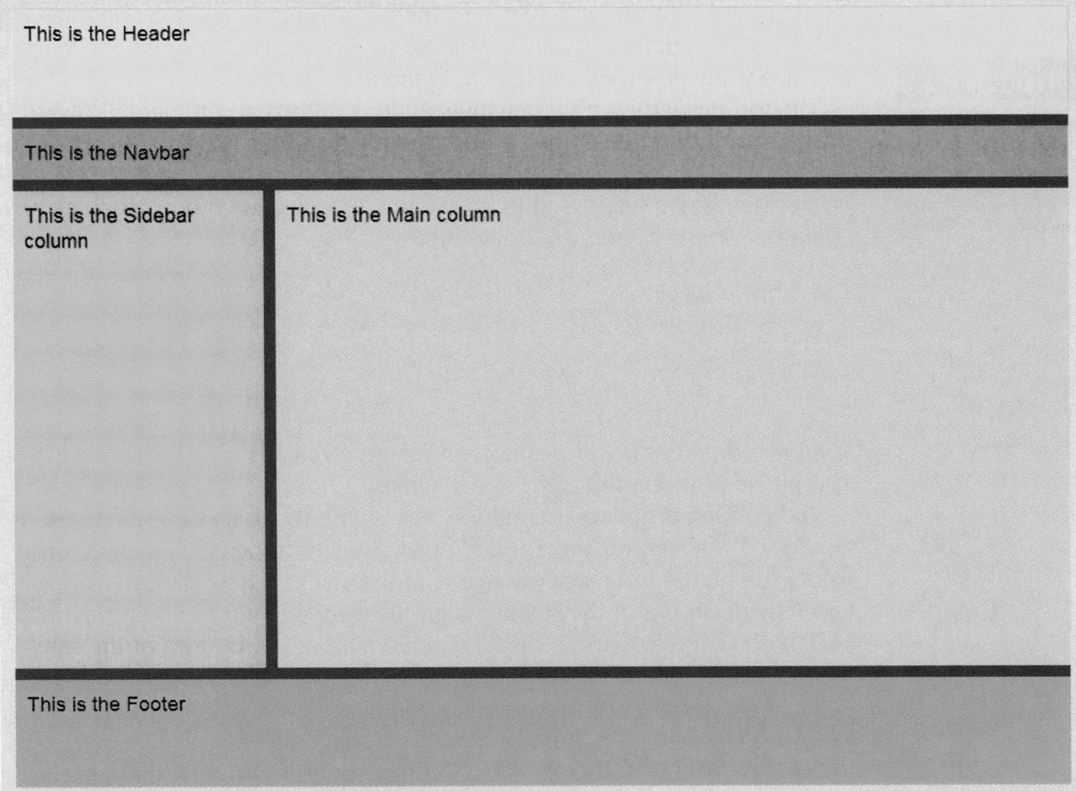

This is the Header

This is the Navbar

This is the Sidebar column

This is the Main column

This is the Footer

▶ **4.** Close the **fixednew.htm** file.

▶ **5.** Submit the results of the **fixednew.htm** file to your instructor, either in printed or electronic form, as requested.

▶ **6.** If you will not be completing the next session, close your text editor and your browser.

An older method of creating page layouts is also available. You want Pierre to know about this method in case he encounters such code when working with someone else's documents, so you briefly will explain the CSS positioning properties.

Using the Positioning Properties

The **document flow** describes how the contents of the page are recognized by the browser. The positioning properties can place any element—images or text—anywhere on the screen regardless of where the element appears in the document flow. When you use **absolute positioning**, the element is displayed in the exact position you specify, no matter what elements surround it. If text or an image already appears in that screen location, the items that have an absolute position may even appear on top of that object. No matter how you revise the page to add or delete text or images, an absolutely positioned element remains in the same position. When you use **relative positioning**, you shift the element's position from the point where it normally would appear in the document flow. Note that floated elements do not get shifted around absolutely positioned elements, which might make elements overlap on the screen.

The **left property** with a positive value positions an element a certain distance from the left edge of the screen, moving the element to the right. The **top property** with a positive value positions an element a certain distance from the top edge of the screen, moving the element down. Although they are not used nearly as often, the **bottom property** and **right property** function in the same way. The bottom property with a positive value moves an element up; the right property with a positive value moves an element to the left. You can also use negative numbers as values for these properties. For example, the left property with a negative value positions an element to the left.

The top property with a negative value positions an element above the normal position. You don't have to use both the left and top properties; you can use either the left property or the right property, or you can use both. The values for the left and top properties can be expressed in any of the CSS measurements, such as pixels, points, percentages, or em values, as shown below:

<div style="float:left; width:200px;">
<p><strong>Tip</strong></p>
<p>Although margins can have negative values, padding can only have positive values or the value of 0.</p>
</div>

```
img.absolute {
  position: absolute;
  top: 40px;
  left: 120px;
}
```

The preceding code will position an image 40 pixels from the top edge of the screen and 120 pixels from the left edge of the screen.

The **z-index property** is used to stack elements on top of each other in the browser window. The value for the z-index property determines the stacking order; the higher the value, the higher the text or image is in the stack. If you want to always display a particular element on top of the stack, assign the z-index value to be a high number, such as 100. If you always want to display an element at the bottom of the stack, assign that element a z-index value of 0. You can have negative values for the z-index property, but negative values are not supported by the Firefox browser. For accessibility reasons, you should avoid using the z-index property in page layouts.

Several years ago, the CSS positioning properties were widely used for creating page layout, but their use in layout has dramatically declined because the positioning properties create major obstacles for screen readers and accessibility. If the user resizes the screen, for example, the positioned elements may overlap other content.

InSight | Using Comments Correctly

It's important to remember that there are two different syntaxes for comments. An XHTML comment has the following syntax:

```
<!-- comment code here -->
```

A CSS comment uses the following syntax:

```
/* comment code here */
```

A common error when creating comments is failing to enter the code to close a comment. If you do not close a comment, all code past that point will be treated as part of the comment and will not take effect.

Besides entering the correct syntax for a comment, you also need to be mindful of when to use each type of comment. Use an XHTML comment *only* in the document body of an XHTML document. Use a CSS comment only in the embedded style sheet code or in an external style sheet document. If you use a CSS comment in the body of an XHTML document, your comment will be treated as text and displayed in the browser. If you use an XHTML comment in an embedded style sheet or an external style sheet, the comment will cause some styles to appear incorrectly, particularly in the Firefox browser. Don't insert a space after the exclamation point in an XHTML comment or after the / in a CSS comment. Your document will not validate if you do.

In this session, you learned that there are many ways to create Web page layouts, including fixed designs and fluid designs. Fixed designs have a fixed page width; fluid designs take advantage of the entire screen width. The id selector is used to create a style that is applied only once on a Web page. The XHTML div element serves as an unformatted, empty container for Web page content.

Review | Session 6.1 Quick Check

1. What term describes layouts that do not function as intended?
2. What are the two major categories of layouts?
3. What is the viewport?
4. What is column drop?
5. How does column width differ from content width?
6. What are the usual five components of any layout?
7. What formatting does the div element apply?

Session 6.2

Creating a Three-Column Layout

Recall that for his real Web page, Pierre would like a three-column layout. You've already created a workable two-column layout. His proposed layout includes a new column named "section," which will list the dates his paintings will be exhibited at the gallery. He wants the new section column to appear on the right. Pierre's first design consideration is whether he wants three columns of equal width or columns of unequal widths. He has decided to give the sidebar and the section columns equal widths, and give the main column more width. The sidebar column will remain on the left, and the main column will be in the center. Pierre has sketched out the proposed layout for the side-by-side columns, as shown in Figure 6-29.

Figure 6-29 ⟩ **Pierre's design for a three-column layout**

Sidebar	Main	Section

Tip

main column need
lways be the center
nn; it is merely the
st column in the
ut.

Pierre has created a file named art.htm, a draft of the Art Gallery Web page. You have modified his initial draft to create start and end div tags in the body section and apply the id selectors, for which you will show Pierre how to create styles. You have created styles for the body, the universal selector, and the container id selector. You will start by opening the art.htm file and saving it with a new filename.

To open the art.htm file and save it with a new filename:

▶ 1. If necessary, open your browser and text editor.

▶ 2. In your text editor, open the **art.htm** file, which is provided in your Data Files in the Tutorial.06\Tutorial folder.

▶ 3. Take time to study the code in the file, and then save the file as **artnew.htm** in the same folder.

▶ 4. In the head section and below the page title, enter your name and today's date in the comment section where noted.

> 5. In your browser, open **artnew.htm** and compare your file to the one shown in Figure 6-30. Depending on your browser and browser version, you may see bullets at the top of the page. Do not concern yourself now with the appearance or the position of the bullets.

Figure 6-30	The draft of the Art Gallery home page

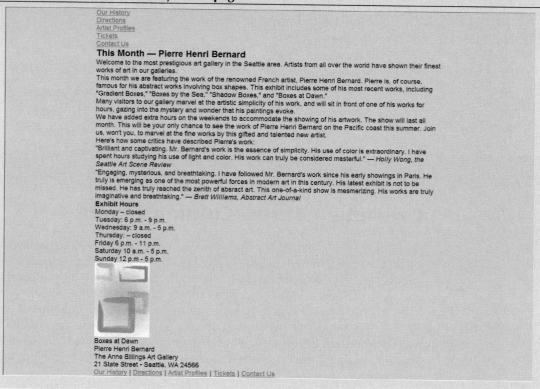

Now that Pierre has grasped the principles of fixed-width design, you are ready to start working with him to design a three-column layout using the real text and graphics for his Web page. When designing layouts, you will use the float element to position divs left or right. Floated elements need to be positioned in the document body in a certain way, so you'll start by explaining the effect of floated elements on the document flow.

Interrupting the Document Flow

The **source order** is the order of the content in the document flow. Normally, the browser reads content from top to bottom and left to right, like a page in a book. However, for columns that are side by side, floated divs must appear before nonfloated divs. You sometimes may have to pull content out of its original source order. The artnew.htm file is a good example of how the source order has been interrupted and the divs do not appear as they would in the normal document flow.

In the artnew.htm document, three divs are side by side: the sidebar div, the main div, and the section div. In the normal document flow, the sidebar div would come first, the main div would be second, and the section div would come next. However, if you floated the sidebar div left and the section div right (and did not float the main div), the divs would have to be arranged like this:

```
<div id="sidebar">
</div>

<div id="section">
</div>
```

```
<div id="main">
</div>
```

The two floated divs would have to appear in the document body before the main div, which might be confusing when someone else has to revise the code. Also, screen readers would read the secondary content (the sidebar and the section) before the main content, which now would come last. To retain the source order, you will float the main div as well.

Creating Styles for the Header Div

For the header id selector, Pierre has decided to use the same content width and column width he used in the practice file. However, he does need to make one adjustment to the code for the header div. In the practice file, the header div contained text, so padding was applied on both the left and the right. The padding width was subtracted from the column width to obtain the value for the content width. In the artnew.htm file, the only content for the header will be an image, artlogo.gif, so there is no need for padding. For the artnew.htm file, the header column width will be equal to the content width. The image has a border, but it is part of the image and was not created with the CSS border property, so the border width will not be taken into account in determining the layout.

In the artnew.htm file, you have already created styles for the body, the universal selector, and the container div. Pierre is familiar with these styles because they are similar to the ones you showed him in the last session. You will show Pierre how to create the header id selector, and you will have him enter the code for the artlogo.gif image in the header div.

To style the header id selector:

▶ **1.** Switch back to your text editor. In the embedded style sheet, position the insertion point below the container id style. On a blank line, type the following code, as shown in Figure 6-31.

```
#header {
    width: 930px;
    background-color: #6e8953;
    margin-bottom: 10px;
}
```

Figure 6-31   **The header id selector code**

```
#container {
   margin: 0 auto;
   width: 930px;
   border-width: 1px; /* needed for Firefox so that when the screen is
enlarged, the document remains centered */
}

#header {
   width: 930px;
   background-color: #6e8953;
   margin-bottom: 10px;
}
```

the header id code

▶ **2.** In the body area, position the insertion point on the blank line below the start <div> tag for the header div. Type the following code, as shown in Figure 6-32.

```
<p><img src="artlogo.gif" alt="Anne Billings Art Gallery
logo" width="930" height="150" /></p>
```

Figure 6-32   **The image code**

the code to insert the
artlogo.gif image

```
<div id="container">

<div id="header">

<p><img src="artlogo.gif" alt="Anne Billings Art Gallery logo"
width="930" height="150" /></p>

</div> <!-- end header -->
```

   3. Save the file.

   4. In your browser, refresh or reload the **artnew.htm** page, and compare your file to
      the one shown in Figure 6-33 to verify that the header has been styled correctly.

Figure 6-33   **The header in the browser**

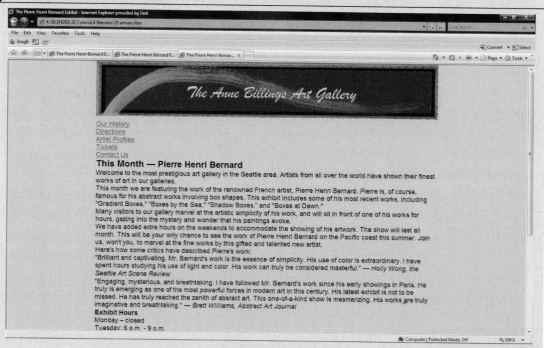

Now that the header has been created, you are ready to start showing Pierre how to
create the column layout. You'll start by working on the design for the sidebar column.

Creating Styles for the Sidebar Column

Pierre is pleased with the appearance of the header div. The sidebar contains an unordered list that will contain links to the other pages at the Art Gallery Web site, which he will link to later. Pierre would like to make those links stand out. You suggest creating some descendant selectors for the sidebar selector to style the list items. The sidebar has a content width of 200px. With a margin of 10px on the right and padding of 10px on both the left and right, the column width is 230px. You will show Pierre how to create some styles for the sidebar column and styles for the links in the sidebar column.

To style the sidebar id selectors:

   1. Switch back to your text editor. Position the insertion point below the header id
      style. On a blank line, type the following code, as shown in Figure 6-34.

```
#sidebar {
  width: 200px;
  margin: 0 10px 10px 0;
  padding: 10px;
  float: left;
}

#sidebar ul {
  font-weight: bold;
  list-style: none;
  text-align: center;
}

#sidebar ul li a {
  padding: 5px;
  background-color: maroon;
  color: yellow;
  display: block;
}

#sidebar ul li a:hover {
  border: dotted thin;
  background: yellow;
  color: navy;
}
```

Figure 6-34 ▷ **The sidebar selectors code**

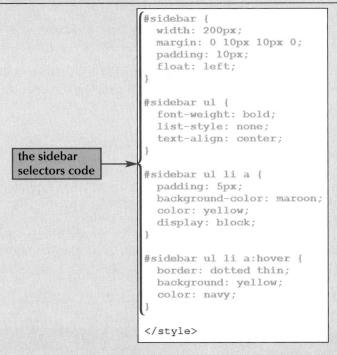

the sidebar selectors code

```
#sidebar {
  width: 200px;
  margin: 0 10px 10px 0;
  padding: 10px;
  float: left;
}

#sidebar ul {
  font-weight: bold;
  list-style: none;
  text-align: center;
}

#sidebar ul li a {
  padding: 5px;
  background-color: maroon;
  color: yellow;
  display: block;
}

#sidebar ul li a:hover {
  border: dotted thin;
  background: yellow;
  color: navy;
}

</style>
```

▶ **2.** Save the file.

▶ **3.** In your browser, refresh or reload the **artnew.htm** page, and compare your file to the one shown in Figure 6-35 to verify that the sidebar column has been styled correctly.

Figure 6-35 The sidebar in the browser

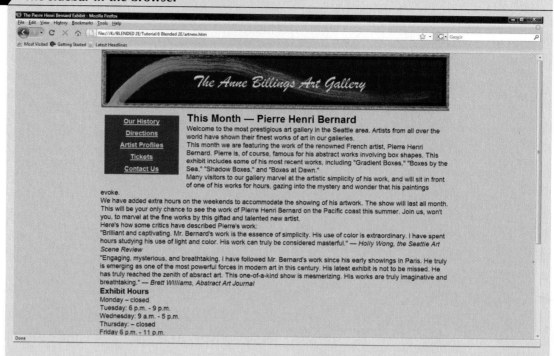

4. Pass the mouse pointer over the links to see if the hover effect is working correctly.

Pierre is pleased with the appearance of the sidebar column, but the main column and the section column still need to be developed. You'll work with Pierre to determine the width of these two columns next.

Creating Styles for the Main Column

To determine the column width and content width for the main column, you have some calculations to perform. The sidebar column currently has a column width of 230px. Pierre wants the new section column on the right to have the same width as the sidebar column, so the section column will also have a width of 230px. The section column will have a left margin to create a gutter between the section column and the main column to its left. The section column will also have 10px of padding on both the left and the right. Figure 6-36 shows the layout plan so far.

Figure 6-36 The layout plan for the main column

Sidebar	Main	Section
margin-left: 0		margin-left: 10
border: 0		border: 0
padding-left: 10		padding-left: 10
content: 200		content: 200
padding-right: 10		padding-right: 10
border: 0		border: 0
margin-right: 10		margin-right: 0
Total: 230px		**Total: 230px**

Now you'll work with Pierre to determine the column width of the main column. The sum of the sidebar and the section columns is 460px. The sidebar column is to the left of the main column and the section column is to the right of the main columns. **Flanking columns** are columns that appear to the left or the right of the main column.

To determine the column width for the main column, subtract the sum of the widths for the flanking columns (460px) from the container width (930px), as shown in Figure 6-37.

Figure 6-37 Determining the column width for the main column

930px	The container width
460px	The sum of the column widths of the two flanking columns
470px	The column width of the main column (930 – 460)

As you can see, the width of the main column will be 470px. To determine the content width for the main column, subtract the combined width of the margins, border, and padding used in the main column from the column width. The main column will have 10px of padding on both the left and the right, and no margins or borders. The main column, therefore, will have a content width of 450px, as shown in Figure 6-38.

Figure 6-38 Determining the content width for the main column

470px	The column width of the main column
20px	The sum of the margins, padding, and border for the main column
450px	The content width of the main column (470 – 20)

You will show Pierre how to enter the code for the main id selector. You will also create a descendant selector for the main div so that paragraph text is indented.

To style the main id selectors:

▶ **1.** Switch back to your text editor. In the embedded style sheet, position the insertion point below the sidebar "ul li a:hover" style. On a blank line, type the following code, as shown in Figure 6-39.

```
#main {
    width: 450px;
    margin: 0 0 10px 0;
    padding: 10px;
    float: left;
    color: white;
}

#main p {
    text-indent: 1.5em;
}
```

Figure 6-39 ▸ **The main id selectors code**

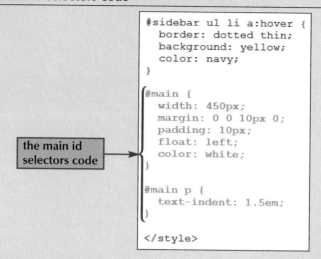

the main id selectors code

```
#sidebar ul li a:hover {
    border: dotted thin;
    background: yellow;
    color: navy;
}

#main {
    width: 450px;
    margin: 0 0 10px 0;
    padding: 10px;
    float: left;
    color: white;
}

#main p {
    text-indent: 1.5em;
}

</style>
```

▸ **2.** Save the file.

▸ **3.** In your browser, refresh or reload the **artnew.htm** page, and compare your file to the one shown in Figure 6-40 to verify that the main column has been styled correctly. Both the section and the footer text will appear to the right of the main column. (Later you'll move the footer so it's below all three columns.)

Figure 6-40 ▸ **The main column styled in the browser**

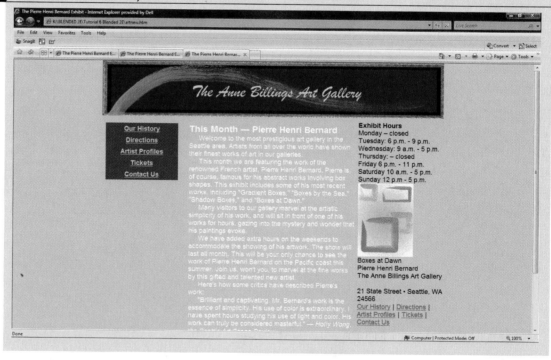

Now that the styles for the main id selector have been created, you will show Pierre how to create styles for the section id selector.

Creating Styles for the Section id Selector

The section div contains information about the show's exhibit hours. The section div will also include an image and a caption for one of Pierre's works, entitled "Boxes at Dawn." The section id selector will be styled to have a width of 200px and to float right. The text for the exhibit hours will appear in bold and italic, so you will create a descendant selector to style just the paragraph text that appears within the section div. You will show Pierre how to enter the code for the section id selector and the descendant selector for the paragraph element.

To style the section id selectors:

▶ 1. Switch back to your text editor. In the embedded style sheet, position the insertion point below the main p style. On a blank line, type the following code, as shown in Figure 6-41.

```
#section {
   width: 200px;
   margin: 0 0 10px 8px;
   padding: 10px;
   float: right;
}

#section p {
   margin: 0.2em;
   font-style: italic;
   font-weight: bold;
   font-size: 0.9em;
}
```

| Figure 6-41 | The section id selectors code |

```
#section {
   width: 200px;
   margin: 0 0 10px 8px;
   padding: 10px;
   float: right;
}

#section p {
   margin: 0.2em;
   font-style: italic;
   font-weight: bold;
   font-size: 0.9em;
}

</style>
```

the section id selectors code →

▶ 2. Save the file.

▶ 3. In your browser, refresh or reload the **artnew.htm** page, and compare your file to the one shown in Figure 6-42 to verify that the section column has been styled correctly. (The section column should shift slightly to the right and down. The footer, however, will still appear as though it is in the section column.)

Figure 6-42 | **The section column styled in the browser**

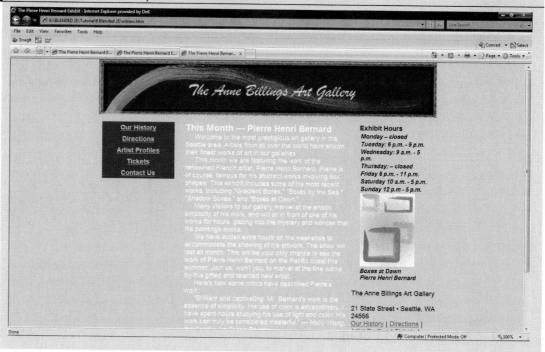

Next, you will show Pierre how to center different types of content for the section div and both the h2 and h3 headings.

Creating Styles for Centering

Pierre would like to center the dawn.gif image that appears in the section div, but there is a problem. First, there isn't a way to float an item that you want centered. Second, you can only center block-level elements, not inline elements, such as the image element. So, to center this image, you will use the display property and change the value for the image to "block." The browser will treat the dawn.gif image as though it were a block-level element, so you will be able to center the image. The caption text, which is contained in its own div, can be centered using the text-align property.

Reference Window | **Centering an Image**

- To center an image, use the declaration:
  ```
  img.classname {
    display: block;
    margin: auto;
  }
  ```
  where *img* is the image element and *classname* is the name of the class.
- Apply the class to the image to be centered.
- To center all images, use the same declarations for the image element selector.

The main div has an h2 heading that Pierre would like to have centered. The section div has an h3 heading, which Pierre also would like centered, so you will create styles to center both the h2 and h3 heading text and make other minor modifications to the margins and padding as well.

To style the selectors to center content:

▶ **1.** Switch back to your text editor. In the embedded style sheet, position the insertion point below the section p style. On a blank line, type the following code, as shown in Figure 6-43.

```
img.center {
  display: block;
  width: auto;
  margin: 10px auto;
}

#caption {
  text-align: center;
}

h2 {
  font-size: 1.4em;
  text-align: center;
  padding-bottom: 0.5em;
}

h3 {
  text-align: center;
  padding-bottom: 0.5em;
}
```

Figure 6-43	The code to center content

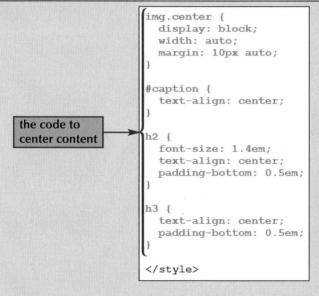

the code to center content

```
img.center {
  display: block;
  width: auto;
  margin: 10px auto;
}

#caption {
  text-align: center;
}

h2 {
  font-size: 1.4em;
  text-align: center;
  padding-bottom: 0.5em;
}

h3 {
  text-align: center;
  padding-bottom: 0.5em;
}

</style>
```

▶ **2.** Save the file.

Now that the styles to center content have been created, you need to show Pierre how to apply the center class to the image code for the dawn.gif image.

To apply the center class:

▶ **1.** Switch back to your text editor. In the document body, scroll down and position the insertion point to the left of the forward slash at the end of the image code for the dawn.gif image.

▶ **2.** Type the following code to apply the center class, as shown in Figure 6-44, and then press the **Spacebar** once.

```
<p><img src="dawn.gif" alt="boxes at dawn" width="150"
height="200" class="center" /></p>
```

Figure 6-44 **Applying the center class**

the center class
applied

```
<p>Saturday 10 a.m. - 5 p.m.</p>
<p>Sunday 12 p.m - 5 p.m.</p>

<p><img src="dawn.gif" alt="boxes at dawn" width="150" height="200"
class="center" /></p>

<div id="caption">
<p>Boxes at Dawn
```

3. Save the file.

4. In your browser, refresh or reload the **artnew.htm** page, and compare your file to the one shown in Figure 6-45 to verify that the h2 and h3 headings, the dawn.gif image, and the two-line caption below the image are centered.

Figure 6-45 **The content centered in the browser**

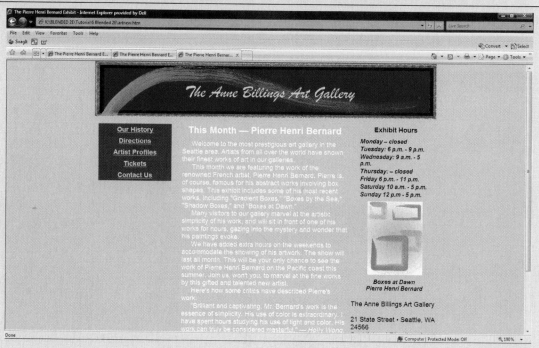

Now that the columns have been styled, you will show Pierre how to create styles for the last section of the layout, the footer div.

Creating Styles for the Footer Div

The last section to style is the footer. The footer contains text, so you will apply 10px of padding on all sides. Because of the padding widths on the left and right, the content width will be 910px, not 930px, which is the width of the header div. Currently, the footer appears below the content for the section div, but you want it below all three columns. Therefore, you will also use the clear property with a value of "both" to ensure that the footer clears all of the columns. You will now show Pierre how to style the footer id selector.

To style the footer id selector:

1. Switch back to your text editor. In the embedded style sheet, position the insertion point below the h3 heading style. On a blank line, type the following code, as shown in Figure 6-46.

```
#footer {
  width: 910px;
  margin: 0;
  padding: 10px;
  background-color: #2e1e6c;
  clear: both;
  color: white;
  text-align: center;
}
```

Figure 6-46 ▸ **The footer id selector code**

the footer id selector code →
```
#footer {
  width: 910px;
  margin: 0;
  padding: 10px;
  background-color: #2e1e6c;
  clear: both;
  color: white;
  text-align: center;
}

</style>
```

2. Save the file.

3. In your browser, refresh or reload the **artnew.htm** page. If necessary, scroll down and compare your file to the one shown in Figure 6-47 to verify that the footer has been styled correctly. Depending on your browser and browser version, the link text may look slightly different than that shown in Figure 6-47.

Figure 6-47 ▸ **The footer styled in the browser**

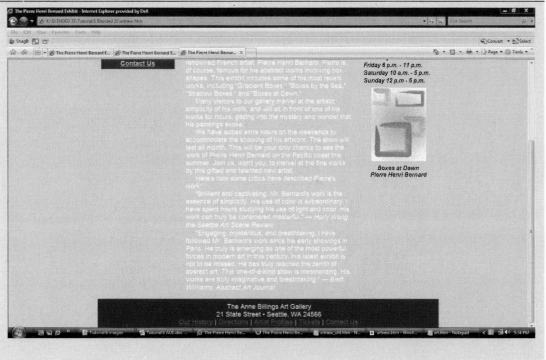

Although HTML has not yet been finalized, a number of new elements that will control page layout have been proposed. If accepted, these elements will replace the need for div tags within the document, and they will help make Web page layout more consistent:

<header>—The header element will be used to enclose the items displayed in the document header of the page, such as logos and banners. Do not confuse the header element with the <head> element, which still will be used as a container for metadata. Instead of creating the header area using div tags such as <div id="header"></div>, you will instead use the start <header> and end </header> tags to enclose the header information. There will be no need to create a header id selector.

<nav>—The nav element will be used anywhere that the document has a group of links. The nav element could be used within the <header> element, in a sidebar, or in the footer.

<section>—The section element indicates a section on the page, either horizontally or vertically. A series of related content will be preceded and followed by <section> </section> tags. You can format and position the section as you want.

<article>—The article element will be used to specify the items on a page that are part of a particular article. You can format and position the article as you want.

<footer>—The footer element will be used to enclose all the information that typically appears in a footer.

Next, you will show Pierre how to use the @import rule to import styles from another style sheet.

Using @import

Over time, you will start to develop a **style sheet library**, a collection of frequently used styles. For example, rather than constantly creating new code for how header text, footer text, or navigational links should appear, you can create separate style sheets with names like header.css, footer.css, and so forth. You can **import** (make use of) those styles into either an embedded or external style sheet using the @import rule. The **@import rule** allows users to import style rules from other style sheets. The @import rule has the following syntax:

```
@import url(stylesheet_filename.css);
```

Importing styles allows you to import one style sheet into another. The @import rule must come after the CSS comment (if there is one) and before any of the styles code in the style sheet. For example, the following code would be correct for an embedded style sheet that imports a style sheet named footer.css.

```
<style type="text/css">

@import url(footer.css);

* {
  margin: 0 auto;
  padding: 0;
}
. . . (other styles here) . . .

</style>
```

You have created a file named navfooter.css that contains styles to format the footer. The styles code appears as shown:

```
#footer a:link {
  color: white;
  text-transform: uppercase;
}

#footer a:visited {
  color: navy;
  background-color: gray;
  text-decoration: none;
}

#footer a:hover {
  background-color: #faf9f6;
}
```

In the navfooter.css code, unvisited links will appear in uppercase. Visited links will appear in navy, with a background color of gray, and without underlining. The hover effect will create a background color for the link text. You will show Pierre how to enter the @import rule at the top of the style sheet to import the navfooter.css file.

To enter the @import rule:

▶ **1.** Switch back to your text editor. Position the insertion point after the end angle bracket (>) following the start <style type="text/css"> code.

▶ **2.** Press the **Enter** key twice.

▶ **3.** Type the following code, as shown in Figure 6-48.

```
@import url(navfooter.css);
```

Figure 6-48 | The @import rule code

```
Today's Date:
Filename: artnew.htm
-->

<style type="text/css">
```

the @import rule code ▶ `@import url(navfooter.css);`

```
body {
    font-size: 1.1em;
    font-family: Arial, Helvetica, sans-serif;
    background-color: #bfe2e5;
}
```

▶ **4.** Save the file.

▶ **5.** In your browser, refresh or reload the **artnew.htm** page. If necessary, scroll down and compare your file to the one shown in Figure 6-49 to verify that the links are styled according to the @import rule. (The link text should now appear in all capital letters.)

Figure 6-49   **The footer in the browser**

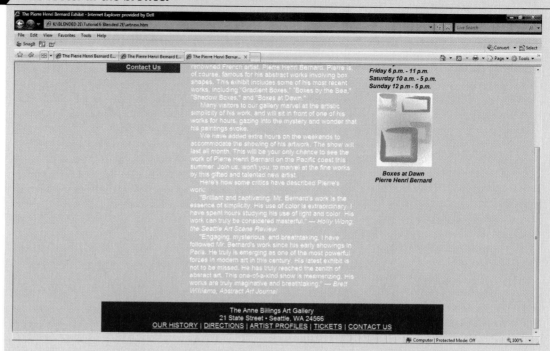

6. Pass the mouse pointer over the links in the footer to see if the hover effect is working correctly. (The link text should be navy and on a white background.)

Throughout this tutorial, you have shown Pierre how to use id selectors. You now will explain to him how style conflicts are resolved when different types of selectors are used in the same style sheet.

Understanding Specificity

In an earlier tutorial, you learned that style precedence is used to resolve conflicts if the same element has been styled more than once. Now that you have learned about id selectors, you need to know how specificity is used to resolve style conflicts. **Specificity** determines priorities and uses a weighting method to calculate which style rule will prevail if there are conflicting rules in the same source.

If there is a conflict within the same style sheet, generally *the style farthest down in the list will prevail*. For example, in the following embedded style sheet code, in what color will the h2 heading text appear in the browser?

```
h2 {
  color: red;
}

em {
  font-style: normal;
}

h2 {
  color: blue;
}
```

In this instance, the h2 heading text will appear in blue because that h2 style is farther down in the list. Bear in mind, though, that specificity applies only to conflicts. In the following code, would the h2 heading text appear in italics or not?

```
h2 {
  color: red;
  font-style: italic;
}

em {
  font-style: normal;
}

h2 {
  color: blue;
}
```

The answer is yes. The h2 heading text will appear in italics and blue, because there is no conflict between font-style properties. Therefore, the property (font-style) and its value (italic) will be carried over from the first h2 style to the second h2 style. Specificity resolves only style conflicts.

In addition to the location of the style in the style sheet, CSS also uses specificity to resolve style conflicts among different *types* of selectors. The World Wide Web Consortium has a weighting methodology for calculating the specificity of particular selectors. Id selectors have a weight of 100, class selectors have a weight of 10, and element selectors (also known as "type" selectors) have a weight of 1. If two styles conflict in the same source, these weighting values will help determine which style will prevail.

For example, in the same embedded style sheet, an id selector (#green), a class selector (h2.yellow), and an element selector (h2) are all attempting to style the same element. Look at the following code and decide what color the words "Please be Specific" will appear in the browser.

```
<style type="text/css">

#green {
  color: green;
}

h2.yellow {
  color: yellow;
}

h2 {
  color: blue;
}

</style>
</head>

<body>

<h2 id="green" class="yellow">Please be Specific</h2>
```

You would expect that because the h2 element selector style is the farthest down in the list, it would prevail and the h2 text would appear in blue. Or, you might think that because the yellow class has been applied last in the start h2 tag, yellow will prevail. However, even though the #green id selector is at the top of the style list, the #green id style will prevail because it has greater numeric specificity than either the class selector or the element selector. In this instance, the words "Please be Specific" will appear in green.

One major detail in the artnew.htm layout remains to be completed. The layout lacks a background. You will next show Pierre how to use a background image to create the illusion that all three columns have an equal height.

Creating Faux Columns

In the earlier session, the sidebar and the main columns were of equal height solely because you used the height property and gave each column the same value of 400px. However, there is a disadvantage to giving each column a fixed height. If one or more of the columns had content that exceeded the 400px height, the content that didn't fit inside the div would appear outside the box contents, as shown in Figure 6-50.

Figure 6-50	Text overflow

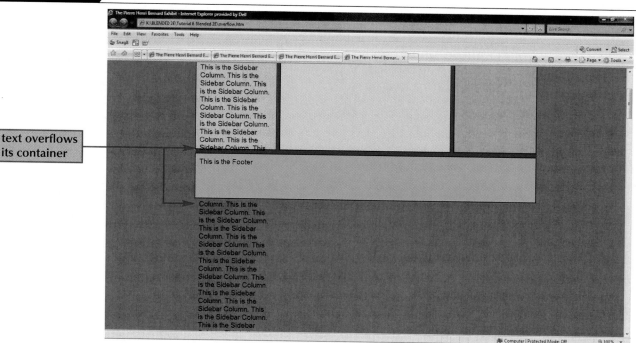

You can partially overcome this problem by using the CSS **overflow property**. The overflow property with a value of "auto" adds a vertical scroll bar as needed, so if the box content exceeds the height, a vertical scroll bar will appear to the right of the column. The overflow property value of "scroll" always creates a vertical scroll bar regardless of the column height. Figure 6-51 shows the same layout as in Figure 6-50, except that the overflow property with a value of auto has been added to the sidebar id selector style. A vertical scroll bar has also been added.

Figure 6-51 ▶ **The overflow property with a value of auto**

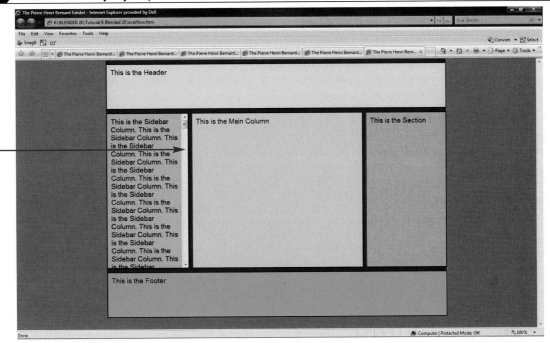

scroll bar has been added

Adding scroll bars sounds like a good workaround, but scroll bars take up approximately 19 pixels of screen space. You have already performed the calculations for the width of the content area. If a scroll bar appears, your calculations for the column widths would be off by 19 pixels, which means that one or more of your columns would no longer fit the container width. In addition, scroll bars detract from the simplicity of your Web site. Many visitors do not like to use vertical scroll bars to view content. Figure 6-52 shows the values for the CSS overflow property.

Figure 6-52 ▶ **Values for the overflow property**

Value	Description
visible	The default value. The content is not clipped, and whatever does not fit in the div will appear outside the div.
hidden	The content is clipped and scroll bars are not added to view the overflow content.
scroll	The content is clipped. The browser displays a scroll bar so that the clipped content can be viewed.
auto	The browser will display a scroll bar only if the content is clipped.

Rather than risk having content overflow, having your document become populated with scroll bars, or breaking the layout, you can create faux columns. This technique is named after Web designer Dan Cederholm's article at the A List Apart Web site (*www.alistapart.com/articles/fauxcolumns/*). **Faux columns** add a background image to create the illusion that the columns have equal height. You do not use the height property when you create id selector styles for faux columns. First, you must create another container, which you will call "wrapper."

Tip

word "faux" means e in French. Faux is ounced "foe."

Creating the Wrapper id Selector

To create the faux column look, you need to locate an appropriate background image, or create one using a graphics editor such as Adobe Illustrator or Expression Design. The width of the background image (and its color) is based on your calculations for the width of each column. You have created a background image named wrapper.gif that Pierre can use for the artnew.htm page. It was designed using the calculations you determined with Pierre for the artnew.htm column layout. The image has a width of 930px, but has a height of only 15px. The image appears in Figure 6-53.

Figure 6-53	The background image for faux columns

image has been created based on the layout calculations

You will enclose the three side-by-side columns in their own container, which you will name "wrapper." The wrapper.gif image will be used as the background image for the wrapper div. When you create the style for the wrapper id selector, you also need to use the overflow property with a value of auto so that the layout will appear correctly in the Firefox browser. The image will be repeated vertically. The longest column will set the height of the background image. You will enter the code for the wrapper id selector below the code for the container id selector.

To style the wrapper id selector:

1. In your text editor, scroll up the embedded style sheet if necessary, and position the insertion point after the end brace for the container id selector.

2. Press the **Enter** key twice.

3. Type the following code and CSS comment, as shown in Figure 6-54.

```
#wrapper {
    width: 930px;
    background-image: url(wrapper.gif);
    background-repeat: repeat-y;
    margin-bottom: 10px;
    overflow: auto; /* needed for Firefox */
}
```

Figure 6-54 ▶ **The wrapper id selector code**

the wrapper id selector code →

```
#wrapper {
    width: 930px;
    background-image: url(wrapper.gif);
    background-repeat: repeat-y;
    margin-bottom: 10px;
    overflow: auto; /* needed for Firefox */
}

#header {
    width: 930px;
    background-color: #6e8953;
    margin-bottom: 10px;
}

#sidebar {
    width: 200px;
    margin: 0 10px 10px 0;
```

▶ **4.** Save the file.

Next, in the body section, you need to insert the code for a start div tag for the wrapper id before the sidebar div. You also need to insert an end div tag after the section div.

To enter the div tags for the wrapper:

▶ **1.** In your text editor, and in the body area of the document, position the insertion point after the following line of code:

```
</div> <!-- end header -->
```

▶ **2.** Press the **Enter** key twice.

▶ **3.** On a blank line, type the following code, as shown in Figure 6-55.

```
<div id="wrapper">
```

Figure 6-55 ▶ **The start wrapper div code**

the start div for the wrapper →

```
<p><img src="artlogo.gif" alt="Anne Billings Art Gallery logo"
width="930" height="150" /></p>

</div> <!-- end header -->

<div id="wrapper">

<div id="sidebar">
<ul>
    <li><a href="#">Our History</a></li>
    <li><a href="#">Directions</a></li>
    <li><a href="#">Artist Profiles</a></li>
    <li><a href="#">Tickets</a></li>
    <li><a href="#">Contact Us</a></li>
</ul>
```

▶ **4.** Position the insertion point after the following line of code:

```
</div> <!-- end section -->
```

▶ **5.** Press the **Enter** key twice.

▶ **6.** On a blank line, type the following code, as shown in Figure 6-56.

```
</div> <!-- end wrapper -->
```

Figure 6-56 The end wrapper div code

```
<div id="caption">
<p>Boxes at Dawn
<br />Pierre Henri Bernard</p>
</div> <!-- end caption -->

</div> <!-- end section -->

</div> <!-- end wrapper -->

<div id="footer">

<p>The Anne Billings Art Gallery
<br />21 State Street &bull; Seattle, WA 24566
<br /><a href="#">Our History</a> | <a href="#">Directions</a> | <a
```

the end div for the wrapper

> **7.** Save the file.

> **8.** Switch to your browser, refresh or reload the page, and then compare your file to Figure 6-57 to confirm that the wrapper div has been styled correctly.

Figure 6-57 The wrapper div in the browser

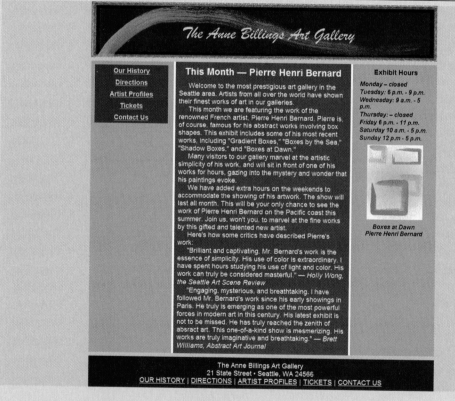

> **9.** If you will not be completing the Review Assignments or the Case Problems, exit your browser and your text editor.

> **10.** If you validate the artnew.htm file for the accuracy of the CSS code, you will receive this warning, which you can ignore: "Imported style sheets are not checked in direct input and file upload modes."

In this session, you learned how to create a three-column layout, learned about document flow, and learned how to use the @import rule to streamline the use of CSS libraries. You also learned about specificity and how to create faux columns to create the illusion of columns having equal height.

Review | **Session 6.2 Quick Check**

1. What is source order?
2. What rule is used to import one style sheet into another?
3. What is specificity?
4. What is another name for an element selector?
5. In determining specificity, which type of selector has the greatest weight? Which has the lowest?
6. What property is used to add scroll bars to a box if needed?
7. What are faux columns?

Review | **Tutorial Summary**

In this tutorial, you learned that there are several different methods to create Web page layouts, and you learned that you should know the most common methods so that you will be comfortable using them in the workplace. None of the methods is standard, and each has its advantages and disadvantages. You learned about fixed-width and fluid layouts. The id selector and the div tag are used to create and apply styles to a particular area of a Web page. You used the float property to position the div elements on the page. The document flow is the order in which the elements on the Web page are read. In addition to style precedence, you learned about specificity, which is used to resolve conflicts when the same element has been styled more than once in the same location. Finally, you used the faux column technique to create the illusion of equal columns.

Key Terms

@import rule
absolute positioning
bottom property
broken layout
column drop
column width
container div
content width
div element
document flow
faux columns
fixed-width layout
flanking columns

fluid layout
footer
gutter
header
import
left property
main content area
navbar
overflow property
parent container width
placeholder text
pull quote

relative positioning
right property
sidebar
source order
specificity
style sheet library
top property
universal selector
viewport
widget sidebars
zero out
z-index property

| Practice | **Review Assignments** |

Take time to practice the skills you learned in the tutorial using the same case scenario.

Data Files needed for the Review Assignments: artlogo.gif, direct.htm

Anne Billings has asked for your assistance in developing more pages at the Anne Billings Gallery Web site, including the important page that gives directions to the gallery. Because of ongoing construction, the Directions page needs extensive revision so that people driving to the gallery will know how to find an alternate route. You have already begun work on the document by styling some selectors and creating several divs in the body of the document. After you create a style in your text editor, save the file, switch to your browser, refresh or reload the page, verify that you entered the style code correctly, and then switch back to your text editor and complete the next step. A preview of the Web page you will create appears in Figure 6-58.

Figure 6-58

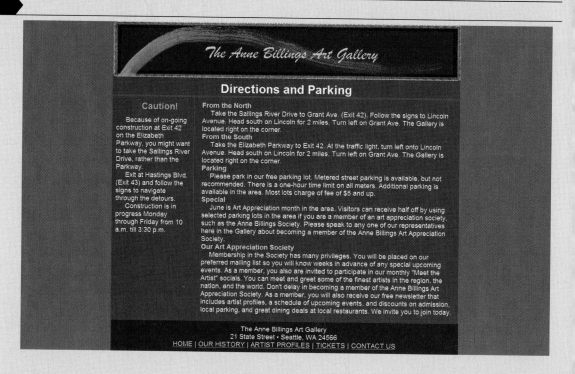

Complete the following:

1. Use your text editor to open the **direct.htm** file, which is provided in your Data Files in the Tutorial.06\Review folder. In the head section and below the page title, enter your name and today's date in the comment section where noted.
2. Save the file as **directnew.htm** in the same folder. Open the file in your browser and observe the appearance of the original file.
3. Switch back to your text editor. In the embedded style sheet and just below the CSS comment /* add new styles below */, style the body element as follows:
   - Set the font size to 1.1em.
   - Have the text appear in Arial, a sans-serif font.
   - Set the text color to white.
   - Set the background color to #6e8953.
4. Save the **directnew.htm** file. Switch back to your browser and refresh or reload the page to verify that the body element style appears correctly in your file.

5. Switch back to your text editor. In the embedded style sheet code, you will continue to add styles below the style for the body element. Create a style for the universal selector to have a margin of 0 and padding of 0.

6. Create a style for the #container id selector as follows:
   - Set the width to 930px.
   - Set the margin to 0 on the top and bottom and "auto" on the left and right.
   - Set the border width to 1px on all sides.
   - Set the background color to #425b5f.

7. Create a style for the #header id selector to have a width of 930px. Set the bottom margin to 10px. Set the background color to #6e8953.

8. Create a style for the #banner id selector to have a bottom border that is solid, thick, and teal. The banner id text should be centered.

9. Create the following styles for the #sidebar id selector:
   - Set the width to 200px.
   - Set the margin to 0 on the top, 10px on the right, 10px on the bottom, and 0 on the left.
   - Add padding of 10px on all sides.
   - Set the border on the right to appear as solid, thin, and teal.
   - Set the value of the float property to left.
   - Set the text indent to 1.4em.

10. Create the following styles for the #main id selector:
    - Set the width to 670px.
    - Set the margins to 0 on the top, 0 on the right, 10px on the bottom, and 0 on the left.
    - Add padding of 10px on all sides.
    - Set the value of the float property to left.

11. Create a descendant selector for the main id selector so that paragraphs in the main div have a text indent of 1.25em.

12. Save the **directnew.htm** file. Switch to your browser and refresh or reload the page. Compare your file to Figure 6-58 to verify that your file is correct.

13. Submit the results of the preceding steps to your instructor, either in printed or electronic form, as requested.

14. If you are not completing the next assignment, close your text editor and your browser.

| Apply | | **Case Problem 1** |

*he skills you
ed in the tutorial
·ate a Web page
business
zine.*

Data Files needed for this Case Problem: biz.htm, bizlogo.gif, cloth.gif

Biz Blizzard Magazine   Each month, Biz Blizzard Magazine, headquartered in San Antonio, Texas, publishes articles of interest to middle-level managers. Sheryl Jones, an editor at the magazine, has asked for your help in putting one of this month's lead stories on the magazine's Web page. The article focuses on how managers can deal with the thorny issue of employee tardiness. After meeting with Sheryl and creating a layout, you have been asked to further develop the Web page. After you complete a step to create a style, verify in your browser that the style code has been entered correctly, and then switch back to your text editor. A preview of the Web page you will create appears in Figure 6-59.

Figure 6-59

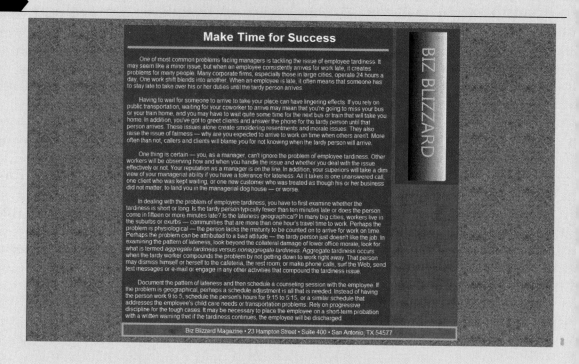

Complete the following:

1. Use your text editor to open the **biz.htm** file, which is provided in your Data Files in the Tutorial.06\Case1 folder. In the head section and below the page title, enter your name and today's date in the comment section where noted.

2. Save the file as **biznew.htm** in the same folder. Open the file in your browser and observe the appearance of the original file.

3. Switch back to your text editor. In the code for the embedded style sheet, style the body element to have text appear in white and in Arial (sans-serif). Use the cloth.gif image as a background image for the body element. The image should repeat.

4. Save the **biznew.htm** file. Switch back to your browser and refresh or reload the page. Verify that the body element style appears correctly in your file.

5. Switch back to your text editor. In the embedded style sheet and below the body style, create the following styles for the #container id selector:
   - Set the width to 900px.
   - Set the margin to 0 on the top and bottom and auto on the left and right.
   - Set the border width to 1px on all sides.
   - Set the background color to #837c63.

6. Create the following styles for the #sidebar id selector:
   - Set the width to 150px.
   - Add padding of 10px on all sides.
   - Have the text appear in white.
   - Set the background color to teal.
   - Set the value of the float property to right.

⊕ **EXPLORE**

7. Create a descendant selector for the sidebar so that images within the sidebar have a margin of 0 on the top and bottom and "auto" on the left and right. Set the display property so that the image is treated as a block-level element.

8. Create the following styles for the #main id selector:
    - Set the width to 700px.
    - Set the margin on the right to 10px.
    - Add padding of 10px on all sides.
    - Set the background color to teal.
    - Set the value of the float property to left.
    - Set the text indent to 2em.

9. Create a descendant selector for the #main id selector so that paragraph text within the main div has a font size of 1em.

10. Create a descendant selector for the #main id selector so that h1 heading text has a bottom border that is solid, thick, and orange. Add padding of 10px on the bottom. Center the h1 text.

11. Create the following styles for the #footer id selector.
    - Set the width to 880px.
    - Set the border on all four sides to be solid, 5px, and orange.
    - Add padding of 5px on all sides.
    - Set the background color to gray.
    - Clear both the left and right margins.
    - Center the footer text.

12. Save the **biznew.htm** file. Switch to your browser and refresh or reload the page. Compare your file to Figure 6-59 to verify that your file is correct. Depending on your browser and browser version, you might not see the same amount of padding as shown in Figure 6-59.

13. Submit the results of the preceding steps to your instructor, either in printed or electronic form, as requested.

14. If you are not completing the next assignment, close your text editor and your browser.

| Apply | **Case Problem 2** |

what you've
ed and expand
skills to create
style a Web page
jewelry store.

Data Files needed for this Case Problem: back.gif, griff.htm, grifflogo.gif, links.css

Griff Jewelers   Ernie Griff is the owner of Griff Jewelers in Little Rock, Arkansas. Griff Jewelers has been in the same location for more than 100 years. The store has built a loyal clientele that seeks gold, silver, or diamond jewelry at a variety of price points. Griff Jewelers has a large assortment of engagement and wedding rings at affordable prices, so the store attracts customers from more than a hundred miles away. Ernie seeks your help in creating a Web page for the store that will highlight the affordability of its jewelry. You will create a Web page using a fixed-width design with faux columns to create the illusion of columns of equal length. You will create a nested div in the sidebar column to call attention to the store's special sale on diamond pendants this month. You will also use an existing file named links.css to apply styles for the navigation bar. After you complete a step to create a style, verify in your browser that the style code has been entered correctly, and then switch back to your text editor. A preview of the Web page you will create appears in Figure 6-60.

Figure 6-60

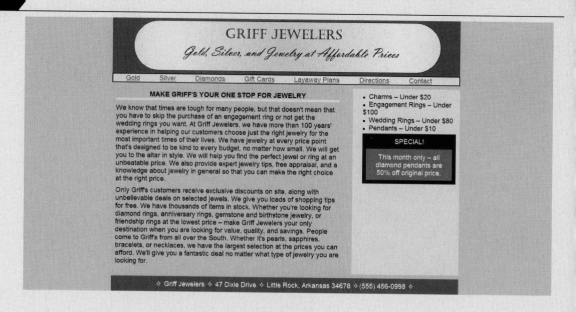

Complete the following:

1. Use your text editor to open the **griff.htm** file, which is provided in your Data Files in the Tutorial.06\Case2 folder. In the head section and below the page title, enter your name and today's date in the comment section where noted.

2. Save the file as **griffnew.htm** in the same folder. Open the file in your browser and observe the appearance of the original file.

EXPLORE

3. Switch back to your text editor. Within the embedded style sheet code, insert the code to import the **links.css** style sheet, which is provided in your Data Files in the Tutorial.06\Case2 folder.

4. Style the body element to have text appear in a font size of 1.1em and in Arial (sans-serif). The text should have a background color of #e1d387.

5. Save the **griffnew.htm** file. Switch back to your browser and refresh or reload the page. Verify that the body element style appears correctly in your file.

6. Switch back to your text editor. In the code for the embedded style sheet and below the body element style, create a style for the universal selector. Set the margin and padding to 0 on all sides.

7. Create a style for the #container id selector. The container should have a width of 940px, margins on the top and bottom of 0, and margins on the left and right set to auto. Set the border width to 1px on all sides.

8. Create the following styles for the #wrapper id selector:
   - Set the width to 930px.
   - Use the back.gif file as the background image for the wrapper.
   - Set the margin on the bottom to 10px.
   - Set the overflow property to have a value of auto. To the right of the auto value, type the following CSS comment: `/* needed for Firefox */`.

9. Create a style for the #header id selector to have a width of 940px.

10. Create the following styles for the #main id selector.
    - Set the width to 600px.
    - Set the margins to 0 on the top, 10px on the right, 10px on the bottom, and 0 on the left.

- Add padding of 10px on all sides.
- Set the value of the float property to left.

EXPLORE   11. Create a descendant selector for the main id selector so that paragraph text has a bottom margin of 10px.

12. Create the following styles for the sidebar id selector:
    - Set the width to 250px.
    - Set the margins to 0 on the top, 0 on the right, 10px on the bottom, and 0 on the left.
    - Add padding of 10px on all sides.
    - Set the value of the float property to right.

13. Create a descendant selector for the sidebar id that creates a style for the unordered list element. The list should have a list style type of square and a list style position of inside. To the right of the value for the list style position, type the following CSS comment: /* needed for IE */.

14. Create the following styles for the #special id selector:
    - Set the top margin to 5px.
    - Add padding of 10px on all sides.
    - Set the text color to white.
    - Set the background color to navy.
    - Center the text.

15. Create the following styles for the #content id selector:
    - Set the top margin to 10px.
    - Add padding of 10px on all sides.
    - Set the text color to white.
    - Set the background color to olive.

16. Create the following styles for the h3 element selector:
    - Set the bottom margin to 10px.
    - Set the bottom border to have values of solid, thick, and yellow.
    - Center the text.
    - Set the text to appear in uppercase.

17. Create the following styles for the #footer id selector:
    - Set the width to 910px.
    - Set the margin to 0 on all sides.
    - Add padding of 10px to all sides.
    - Set the color to white.
    - Set the background color to #595959.
    - Clear all elements on both the left and the right.
    - Center the text.

18. Save the **griffnew.htm** file.

19. Switch to your browser and refresh or reload the page. Compare your file to Figure 6-60 to verify that your file is correct.

20. Submit the results of the **griffnew.htm** file to your instructor, either in printed or electronic form, as requested.

21. If you are not completing the next assignment, close your text editor and your browser.

Challenge | Case Problem 3

Use the skills you learned in the tutorial to create and style a Web page for a financial newsletter.

Data Files needed for this Case Problem: footer.css, greenback.gif, ziller.htm, zillerstyles.css

The Ziller Financial Group The Ziller Financial Group ("the Ziller Group") is an investment firm in Strasbourg, Pennsylvania. In the past, the Ziller Group has relied upon a printed publication to address its audience, which is a savvy group of financial investors. The Ziller Group now wants to establish a Web presence. You have been asked to create a Web page that closely matches the format of the firm's printed publication. To do so, you will create a three-column fixed-width layout. After you complete a step to create a style, verify in your browser that the style code has been entered correctly, and then switch back to your text editor. A preview of the Web page you will create appears in Figure 6-61.

Figure 6-61

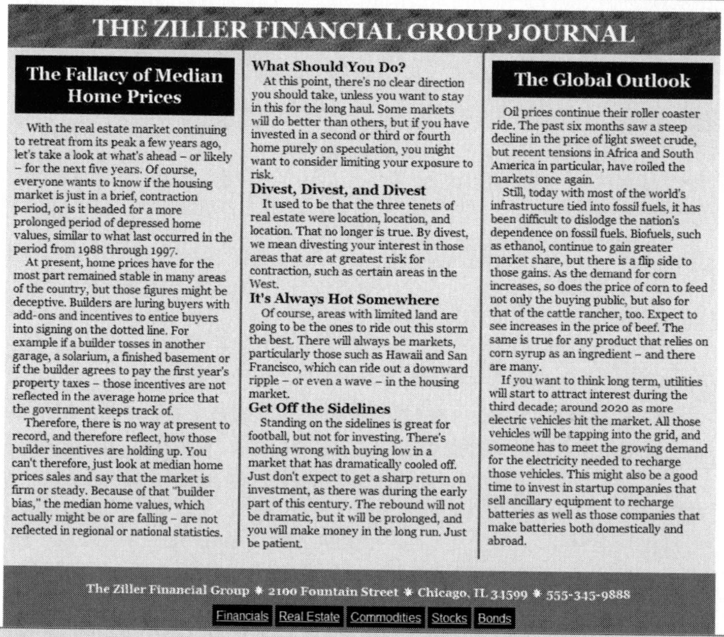

THE ZILLER FINANCIAL GROUP JOURNAL

The Fallacy of Median Home Prices

With the real estate market continuing to retreat from its peak a few years ago, let's take a look at what's ahead – or likely – for the next five years. Of course, everyone wants to know if the housing market is just in a brief, contraction period, or is it headed for a more prolonged period of depressed home values, similar to what last occurred in the period from 1988 through 1997.

At present, home prices have for the most part remained stable in many areas of the country, but those figures might be deceptive. Builders are luring buyers with add-ons and incentives to entice buyers into signing on the dotted line. For example if a builder tosses in another garage, a solarium, a finished basement or if the builder agrees to pay the first year's property taxes – those incentives are not reflected in the average home price that the government keeps track of.

Therefore, there is no way at present to record, and therefore reflect, how those builder incentives are holding up. You can't therefore, just look at median home prices sales and say that the market is firm or steady. Because of that "builder bias," the median home values, which actually might be or are falling – are not reflected in regional or national statistics.

What Should You Do?

At this point, there's no clear direction you should take, unless you want to stay in this for the long haul. Some markets will do better than others, but if you have invested in a second or third or fourth home purely on speculation, you might want to consider limiting your exposure to risk.

Divest, Divest, and Divest

It used to be that the three tenets of real estate were location, location, and location. That no longer is true. By divest, we mean divesting your interest in those areas that are at greatest risk for contraction, such as certain areas in the West.

It's Always Hot Somewhere

Of course, areas with limited land are going to be the ones to ride out this storm the best. There will always be markets, particularly those such as Hawaii and San Francisco, which can ride out a downward ripple – or even a wave – in the housing market.

Get Off the Sidelines

Standing on the sidelines is great for football, but not for investing. There's nothing wrong with buying low in a market that has dramatically cooled off. Just don't expect to get a sharp return on investment, as there was during the early part of this century. The rebound will not be dramatic, but it will be prolonged, and you will make money in the long run. Just be patient.

The Global Outlook

Oil prices continue their roller coaster ride. The past six months saw a steep decline in the price of light sweet crude, but recent tensions in Africa and South America in particular, have roiled the markets once again.

Still, today with most of the world's infrastructure tied into fossil fuels, it has been difficult to dislodge the nation's dependence on fossil fuels. Biofuels, such as ethanol, continue to gain greater market share, but there is a flip side to those gains. As the demand for corn increases, so does the price of corn to feed not only the buying public, but also for that of the cattle rancher, too. Expect to see increases in the price of beef. The same is true for any product that relies on corn syrup as an ingredient – and there are many.

If you want to think long term, utilities will start to attract interest during the third decade; around 2020 as more electric vehicles hit the market. All those vehicles will be tapping into the grid, and someone has to meet the growing demand for the electricity needed to recharge those vehicles. This might also be a good time to invest in startup companies that sell ancillary equipment to recharge batteries as well as those companies that make batteries both domestically and abroad.

The Ziller Financial Group ✱ 2100 Fountain Street ✱ Chicago, IL 34599 ✱ 555-345-9888

Financials | Real Estate | Commodities | Stocks | Bonds

Complete the following:

1. Use your text editor to open the **ziller.htm** file, which is provided in your Data Files in the Tutorial.06\Case3 folder. In the head section and below the page title, enter your name and today's date in the comment section where noted.
2. Save the file as **zillernew.htm** in the same folder. Open the file in your browser and observe the appearance of the original file.
3. Switch back to your text editor. Just below the start style tag, enter the @import rule to import the footer.css file, which is provided in your Data Files in the Tutorial.06\Case3 folder.
4. Style the body element as follows:
   - Set the font size to 1em.
   - Set the font to Georgia, a serif font.
   - Set the top margin to 1em.
5. Save the **zillernew.htm** file. Switch back to your browser and refresh or reload the page. Verify that the body element style appears correctly in your file.

6. Switch back to your text editor. Below the body element style, style the universal selector to have margins set to 0 and padding set to 0.

7. Style the #container id as follows:
   - Set the width to 960px.
   - Set the margin to 0 on the top and bottom and auto on the left and right.
   - Set the border width to 1px on all sides.
   - Set the background color to #f3f6e9.

8. Style the #header id selector to have a width of 960px.

9. Style the #left id selector as follows:
   - Enter the width property, but leave its value blank for now.
   - Add padding of 10px to all sides.
   - Create a border on the right that is solid, 3px, and teal.
   - Set the value of the float property to left.

10. Style the #middle id selector just as you did the #left id selector. (Again, leave the value for the width property blank for now.)

11. Style the #right id selector just as you styled the #left id and #middle id selectors, but do not create a border.

EXPLORE 12. The three columns should be of equal width. Using the information supplied in the #container, #left, #middle, and #right id selectors, determine values for the width property for each of the left, middle, and right columns. After you complete your calculations, enter the width value in the code for each of the #left, #middle, and #right id selectors.

13. Style the h1 heading element as follows:
   - Add padding of 10px to all sides.
   - Have text appear in white.
   - Center the h1 text.
   - Using the background shorthand property to write one declaration, use the greenback.gif image as a background image. The background color should be teal. Repeat the image both horizontally and vertically.
   - Have the h1 text appear in uppercase.

14. Style the h2 heading element as follows:
   - Add padding of 10px to all sides.
   - Set the bottom margin to 10px.
   - Have text appear in white.
   - Set the background color to navy.
   - Center the h2 text.

15. Style the p element to have a text indent of 1em.

16. Save the **zillernew.htm** file. Switch to your browser and refresh or reload the page. Compare your file to Figure 6-61 to verify that your file is correct.

17. Switch back to your text editor. In the embedded style sheet, delete all of the code for the start <style> tag. Delete the end </style> tag. Select all of the remaining CSS code for the embedded style sheet. Press the Ctrl+X keys to cut the CSS code.

18. In the head section and on a blank line below the page title, enter the code to link to a CSS file named **zillerstylesnew.css**.

19. Save and then close the **zillernew.htm** file.

20. In your text editor, open the **zillerstyles.css** file, which is provided in your Data Files in the Tutorial.06\Case3 folder. Enter your name and today's date in the comment section where noted.

21. On a blank line below the comment code, paste the CSS code that you cut from zillernew.htm.

22. Save the file as **zillerstylesnew.css** in the same folder.

23. Switch to your browser and refresh or reload the **zillernew.htm** page. Compare your file to Figure 6-61 to verify that your file is correct.

24. In your browser, go to *http://validator.w3.org* to open the W3C validator. Validate the **zillernew.htm** file by using the Validate by File Upload method. Note any errors and correct them in your file if necessary.

25. In your browser, navigate to *http://jigsaw.w3.org/css-validator*. Validate the **zillerstylesnew.css** file by using the By file upload method. Note any errors and correct them in your file if necessary. You can ignore the following warning you will receive regarding the imported style sheet: "Imported style sheets are not checked in direct input and file upload modes."

26. Submit the results of the **zillernew.htm** and **zillerstylesnew.css** files to your instructor, either in printed or electronic form, as requested.

27. If you are not completing the next assignment, close your text editor and your browser.

Create	**Case Problem 4**

Create a Web page for a corporate travel agency.

Data Files needed for this Case Problem: rounded.png, travel.css, travel.htm, triangle.gif

Triangle Travel Planners Olivia Henry is the owner of Triangle Travel Planners ("Triangle"), a corporate travel agency in Manhattan, New York. Triangle specializes in sending weary executives and their families to exotic locales across the globe. Olivia wants your help in choosing several new travel destinations. She would like you to research new places to travel, and then create a Web page for the Triangle Web site that lists the exciting places you selected based on your research. An image named triangle.gif has been provided for the banner, and several styles for the sidebar have been created for you. The rounded.png image is used in the sidebar column to create a tab with rounded corners. In the travel.htm file, use the comments as your guide to structure the Web page.

Complete the following:

1. Use your text editor to open the **travel.htm** file, which is provided in your Data Files in the Tutorial.06\Case4 folder. In the head section, give your page an appropriate title. Below the page title, enter your name and today's date in the comment section where noted.

2. Save the file as **travelnew.htm** in the same folder.

3. Within the tags for the embedded style sheet, format the body element with the text size, font, color, and background color of your choice.

4. In the body section, enter at least five paragraphs of text that describe the destinations you have chosen.

5. Plan a fixed-width layout for the travelnew.htm file. The layout should be 900px wide and have two columns. The layout should have divs for a header, sidebar, main section, and footer. The sidebar id selector has already been styled, and the sidebar div has already been created for you. Use the triangle.gif image in the header div. Include margins and padding as appropriate in your layout to make it attractive and readable.

6. Create styles for all the id selectors.

7. In the body section, create divs as necessary. Apply the id selectors to your divs as appropriate.

8. Create a container div for your layout. Create styles for the container div so that the page is centered horizontally in the browser.

9. Include at least one example of the use of a descendant selector.
10. Save the **travelnew.htm** file. Switch to your browser and refresh or reload the page. Verify that all styles work correctly.
11. Switch back to the **travelnew.htm** file in your text editor.
12. In the **travelnew.htm** file, delete the start and end style tags in the embedded style sheet.
13. In the head section, use the link element to create a link to a CSS file named **travelnew.css**.
14. Cut the remaining embedded style sheet code from the travelnew.htm file.
15. Save the **travelnew.htm** file. Close the file.
16. In your text editor, open the **travel.css** file, which is provided in your Data Files in the Tutorial.06\Case4 folder.
17. Below the CSS comment code, paste the CSS code that you cut from the travelnew.htm file. Enter your name and today's date in the CSS comment section where noted.
18. Save the CSS file as **travelnew.css**. Close the file.
19. Open your browser and go to *http://validator.w3.org*. Use the Validate by File Upload method to check the **travelnew.htm** document and ensure that the XHTML code is correct. If necessary, correct any errors detected by the validation, and then open the file in the browser to confirm that the file is correct.
20. In your browser, go to *http://jigsaw.w3.org/css-validator*. Use the By file upload method to check the **travelnew.css** file and ensure that the CSS code is correct. If necessary, correct any errors detected by the validation.
21. Submit the results of the **travelnew.htm** and **travelnew.css** files to your instructor, either in printed or electronic form, as requested.
22. Close your text editor and your browser. Close all open windows.

Review | Quick Check Answers

Session 6.1

1. The layout is said to be broken.
2. fixed-width and fluid
3. the document window
4. When there is not enough room for the column to fit, it will drop below where it was designed to appear.
5. Content width is the width of the content alone; column width is the combined width of the content, the left and right margins, borders, and padding.
6. header, navbar, sidebar, main, and footer
7. none

Session 6.2

1. the order of the content in the document flow
2. @import
3. Specificity determines priorities and uses a weighting method to calculate which style rule will prevail if there are conflicting rules in the same source.
4. type selector
5. The id selector has the greatest weight, and the element selector has the lowest.
6. overflow
7. added background images to create the illusion that columns have equal height

Ending Data Files

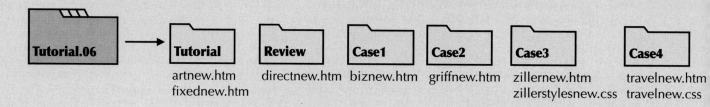

Tutorial.06 → **Tutorial**

artnew.htm
fixednew.htm

Review

directnew.htm

Case1

biznew.htm

Case2

griffnew.htm

Case3

zillernew.htm
zillerstylesnew.css

Case4

travelnew.htm
travelnew.css

Creating Liquid Layouts

Creating Flexible Widths for Layouts

Case | The Sundown Spa and Resort

The Sundown Spa and Resort, about a two-hour drive north of Augusta, Maine, has long been noted as a retreat for people who want to get away from the demands and stresses of city life. The company's business and marketing offices, however, are in Augusta. Nestled deep in the pristine and peaceful Maine woods, the Sundown Spa and Resort (the "Sundown Spa") attracts affluent visitors from all over the United States. Local residents take advantage of reduced off-season rates. Although the natural beauty of the lakes and woodlands are major attractions, there is more to the spa than fantastic scenery. The Sundown Spa has customized programs so that the nutritional and health needs of each guest are looked after as well. The owner, Paula Dodd, has asked for your assistance in creating a new home page for the Sundown Spa and Resort Web site.

Starting Data Files

Tutorial.07

Tutorial
button.gif
carnation.gif
glade.jpg
liquid.htm
printstyles.css
spa.htm
spalogo.gif
sunflower.gif

Review
gift.htm
giftlogo.gif

Case1
car.jpg
reddie.htm
reddielogo.gif

Case2
block.gif
letter.htm
modblock.gif
printstyles.css

Case3
lana.htm
lanalogo.gif
navbar.css
tailfin.gif

Case4
hooks.htm
hookslogo.gif

Session 7.1

Creating a Two-Column Liquid Layout

Over the last few years, wide-screen monitors have become quite popular, but such monitors have created a design challenge: whether to design for the traditional **portrait orientation**, in which the page is taller than it is wide, or to design for a **landscape orientation**, in which the page is wider than it is long. In the past, most Web pages were designed based on a screen resolution of 800×600 pixels, but most Web pages today are designed based on a screen resolution of 1024×768 pixels or greater.

In designing a Web page for a landscape orientation, you must ensure that the Web page is not only aesthetically pleasing, but readable. Long lines of text are harder to read, which is why newspapers and magazines have several narrow columns of text on a page rather than one wide column. Opinions vary about the optimal line lengths for Web pages; a safe rule is to have columns with line lengths of 60 to 80 characters.

In the last tutorial, you used fixed-width layouts and calculated how wide you wanted the content to be, but those layouts were based on an educated guess about the user's screen resolution. If the user's resolution is far greater than 1024 pixels, your design might waste a lot of space that you could fill with content instead. By designing for a wider page layout, you ensure that the user does not have to scroll down the page to view additional content. The great advantage of fluid layouts is that you don't have to guess about the width of the user's viewport.

The two most common types of fluid layouts are liquid layouts and elastic layouts. A **liquid layout** is a design that expands or contracts in proportion to the size of the user's viewport. In a liquid layout, the column widths are determined using percentage values, not pixel values. Just as with fixed layouts, you must consider the widths of the margins, padding, and borders for each column. Then you choose how much of the screen width to use—you can use the entire screen width or restrict the screen width to a certain percentage of the viewport. By restricting the screen width, you can center the layout horizontally and have greater assurance that line lengths will not be an issue.

In an **elastic layout**, em values are used instead of percentage values to determine column widths. Elastic layouts work well because ems are relative units, so text becomes larger or smaller based on user preferences set in the browser. The disadvantage to elastic layouts is that you must convert pixels to em units.

In a **hybrid layout**, part of the content (such as the header and navbar) may have a liquid layout and occupy the entire screen width, while the remainder of the content may have a fixed-width layout. Figure 7-1 summarizes the different categories of Web page layouts.

Tip

Most computer monitors sold today have a resolution greater than 1024px.

Tip

Fluid layouts are also known as flexible layouts.

Figure 7-1	The different categories of Web page layouts

Layout	Approach
Elastic	Measurements are in em values. If you want, the layout can use the entire screen width.
Fixed Width	Measurements are in pixels. The layout has a fixed screen width and usually does not occupy the entire screen width.
Hybrid	Both fixed-width and fluid layouts exist on the same Web page.
Liquid	Measurements are in percentages. If you want, the layout can use the entire screen width.

You have decided to show Paula how to create a liquid layout. You'll start in this session with a practice file named liquid.htm, and then in the next session you'll use the principles of liquid design to help her create a home page for the Sundown Spa. You'll show Paula how to open the file you have created, enter a comment, and then save the file with a new filename.

To open the liquid.htm file and save it with a new filename:

▶ **1.** In your text editor, open the **liquid.htm** file, which is located in the Tutorial.07\ Tutorial folder included with your Data Files. In the head section and below the page title, enter your name and today's date in the comment section where noted.

▶ **2.** Save the file as **liquidnew.htm** in the same folder.

Next, you'll start the practice layout by creating a header id selector for the document.

Adding a Header to the Document

Unlike a fixed-width layout, you don't specify a width for the header div in a liquid layout. The header has some text, so you will specify some padding in the header id selector. You'll also give the header a bottom margin to create some breathing room between the header and the content that follows. As you create these styles, note that the padding and margin values will be expressed in percentages (which are relative values), not pixels (which are absolute values). In the liquid.htm file, the code to style the universal selector to "zero out" the margins has already been entered. The universal selector also plays an important part in preventing **column droop**, in which the top of one or more columns is slightly lower than the other columns. Column droop occurs when the bottom margin of a div element competes for the same space as the top margin of another block-level element, such as a paragraph or heading (recall that most columns begin with a block-level element). By using the universal selector to zero out the margins of all block-level elements, you eliminate the competition for margin space, and you should not see column droop in your layouts.

You will now show Paula how to enter the code for the header id selector.

To style the header id selector:

▶ **1.** In your text editor, within the embedded style sheet and on a blank line below the end brace for the body element style code, type the following code, as shown in Figure 7-2.

```
#header {
  padding: 0.5%;
  margin-bottom: 0.5%;
  background-color: #d7d556;
}
```

Figure 7-2	The header id selector code

```
body {
  font-size: 1.1em;
  font-family: Arial, Helvetica, sans-serif;
  background-color: #ece1ef;
}

#header {
  padding: 0.5%;
  margin-bottom: 0.5%;
  background-color: #d7d556;
}
```

the header id selector code

▶ **2.** Save the file.

▶ **3.** Switch to your browser and open the **liquidnew.htm** page. Compare your file with the one shown in Figure 7-3 to verify that the header has been styled correctly.

Figure 7-3 **The header styled in the browser**

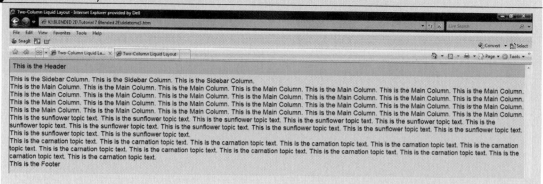

Next, you'll show Paula how to create the layout by planning the sidebar and main columns.

Creating the Sidebar and Main Columns

Paula wants the layout to consist of two columns: a narrow sidebar column on the left and a wider main column on the right. Although it is common to place a list of links in a navbar, you will instead create a navbar row later below the header, which also is common in layouts. You have already created the div sections and entered appropriate comments to denote the location of the divs in the body section of the liquidnew.htm document.

Reference Window | **Creating Two-Column Liquid Layouts**

To create a two-column liquid layout:

- Decide the width (in percentages) of the narrower of the two columns. Generally, the sidebar column is narrow and the main column is wide.
- Decide whether you want the sidebar column to appear on the left or the right.
- In the style sheet, enter the code for the sidebar and main id selectors. Assign a width (as a percentage) to the sidebar column. Do not assign a width to the main column.
- In the document body, enter start and end div tags for the sidebar and main divs.
- If you are not floating all the id selectors, change the source order so that the floated content appears before nonfloated content.

Paula wants the sidebar column to be floated left. Any element that is floated must have a width, so you will assign a width of 25% for the sidebar column. By establishing a width for the sidebar column, you ensure that the column will remain narrow, as intended. The remainder of the screen width will be occupied by the main column. You will not give the main column a width and you will not float it. You will now show Paula how to create the id selectors for the sidebar and main columns. You'll give each column a different background color so you can quickly tell if the layout is correct.

To style the sidebar and main id selectors:

  1. In your text editor, on a blank line below the header id selector style code, type the following code, as shown in Figure 7-4.

```
#sidebar {
  width: 25%;
  background-color: orange;
  float: left;
}

#main {
  background-color: aqua;
}
```

Figure 7-4 | **The sidebar and main id selector code**

the sidebar and main id selector code →

```
#sidebar {
  width: 25%;
  background-color: orange;
  float: left;
}

#main {
  background-color: aqua;
}

</style>
```

▶ **2.** Save the file.

▶ **3.** Switch to your browser and refresh or reload the **liquidnew.htm** page. Compare your file with the one shown in Figure 7-5. Depending on your browser and browser version, your file may look somewhat different from the one in Figure 7-5.

Figure 7-5 | **The sidebar and main columns in the browser**

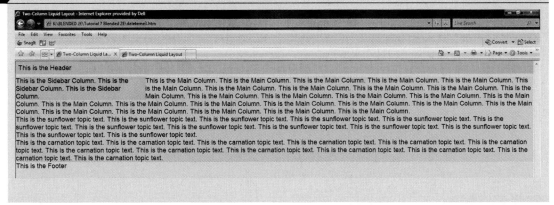

InSight | **Using the Span Element**

The **span element** is an inline element. Like the block-level div element, it does not create any formatting of its own. You style the span element as you would any other element. To apply the span style, however, you surround the inline content with start and end span tags, as shown in the following code:

`<span>content</span>`

Some Web designers use the span element as a means of developing layout, especially to position a particular object on the page. To keep your presentation and document structure separate, it's a good idea to limit or avoid the use of the span element on your Web pages. Use the box properties and the classification properties to format and position elements. Similar to inline styles, you don't want to populate the body of your documents with formatting-specific structures or styles.

Although the sidebar column floats to the left, and the text for the main column wraps to the right of the sidebar column, there is an obvious problem: neither of these columns looks like a column. To correctly position the main column, you have to establish some distance between it and the sidebar column. To do that, you will create a left margin for the main id selector that is at least equal to the width of the sidebar id selector. The sidebar is currently 25% of the screen width, so you will show Paula how to add a left margin of 25% to the main id selector code.

To create a left margin for the main column:

1. Switch back to your text editor, and position the insertion point after the start brace ({) in the main id selector code.

2. Press the **Enter** key to create a new line and then press the **Spacebar** twice.

3. Type the following line of code, as shown in Figure 7-6.

```
#main {
  margin-left: 25%;
  background-color: aqua;
}
```

| Figure 7-6 | The margin-left declaration for the main id selector |

```
#sidebar {
  width: 25%;
  background-color: orange;
  float: left;
}

#main {
  margin-left: 25%;
  background-color: aqua;
}
```

left margin is set to 25% →

4. Save the file.

5. Switch to your browser and refresh or reload the **liquidnew.htm** page. Compare your file with the one shown in Figure 7-7 to confirm that the main column has been repositioned to the right. Depending on your browser and browser version, your file may look somewhat different from the one in Figure 7-7.

| Figure 7-7 | The main column repositioned |

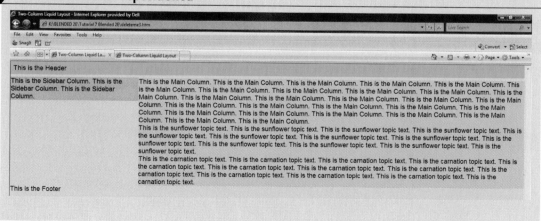

Tip

uid layouts, use per-
values for padding
margins.

Recall that the margins and padding have been zeroed out in the style for the universal selector, so the column text does not have any surrounding white space. Borders present a problem, though, because browsers do not recognize percentage values for border widths, and em values do not display correctly for border widths. In addition, browsers differ on the thicknesses of the keyword values "thin," "medium," and "thick." You can use keywords or pixel values to set border widths, but preview your file in several contemporary browsers to see if you need to modify the border widths. If you do use borders in a liquid layout, make sure that the total of your column widths (in percentages) is slightly less than 100%. If you don't account for the border widths, your layout will break.

Paula would like to add padding of 0.5% to all sides of both the sidebar and main columns, so there will be 0.5% padding on the left and on the right—a total of 1%. You will show her how to add the padding declarations now.

Tip

you use borders to
e vertical lines
een columns, apply
orders to the left or
sides of the longest
nns in the layout.

To add padding to the columns:

▶ 1. Switch back to your text editor, and position the insertion point after the semicolon in the `width: 25%;` declaration in the sidebar id selector code.

▶ 2. Press the **Enter** key to create a new line, and then press the **Spacebar** twice.

▶ 3. Type the following code, as shown in Figure 7-8.

```
#sidebar {
  width: 25%;
  padding: 0.5%;
  background-color: orange;
  float: left;
}
```

Figure 7-8 ▶ **The padding declaration for the sidebar id selector**

padding of 0.5% is
added to the sidebar

```
#sidebar {
  width: 25%;
  padding: 0.5%;
  background-color: orange;
  float: left;
}
```

▶ 4. Position the insertion point after the margin-left declaration in the main id selector style.

▶ 5. Press the **Enter** key to create a new line, and then press the **Spacebar** twice.

▶ 6. Type the following code, as shown in Figure 7-9.

```
#main {
  margin-left: 25%;
  padding: 0.5%;
  background-color: aqua;
}
```

Figure 7-9 ▶ **The padding declaration for the main id selector**

padding of 0.5%
added to the
main id selector

```
#main {
  margin-left: 25%;
  padding: 0.5%;
  background-color: aqua;
}
```

▶ 7. Save the file.

8. Switch to your browser and refresh or reload the **liquidnew.htm** page. Compare your file with the one shown in Figure 7-10 to confirm that padding has been added to both the sidebar and the main divs. (Don't be concerned if the sidebar column slightly overlaps the main column; you'll fix that in a moment.)

Figure 7-10 **The padding in the browser**

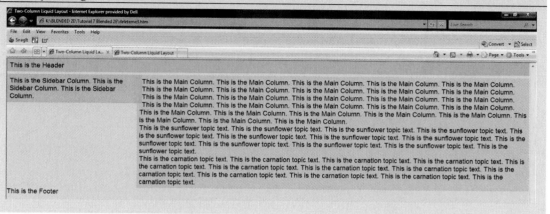

Although padding has been added, you see a new problem. There isn't any gutter space between the columns. The sidebar column is overlapping the main column. To create some gutter space between the columns, you must change the value for the left margin property of the main id selector. Padding totaling 1% was added to the left and the right of the sidebar column, so you will show Paula how to change the value for the margin-left property from 25% to 27%, which will be enough space to create a gutter between the two columns.

To edit the margin-left property for the main id selector:

1. Switch back to your text editor, and change the value for the margin-left property in the main id selector from 25% to 27%, as shown in Figure 7-11.

```
#main {
    margin-left: 27%;
    padding: 0.5%;
    background-color: aqua;
}
```

Figure 7-11 **The value for the margin-left property increased to 27%**

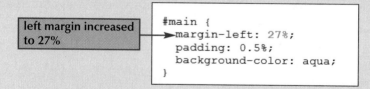

left margin increased to 27%

```
#main {
    margin-left: 27%;
    padding: 0.5%;
    background-color: aqua;
}
```

Trouble? If there still is not enough white space between the columns, increase the value for the margin-left property by an additional 1 or 2 percent.

2. Save the file.

3. Switch to your browser and refresh or reload the **liquidnew.htm** page. Compare your file with the one shown in Figure 7-12 to confirm that gutter space now exists between the sidebar and main columns.

Figure 7-12   **Gutter space added between the columns**

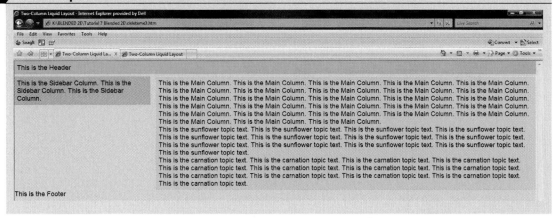

Paula is curious to know if the layout can be changed so that the sidebar column is on the right rather than the left. You will show her how easy it is to rearrange the order of the columns.

Repositioning the Sidebar Column

You tell Paula that it will take just two changes to flip the order of the columns. You will float the sidebar column right, and you will give the main column a margin on the right instead of on the left. You will show Paula how to make these two revisions to the id selector code now.

To edit the code for the sidebar and main id selectors:

1. Switch back to your text editor. In the sidebar id selector code, change the value for the float property to "right," as shown in Figure 7-13.

```
#sidebar {
   width: 25%;
   padding: 0.5%;
   background-color: orange;
   float: right;
}
```

2. In the main id selector code, change the margin-left property to the margin-right property, as shown in Figure 7-13.

```
#main {
   margin-right: 27%;
   padding: 0.5%;
   background-color: aqua;
}
```

Figure 7-13 > **Revisions made to the sidebar and main id selectors**

> sidebar will now be floated right and main id selector now has a right margin

```
#sidebar {
    width: 25%;
    padding: 0.5%;
    background-color: orange;
    float: right;
}

#main {
    margin-right: 27%;
    padding: 0.5%;
    background-color: aqua;
}
```

> **3.** Save the file.

> **4.** Switch to your browser and refresh or reload the **liquidnew.htm** page. Compare your file with the one shown in Figure 7-14 to confirm that the sidebar is now on the right.

Figure 7-14 > **The sidebar repositioned to the right**

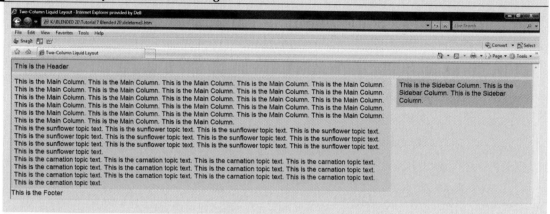

Paula likes the sidebar in the new position, so now that the layout has been determined, you will show her how to develop some of the other parts of the page.

Creating a Navigation Bar

Paula would like to know how to position a navigation bar below the header. To create a style for the navigation bar, you first will show Paula how to enter an unordered list. The list items in the unordered list will serve as the link text. The links are just placeholder links for now; the actual target pages will be added later as the site is developed further.

To insert the code for the navbar div:

> **1.** Switch back to your text editor. In the document body, on a blank line below the end </div> tag and the comment for the header div, type the following code, as shown in Figure 7-15.

```
<div id="navbar">
<ul>
  <li><a href="#">first link text</a></li>
  <li><a href="#">second link text</a></li>
  <li><a href="#">third link text</a></li>
</ul>
</div> <!-- end navbar -->
```

Figure 7-15 ▶ **The navbar div code**

```
<div id="header">
<p>This is the Header</p>
</div> <!-- end header -->

<div id="navbar">
<ul>
  <li><a href="#">first link text</a></li>
  <li><a href="#">second link text</a></li>
  <li><a href="#">third link text</a></li>
</ul>
</div> <!—end navbar -->
```

unordered list code for the navigation bar

▶ **2.** Save the file.

Next, you will create the style for an id selector named "navbar," which will be used to style the links. You'll set the value for the list style type property to "none" because you do not want any list item markers, such as bullets, in the navigation bar. You'll also display the list horizontally rather than vertically. To create the illusion of a button, you will show Paula how to use the background property to create a background for the link text. The links use a file named button.gif as a background image. You'll choose not to have the image repeat. You'll also center the image horizontally and vertically by using the keywords "center center," and you'll add a margin on the right to create some distance between the links.

To style the navbar links:

▶ **1.** In your text editor and on a blank line below the main id selector code, type the following code, as shown in Figure 7-16.

```
#navbar ul li {
   margin-right: 1em;
   background: url(button.gif) no-repeat center center;
   display: inline;
   list-style-type: none;
}

#navbar li a {
   padding: 1em;
   color: white;
   text-decoration: none;
}
```

Figure 7-16 The navbar id selectors code

```
#main {
  margin-right: 27%;
  padding: 0.5%;
  background-color: aqua;
}

#navbar ul li {
  margin-right: 1em;
  background: url(button.gif) no-repeat center center;
  display: inline;
  list-style-type: none;
}

#navbar li a {
  padding: 1em;
  color: white;
  text-decoration: none;
}
```

list items will display inline to create the navigation bar effect

▶ **2.** Save the file.

▶ **3.** Switch to your browser and refresh or reload the **liquidnew.htm** page. Compare your file with the one shown in Figure 7-17 to confirm that links now appear below the header.

Figure 7-17 The link text in the browser

link text

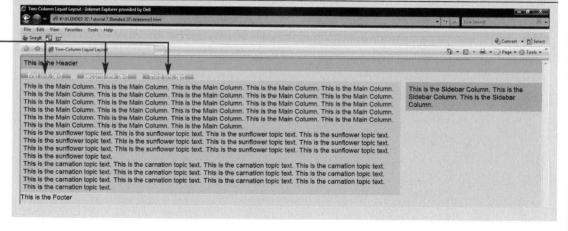

You tell Paula that she can give the links greater visual interest by creating a hover effect for them. She can create this effect by changing the link text color to yellow and underlining the text.

To create the hover effect:

▶ **1.** In your text editor and on a blank line below the navbar li a id selector code, type the following code, as shown in Figure 7-18.

```
#navbar li a:hover {
  color: yellow;
  text-decoration: underline;
}
```

Figure 7-18 | The hover effect code

```
#navbar li a {
   padding: 1em;
   color: white;
   text-decoration: none;
}

#navbar li a:hover {
   color: yellow;
   text-decoration: underline;
}

</style>
```

the hover effect is created

▶ **2.** Save the file.

▶ **3.** Switch to your browser and refresh or reload the **liquidnew.htm** page. Pass the mouse pointer over any of the links to confirm that the hover effect is working properly, and that the link text appears in yellow when the mouse passes over it, as shown in Figure 7-19.

Figure 7-19 | The hover effect in the browser

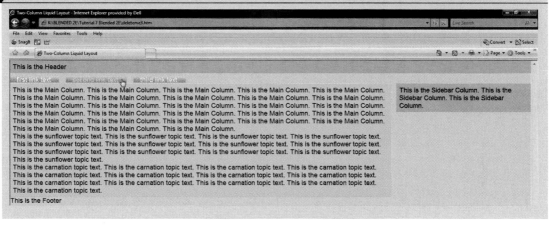

You will now show Paula how to add a footer to the layout.

Creating a Footer

Paula would like a footer to appear below both the main column and the sidebar column. The footer is primarily used for address and contact information, but you will enter only placeholder text for this practice document. The footer must clear the longest column, which currently is the main column, on the left. Instead of using "left" as the value for the clear property, you will use the value of "both." The advantage of this approach is that no matter how the columns are positioned, the value of "both" will always work, whereas the value of "left" or "right" will only clear the footer div based on what is currently the longer column.

To insert the code for the footer id selector:

▶ **1.** In your text editor and on a blank line below the code for the navbar li a:hover id selector, type the following code, as shown in Figure 7-20.

```
#footer {
  margin: 0.5% 0 0 0;
  border-top: solid thick teal;
  padding: 0.5%;
  background-color: lime;
  clear: both;
}
```

Figure 7-20 ▶ **The footer id selector code**

```
#navbar li a:hover {
  color: yellow;
  text-decoration: underline;
}

#footer {
  margin: 0.5% 0 0 0;
  border-top: solid thick teal;
  padding: 0.5%;
  background-color: lime;
  clear: both;
}

</style>
```

code to style the footer

2. Save the file.

3. Switch to your browser and refresh or reload the **liquidnew.htm** page. Compare your file with the one shown in Figure 7-21 to confirm that the footer appears below the main column and is clear of the main column.

Figure 7-21 ▶ **The footer in the browser**

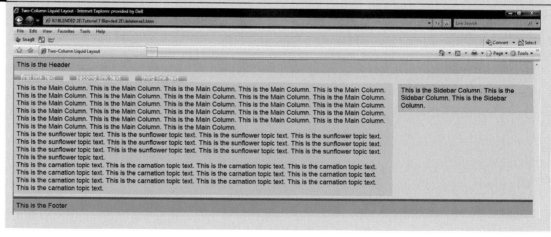

You'll next show Paula how to group related content by placing one div inside another.

Creating Nested Divs

When creating liquid layouts, it is quite common to create a nested div—a div within another div. In the next session, you will show Paula how to use a nested div in a sidebar column to group common elements. You nested divs in an earlier tutorial to create a structure with container and wrapper divs. In addition to creating structure, you can create nested divs to group content within related content. For example, you might want to create a main category such as "flowers," and then nest divs in it that relate to different types of flowers. By including an image or a background image, you can create a gallery of different flowers and a description of each. You can use a background color or border for the main container div to establish that its subsections are part of a larger category. The nested divs can have a similar appearance or look completely different; the choice is up to you as the designer.

You will show Paula how to create two divs nested inside the main div. For this practice document, you will show Paula how to nest two divs that contain images. The topic for the first div is sunflowers; the topic for the second div is carnations. The divs have already been created in the main div in the liquid.htm document, and the id selectors have been applied to each appropriate div. First you will show Paula how to style the topic id selector. You will use the background shorthand property and style the id selector to have a yellow background and a solid, 1px-wide, black border. The div will have a background image named sunflower.gif. The image will be positioned 1% from the left edge of the div and 50% down from the top of the div. Recall that when positioning a background image, the first two values indicate the position from the left and top edges of the container, respectively. The image will not be repeated. The topic div will have a background color of navy. You will use the background shorthand property to set all of the values for the background property—image, position, repeat, and color—in one declaration.

To insert the code for the topic id selector:

▶ **1.** In your text editor and on a blank line below the code for the footer id selector, type the following code, as shown in Figure 7-22.

```
#topic {
  margin-top: 1%;
  border: solid 1px black;
  padding: 0.5% 0.5% 0.5% 7.5%;
  color: yellow;
  background: url(sunflower.gif) 1% 50% no-repeat navy;
}
```

Figure 7-22	The topic id selector code

```
#footer {
  margin: 0.5% 0 0 0;
  border-top: solid thick teal;
  padding: 0.5%;
  background-color: lime;
  clear: both;
}

#topic {
  margin-top: 1%;
  border: solid 1px black;
  padding: 0.5% 0.5% 0.5% 7.5%;
  color: yellow;
  background: url(sunflower.gif) 1% 50% no-repeat navy;
}

</style>
```

the first topic code

▶ **2.** Save the file.

▶ **3.** Switch to your browser and refresh or reload the **liquidnew.htm** page. Compare your file with the one shown in Figure 7-23 to confirm that the topic div appears correctly in the main div. Depending on your browser and browser version, the sunflower.gif image may appear closer to the text than it does in Figure 7-23.

Figure 7-23

The topic div text in the browser

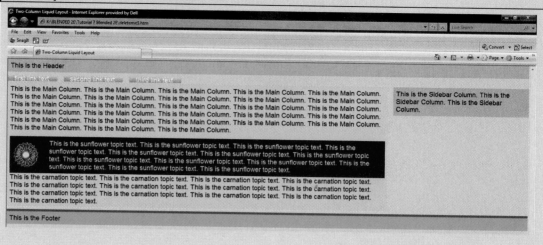

In the layouts you have created so far, one column was floated and the other was not. The advantage to this method is that the layout should not break because not all the columns have a width. The disadvantage is that you may not have the desired source order in the document body. The source order, as you learned in an earlier tutorial, is the order of the content in the document flow. In the document flow, floated columns must precede columns that are not floated, so floating all of the columns is one way to preserve their source order.

If you float all of the columns, however, you have to be certain of your math: all of the columns will have a specified width, so you must make sure that your layout doesn't break as a result of the browser rounding up or down the values you have listed (in percentages) for the column widths. Browsers convert percentage widths to pixel values, so some rounding of pixel values is bound to occur as a result. If you haven't left any extra space in your layout between the columns, it takes only one pixel too many to break the layout. Therefore, it's a good idea to accommodate rounding by building a small amount of extra space between the columns. Also, don't forget that subsequent changes to the margin, padding, and border values will affect the layout width.

The direction that the columns float determines where any extra space will appear to the left or the right of the columns. For example, if you had a layout with three columns and you floated each column "left," any extra space would appear to the right of column 3. On the other hand, if you floated all three columns "right," any extra space would appear before column 1. If you floated the columns in different directions, the extra space would be placed where the columns change direction. For example, if you floated column 1 and column 2 "left" and you floated column 3 "right," any extra space would appear between column 2 and column 3.

For accessibility purposes, consider floating all your columns to retain the source order. Some Web designers argue that it's important to have the sidebar column (with links) in the left column; others argue that the most accessible layouts are those with the main column on the left (which has the most important information to convey to the user) and sidebar columns to the right of the main column.

Next, you will show Paula how to style the topic2 id selector, which is the second id selector that will be nested in the main div. To create visual interest, you will change the color and background color for the topic2 div. You will also position the background image 99% from the left and 50% down from the top. You will again use the background shorthand property to set all of the values for the background property.

To style the topic2 id selector:

1. In your text editor and on a blank line below the code for the topic id selector, type the following code, as shown in Figure 7-24.

```
#topic2 {
  margin-bottom: 1%;
  border: solid 1px black;
  padding: 0.5% 7.5% 0.5% 0.5%;
  color: maroon;
  background: url(carnation.gif) 99% 50% no-repeat #eb9ebc;
}
```

Figure 7-24 — The topic2 id selector code

```
#topic {
  margin-top: 1%;
  border: solid 1px black;
  padding: 0.5% 0.5% 0.5% 7.5%;
  color: yellow;
  background: url(sunflower.gif) 1% 50% no-repeat navy;
}

#topic2 {
  margin-bottom: 1%;
  border: solid 1px black;
  padding: 0.5% 7.5% 0.5% 0.5%;
  color: maroon;
  background: url(carnation.gif) 99% 50% no-repeat #eb9ebc;
}
```

the second topic code →

2. Save the file.

3. Switch to your browser and refresh or reload the **liquidnew.htm** page. Compare your file with the one shown in Figure 7-25 to confirm that the topic2 div appears correctly in the main div. Depending on your browser and browser version, the carnation.gif image may appear closer to the text than it does in Figure 7-25.

Figure 7-25 — The topic2 div text in the browser

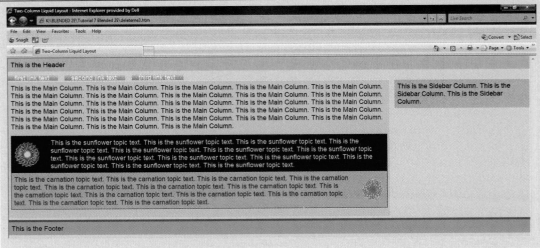

One change you suggest to Paula is to give the footer the same right margin as the main div. By conforming the footer width to the main column width, the footer will not be perceived as being part of the sidebar column. The main div has a right margin of 27%. You will show Paula how to assign the same right margin value to the footer.

To edit the right margin for the footer:

1. In your text editor, in the values for the margin property for the footer ID selector, delete the second value and replace it with 27%, as shown in Figure 7-26.

```
#footer {
    margin: 0.5% 27% 0 0;
    border-top: solid thick teal;
    padding: 0.5%;
    background-color: lime;
    clear: both;
}
```

| Figure 7-26 | The right margin changed to 27% |

right margin is changed to 27% to match that of the main div

```
#footer {
    margin: 0.5% 27% 0 0;
    border-top: solid thick teal;
    padding: 0.5%;
    background-color: lime;
    clear: both;
}
```

2. Save the file.

3. Switch to your browser and refresh or reload the **liquidnew.htm** page. Compare your file with the one shown in Figure 7-27 to confirm that the right margin for the footer has been adjusted correctly.

| Figure 7-27 | The revised right margin for the footer in the browser |

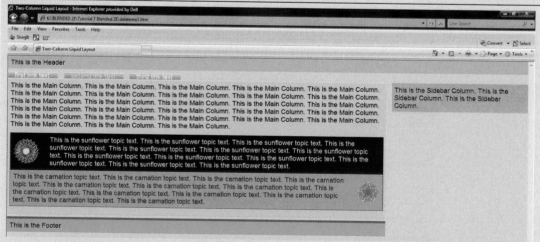

4. Submit the results of the **liquidnew.htm** file to your instructor, either in printed or electronic form, as requested.

5. If you will not be completing the next session, close your text editor and your browser.

In this session, you learned that liquid layouts are determined by percentages. Liquid layouts take full advantage of wide-screen monitors, which have become very popular over the past few years. You can create nested divs so that related content can be grouped together. You also learned that you can adjust the width of the footer to conform to the width of the main column above it.

1. What is portrait orientation?
2. What is landscape orientation?
3. What is a liquid layout?
4. What is an elastic layout?
5. What is a nested div?
6. What is the purpose of a nested div?

Session 7.2

Creating Three-Column Liquid Layouts

Now that Paula has worked with a document that contains placeholder text, you can show her how to create a liquid layout for the Sundown Spa and Resort home page. Paula thinks that a three-column layout would work well. She wants to include a sidebar column on the left that lists some outdoor activities for guests. A main column to the right of the sidebar will serve as an introduction to the resort. A third column to the right of the main column will highlight the spa's amenities. You have already created a document named spa.htm that contains the content for the body. You are ready to begin creating styles for the Sundown Spa and Resort home page.

To open the spa.htm file and save it with a new filename:

▶ 1. In your text editor, open the **spa.htm** file, which is located in the Tutorial.07\ Tutorial folder included with your Data Files. In the head section and below the page title, enter your name and today's date in the comment section where noted.

▶ 2. Save the file as **spanew.htm** in the same folder.

▶ 3. Open **spanew.htm** in your browser and view the initial file, as shown in Figure 7-28.

Figure 7-28 The initial spanew.htm file

Summer is Here

Tennis

We have a dozen tennis courts for our guests. Six of the courts are available by reservation only. If you wish to reserve a tennis court, please see the front desk to check for dates and times of availability. We also have six tennis courts available "under the bubble" for year-round and inclement weather use.

Pools

The Dolphin pool, which is an Olympic-sized pool and the smaller Cove pool are now open from 9 a.m. till sunset. The Tykes pool, which is available for children aged 6 and under, will be open starting tomorrow.

Golf

Both the Champions golf course and the Links golf course are open. Both courses open from 8 a.m. till sunset. Please call the front desk for waiting times and additional fees for the use of the golf courses.

Baseball and Soccer

All six baseball fields and all three soccer fields will be open starting Monday of next week. We have completely renovated the grounds with new sod on all nine fields.

Skiing and Hiking

Ski season has ended. Hiking is now available along our wooded trails.

Get Spa-tacular

- Our spa facilities are open all year long to provide you with the ultimate in pampering and comfort.
- We offer several types of massage, including Swedish massage, deep tissue massage, and aromatherapy massage. For rejuvenating your body, we offer both a hydrating body wrap and an exfoliating body wrap.
- We also offer facials for both men and women. For women, we not only offer haircutting services, but we will also wash and condition your hair with many of the exotic oils and creams we have on hand. We have both curling and flat iron treatments for styling your hair. We also offer haircuts and facial trims for men.

Welcome to our Spa and Resort

If you are looking for the perfect getaway, the Sundown Spa and Resort is the place to be. We offer spacious rooms from small and cozy to grand and luxurious. If you are just looking to relax, we have fabulous 4-star dining, quiet trails to enjoy hiking along Pine Valley, or enjoy tranquil sailing on Blue Lake. If you are the active type, then join the other guests for golfing, tennis, and swimming in one of our outdoor or indoor pools. Go sailing or canoeing on nearby Lake Meade. When you work up an appetite, order a delicious brunch served in your room or visit any one of our three restaurants.

Our guest accommodations are the finest at every price point. You will have a great night's sleep in one of our king-sized beds. Each room has a spa-like tub where you can relax your troubles away for as long as you wish. You can also visit our sauna or relax in one of our many indoor heated whirlpools. All walls and windows are double-insulated, so don't worry about the outside world creeping in; you'll be in your own world of peace, quiet, and relaxation.

Of course, all of these features do come at a price, but you'll be pleasantly surprised at how affordable our room rates are. Reservations must be made at least 30 days in advance, so don't put off joining us here at the Sundown Spa and Resort. After one visit, you'll see what you have been missing for too long. The Sundown Spa and Resort — let your dreams soar here. We hope to see you soon.

The Sundown Spa and Resort ✻ 24 Hillside Way ✻ Augusta, ME 04999

Directions ▪ Reservations ▪ Lunch Menu ▪ Dinner Menu ▪ Gift Cards ▪ Contact Us

You'll begin by showing Paula how to zero out the padding and margins for all elements on the Web page by using the universal selector. By creating this style, you will override the browser defaults, thereby establishing a more consistent layout when the page is viewed in different browsers. Later, you will add padding and margins only to selected elements.

To create a style for the universal selector:

▶ 1. Switch back to your text editor. Position the insertion point on a blank line below the start <style> tag in the embedded style sheet code. Type the following code, as shown in Figure 7-29.

```
* {
  margin: 0;
  padding: 0;
}
```

Figure 7-29 | The universal selector code

```
<style type="text/css">

*  {
   margin: 0;
   padding: 0;
}

</style>
```

margins and padding are zeroed out

▶ **2.** Save the file.

Paula has chosen a Verdana font for the text. She'd like a background color for the page that complements the Spa's logo, which contains mostly red and orange colors. You will show Paula how to style the body element to create styles for the font size, font family, and background color.

To style the body element:

▶ **1.** In your text editor, position the insertion point below the style for the universal selector.

▶ **2.** Press the **Enter** key.

▶ **3.** On a blank line, type the following code, as shown in Figure 7-30.

```
body {
   background-color: #ebbe8d;
   font-size: 0.9em;
   font-family: Verdana, sans-serif;
}
```

Figure 7-30 | The body element selector code

```
*  {
   margin: 0;
   padding: 0;
}

body {
   background-color: #ebbe8d;
   font-size: 0.9em;
   font-family: Verdana, sans-serif;
}

</style>
```

code to style the body is entered

▶ **4.** Save the file.

▶ **5.** Switch to your browser, refresh or reload the **spanew.htm** page, and then compare your file to Figure 7-31 to confirm that the body element has been styled correctly.

Figure 7-31

The document with the body styled in the browser

Summer is Here

Tennis
We have a dozen tennis courts for our guests. Six of the courts are available by reservation only. If you wish to reserve a tennis court, please see the front desk to check for dates and times of availability. We also have six tennis courts available "under the bubble" for year-round and inclement weather use.

Pools
The Dolphin pool, which is an Olympic-sized pool, and the smaller Cove pool are now open from 9 a.m. until sunset. The Tykes pool, which is available for children aged 6 and under, will be open starting June 1.

Golf
Both the Champions golf course and the Links golf course are open. You can golf each day from 7 a.m. until sunset. Please call the front desk for waiting times and additional fees for the use of the golf courses.

Baseball and Soccer
All six baseball fields and all three soccer fields will be open starting May 1. We have completely renovated the grounds with new sod on all nine fields.

Skiing and Hiking
Ski season has ended. Hiking is now available along our wooded trails.

Get Spa-tacular
Our spa facilities are open all year to provide you with the ultimate in pampering and comfort.
We offer several types of massage, including Swedish massage, deep tissue massage, and aromatherapy massage. For rejuvenating your body, we offer both a hydrating body wrap and an exfoliating body wrap.
We also offer facials for both men and women. For women, we not only offer haircutting services, but we will also wash and condition your hair with many of the exotic oils and creams we have on hand. We have both curling and flat iron treatments for styling your hair. We also offer haircuts and facial trims for men.

Welcome to our Spa and Resort
If you are looking for the perfect getaway, the Sundown Spa and Resort is the place to be. We offer spacious rooms from small and cozy to grand and luxurious. If you are just looking to relax, we have fabulous 4-star dining, quiet trails for hiking along Pine Valley, and tranquil sailing on Blue Lake. If you are the active type, then join the other guests for golfing, tennis, and swimming in one of our outdoor or indoor pools. Go sailing or canoeing on nearby Lake Meade. When you work up an appetite, order a delicious brunch served in your room or visit any one of our three restaurants.
Our guest accommodations are the finest at every price point. You will have a great night's sleep in one of our king-sized beds. Each room has a spa-like tub where you can relax your troubles away in; you'll be in your own world of peace, quiet, and relaxation.
Of course, all of these features do come at a price, but you'll be pleasantly surprised at how affordable our room rates are. Reservations must be made at least 30 days in advance, so don't put off joining us here at the Sundown Spa and Resort. After one visit, you'll see what you have been missing for too long. The Sundown Spa and Resort — let your dreams soar here. We hope to see you soon.

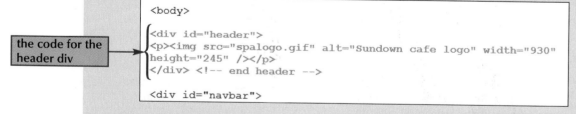

The Sundown Spa and Resort ✳ 24 Hillside Way ✳ Augusta, ME 04999
Directions ▌ Reservations ▌ Lunch Menu ▌ Dinner Menu ▌ Gift Cards ▌ Contact Us

You have created a logo, spalogo.gif, for the Sundown Spa and Resort. You will now show Paula how to enter the code for the header div at the top of the page in the body section. The header div will contain the code for the spalogo.gif image.

To enter the code for the header div:

1. Switch back to your text editor and position the insertion point on a blank line below the start <body> tag. Type the following code, as shown in Figure 7-32.

```
<div id="header">
<p><img src="spalogo.gif" alt="Sundown cafe logo"
width="930" height="245" /></p>
</div> <!-- end header -->
```

Figure 7-32

The header div code

the code for the header div →

```
<body>

<div id="header">
<p><img src="spalogo.gif" alt="Sundown cafe logo" width="930"
height="245" /></p>
</div> <!-- end header -->

<div id="navbar">
```

2. Save the file.

3. Switch to your browser, refresh or reload the **spanew.htm** page, and then compare your file to Figure 7-33 to confirm that the spalogo.gif image code has been entered correctly.

Figure 7-33 ▶ **The spalogo.gif image in the browser**

Now that the image has been inserted and a div has been created for the header, you will show Paula how to style the header id selector. She would like a background color that blends in well with the spalogo.gif image.

To enter the code for the header id selector:

▶ **1.** Switch back to your text editor, and position the insertion point on a blank line below the end brace for the body id selector.

▶ **2.** Type the following code, as shown in Figure 7-34.

```
#header {
   background-color: #ba3323;
}
```

Figure 7-34 ▶ **The header id selector code**

the header will have a background color that blends into the image in the header →

```
body {
   font-size: 0.9em;
   font-family: Verdana, sans-serif;
   background-color: #ebbe8d;
}

#header {
   background-color: #ba3323;
}

</style>
```

▶ **3.** Save the file.

▶ **4.** Switch to your browser, refresh or reload the **spanew.htm** page, and then compare your file to Figure 7-35 to confirm that the header now has a background color that extends the full screen width.

Figure 7-35 The header styled in the browser

Paula would like a navigation bar below the header. She has not yet developed all the pages at the Sundown Spa Web site, but you will show her how to create links using the # symbol placeholder character. The code for the links will be part of an unordered list. You will show Paula how to create a new navbar div just below the header div.

To enter the code for the navbar div:

▶ 1. Switch back to your text editor. In the document body, position the insertion point after the comment for the end </div> tag of the header div.

▶ 2. Press the **Enter** key twice.

▶ 3. On a blank line, type the following code, as shown in Figure 7-36.

```
<div id="navbar">
<ul>
  <li><a href="#">Directions</a></li>
  <li><a href="#">Reservations</a></li>
  <li><a href="#">Lunch Menu</a></li>
  <li><a href="#">Dinner Menu</a></li>
  <li><a href="#">Gift Shop</a></li>
  <li><a href="#">Contact Us</a></li>
</ul>
</div> <!-- end navbar -->
```

Figure 7-36 The navbar div code

```
<div id="header">
<p><img src="spalogo.gif" alt="Sundown cafe logo" width="930"
height="245" /></p>
</div> <!-- end header -->

<div id="navbar">
<ul>
  <li><a href="#">Directions</a></li>
  <li><a href="#">Reservations</a></li>
  <li><a href="#">Lunch Menu</a></li>
  <li><a href="#">Dinner Menu</a></li>
  <li><a href="#">Gift Shop</a></li>
  <li><a href="#">Contact Us</a></li>
</ul>
</div> <!-- end navbar -->

<div id="left">
<h2>Summer is Here</h2>
```

the navbar code with placeholder data

▶ 4. Save the file.

▶ **5.** Switch to your browser, refresh or reload the **spanew.htm** page, and then compare your file to Figure 7-37 to confirm that the unordered list containing the link code has been entered correctly.

Figure 7-37 ▶ **The unordered list in the browser**

Of course, the list items in the navbar do not look much like a navbar at this point. The list items appear vertically because by default, the value for the display property is "block." To make the list of links appear horizontally, you'll use the display property and assign a value of "inline." You'll also give the navbar a background color, make sure the contents are centered, and add some padding to create some white space around the links. You'll show Paula how to style the navbar now.

To style the navbar id selector:

▶ **1.** Switch back to your text editor, and in the embedded style sheet, position the insertion point on a blank line below the end brace for the header id selector.

▶ **2.** Type the following code, as shown in Figure 7-38.

```
#navbar {
  padding: 0.5em;
  background-color: black;
  text-align: center;
}

#navbar ul li {
  display: inline;
  list-style-type: none;
}
```

Figure 7-38 ▶ **The navbar id selector code**

```
#header {
  background-color: #ba3323;
}

#navbar {
  padding: 0.5em;
  background-color: black;
  text-align: center;
}

#navbar ul li {
  display: inline;
  list-style-type: none;
}
```

the navbar is styled →

▶ **3.** Save the file.

▶ **4.** Switch to your browser, refresh or reload the **spanew.htm** page, and then compare your file to Figure 7-39 to confirm that the navbar now displays the links horizontally and just below the spalogo.gif image.

Figure 7-39 The navbar styled in the browser

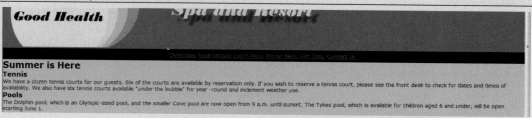

The navbar link text is a little difficult to read on a black background, so you want to address that issue with Paula now. You also want to show Paula how to style unvisited links and how to create a hover effect when the mouse pointer passes over a link in the navbar. You will again use colors that complement the colors in the spalogo.gif image.

To create the hover effect:

▶ **1.** Switch back to your text editor, and in the embedded style sheet, position the insertion point on a blank line below the end brace for the `navbar ul li` id selector.

▶ **2.** Type the following code, as shown in Figure 7-40.

```
#navbar ul li a {
   padding: 0.25em;
   color: white;
   background-color: orange;
   font-weight: bold;
}

#navbar ul li a:hover {
   color: black;
   background-color: yellow;
}
```

Figure 7-40 The navbar links code

```
#navbar ul li {
   display: inline;
   list-style-type: none;
}

#navbar ul li a {
   padding: 0.25em;
   color: white;
   background-color: orange;
   font-weight: bold;
}

#navbar ul li a:hover {
   color: black;
   background-color: yellow;
}
```

the hover effect is created

▶ **3.** Save the file.

▶ **4.** Switch to your browser, refresh or reload the **spanew.htm** page, and then compare your file to Figure 7-41 to confirm that the navbar has been styled correctly.

Figure 7-41 **The links styled in the browser**

5. Pass the mouse pointer over any of the links to confirm that the hover effect is working properly.

The setup for the header and the navbar are complete. Now you will begin showing Paula how to create a three-column liquid layout for the Sundown Spa home page.

Creating Styles for the Left Column

You are ready to determine the column widths for the three columns, which you will name "left," "middle," and "right." Paula wants the left and right columns to be narrow, so you will assign each a width of 20%.

ference Window | **Creating Three-Column Liquid Layouts**

To create a three-column liquid layout:
- Decide on the width (in percentages) for each of the narrower two sidebar columns.
- Decide how you want the sidebar columns to float.
- In the style sheet, enter the code for the sidebar and main id selectors. Assign widths to both sidebar columns. Do not assign a width to the main column.
- In the document body, enter start and end div tags for the sidebars and the main divs.
- If necessary, change the source order so that the floated content appears before non-floated content.

The middle column will not have a set width—its width will expand or collapse based on the screen resolution. The left column will be floated left, and the right column will be floated right. In the body section, the divs are currently in the following source order. Note that the middle div follows both the left and the right div:

1. header
2. navbar
3. left
4. right
5. middle
6. footer

Recall that when divs appear side by side, floated divs must appear before divs that are not floated, which is why the preceding source order seems incorrect (the divs appear as left, right, and middle, rather than left, middle, and right). The left and middle columns will have the same background color. To provide separation among the columns, you will give the left column a border on the right, which will create the appearance of a vertical ruled line. For the left column, you will create a descendant selector style for the h2 element, which means h2 headings in the left column will look different from the other h2 headings in the document. You will show Paula how to create styles for the left column now.

To enter the left column id selectors code:

▶ **1.** Switch back to your text editor, and in the embedded style sheet, position the insertion point on a blank line below the end brace for the `navbar ul li a:hover` style.

▶ **2.** Type the following code, as shown in Figure 7-42.

```
#left {
   width: 20%;
   border-right: solid thin black;
   float: left;
}

#left h2 {
   margin-bottom: 0.5em;
   color: white;
   background-color: maroon;
   text-align: center;
   text-transform: uppercase;
}

#left p {
   padding: 0 1% 1% 0;
}
```

Figure 7-42 ▶ **The left column id selectors code**

the left column is styled; descendant selectors are created for the heading and paragraph text →

```
#left {
   width: 20%;
   border-right: solid thin black;
   float: left;
}

#left h2 {
   margin-bottom: 0.5em;
   color: white;
   background-color: maroon;
   text-align: center;
   text-transform: uppercase;
}

#left p {
   padding: 0 1% 1% 0;
}
```

▶ **3.** Save the file.

▶ **4.** Switch to your browser, refresh or reload the **spanew.htm** page, and then compare your file to Figure 7-43 to confirm that the left column has been styled correctly. The columns will appear too close and the bullets in the main column may overlap the sidebar column, but you will address those issues with Paula later.

Figure 7-43 The left column styled in the browser

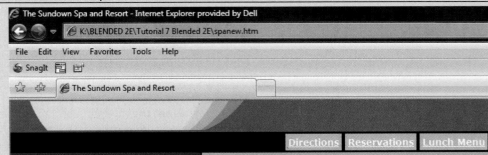

The Sundown Spa and Resort - Internet Explorer provided by Dell

K:\BLENDED 2E\Tutorial 7 Blended 2E\spanew.htm

File   Edit   View   Favorites   Tools   Help

SnagIt

The Sundown Spa and Resort

Directions   Reservations   Lunch Menu

SUMMER IS HERE

Tennis
We have a dozen tennis courts for our guests. Six of the courts are available by reservation only. If you wish to reserve a tennis court, please see the front desk to check for dates and times of availability. We also have six tennis courts available "under the bubble" for year -round and inclement weather use.

Pools
The Dolphin pool, which is an Olympic-sized pool, and the smaller Cove pool are now open from 9 a.m. until sunset. The Tykes pool, which is available for children aged 6 and under, will be open starting June 1.

Golf
Both the Champions golf course and the Links golf course are open. You can golf each day from 7 a.m. until sunset. Please call the front desk for waiting times and additional fees for the use of the golf courses.

Baseball and Soccer
All six baseball fields and all three soccer fields will be open starting May 1. We have completely renovated the grounds with new sod on all nine fields.

Skiing and Hiking
Ski season has ended. Hiking is now available along our wooded trails.

Get Spa-tacular
- Our spa facilities are open all year to provide you with the ulti
- We offer several types of massage, including Swedish massa hydrating body wrap and an exfoliating body wrap.
- We also offer facials for both men and women. For women, w exotic oils and creams we have on hand. We have both curlin

Welcome to our Spa and
If you are looking for the perfect getaway, the Sundown Spa luxurious. If you are just looking to relax, we have fabulous the active type, then join the other guests for golfing, tennis Meade. When you work up an appetite, order a delicious brun Our guest accommodations are the finest at every price point where you can relax your troubles away for as long as you wi windows are double-insulated, so don't worry about the outs Of course, all of these features do come at a price, but you'll 30 days in advance, so don't put off joining us here at the S Sundown Spa and Resort — let your dreams soar here. We h

The Sundown Spa and Resort ✳ 24 Hillside Way ✳ Augusta,

Directions I Reservations I Lunch Menu I Dinner Menu I Gift Cards I Contact Us

When creating a design with a fluid layout, you must be wary of objects that have a fixed width, such as an image, a table, a form, or a multimedia control. These types of objects may prevent a column from resizing when you make the viewport narrower. When designing a Web page with fixed-width content, try to place such objects into the widest column and assign these objects a generous amount of white space on the left and right so that the columns can be resized to some extent.

The min-width and max-width properties set the minimum and maximum width of an element, respectively. The minimum and maximum widths are for the content only, and do not include the widths of margins, borders, or padding. You can apply the min-width or max-width property to the div element to keep the layout from expanding or contracting too much. If the document body contains fixed-width content, such as an image, you don't want to have overlapping content if the user has a small screen or resizes the screen to be smaller. The min-width value, therefore, could be set to the width of the image element in that particular div. Similarly, the max-width property could be used to limit how large the layout could appear. At some point, the layout may contain too much white space. Set the max-width property to the limit at which you want users to maximize the screen. This limit will depend on the number of columns and content in your layout.

Now that the left column has been styled, you will help Paula create styles for the middle column.

Creating Styles for the Middle Column

Recall that the left column and right column both have a width of 20%. The middle column will occupy the remaining space between those columns. Right now, the sidebar column and the main column are far too close to each other, so you need to move the contents of the middle column over from the left. You also need to move the middle column over from the right to create space for the right column. To ensure adequate space between the columns, you will assign the middle column a left and right margin of 22% each. This margin space will create a gutter between the middle column and its flanking columns. Paula would also like h1 heading text centered, so you will create a descendant selector for the h1 element. Last, you will create some white space below the h1 heading by giving it a bottom margin of 1em.

To enter the middle column id selectors code:

▶ **1.** Switch back to your text editor, and in the embedded style sheet, position the insertion point on a blank line below the end brace for the `left p` style.

▶ **2.** Type the following code, as shown in Figure 7-44.

```
#middle {
  margin-left: 22%;
  margin-right: 22%;
  padding: 0.5%;
}

#middle h1 {
  margin-bottom: 1em;
  text-align: center;
}
```

Figure 7-44 ▶ **The middle column id selectors code**

the middle column
is styled

```
#left p {
   padding: 0 1% 1% 0;
}

#middle {
   margin-left: 22%;
   margin-right: 22%;
   padding: 0.5%;
}

#middle h1 {
   margin-bottom: 1em;
   text-align: center;
}
```

▶ **3.** Save the file.

▶ **4.** Switch to your browser, refresh or reload the **spanew.htm** page, and then compare your file to Figure 7-45 to confirm that the middle column and the h1 element have been styled correctly.

Figure 7-45 ▶ **The middle column styled in the browser**

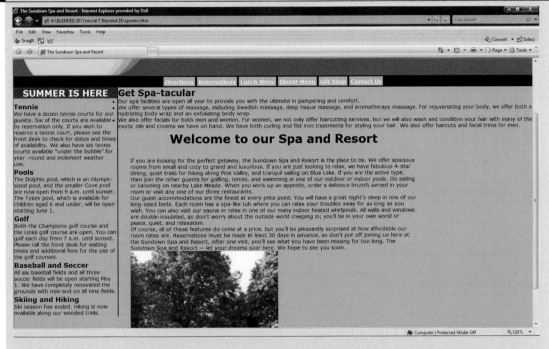

Trouble? If the columns appear too close in some sections and the bullets in the main column overlap the sidebar column, do not be concerned. You will address these problems in upcoming steps.

You will now show Paula that id selectors can be grouped. Because margins and padding were zeroed out by the universal selector, there isn't any white space between the paragraphs in the left or middle column. You've already defined the paragraphs in the left div to have some padding. Now you'll show Paula how to further refine the appearance of the left div paragraphs. To give some white space to the paragraph text, you will show Paula how to create a style for the left and middle column paragraph elements that will indent the text and create a bottom margin.

To enter the grouped id selectors code:

▶ 1. Switch back to your text editor, and in the embedded style sheet, position the insertion point on a blank line below the end brace for the #middle h1 style.

▶ 2. Type the following code, as shown in Figure 7-46.

```
#left p, #middle p {
  margin-bottom: 1em;
  text-indent: 2em;
}
```

Figure 7-46 ▶ **The grouped id selectors code**

margins and text indent are established for both the left and the middle column text

```
#middle h1 {
  margin-bottom: 1em;
  text-align: center;
}

#left p, #middle p {
  margin-bottom: 1em;
  text-indent: 2em;
}
```

▶ 3. Save the file.

▶ 4. Switch to your browser, refresh or reload the **spanew.htm** page, and then compare your file to Figure 7-47 to confirm that the paragraphs in the left and middle columns have been styled correctly. (The paragraphs should now have some space between them and have a text indent.)

Figure 7-47 ▶ **The left and middle columns styled in the browser**

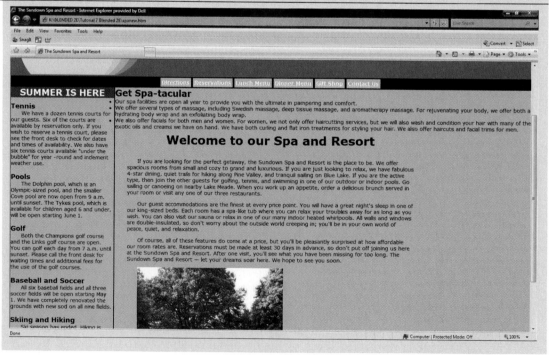

Now that the left and middle columns have been styled, you will work with Paula to create styles for the right column and resolve the lingering overlap problems between the columns.

Creating Styles for the Right Column

Paula wants a different appearance for the right column so that the reader's attention is drawn to the spa's numerous amenities. She also wants the column to be floated right and to have some contrasting colors. In addition, Paula wants the h2 heading in this div to look different from the h2 headings in other parts of the document, so you will show her how to create a descendant style for the h2 selector in the right column.

To enter the right column id selectors code:

▶ **1.** Switch back to your text editor, and in the embedded style sheet, position the insertion point on a blank line below the end brace for the #left p, #middle p grouped id selectors.

▶ **2.** Type the following code, as shown in Figure 7-48.

```
#right {
  width: 20%;
  color: white;
  background-color: maroon;
  float: right;
}

#right h2 {
  margin-bottom: 0.5em;
  color: maroon;
  background-color: white;
  text-align: center;
  text-transform: uppercase;
}

#right p {
  padding: 0 1% 1% 1%;
}
```

Figure 7-48	The right column id selectors code

```
#left p, #middle p {
  margin-bottom: 1em;
  text-indent: 2em;
}

#right {
  width: 20%;
  color: white;
  background-color: maroon;
  float: right;
}

#right h2 {
  margin-bottom: 0.5em;
  color: maroon;
  background-color: white;
  text-align: center;
  text-transform: uppercase;
}

#right p {
  padding: 0 1% 1% 1%;
}
```

code to style the right column

▶ **3.** Save the file.

4. Switch to your browser, refresh or reload the **spanew.htm** page, and then compare your file to Figure 7-49 to confirm that the right column has been styled correctly. Depending on your browser and browser version, you may not see the bullets for the unordered list in the right column or you may not see any bullets at all in the right column. You will address these problems shortly.

Figure 7-49 | **The right column styled in the browser**

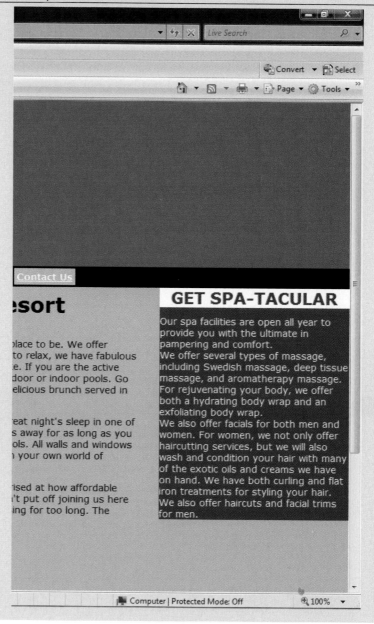

You have already styled an unordered list for the navbar, so you will show Paula how to create id selectors to style the unordered list in the right column to look different from the unordered list items in the navbar.

To address the problems with the list markers in the right columns, you will change the list style position to create an indent, and provide some white space by creating a margin below each list item. In addition, Paula prefers square list markers, so you will change the list style type as well.

Tip

ent browsers and
ent versions of the
browser provide
ent amounts of pad-
and margin space for
arkers, so always
your lists in several
sers and browser
ns. Adjust margins
dding as needed.

To enter the unordered list code in the right column:

1. Switch back to your text editor, and in the embedded style sheet, position the insertion point on a blank line below the end brace for the #right p selector.

2. Type the following code, as shown in Figure 7-50.

```
#right ul {
  padding: 1em;
  list-style-type: square;
  list-style-position: inside;
}

#right ul li {
  margin-bottom: 1em;
}
```

Figure 7-50   **The right column unordered list descendant selectors code**

```
#right p {
  padding: 0 1% 1% 1%;
}

#right ul {
  padding: 1em;
  list-style-type: square;
  list-style-position: inside;
}

#right ul li {
  margin-bottom: 1em;
}
```

the unordered list in
the right column will
have square bullets

3. Save the file.

4. Switch to your browser, refresh or reload the **spanew.htm** page, and then compare your file to Figure 7-51 to confirm that the list markers have been styled correctly. The list markers should now be visible (if they were not before), and they should appear inside the right column.

Figure 7-51   **The right column list markers styled in the browser**

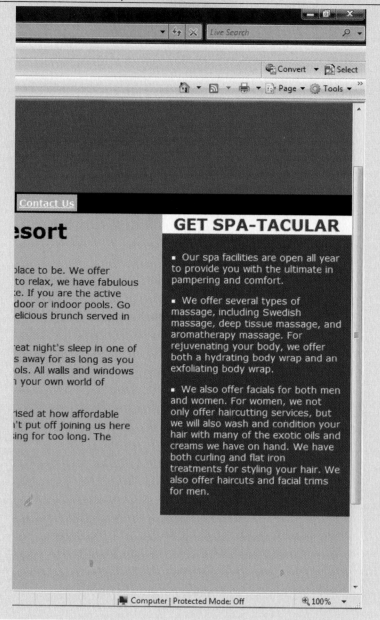

The last task is to show Paula how to create styles for the site footer.

Creating Styles for the Footer

The footer must clear all columns, and Paula also wants to center the footer content. You will also show Paula how to give the footer some white space by providing margin space and padding on the top.

To enter the footer id selector code:

▶ **1.** Switch back to your text editor, and in the embedded style sheet, position the insertion point on a blank line below the end brace for the #right ul li id selectors.

▶ **2.** Type the following code, as shown in Figure 7-52.

```
#footer {
  margin-top: 1em;
  border-top: solid thick maroon;
  clear: both;
  font-weight: bold;
  text-align: center;
}
```

Figure 7-52   **The footer id selector code**

```
#right ul li {
  margin-bottom: 1em;
}

#footer {
  margin-top: 1em;
  border-top: solid thick maroon;
  clear: both;
  font-weight: bold;
  text-align: center;
}
```

the footer selector code

3. Save the file.

4. Switch to your browser, refresh or reload the **spanew.htm** page. Scroll down the page if necessary, and then compare your file to Figure 7-53 to confirm that the footer div has been styled correctly.

Figure 7-53   **The footer div styled in the browser**

Baseball and Soccer
All six baseball fields and all three soccer fields will be open starting May 1. We have completely renovated the grounds with new sod on all nine fields.

Skiing and Hiking
Ski season has ended. Hiking is now available along our wooded trails.

The Sundown Spa and Resort ✿ 24 Hillside Way ✿ Augusta, ME 04999
Directions ❚ Reservations ❚ Lunch Menu ❚ Dinner Menu ❚ Gift Cards ❚ Contact Us

Computer | Protected Mode: Off   100%

Paula is curious to know how liquid layouts can be constrained so that the layout is centered and does not occupy the entire screen width. You will next explain to Paula how to constrain a liquid layout.

Modifying the Layout Width

Paula is curious to know how she can constrain (limit) the layout from spanning the entire screen width because she'd like to center the layout horizontally, which will result in shorter, more readable lines in the main column. To limit the layout width, just create a container div in the body of the document, and style the container id selector to have the desired width.

You will now show Paula how to constrain the layout to 90% of the screen width. You'll also show her where to enter the <div> tags for the container div.

Tip

common to constrain
d layouts to 70-90%
e screen width.

To enter the container div code:

1. Switch back to your text editor. In the document body, position the insertion point after the right angle bracket in the start <body> tag.

2. Press the **Enter** key twice.

▶ **3.** On a blank line, type the following code, as shown in Figure 7-54.

```
<div id="container">
```

Figure 7-54 **The start div tag for the container**

the start div tag
for the container

```
<body>

<div id="container">

<div id="header">
<p><img src="spalogo.gif" alt="Sundown cafe logo" width="930"
height="245" /</p>
</div> <!-- end header -->

<div id="navbar">
```

▶ **4.** Scroll down and position the insertion point on a blank line before the end </body> tag.

▶ **5.** On a blank line, type the following code, as shown in Figure 7-55.

```
</div> <!-- end container -->
```

Figure 7-55 **The end div tag and comment for the container**

```
<p><a href="#">Directions</a> &#10074; <a href="#">Reservations</a> &#
10074; <a href="#">Lunch Menu</a> &#10074; <a href="#">Dinner Menu</a> &#
10074; <a href="#">Gift Cards</a> &#10074; <a href="#">Contact Us</a></p>
</div> <!-- end footer -->

</div> <!-- end container -->

</body>
</html>
```

the end div tag
for the container

▶ **6.** Save the file.

Now that the container div has been created, you are ready to show Paula how to style the container id selector. Because the container id affects the positioning of the document in the browser, you want to enter this code after the body element selector style.

To style the container id selector:

▶ **1.** Switch back to your text editor. In the embedded style sheet, position the insertion point after the end } brace after the body element style.

▶ **2.** Press the **Enter** key twice.

▶ **3.** On a blank line, type the following code, as shown in Figure 7-56.

```
#container {
  width: 90%;
  margin: 0 auto;
  border-width: 1px;
}
```

Figure 7-56 | The container id selector code

```
body {
    font-size: 0.9em;
    font-family: Verdana, sans-serif;
    background-color: #ebbe8d;
}

#container {
    width: 90%;
    margin: 0 auto;
    border-width: 1px;
}
```

the container width is set to 90% of the viewport

▶ **4.** Save the file.

▶ **5.** Switch to your browser, refresh or reload the **spanew.htm** page, and then compare your file to Figure 7-57 to confirm that the layout width is now 90% of the screen width.

Figure 7-57 | The modified layout width in the browser

Paula has noticed that the glade.jpg image is not centered in the middle column. She thinks that centering the image would make the content appear more balanced. She also would like to center the logo image in the header. You will show Paula how to style the img element so that all the images on the page are centered.

To center the images:

▶ **1.** Switch back to your text editor. In the embedded style sheet, scroll down and position the insertion point on a blank line after the footer id style code.

▶ **2.** Type the following code, as shown in Figure 7-58.

```
img {
    margin: 0 auto;
    display: block;
}
```

Figure 7-58 ▶ **The image style code to center images**

```
#footer {
    clear: both;
    text-align: center;
    font-weight: bold;
    border-top: solid thick maroon;
    margin-top: 1em;
}

img {
    margin: 0 auto;
    display: block;
}
```

the code to center the images

▶ **3.** Save the file.

▶ **4.** Switch to your browser, refresh or reload the **spanew.htm** page, and then compare your file to Figure 7-59 to confirm that the images have been centered.

Figure 7-59 ▶ **The images centered in the browser**

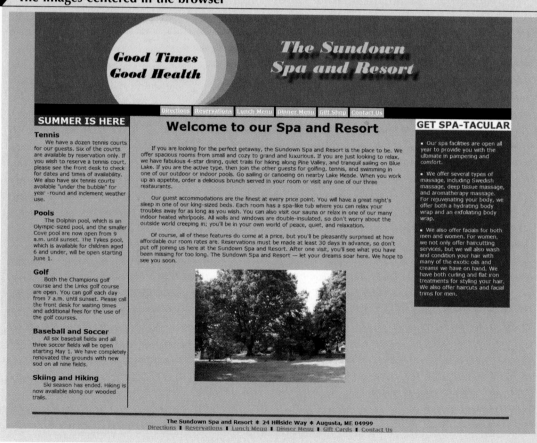

Paula wants to know if it's possible to print just the text of the document. She's concerned that the document may be too wide to print. She also thinks that it might take too long to print the header and the navbar. You'll next show Paula how to print selected parts of a Web page.

Using Print Styles

Printing a three-column or even a two-column layout Web page can be problematic. To make sure a Web page prints correctly for your users, as a Web page designer you need to create a **print style**, which is a style designed to create output for printed copy. When you create a print style, you should hide individual elements or even entire page divisions so that only the text content is printed. You usually don't want users to have to print the navbar, the banner, or the images.

erence Window | **Creating an External Print Style Sheet**

To create print styles:
- Change the text color to black and the background color to white.
- Specify a font size in points.
- Specify the font family as a serif font.
- Style the navbar, banner, and images to have a display property value of none.
- Set the line height to 120% or greater.
- Use the @page rule to set the page size and margin.

To avoid confusion between which elements you want to print and exclude from printing, it's best to create print styles in an external style sheet rather than mixing them in the same embedded style sheet. Therefore, you need to use the link element to create a link to the external style sheet that contains the print styles. You have already worked with the link element to create a link to an external style sheet. The code to link to an external print style sheet is similar to the following:

```
<link rel="stylesheet" href="printstyles.css" type="text/css" />
```

To create a link to a print style sheet, you need to enter the code for the link element and add the media attribute and value to the link element code. The **media attribute** determines where output will be directed. The media attribute has 10 values, but the most common (and most browser-supported) values are as follows:

- all (the default choice)—Styles are applied to all devices.
- screen—Limits output to the screen and tells the browser to apply the styles only when displaying the page in the browser.
- print—Sends output to the printer and tells the browser to apply the assigned set of styles only when the document prints.
- handheld—For output on mobile devices, such as cell phones.

For example, if you wanted to have two style sheets—one for the screen styles and one for the link styles—you would enter code similar to that shown below. Note the two different values for the media attribute.

```
<link rel="stylesheet" href="mystyles.css" type="text/css"
media="screen" />

<link rel="stylesheet" href="printstyles.css" type="text/css"
media="print" />
```

If you do not want to create a separate style sheet for the CSS screen styles, you could merely add the media attribute and its value to the start style tag for the embedded style sheet, as shown in the following code.

Tip

With the exception of "print," "screen," and "all," most values for the media attribute are not supported by all browsers.

```
<style type="text/css" media="screen">
```

Whenever you have more than one set of links to external style sheets, it's a good coding practice to add the media attribute and its value to each of the link element codes. You will thus avoid confusion about the purpose of the style sheet. You also must be concerned with the order of the link tags in the head area. If you have more than one link element, the link elements further down the list have greater precedence.

After you create the link to the print style sheet, obviously you must create the external print style sheet. Now you have to choose what you don't want to be printed when a user prints your Web page. You don't want the header and navbar to print, because no one wants to print banner ads, search bars, and logos, so you'll hide those divs by creating grouped selectors and using the display property with a value of "none." It's a good coding practice to document your code by using comments, so that other designers know what you specify for printing. The grouped selector would be similar to the following code:

```
/* hides unwanted divs */

#nav, #header {
   display: none;
}
```

You would build on this list of hiding id selectors based on the complexity of your document. For example, you may have a sidebar or section that has banner ads or a list of links—you'd want to hide those divs as well.

The **@page rule** is used to determine the size of the print area and the margins for printing. Use the **size property** to determine the size of the page. Use inches as the unit measurement instead of pixels, percentages, or em values. The @page rule for this print style sheet would be set as shown in the following code:

```
@page {
   size: 8.5in 11in;
   margin: 0.5in;
}
```

Tip

The size property is always used with the @page rule.

Your next task is to create a style for the body element that is printer friendly. To start, change the text color to black, the background color to white, and the background-image property to a value of "none." Set the font size to the default size, which is 12pt. You will use points instead of em values for the print style sheet because printers use point values by default. Use a serif font, which is easier to read on a printed page. Increase the line height to 120% or more to create some breathing room between the lines of text, as shown in the following code.

```
/* print designed for accessibility */

body {
   color: black;
   background-color: white;
   background-image: none;
   font-size: 12pt;
   font-family: "Times New Roman", Times, serif;
   line-height: 120%;
}
```

Links should be underscored. If you want, you can also change the link color to blue for users who have color printers.

```
/* sets links to default colors */

a {
  text-decoration: underline;
  color: blue;
}
```

If you do not want images to print, either because it takes too much time to print or takes up too much space on the page, then style the img element to have a display property value of "none," as shown in the following code.

```
/* removes images from print out */

img {
  display: none;
}
```

You should always verify your style sheet code by printing pages from several different browsers and browser versions. The print preview feature of most browsers provides a *likeness* of how the page will print. To be certain that your print styles are correct, you should print from several different browsers, browser versions, and printers, analyze the results, and adjust your styles accordingly.

You have already created a print style sheet named printstyles.css. You will show Paula how to add the link code to link the spanew.htm file to the printstyles.css file.

Tip

an adjust the page ins in the Internet rer print preview.

To enter the code to link to the printstyles.css style sheet:

1. Switch back to your text editor. In the embedded style sheet, scroll up and position the insertion point on a blank line after the page title code in the head section.

2. Type the following code, as shown in Figure 7-60.

   ```
   <link rel="stylesheet" href="printstyles.css"
   type="text/css" media="print" />
   ```

Figure 7-60	The link code for the printstyles.css style sheet

```
<!DOCTYPE html PUBLIC "-//W3C//DTD XHTML 1.0 Strict//EN"
    "http://www.w3.org/TR/xhtml1/DTD/xhtml1-strict.dtd">
<html xmlns="http://www.w3.org/1999/xhtml" lang="en" xml:lang="en">
<head>
<meta http-equiv="Content-Type" content="text/html; charset=ISO-8859-1" />
<title>The Sundown Spa and Resort</title>

<link rel="stylesheet" href="printstyles.css" type="text/css"
media="print" />
```

e link to the print
vle sheet

3. In the embedded style sheet, position the insertion point before the end angle bracket in the start `<style type="text/css">` tag.

4. Press the **Spacebar** once.

5. Type the following code, as shown in Figure 7-61.

   ```
   <style type="text/css" media="screen">
   ```

Figure 7-61 The media attribute and value added to the start style tag

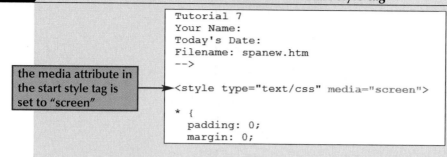

```
Tutorial 7
Your Name:
Today's Date:
Filename: spanew.htm
-->

<style type="text/css" media="screen">

*  {
  padding: 0;
  margin: 0;
```

the media attribute in the start style tag is set to "screen"

6. Save the file.

Now that the link has been established and the edits have been made to the start style tag in the embedded style sheet, you will show Paula how to use the print preview feature of your browser to see how the page should print. The print preview is entirely browser dependent, and browsers preview pages in significantly different ways. Figure 7-62 shows the print preview for Internet Explorer. The print preview for the same document in the Firefox browser, for example, will look quite different.

To use the print preview feature of the browser:

1. Switch to your browser and refresh or reload the **spanew.htm** page.

2. Click **File** on the menu bar, and then click **Print Preview**.

3. If you're using Firefox, click the Scale list arrow and click 100%. If you're using Internet Explorer, click the Change Print Size list arrow and click 100%. In Internet Explorer, the print preview should look similar to the one shown in Figure 7-62.

Trouble? If necessary, press the Alt key to display the menu bar or click the Print button list arrow on the command bar, and then click Print Preview.

Figure 7-62 The print preview in Internet Explorer

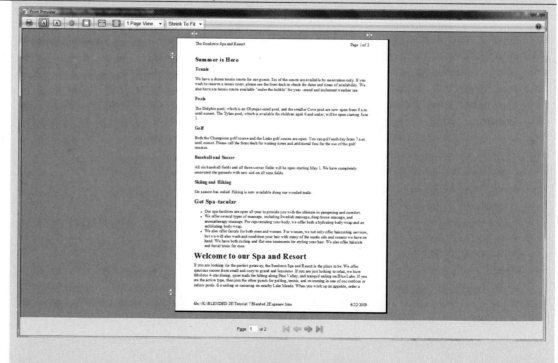

▶ **4.** Click the **Close** button ▨ to close the print preview.

▶ **5.** Submit the results of the **spanew.htm** file to your instructor, either in printed or electronic form, as requested.

▶ **6.** If you are not completing the Review Assignments or the Case Problems, close your text editor and your browser.

In this session you learned how to create a three-column liquid layout. You created styles for each of the three columns, as well as for a navigation bar and the site footer. You also learned about print styles, which are contained in an external style sheet. Finally, you learned how to use the media attribute when creating print styles.

Review | Session 7.2 Quick Check

1. What does it mean to "constrain" a liquid layout?
2. What id selector is commonly used to constrain the liquid layout?
3. What is a print style?
4. In what type of style sheet should print styles be entered?
5. What attribute and value are used in the link tag to link to a print style sheet?
6. What rule is commonly used with print style sheets?

Review | Tutorial Summary

In this tutorial, you learned about the differences among various types of layouts. You learned that liquid layouts use percentages rather than pixels to determine the layout width. You also created a nested div, a div within another div. You worked with three-column layouts. You learned the importance of source order when you float divs. You created print styles and you used the link element to link to an external style sheet that contained print styles. Finally, you learned about the media attribute and how output can be directed to a printer or a screen.

Key Terms

@page rule	landscape orientation	print style
column droop	liquid layout	size property
elastic layout	media attribute	span element
hybrid layout	portrait orientation	

Take time to practice the skills you learned in the tutorial using the same case scenario.

Data Files needed for the Review Assignments: gift.htm, giftlogo.gif

Paula has asked for your assistance in developing other pages at the Sundown Spa and Resort Web site. The resort has recently constructed a new gift shop, so Paula would like to announce its grand opening, which will occur in a few weeks. The gift shop will stock all sorts of items, ranging from fashion to food, and it will be the primary seller of the resort's gift cards. You have begun working on a document about the gift shop that you think Paula will like. After each step, save the file, switch to your browser, refresh or reload the page, verify that you entered the style code correctly, and then switch back to your text editor and complete the next step. A preview of the Web page you will create appears in Figure 7-63.

Figure 7-63

Complete the following:

1. Use your text editor to open the **gift.htm** file, which is provided in your Data Files in the Tutorial.07\Review folder. In the head section and below the page title, enter your name and today's date in the comment section where noted.
2. Save the file as **giftnew.htm** in the same folder. Open the file in your browser and observe the appearance of the original file.
3. Switch back to your text editor. In the embedded style sheet and below the comment "add new styles below," style the body element to have a font size of 1em and appear in Arial (sans-serif). The body should have a background color of black.
4. Save the **giftnew.htm** file. Switch back to your browser and refresh or reload the page. Verify that the body element style appears correctly in your file.
5. Switch back to your text editor. In the embedded style sheet code, you will continue to add styles below the style for the body element. Create a style for the universal selector to have a margin of 0 and padding of 0.
6. Create a style for the #container id selector as follows:
   - Set the width to 90%.
   - Set the margin to 0 on the top and bottom and "auto" on the left and right.

7. Create a style for the #header id selector to add padding of 0.5% on all sides. Set the background color to #cbbf8b.

8. Create a descendant selector for the header id selector so that the image element has margins of 0 on the top and bottom, and margins of "auto" on the left and right. Set the display value to "block."

9. Create the following styles for the #sidebar id selector:
   - Set the width to 30%.
   - Add padding of 0.75% on all sides.
   - Set the background color to #f3da79.
   - Float the sidebar "left."

10. Create the following styles for the #main id selector:
    - Set the margin on the left to 33%.
    - Add padding of 0.75% on all sides.
    - Set the background color to #f3da79.

11. Create the following styles for the #footer id selector:
    - Set the margins to 1% on the top, 0 on the right, 1% on the bottom, and 33% on the left.
    - Create a border on the top that is solid, thick, and black.
    - Add padding of 1% on the bottom.
    - Set the background color to #cbbf8b.
    - Clear all elements on both the left and right.
    - Center the footer text.

12. Save the **giftnew.htm** file. Switch to your browser and refresh or reload the page. Compare your file to Figure 7-63 to verify that your file is correct.

13. Submit the results of the preceding steps to your instructor, either in printed or electronic form, as requested.

14. If you are not completing the next assignment, close your text editor and your browser.

Apply | **Case Problem 1**

*what you've
ed and expand
skills to create
style a Web page
n auto repair
ce.*

Data Files needed for this Case Problem: car.jpg, reddie.htm, reddielogo.gif

Reddie Motors and Repair   Reddie Motors and Repair is a national chain of auto repair shops headquartered in St. Louis, Missouri. Reddie Motors has built its reputation on being able to service almost any vehicle on the road. Because it has been able to offer car repair as a commodity, the franchise is becoming more popular every day. Ken Cole, the general manager of Reddie Motors, has asked you to create a new layout and home page for their Web site. You have decided on a two-column layout. After you complete a step to create a style, verify in your browser that the style code has been entered correctly, and then switch back to your text editor. A preview of the Web page you will create appears in Figure 7-64.

Figure 7-64

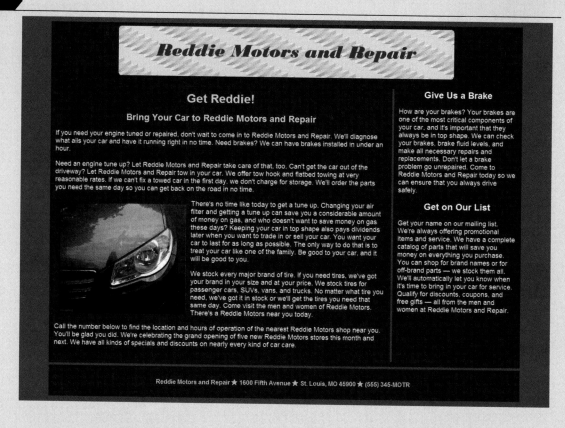

Complete the following:

1. Use your text editor to open the **reddie.htm** file, which is provided in your Data Files in the Tutorial.07\Case1 folder. In the head section and below the page title, enter your name and today's date in the comment section where noted.

2. Save the file as **reddienew.htm** in the same folder. Open the file in your browser and observe the appearance of the original file.

3. Switch back to your text editor. Within the tags for the embedded style sheet, style the body element to have text appear in a font size of 1.1em and in Arial (sans-serif). The text should be white with a background color of #5d4190.

4. Save the **reddienew.htm** file. Switch back to your browser and refresh or reload the page. Verify that the body element style appears correctly in your file.

5. Switch back to your text editor. In the code for the embedded style sheet and below the body element style, create a style for the #container id selector as follows:
   - Set the width to 90%.
   - Create margins on the top and bottom of 0, and margins on the left and right set to "auto."
   - Set the background color to #38265a.

⊕ EXPLORE

6. Create a descendant style for the #header id selector using the margin property and the display property so that images within the header div are centered.

7. Create the following styles for the sidebar id selector:
   - Set the width to 25%.
   - Add padding of 0 on the top, and 1% on the right, bottom, and left sides.
   - Float the sidebar "right."

8. Create a descendant style for the #sidebar id selector so that h2 text appears as white text.

9. Create the following styles for the #main id selector:
   - Set the margin on the right to 27%.
   - Create a border on the right that is solid, 5px, and purple.
   - Add padding of 1% on all sides.
   - Set the color to white.

⊕ EXPLORE 10. For the #main id selector, create a descendant grouped selector to style both the h1 and h2 elements in the main div to appear with a margin on the top of 0. The h1 and h2 text should appear in yellow and should be centered.

11. Create a descendant style for the #main id selector so that images within the main div have margins of 1% on all sides and float "left."

12. Create the following styles for the #footer id selector:
    - Create a margin on the top of 1%.
    - Create a border on the top that is solid, thick, and purple.
    - Add padding of 1% on all sides.
    - Clear elements on both the left and the right.
    - Set the color to #ffc800.
    - Center the footer text.

13. Save the **reddienew.htm** file.

14. Switch to your browser and refresh or reload the page. Compare your file to Figure 7-64 to verify that your file is correct.

15. Submit the results of the **reddienew.htm** file to your instructor, either in printed or electronic form, as requested.

16. If you are not completing the next assignment, close your text editor and your browser.

| Apply | **Case Problem 2** |

*he skills you
ed in the tutorial
ate a Web page
college Business
munications
e.*

Data Files needed for this Case Problem: block.gif, letter.htm, modblock.gif, printstyles.css

Writing Effective Business Communications   Professor Janet Shah, chair of the English Department at Canyon Lake College in Davis, Oklahoma, teaches several sections of her English 245 class, Writing Effective Business Communications. She has asked you to create a new Web page for this course. You will create a three-column liquid layout that has nested divs in the center column. After you complete a step to create a style, verify in your browser that the style code has been entered correctly, and then switch back to your text editor. A preview of the Web page you will create appears in Figure 7-65.

Figure 7-65

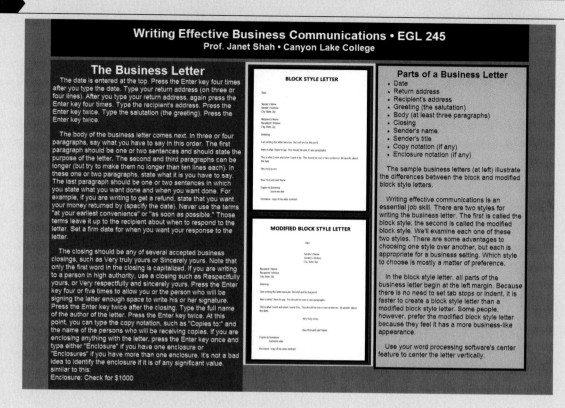

Complete the following:

1. Use your text editor to open the **letter.htm** file, which is provided in your Data Files in the Tutorial.07\Case2 folder. In the head section and below the page title, enter your name and today's date in the comment section where noted.

2. Save the file as **letternew.htm** in the same folder. Open the file in your browser and observe the appearance of the original file.

3. Switch back to your text editor. In the code for the embedded style sheet, style the universal selector to have margins of 0 and padding of 0.

4. Style the body element to have text appear with a font size of 1.1em in Arial (a sans-serif font). Set the background color to #818039.

5. Save the **letternew.htm** file. Switch back to your browser and refresh or reload the page. Verify that the body element style appears correctly in your file.

6. Switch back to your text editor. In the head section and below the page title, use the link element to create a link to the printstyles.css file. Insert the appropriate value for the media attribute in the link tag.

7. In the start style tag, add the media attribute with a value of "screen" to the right of the "text/css" value.

8. In the embedded style sheet and below the body style, create the following styles for the #container id selector:
   - Set the width to 90%.
   - Set the margin to 0 on the top and bottom and "auto" on the left and right.

9. Create the following styles for the #header id selector:
   - Set the margin on the bottom to 0.5em.
   - Add padding of 1em on all sides.

- Set the text color to white.
- Set the background color to black.

10. Create the following styles for the #main id selector:
    - Set the width to 40%.
    - Add padding of 0.5% on all sides.
    - Set the text color to white.
    - Set the background color to #48332f.
    - Float the contents "left."

11. Create the following styles for the #sidebar id selector:
    - Set the margin on the left to 41%.
    - Set the margin on the right to 32%.
    - Add padding of 0.5% on all sides.
    - Set the background color to yellow.

12. Create the following styles for the #section id selector:
    - Set the width to 30%.
    - Create a border that is solid, thick, and black.
    - Add padding of 0.5% on all sides.
    - Set the background color to orange.
    - Float the contents "right."

⊕ EXPLORE 13. Create a grouped descendant selector for the #main id selector and the #section id selector so that paragraph text appears with a margin of 1em on the bottom and a text indent of 1em.

⊕ EXPLORE 14. Create a grouped selector to style the #block id selector and the #modblock id selector as follows:
    - Create a border that is solid, thick, and navy.
    - Add padding of 0.5% on all sides.
    - Set the background color to black.

15. Create a style for the image element to have margins of 0 on the top and bottom and "auto" on the left and right. Set the display value to "block."

16. Style the ul element selector to have a margin on the left of 2em and a margin on the bottom of 1em.

17. Create a grouped selector to style both the h1 and h2 element selectors so that h1 and h2 text is centered.

18. Save the **letternew.htm** file. Switch to your browser and refresh or reload the page. Compare your file to Figure 7-65 to verify that your file is correct.

19. From the menu bar, click File and then click Print Preview. Preview the print style that has been created. Exit Print Preview.

20. Submit the results of the preceding steps to your instructor, either in printed or electronic form, as requested.

21. If you are not completing the next assignment, close your text editor and your browser.

Challenge | Case Problem 3

Use the skills you learned in the tutorial to create and style a Web page for a bowling alley and entertainment center.

Data Files needed for this Case Problem: lana.htm, lanalogo.gif, navbar.css, tailfin.gif

Lana Lanes Lana Lanes is a large bowling and entertainment complex on the outskirts of Fargo, North Dakota. The bowling alley, restaurants, game rooms, and party room are all designed with a 1950s retro-style décor to attract customers. Lana Lanes is opening a new restaurant called the Strike 'n Spare and a new dance club called the Tailfin Lounge. Lana Clark, the owner of Lana Lanes, has asked you to develop a new home page for the company's Web site. You will create a three-column liquid layout. After you complete a step to create a style, verify in your browser that the style code has been entered correctly, and then switch back to your text editor. A preview of the Web page you will create appears in Figure 7-66.

Figure 7-66

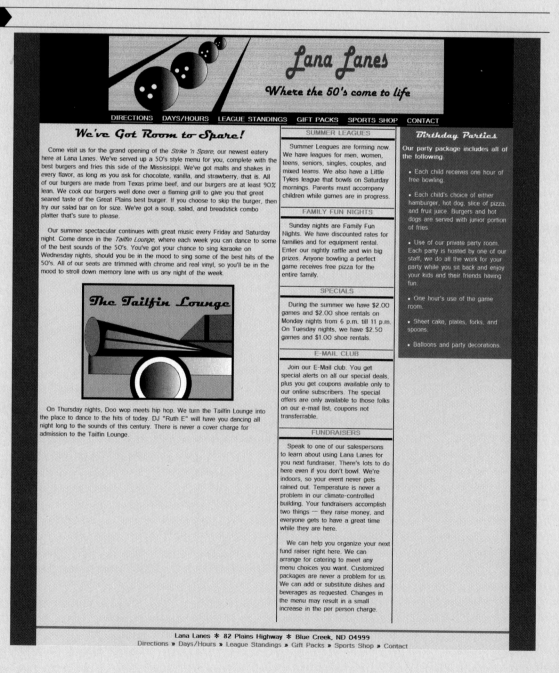

Complete the following:

1. Use your text editor to open the **lana.htm** file, which is provided in your Data Files in the Tutorial.07\Case3 folder. In the head section and below the page title, enter your name and today's date in the comment section where noted.

2. Save the file as **lananew.htm** in the same folder. Open the file in your browser and observe the appearance of the original file.

EXPLORE

3. Switch back to your text editor. Just below the start style tag, enter the @import rule to import the navbar.css file, which is provided in your Data Files in the Tutorial.07\Case3 folder.

4. Style the body element as follows:
   - Set the font size to 1.1em.
   - Set the font to Shruti (sans-serif).
   - Set the background color to #0d4a2c.
   - Set the line height to 1.25.

5. Save the **lananew.htm** file. Switch back to your browser and refresh or reload the page. Verify that the body element style appears correctly in your file.

6. Switch back to your text editor. Below the body element style, style the universal selector to have margins of 0 and padding of 0.

7. Style the #container id as follows:
   - Set the width to 90%.
   - Set the margin to 0 on the top and bottom and "auto" on the left and right.
   - Set the border width to 1px on all sides.
   - Set the background color to #c2efd8.

8. Style the #header id selector to have a background color of black.

9. Style the #left id selector as follows:
   - Set the width to 50%.
   - Add padding of 0.5% on all sides.
   - Float the contents "left."

10. Create a descendant selector for the #left id selector so that h1 text appears as follows:
    - Set the bottom margin to 0.5em.
    - Set the font family to Magneto (a serif font).
    - Center the h1 text.

EXPLORE

11. Create a grouped style for the #left p and #middle p selectors so that paragraph text in both the left and middle columns appears as follows:
    - Set the margin on the bottom to 1em.
    - Set the text indent to 1em.

12. Style the #middle id selector as follows:
    - Set the width to 23%.
    - Set the border on the left to solid, thin, and black.
    - Set the border on the right to solid, thin, and black.
    - Add padding of 0.5% on all sides.
    - Float the contents "left."

13. Style the #right id selector as follows:
    - Set the width to 23%.
    - Add padding of 0.5% on all sides.
    - Set the text color to white.

- Set the background color to green.
- Float the contents "right."

14. Create a descendant selector for the #right id selector so that unordered list items appear as follows:
    - Set the margin on the left to 1em.
    - Set padding on the top to 0.
    - Set the list style type to square.
    - Set the list style position to inside.

EXPLORE

15. Create a descendant selector for the #right id selector so that list items within unordered lists have a margin of 1em on the top and bottom and 0 on the left and right.

16. Style the #footer id selector as follows:
    - Set the margin on the top to 1em.
    - Set the border on the top to solid, thick, and green.
    - Clear the contents of the footer on both the left and the right.
    - Set the font weight to bold.
    - Center the contents of the footer.

17. Style the h2 heading element selector as follows:
    - Set the margin on the bottom to 0.5em.
    - Set the font family to Magneto (a serif font).
    - Center the h2 text.

18. Set the h3 heading element selector as follows:
    - Set the margin on the bottom to 0.5em.
    - Set the border on the top to solid, thin, and black.
    - Set the border on the bottom to solid, thick, and black.
    - Set the text color to #68964c.
    - Center the h3 text.
    - Have the h3 text appear in uppercase.

19. Style the image element selector as follows:
    - Set margins to 0 on the top and bottom and "auto" on the left and right.
    - Set the border to solid, thick, and black.
    - Set the value for the display property to "block."

20. Save the **lananew.htm** file. Switch to your browser and refresh or reload the page. Compare your file to Figure 7-66 to verify that your file is correct.

21. In your browser, go to *http://validator.w3.org* to open the W3C validator. Validate the **lananew.htm** file by using the Validate by File Upload method. Note any errors and correct them in your file if necessary.

22. In your browser, navigate to *http://jigsaw.w3.org/css-validator*. Validate the **lananew.htm** file by using the By file upload method. Note any errors and correct them in your file if necessary. You can ignore the following warning, which you will see regarding the imported style sheet: "Imported style sheets are not checked in direct input and file upload modes."

23. Submit the results of the **lananew.htm** file to your instructor, either in printed or electronic form, as requested.

24. If you are not completing the next assignment, close your text editor and your browser.

Create	**| Case Problem 4**

e a Web page to
ote a new
food.

Data Files needed for this Case Problem: hooks.htm, hookslogo.gif

Hooks, Wheels, and Ladders   The latest entry into the snack food industry is a health-conscious offering named Hooks, Wheels, and Ladders. Each box mixes several flavors, such as ranch, cheddar, and salsa. The snack is designed to appeal to kids based on the snack shapes; however, the company hopes to appeal to adults as well, based on taste, variety, and ingredients. Maye Hanley, the senior marketing manager, has asked you to create a Web site to promote Hooks, Wheels, and Ladders. She has given you some promotional copy that you incorporated into a basic Web page, and now she wants you to create an attractive layout for the page.

Complete the following:

1. Use your text editor to open the **hooks.htm** file, which is provided in your Data Files in the Tutorial.07\Case4 folder. In the head section, give your page an appropriate title. Below the page title, enter your name and today's date in the comment section where noted.
2. Save the file as **hooksnew.htm** in the same folder.
3. Create the tags for an embedded style sheet. Within these tags, format the body element with the text size, font, color, and background color of your choice.
4. Plan a liquid layout for the **hooksnew.htm** file. The layout should have divs for a header, a sidebar, a main section, and a footer. Use the **hookslogo.gif** image in the header div. Include margins and padding as appropriate in your layout.
5. Create styles for all the id selectors and all other selectors.
6. In the body section, create divs as necessary. Apply the id selectors to your divs as appropriate.
7. Create a container div for your layout. Create styles for the container div so that the page is centered horizontally in the browser.
8. Include at least one example of the use of a descendant selector.
9. Feel free to add other images and text content (as appropriate) to the Web page.
10. Save the **hooksnew.htm** file. Switch to your browser and refresh or reload the page. Verify that all styles work correctly.
11. Open your browser and go to *http://validator.w3.org*. Use the Validate by File Upload method to check the **hooksnew.htm** document and ensure that the HTML code is correct. If necessary, correct any errors detected by the validation.
12. In your browser, go to *http://jigsaw.w3.org/css-validator*. Use the By file upload method to check the **hooksnew.htm** file and ensure that the CSS code is correct. If necessary, correct any errors detected by the validation.
13. Submit the results of the **hooksnew.htm** file to your instructor, either in printed or electronic form, as requested.
14. Close your text editor and your browser. Close all open windows.

Review	**| Quick Check Answers**

Session 7.1

1. a layout in which the page is taller than it is wide
2. a layout in which the page is wider than it is tall
3. a layout that expands or contracts in proportion to the size of the viewport
4. a layout using em values

5. a div within a div
6. to group related content or to create additional structure

Session 7.2

1. to limit its width
2. container
3. a style designed to print only the Web page text
4. external
5. media="print"
6. @page rule

Ending Data Files

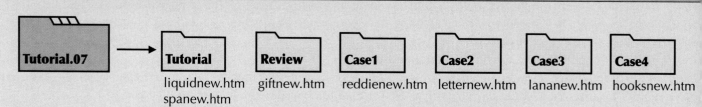

Tutorial.07 → Tutorial   Review   Case1   Case2   Case3   Case4

liquidnew.htm   giftnew.htm   reddienew.htm   letternew.htm   lananew.htm   hooksnew.htm
spanew.htm

Creating Data Tables

Using Tables to Display Data

Case | Devon Valley Summer Film Festival

The Devon Valley Summer Film Festival attracts visitors from all over the United States and around the world. The festival typically is hosted by the small town of Billings Bluff, which is about 100 miles north of Salt Lake City, Utah. During the first week of July each year, thousands of people flock to Billings Bluff to enjoy films that showcase major stars in small-budget movies. Sometimes the movies shown at the festival become commercial hits in their own right. Ben Goldstein, the producer of this year's festival, has asked for your help in creating a Web site to promote the festival.

Ben is familiar with HTML, and he has started work on a Web page that describes the festival. In the first session, you will use a file named table.htm to list some of the noteworthy films that will be shown. The home page will be updated each day during the film festival. You will work with Ben to create the data table for the film schedule. In the second session, you will show Ben how to format the table using CSS styles.

Starting Data Files

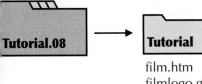

Tutorial.08 →	Tutorial	Review	Case1	Case2	Case3	Case4
	film.htm	lodge.htm	body.htm	berst.htm	admit.htm	personal.htm
	filmlogo.gif	lodgelogo.gif		berstlogo.gif	back.png	
	filmstyles.css				baxter.htm	
	table.htm					

Creating a Table to Display and Organize Data

If you are familiar with the table feature of a word-processing program, you know that you can create tables made up of columns and rows that display data in an organized manner. To organize data for a Web page, you create a **data table**, which is a table used to align Web content in columns and rows. You might also know how easy it is to create tables using a "quick create" or "table draw" feature in a word-processing program. HTML, however, does not have a quick means to create tables. HTML table columns and rows have to be entered one cell at a time. (A **cell** is the intersection of a column and row.)

You might also be familiar with a spreadsheet program, such as Microsoft Excel, which uses columns and rows to organize data. A spreadsheet program has extensive math, formula creation, and charting features, but HTML does not. HTML also does not have cell addresses. For example, the intersection of column C and row 2 is referred to as cell address C2 in a spreadsheet program, but when you refer to a cell in HTML, you just describe its location in the table, such as "the third cell in the second row."

Until a few years ago, HTML tables were used both as a means for organizing data and creating page layout. A **layout table** is a table in which the code is used for page layout. Because tables require a substantial amount of code and can be a barrier to accessibility, the use of layout tables has declined dramatically over the past few years. Although HTML tables are still used to organize data, you should no longer use tables for page layout; CSS is now the preferred method instead.

Similarly, until just a few years ago, HTML frames were also commonly used for page layout. **Frames** present documents in multiple views as either independent windows or subwindows, but frames pose a significant challenge for screen reader software. The use of frames for page layout has been discouraged by the World Wide Web Consortium (the W3C) for more than a decade, and frames are not supported in HTML 5.0. As a result, today you will rarely encounter a Web site with a layout created with HTML frames. For accessibility reasons alone, you should convert any existing pages created with frames into pages with layout created by CSS code. Layout tables and frames today are considered **legacy code**—outdated code that should be replaced with the more contemporary CSS code.

Ben has typed a draft of the content for the film festival Web page, as shown in Figure 8-1.

Figure 8-1 **Ben's typed draft of the film festival Web page**

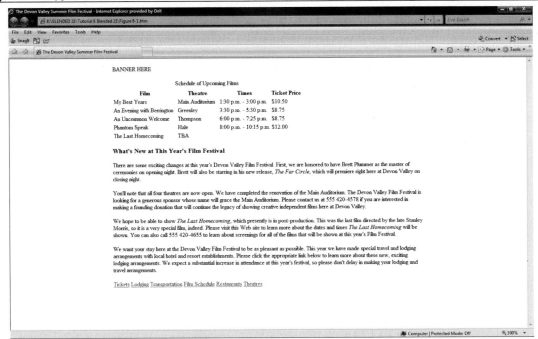

You will begin by opening a file in which you will create the data table for the Devon Valley Film Festival home page.

To open the table.htm file and save it with a new filename:

1. In your text editor, open the **table.htm** file, which is located in the Tutorial.08\ Tutorial folder included with your Data Files. The contents of this file will be copied and pasted into the film.htm file, so you will not create a page title for this file. In the head section, enter your name and today's date in the comment section where noted.

2. Save the file as **tablenew.htm** in the same folder.

Next, you will show Ben how to enter the table tags and give the table a title.

Entering the Table Tags and Creating a Table Title

The **table element** is used to create an HTML table. Tables begin with the start <table> tag and end with the closing </table> tag. Tables can be placed anywhere within the <body> </body> tags, as shown in the following code:

```
<body>

<table>
   . . . table code goes here . . .
</table>

</body>
```

You can use the title attribute to give a title to your table to describe the table content. If you do, and the user passes the mouse pointer over the table, a ScreenTip will display the title. The **summary attribute**, which was used to provide a detailed description of the table, is deprecated in HTML 5.0.

Reference Window		**Creating a Table**

- To create a table, enter the following code:
  ```
  <table title="tabletitle">
  </table>
  ```
  where <table> is the start table tag, title is the title attribute, *tabletitle*
  is a brief description of the table to be used as a ScreenTip, and </table> is the end
  table tag.

You will show Ben how to enter code for the start <table> tag, the title attribute and
its value, and the end </table> tag.

To enter code for the table tags and the title attribute:

▶ **1.** In the tablenew.htm document, below the start <body> tag, type the following
   code, as shown in Figure 8-2.

   ```
   <table title="The Devon Valley Film Festival Schedule">
   ```

▶ **2.** Press the **Enter** key four times.

▶ **3.** Type the following code, as shown in Figure 8-2.

   ```
   </table>
   ```

Figure 8-2	▶	**The table code**

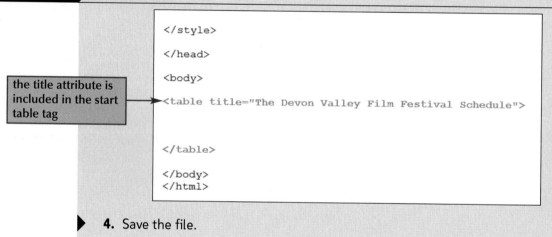

```
</style>

</head>

<body>

the title attribute is    <table title="The Devon Valley Film Festival Schedule">
included in the start
table tag

</table>

</body>
</html>
```

▶ **4.** Save the file.

Now that you have entered the start and end table tags, you're ready to show Ben how
to add a descriptive caption to the table.

Because tables involve a considerable amount of code, it can be difficult to debug a problem in your table code. Here's a good strategy for creating tables:

- Sketch out the table using a pencil and paper. Give each cell a number, starting with cell 1 in the upper-left corner and continuing from left to right and top to bottom. You might even consider labeling the cells as they would appear in a spreadsheet program, such as A1, B1, C1, and so on for the first row, and A2, B2, C2, and so on for the second row.
- In your text editor, create an embedded style sheet and enter styles to make the table borders visible.
- In the document body, enter the start and end table tags, along with the title attribute and its value.
- Type the code for the first row of the table. Use the same placeholder data in all the cells. (You can type anything in the cell, including the word "placeholder," as long as each cell has the same placeholder data so you can globally replace the data later.)
- Name and save the file.
- Open the file in the browser. Observe the result. Debug as necessary.
- Copy the table row code and table data code and paste it in each row you will need for the table.
- If you merge cells, perform one merge at a time. Save the file after each merge. View the result in the browser, and debug as necessary.
- When you are satisfied that the table structure is correct, delete the placeholder data. (Globally delete the placeholder text and replace it with nothing.)
- Type the actual table data in each cell.
- After you enter the table data and verify that the table code is correct, create styles for the table elements.

Creating a Caption

A **caption** is a brief description of a table. You have already entered a title to describe a table when the mouse pointer passes over it. The caption text, however, appears as part of the table and remains visible in the browser at all times. The caption text can be as brief as the words "Figure 1" or it can be more descriptive, such as "Profit and Loss Statement for the Last Two Quarters of the Current Fiscal Year." A table caption is optional, but it helps describe the table data, especially if the table is complex and has a great deal of numeric data. You use the **caption element** to provide a data table with a caption.

- To create a table caption, enter the following code:
  ```
  <caption>captiontext</caption>
  ```
  where `<caption>` is the start caption tag, *captiontext* is the text in the caption, and `</caption>` is the end caption tag.

If you include a table caption, the caption tags must follow the start <table> tag, because the caption is part of the table. For example, if you set the table style to display text in the Arial font, the caption text will also appear in Arial. The end </caption> tag does not have to be placed on a separate line; it can follow the caption text, similar to how you insert the end </title> tag after entering the title text. The code for a table caption would look similar to the following code:

```
<table title="The Devon Valley Film Festival Schedule">
<caption>Schedule of Upcoming Films</caption>

</table>
```

By default, the caption text is centered and is placed above the table. If you don't want the caption to be centered, create a style for the caption property and style the caption to align with the left edge of the table. You also can use the CSS **caption-side property** to position a caption above or below a table. Unfortunately, the caption-side property does not yet have full browser support. It is supported by the Firefox browser, but not by Internet Explorer versions 7 and earlier. The caption-side property takes the values shown in Figure 8-3.

Figure 8-3 ▶ **The caption-side property values**

Value	Purpose
top	The default value. The caption is displayed above the table and is centered.
bottom	The caption is displayed below the table and is centered.

If you must position a caption below a table and you want full browser support, you will have to use the deprecated align attribute with a value of "bottom" in the start <caption> tag, as shown in the following code:

```
<table title="The Devon Valley Film Festival Schedule">
<caption align="bottom">Schedule of Upcoming Films</caption>
</table>
```

Ben does not want to use deprecated code, so he will use the default value and have the caption appear above the table. You will now show Ben how to enter the table caption.

To enter the table caption:

▶ **1.** In your text editor, position the insertion point on a blank line below the start <table> tag. Type the following code, as shown in Figure 8-4.

```
<caption>Schedule of Upcoming Films</caption>
```

Figure 8-4 ▶ **The caption code**

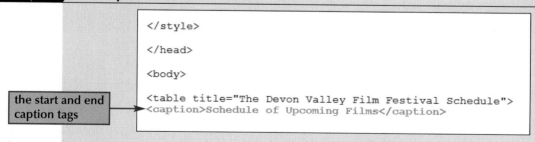

```
</style>

</head>

<body>

<table title="The Devon Valley Film Festival Schedule">
<caption>Schedule of Upcoming Films</caption>
```

the start and end caption tags

▶ **2.** Save the file.

Next, you'll show Ben how to create rows and cells for the table.

Creating Table Rows and Table Data

Tip

ending </tr> tag is
ted, data that you
ed to appear in a cell
e displayed outside
able structure, which
ually above the table.

The **table row element** is used to create table rows. It's good coding practice to type the start <tr> tag and the end </tr> tag at the same time, so you don't forget to insert the </tr> tag after entering the table data into the row. If you fail to enter an end </tr> tag, you won't get the structure for the table that you intended.

To make the table row code easier to read, enter the code for the table row tags on separate lines, as shown in the following code.

```
<tr>
   table data will go here . . .
</tr>
```

Reference Window | Creating Table Rows

- To create table rows, enter the following code:
  ```
  <tr>
     <td>tabledata</td>
  </tr>
  ```
  where <tr> is the start table row tag, <td> is the start table data tag, *tabledata* is the data for the cell, </td> is the end table data tag, and </tr> is the end table row tag.

You enter the content for a cell using the **table data element**. It's common practice to indent the table data code by at least two spaces to make it easier to see the start and end table row tags that enclose the table data tags. The data table for the film festival initially will consist of six rows, each with four columns—a total of 24 cells. You can use the **table header element** to format the first row of a table, which often describes the contents of the rows below. By default, the table header element centers text and makes text bold. In addition to creating the table header cells, you will add an attribute that aids in accessibility (the scope attribute) to the table header code.

The **scope attribute** and its value determine which adjacent cells are associated with a particular cell. This attribute is used by screen readers to help read content down a column or across a row. The scope attribute determines whether a cell is a header for a column, a row, a group of columns, or a group of rows. This attribute does not affect the table's appearance in the browser. The scope attribute takes the values shown in Figure 8-5.

Figure 8-5 ▶ Values for the scope attribute

Scope Attribute Value	Indicates Cell Is Associated With
col	column
row	row
colgroup	a group of columns (seldom used)
rowgroup	a group of rows

Table header tags can also be placed at the start of each row to create row headings rather than column headings. If you want to style the table to mimic the appearance of a spreadsheet, use th (table header) tags rather than td (table data) tags for the first cell in each of the remaining rows as well, as shown in the following code.

```
<tr>
  <th>Last Year</th>
  <td>900,000</td>
  <td>500,000</td>
  <td>2,000,000</td>
</tr>
```

```
<tr>
  <th>This Year</th>
  <td>1,250,000</td>
  <td>1,600,000</td>
  <td>1,800,000</td>
</tr>
```

You could then create a style for the table header element (usually to change the color and background color) and create a different style for the table data element, aligning the contents "right," as shown in the following code.

```
th {
  color: white;
  background-color: navy;
}

td {
  text-align: right;
}
```

The completed table would appear as shown in Figure 8-6.

Figure 8-6	Table with both column and row headers

	Jones	Smith	Rollings
Last Year	900,000	500,000	2,000,000
This Year	1,250,000	1,600,000	1,800,000

When you create the structure for a table, it's a good idea to enter the table data for the first row, save the file, and then open the file in the browser to see the result. If there are any problems with the table structure, it's much easier to correct code errors early, before you create dozens or hundreds of rows in the table. You will show Ben how to enter the table data for the first row.

To enter the table header data:

▶ 1. In your text editor, position the insertion point on a blank line below the caption code. Type the following code, as shown in Figure 8-7.

```
<tr>
  <th scope="col">Film</th>
  <th scope="col">Theatre</th>
  <th scope="col">Times</th>
  <th scope="col">Ticket Price</th>
</tr>
```

Figure 8-7	The table header code

the table header tags and the scope attribute with a value of "col"

```
<table title="The Devon Valley Film Festival Schedule">
<caption>Schedule of Upcoming Films</caption>

<tr>
  <th scope="col">Film</th>
  <th scope="col">Theatre</th>
  <th scope="col">Times</th>
  <th scope="col">Ticket Price</th>
</tr>

</table>
```

▶ **2.** Save the file.

▶ **3.** Open the **tablenew.htm** file in your browser. Compare your file with the one shown in Figure 8-8 to confirm that the code has been entered correctly.

Figure 8-8 ▶ **The table in the browser**

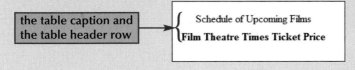

Although the table has content, it does not have any horizontal or vertical ruled lines, so it's not easy to see the boundaries of the table cells. You will show Ben how to create the ruled lines for the table.

Creating Table Borders

Table borders are the horizontal and vertical lines that surround the table. You use the border property and a value in pixels to create the table borders. The table element does not create a table border, so you must use CSS styles to create it. **Gridlines** are the horizontal and vertical lines that appear within the table. By default, a table does not show the gridlines in the browser; so again, you need to use CSS styles to create the gridlines.

erence Window | **Creating Table Borders**

- To create external borders, enter the following CSS code:
  ```
  table {
     border: value;
  }
  ```
  where *table* is the table element, *border* is the border property, and *value* is any CSS unit measurement.
- To create gridlines, enter the following CSS code:
  ```
  th, td {
     border: value;
  }
  ```
  where *th, td* are the table header and table data selectors, *border* is the border property, and *value* is any CSS unit measurement.

When you first create a data table, it's useful to display the table borders and gridlines so you can clearly see the table structure. If you create a style for the table element and use the border property with a pixel value of 1 or greater, you will see the table borders in the browser. Use pixel values rather than keywords to specify a border width, because browsers interpret the keywords "thin," "medium," and "thick" differently. For example, if you specify keywords for border thickness, your borders will appear at least 1px thicker in Internet Explorer than they will in other browsers.

When you create a CSS border style for the table element, you affect only the appearance of the outer borders. To have the table gridlines appear within the table, you must also create styles for the table header and table data elements. You will show Ben how to create styles for the table element, the table header element, and the table data element so that a border appears around the table and gridlines appear within the table.

To show the table borders and table gridlines:

▶ **1.** In your text editor, within the embedded style sheet and below the start <style> tag code, type the following code, as shown in Figure 8-9.

```
table {
  border: solid 6px navy;
}

th, td {
  border: solid 2px orange;
}
```

Figure 8-9	The code to display the table borders

```
<style type="text/css">

table {
  border: solid 6px navy;
}

th, td {
  border: solid 2px orange;
}

</style>
```

the table th and td elements styled

▶ **2.** Save the file.

▶ **3.** Switch to your browser and refresh or reload the **tablenew.htm** page. Compare your file with the one shown in Figure 8-10 to confirm that the table borders and gridlines appear.

Figure 8-10	The table borders and gridlines in the browser

the table borders and gridlines are established

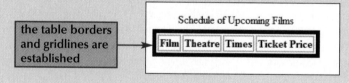

Schedule of Upcoming Films

| Film | Theatre | Times | Ticket Price |

You will now show Ben how to insert the remaining rows of the table.

To enter the table data tags:

▶ **1.** Switch back to your text editor. On a blank line below the end </tr> tag for the table header row, type the following code, as shown in Figure 8-11.

```
<tr>
  <td></td>
  <td></td>
  <td></td>
  <td></td>
</tr>
```

Figure 8-11 | **The table cells code**

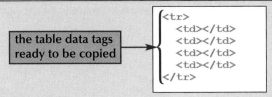

the table data tags
ready to be copied

```
<tr>
  <td></td>
  <td></td>
  <td></td>
  <td></td>
</tr>
```

▶ **2.** Save the file.

▶ **3.** Select the code you just typed.

▶ **4.** Press the **Ctrl+C** keys to copy the code.

▶ **5.** On a blank line below the end </tr> tag for the table data code you just typed, press the **Ctrl+V** keys to paste the code.

▶ **6.** Repeat the preceding step three times to make three more copies of the table row and table data tags. (Make sure to include a blank line between each set of <tr> and </tr> tags to separate each group of table row code.)

▶ **7.** Type the following code between the <td> and </td> tags for each row, as shown in Figure 8-12. Note that there is no content for the last two cells in the last row.

```
<tr>
  <td>My Best Years</td>
  <td>Main Auditorium</td>
  <td>1:30 p.m. - 3:00 p.m.</td>
  <td>$10.50</td>
</tr>

<tr>
  <td>An Evening with Berrington</td>
  <td>Greenley</td>
  <td>3:30 p.m. - 5:30 p.m.</td>
  <td>$8.75</td>
</tr>

<tr>
  <td>An Uncommon Welcome</td>
  <td>Thompson</td>
  <td>6:00 p.m. - 7:25 p.m.</td>
  <td>$8.75</td>
</tr>

<tr>
  <td>Phantom Speak</td>
  <td>Hale</td>
  <td>8:00 p.m. - 10:15 p.m.</td>
  <td>$12.00</td>
</tr>

<tr>
  <td>The Last Homecoming</td>
  <td>TBA</td>
  <td></td>
  <td></td>
</tr>
```

Figure 8-12   The table data cells code

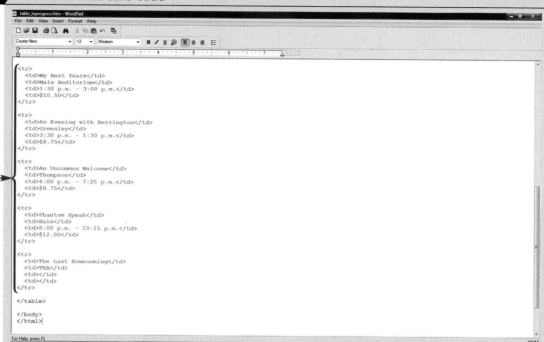

the table data

8. Save the file.

9. Switch to your browser and refresh or reload the **tablenew.htm** page. Compare your file with the one shown in Figure 8-13 to confirm that the table code has been entered correctly. Depending on your browser and browser version, the two cells without content in the last row might not have a border, as shown in Figure 8-13.

Figure 8-13   The table data in the browser

Schedule of Upcoming Films

Film	Theatre	Times	Ticket Price
My Best Years	Main Auditorium	1:30 p.m. - 3:00 p.m.	$10.50
An Evening with Berrington	Greenley	3:30 p.m. - 5:30 p.m.	$8.75
An Uncommon Welcome	Thompson	6:00 p.m. - 7:25 p.m.	$8.75
Phantom Speak	Hale	8:00 p.m. - 10:15 p.m.	$12.00
The Last Homecoming	TBA		

InSight | *Displaying Empty Cells*

An **empty cell** is a cell without content. Depending on your browser and browser version, you may not see gridlines around empty cells. CSS has an **empty-cells property**, which can create gridlines around empty cells. The empty-cells property takes either the "show" value, in which gridlines are drawn around an empty cell, or "hide," in which gridlines are not drawn around an empty cell. To always show a border even if the cell is empty, set the following style for the td element selector:

```
td {
    empty-cells: show;
}
```

By default, cells without content appear with a border in some contemporary browsers. However, in some versions of Internet Explorer, you must enter the   character entity to have empty cells appear with a border. By using the empty-cells property and setting the style for the td element to always show borders, you don't have to include the   character entity in each empty cell.

Ben noticed that the last two cells of the table do not have any content. He'd like to combine the cell that contains "TBA" (an acronym for "To Be Announced") with the cells without content to create a single cell. You will next show Ben how to merge cells in columns.

Merging Cells in Columns

Two HTML attributes are used to merge (combine) cells: colspan and rowspan. The **colspan attribute** is used to merge cells across columns. This attribute can cause accessibility problems for screen readers, unless you merge the entire column or merge all of the cells to the right of a particular data cell. You enter the colspan attribute in the start td tag where you want the column merge to begin. You then delete the <td></td> tags for the number of additional cells the column spans. The colspan code for The Last Homecoming column would appear as shown below. Note that the cells without content have been deleted.

```
<tr>
    <td>The Last Homecoming</td>
    <td colspan="3">TBA</td>
</tr>
```

Figure 8-14 shows an example of the colspan attribute. Note that the last three cells in the table have been merged across the columns.

| **Figure 8-14** | **The colspan attribute in the last row** |

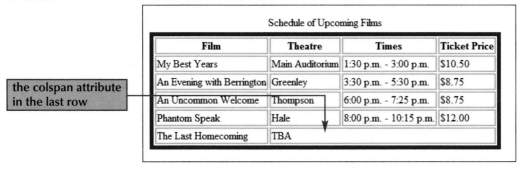

the colspan attribute in the last row

- To span a cell across columns, enter the following code:

  `<td colspan="value">`

  where *colspan* is the colspan attribute and *value* is the number of columns that will be spanned. The colspan attribute and its value must be placed in the cell in which the column merge should begin. All empty spanned table data cells should be deleted.

The **rowspan attribute** is used to merge cells across rows. Be judicious in your use of the rowspan attribute because it can create problems for screen readers. If you must merge rows, merge the cells in each row. In the following example, note that the `<td></td>` tags for the cells to be merged (the cells with the other ticket prices) have been deleted.

```
<tr>
  <td>My Best Years</td>
  <td>Main Auditorium</td>
  <td>1:30 p.m. - 3:00 p.m.</td>
  <td rowspan="4">$10.00</td>
</tr>
```

Figure 8-15 illustrates an example of a table in which the last three columns are merged and four of the rows in the last column are merged.

Figure 8-15 ⟩ **Examples of colspan and rowspan attributes**

You always enter the colspan attribute and its value in the **key cell**, which is the cell where the cells begin to merge. In this instance the key cell is the "TBA" cell. The cells that do not have content will be deleted. You will now show Ben how to merge three cells in the last row and delete the table data cells that are no longer needed.

To merge the cells:

▶ 1. Switch back to your text editor. Position the insertion point in the start `<td>` tag before the right angle bracket in the "TBA" cell.

▶ 2. Press the **Spacebar** once.

▶ 3. Type **colspan="3"**

▶ 4. Delete the `<td></td>` tags for the two cells that do not have any content. Your code should look similar to that in Figure 8-16.

Figure 8-16 ▷ **The colspan code**

```
<tr>
  <td>The Last Homecoming</td>
  <td colspan="3">TBA</td>
</tr>

</table>
```

> the column merge set
> to span three columns

▷ **5.** Save the file.

▷ **6.** Switch to your browser and refresh or reload the **tablenew.htm** page. Compare your file with the one shown in Figure 8-17 to confirm that the colspan code has been entered correctly.

Figure 8-17 ▷ **The colspan in the browser**

Schedule of Upcoming Films

Film	Theatre	Times	Ticket Price
My Best Years	Main Auditorium	1:30 p.m. - 3:00 p.m.	$10.50
An Evening with Berrington	Greenley	3:30 p.m. - 5:30 p.m.	$8.75
An Uncommon Welcome	Thompson	6:00 p.m. - 7:25 p.m.	$8.75
Phantom Speak	Hale	8:00 p.m. - 10:15 p.m.	$12.00
The Last Homecoming	TBA		

By default, the text in merged cells is not formatted. Ben thinks the spanned text would look better if it were centered and appeared in italic. You will show Ben how to create an independent class to format the text and then apply the class to the key cell.

To format the data in the merged cells:

▷ **1.** Switch back to your text editor. Position the insertion point on a blank line after the th, td grouped selector. Type the following code, as shown in Figure 8-18.

```
.center {
  font-style: italic;
  text-align: center;
}
```

Figure 8-18 ▷ **The .center independent class**

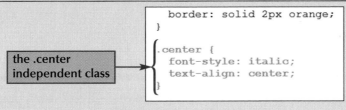

```
    border: solid 2px orange;
}

.center {
  font-style: italic;
  text-align: center;
}
```

> the .center
> independent class

▶ **2.** In the document body, position the insertion point to the right of the closing quote in the colspan="3" code.

▶ **3.** Press the **Spacebar** once.

▶ **4.** Type **class="center"**

Your code should look similar to that in Figure 8-19.

Figure 8-19 ▶ **The center class applied**

```
</tr>

<tr>
  <td>The Last Homecoming</td>
  <td colspan="3" class="center">TBA</td>
</tr>

</table>
```

applying the center class to the colspan row

▶ **5.** Save the file.

▶ **6.** Switch to your browser and refresh or reload the **tablenew.htm** page. Compare your file with the one shown in Figure 8-20 to confirm that the colspan text has been centered and appears in italics.

Figure 8-20 ▶ **The colspan text formatted in the browser**

Schedule of Upcoming Films			
Film	**Theatre**	**Times**	**Ticket Price**
My Best Years	Main Auditorium	1:30 p.m. - 3:00 p.m.	$10.50
An Evening with Berrington	Greenley	3:30 p.m. - 5:30 p.m.	$8.75
An Uncommon Welcome	Thompson	6:00 p.m. - 7:25 p.m.	$8.75
Phantom Speak	Hale	8:00 p.m. - 10:15 p.m.	$12.00
The Last Homecoming	*TBA*		

Grouping Rows

Table rows can be grouped into a table header, a table footer, or into one or more table body sections. The elements used to group table row content are thead, tfoot, and tbody. The thead and tfoot elements are useful when you expect users will want to print tables that are longer than one page—the table header and footer information can be printed on each page that contains table data, similar to a header row in Microsoft Word or Excel. However, if you use all three of these elements in your table code, you must disrupt the source order in the table code, which is why these tags are not often used. If you do use these tags, you must list the thead tag followed by the tfoot tag, and then list the code for the tbody tag, as shown in the following example. Note the source order of the tags.

```
<table>
<caption>caption text here</caption>

<thead>
    ...header row code and content ...
</thead>

<tfoot>
    ...footer row code and content ...
</tfoot>

<tbody>
    ...first row of code and content ...
    ...second row of code and content ...
</tbody>

</table>
```

Although the <tfoot> tag does upset the source order, placing the contents of the <tfoot> tag before the contents of the <tbody> tag will have no effect on how the content appears in the browser.

Ben is curious about the appearance of the gridlines. They do not appear as they would in a word-processing table. He wants to know if he can eliminate some of the gridlines to create a single line between cells. You will next show Ben how to collapse table gridlines.

Collapsing Internal Borders

The **border-collapse property** is used to change the appearance of the table gridlines (the internal borders). By default, each cell has its own border, so each gridline appears as a double ruled line rather than a single ruled line. The double ruled lines tend to compete for attention with the cell contents. To give the table a cleaner, simpler appearance, you can change the cell borders to single rules by using the border-collapse property and assigning a value of "collapse." The default value, "separate," creates a double ruled line. You will show Ben how to add a declaration to the table element style that collapses the table gridlines and simplifies the table's appearance.

To collapse the internal borders:

▶ **1.** Switch back to your text editor. Position the insertion point after the semicolon in the border declaration of the table element style.

▶ **2.** Press the **Enter** key.

> **3.** Press the **Spacebar** twice.

> **4.** Type the following declaration shown in bold and in Figure 8-21.
>
> ```
> table {
>     border: solid 6px navy;
>     border-collapse: collapse;
> }
> ```

Figure 8-21 | **The border-collapse declaration**

borders are set
to collapse

```
<style type="text/css">

table {
    border: solid 6px navy;
    border-collapse: collapse;
}

th, td {
```

> **5.** Save the file.

> **6.** Switch to your browser and refresh or reload the **tablenew.htm** page. Compare your file with the one shown in Figure 8-22 to confirm that the internal table borders now appear as single rules rather than double rules.

Figure 8-22 | **The border collapse in the browser**

Schedule of Upcoming Films			
Film	**Theatre**	**Times**	**Ticket Price**
My Best Years	Main Auditorium	1:30 p.m. - 3:00 p.m.	$10.50
An Evening with Berrington	Greenley	3:30 p.m. - 5:30 p.m.	$8.75
An Uncommon Welcome	Thompson	6:00 p.m. - 7:25 p.m.	$8.75
Phantom Speak	Hale	8:00 p.m. - 10:15 p.m.	$12.00
The Last Homecoming	*TBA*		

> **7.** If you will not be completing the next session, close your text editor and your browser.

InSight | **Using the border-spacing Property**

Although it is not supported by all browsers, the **border-spacing property** can be used to add white space around cells, similar to the deprecated HTML cellspacing property. Border spacing specifies the distance between the borders of adjacent cells. Values can be expressed in any CSS unit of measurement, but negative values are not allowed. If one value is specified, it sets both the horizontal and vertical spacing. If two length values are specified, the first value sets the horizontal spacing and the second value sets the vertical spacing. You must use the border-collapse property of "separate" for the border-spacing property to work, as shown in the following code. In this instance, 5px of border spacing will be added on the top and bottom and 10px of border spacing will be added on the left and right.

```
table {
    border-spacing: 5px 10px;
    border-collapse: separate;
}
```

Last, you want to give Ben some pointers about what not to include in HTML tables.

Separating Presentation from Structure

Remember that your goal as a Web page designer is to separate presentation from structure. Don't use HTML attributes and values within the table element to format a table, as shown in the following code.

```
<table border="1" cellspacing="4" cellpadding="5">
```

Instead, create CSS styles to format your table. You also want to make your Web page content accessible. Some table elements, such as <thead> and <tfoot>, can easily be replaced by the use of CSS classes. In general, you should keep your tables simple and rely on CSS to format them. Above all, do not use tables for Web page layout. Figure 8-23 is an extensive list of the attributes used with table elements that are deprecated in HTML 5.0.

Figure 8-23 | List of HTML 5.0 deprecated table attributes

Attribute	Deprecated for Use With
align	caption element
border	table element
cellpadding	table element
cellspacing	table element
height	td and th elements
nowrap	td and th elements
rules	table element
summary	table element
valign	all table elements
width	all table elements

In this session, you learned that a data table is used to organize data. The title attribute is used to create a ScreenTip for the table. An optional caption tag can be used to provide the table with a description that will be displayed in the browser. Table rows are created by entering a pair of <tr> </tr> tags. The <td> </td> or <th> </th> tags enclose the contents of cells. The table header tags make text bold and centered. You can use the colspan attribute to merge cells across columns and the rowspan attribute to merge cells across rows, although you must use these carefully to make your table accessible. The border-collapse property is used to change the border default from a double ruled line to a single ruled line.

Review | **Session 8.1 Quick Check**

1. What is the purpose of a data table?
2. What is the effect of the title attribute when used with a table?
3. What is the purpose of a table caption?
4. What types of data can be placed into a table cell?
5. How does a table header cell differ from a table data cell?
6. What attribute is used to merge columns?
7. What is a key cell?

Session 8.2

Using CSS to Format Tables

In the past, it was common to format a table using HTML attributes and values. Today, however, most Web designers use CSS to format tables—this allows designers to separate presentation from the table structure. Although you will show Ben how to format only a single table, you can have more than one table on a Web page by using the div element to create page divisions. Create and apply id selectors to the div elements, just as you did in the previous tutorials on page layout.

You have already worked with Ben to create some simple styles for the table so that you could see the table border and the table gridlines. Ben's Web page, film.htm, will serve as the home page for the Devon Valley Film Festival Web site. Now that you have worked with him to create a separate file for the table and you know the table code is correct, you can copy and paste the table code into the film.htm page. Afterward, you will work with Ben to create some CSS styles that will improve the overall appearance of the table, not just enable visitors to see the table borders and gridlines.

To copy and paste the table code:

▶ 1. If necessary, open your browser. If necessary, open the **tablenew.htm** file in your text editor.

▶ 2. In the tablenew.htm file, select all the table code from the start <table> tag through the end </table> tag. Select only the table code.

▶ 3. Press the **Ctrl+C** keys to copy all the table code to the clipboard.

▶ 4. Close the **tablenew.htm** file *without saving changes*.

▶ 5. In your text editor, open the **film.htm** file, which is located in the Tutorial.08\ Tutorial folder included with your Data Files. In the head section and below the page title, enter your name and today's date in the comment section where noted.

▶ 6. In the document body, scroll down. Below the HTML comment to "paste the table code from tablenew.htm below," press the **Ctrl+V** keys to paste the table code from the tablenew.htm file.

▶ 7. Save the file as **filmnew.htm** in the same folder.

▶ 8. Switch to your browser and open the **filmnew.htm** page. Compare your file with the one shown in Figure 8-24 to confirm that the table appears correctly in the filmnew.htm file.

Figure 8-24 **The table in the filmnew.htm file**

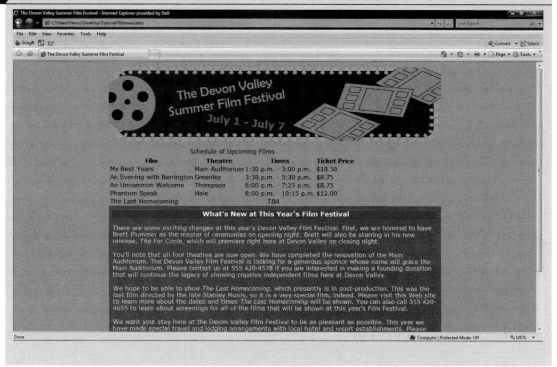

Tip

s can be floated left
ght.

The filmnew.htm file already has several styles to format the document, but it does not have any styles to enhance the appearance of the table. You will work with Ben to create several styles that will add more visual interest to the table. You'll begin by showing him how to style the table element.

Styling the Table Element

The table element can be styled to affect the appearance of the table and its contents. Generally, you want to style the table element to set the table width and determine whether you want to see the table borders. By default, a table is as wide as the sum of the longest lines in each column. The table will expand horizontally until it reaches the full browser width, at which time the text in the cells will begin to wrap. Depending on the length of the data in the longest line in each column, the table might appear too narrow or too wide. Tables can also be floated to wrap content around the table. If you are floating the table, it's a good idea to give the table an appropriate width (50 percent or less) so text can wrap around it.

erence Window | Setting the Table Width

- To set the table width, enter the following CSS styles code:
  ```
  table {
     width: value;
  }
  ```
  where *table* is the table element selector, *width* is the width property, and *value* is a value for the table width expressed in any of the CSS units of measurement.

You will use the width property when you style the table element. The value for the width property is a percentage based on the table's parent container. This page has a container div, which sets the page width to 900px. The table will be 100 percent of the container div width, so the table will also be 900px wide, regardless of the length of the longest lines in each column. If necessary, more space will be added between the columns to expand the table width to match that of the container div width. Tables sized by using a percentage will expand or contract as the browser window is resized. Tables sized using pixels will not expand or contract, so it's a good idea to use percentages as the value for the table width. Tables can be contracted only up to a certain point; the browser will ignore a width value that is too small to display the table contents. Also, if you include an image in a table cell, the table will not scale (contract or expand) the image.

You created some practice styles to style the table in the tablenew.htm file. You will enter new table styles in the filmnew.htm file so that you can style Ben's file. In addition to setting the table width, you will create 10px of margin space on the top and the bottom of the table. The margin value of "auto" for the left and right margins will center the table horizontally. You will give the table a 3px border, and you will use the border-collapse property to collapse the table gridlines. Last, you'll give the table a background color so it will contrast with the body style color.

To style the table element:

▶ 1. Switch back to your text editor. In the embedded style sheet, position the insertion point on a blank line below the CSS comment "enter the code for table styles below."

▶ 2. Type the following code, as shown in Figure 8-25.

```
table {
   width: 100%;
   margin: 10px auto;
   border: solid 3px black;
   border-collapse: collapse;
   background-color: #e9dfc6;
}
```

Figure 8-25	The table element code

```
/* enter the code for table styles below */

table {
   width: 100%;
   margin: 10px auto;
   border: solid 3px black;
   border-collapse: collapse;
   background-color: #e9dfc6;
}

</style>
```

the code to style the table element

▶ 3. Save the file.

▶ 4. Switch to your browser and refresh or reload the **filmnew.htm** page. Compare your file with the one shown in Figure 8-26 to confirm that the table has the correct width, margin, border, and background color.

Figure 8-26 **The table styled in the browser**

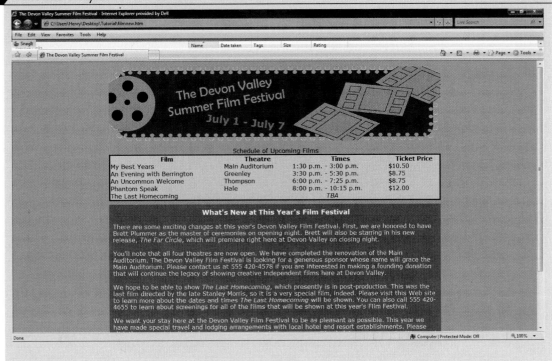

Next, you will show Ben how to create a style for the table caption.

Creating a Style for the Table Caption

Recall that the table caption is part of the table, so any styles you have created for the table element will also be applied to the table caption. Also, remember that the caption is centered by default. You can, however, style the caption element to have a different appearance from that of the table. For example, your table can have a background color of aqua, but your caption can have a background color of maroon. Ben has suggested specifying several of the caption's font properties and color properties to make the caption stand out from the rest of the table, so you will show him how to style the table caption.

To style the table caption:

1. Switch back to your text editor. In the embedded style sheet, position the insertion point on a blank line below the table element style.

2. Type the following code, as shown in Figure 8-27.

```
caption {
  padding: 4px;
  color: white;
  background-color: maroon;
  font-style: italic;
  font-size: 1.2em;
}
```

Figure 8-27 ▶ **The caption code**

```
    width: 100%;
    margin: 10px auto;
    border: solid 3px black;
    border-collapse: collapse;
    background-color: #e9dfc6;
}

caption {
    padding: 4px;
    color: white;
    background-color: maroon;
    font-style: italic;
    font-size: 1.2em;
}
```

the caption styles

▶ **3.** Save the file.

▶ **4.** Switch to your browser and refresh or reload the **filmnew.htm** page. Compare your file with the one shown in Figure 8-28 to confirm that the table caption has been formatted correctly. Depending on your browser and browser version, you may or may not see space between the caption and the table.

Figure 8-28 ▶ **The table caption styled in the browser**

Next, you will show Ben how to create a style for the table data.

Creating a Style for the Table Data

You have already created a style for the table border, but Ben would also like to see the table gridlines. Creating a style for the table data element will create a border style for the table gridlines. Because you will make the gridlines visible, you also want to add some padding to create some white space between the cell content and the table gridlines. You will show Ben how to create a style for the table data element.

To style the table data:

▶ **1.** Switch back to your text editor. In the embedded style sheet, position the insertion point on a blank line below the caption style.

2. Type the following code, as shown in Figure 8-29.

```
td {
    padding: 6px;
    border: solid 1px black;
}
```

Figure 8-29	The table data style code

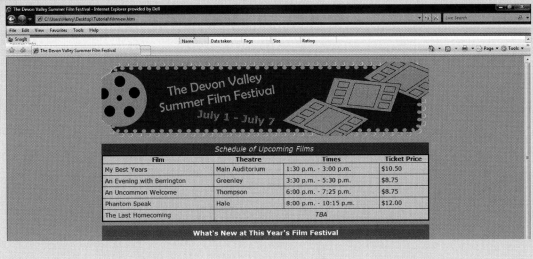

the styles for the
table data element

```
caption {
    padding: 4px;
    color: white;
    background-color: maroon;
    font-style: italic;
    font-size: 1.2em;
}

td {
    padding: 6px;
    border: solid 1px black;
}
```

3. Save the file.

4. Switch to your browser and refresh or reload the **filmnew.htm** page. Compare your file with the one shown in Figure 8-30 to confirm that the table cells now have padding and a border.

Figure 8-30	The table cells with padding and a border

Tip

common practice to
your cells padding if
cells contain text.

Next, you will show Ben how to format one or more table rows so that they contrast in appearance and stand out from each other.

Striping Rows

Row striping alternates the background color of the rows in a table, making the rows easier to locate and read. You accomplish row striping by creating a CSS class and applying the class to every other row.

Creating Row Striping

- To create row striping, enter the following code:
  ```
  tr.stripe {
  styles
  }
  ```
  where `tr` is the table row element, `stripe` is a dependent class name, and `styles` are the styles to change the appearance of an alternate row of the table.
- Within the start <tr> tag, apply the stripe class to each alternate row in the table.

Don't name the class "odd" or "even." As a table grows in complexity and more rows are added, it becomes more difficult to determine an odd or even row. In this instance, you suggest to Ben that the class be named "stripe."

To create the stripe dependent class:

1. Switch back to your text editor. In the embedded style sheet, position the insertion point on a blank line below the table data style.

2. Type the following code, as shown in Figure 8-31.

   ```
   tr.stripe {
      background-color: orange;
   }
   ```

Figure 8-31 | The stripe dependent class code

```
td {
   padding: 6px;
   border: solid 1px black;
}

tr.stripe {
   background-color: orange;
}
```

the stripe dependent class

3. Position the insertion point to the left of the end angle bracket of the <tr> tag in the second row of the table. Press the **Spacebar** once.

4. Type the following code shown in bold and in Figure 8-32.

   ```
   <tr class="stripe">
     <td>My Best Years</td>
     <td>Main Auditorium</td>
     <td>1:30 p.m. - 3:00 p.m.</td>
     <td>$10.50</td>
   </tr>
   ```

Figure 8-32 | Applying the stripe class

the stripe class applied to the second row

```
</tr>

<tr class="stripe">
  <td>My Best Years</td>
  <td>Main Auditorium</td>
  <td>1:30 p.m. - 3:00 p.m.</td>
  <td>$10.50</td>
</tr>
```

▶ **5.** Repeat the procedure to apply the stripe dependent class, but this time apply the class to the fourth and sixth rows of the table, as shown in Figure 8-33.

```
<tr class="stripe">
  <td>An Uncommon Welcome</td>
  <td>Thompson</td>
  <td>6:00 p.m. - 7:25 p.m.</td>
  <td>$8.75</td>
</tr>

<tr>
  <td>Phantom Speak</td>
  <td>Hale</td>
  <td>8:00 p.m. - 10:15 p.m.</td>
  <td>$12.00</td>
</tr>

<tr class="stripe">
  <td>The Last Homecoming</td>
  <td colspan="3" class="center">TBA</td>
</tr>
```

Figure 8-33   **The stripe class applied to alternate rows**

```
</tr>

<tr class="stripe">
  <td>An Uncommon Welcome</td>
  <td>Thompson</td>
  <td>6:00 p.m. - 7:25 p.m.</td>
  <td>$8.75</td>
</tr>

<tr>
  <td>Phantom Speak</td>
  <td>Hale</td>
  <td>8:00 p.m. - 10:15 p.m.</td>
  <td>$12.00</td>
</tr>

<tr class="stripe">
  <td>The Last Homecoming</td>
  <td colspan="3" class="center">TBA</td>
</tr>
```

the stripe class applied to alternate rows to create the row stripe effect

▶ **6.** Save the file.

▶ **7.** Switch to your browser and refresh or reload the **filmnew.htm** page. Compare your file with the one shown in Figure 8-34 to confirm that the rows have striping.

Figure 8-34

The row striping in the browser

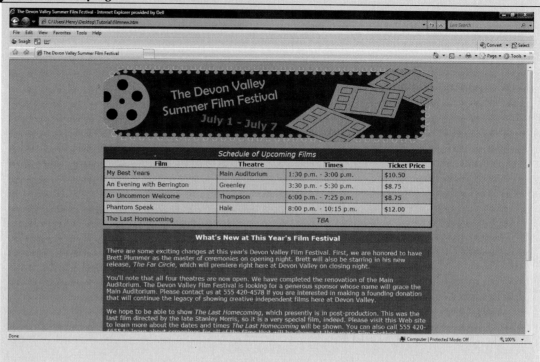

InSight | **Keeping Your Tables Accessible**

Tables can pose a significant barrier for screen reader software. To make your tables as accessible as possible, follow these tips:

- Do not use tables for layout. Create data tables only.
- Do not nest tables (placing another table within a table).
- Don't use background images for content in a table. Background images can't be used with the alt attribute, which a screen reader needs to describe the image. If you use background images for the content of your table cells, you might be making the data inaccessible.
- If you must use the colspan attribute, complete the span across all the columns. A screen reader can also read the table if you span all the cells to the right of a particular cell.
- Limit or avoid using the rowspan attribute. A screen reader will have difficulty interpreting cells merged across rows.
- Use the scope attribute to let the screen reader software know the association between the table data and the cells below or to its right.
- In the start table tag, include only the title attribute and its value. Do not include any other HTML attributes and values.

Now that you have created styles for the table rows and created row striping, you want to show Ben how to create a hover effect for the table rows.

Creating a Hover Effect for the Table Rows

Besides row striping, another common means of calling attention to an individual row is to create a hover effect, so that when the mouse pointer passes over a row, the row will have different text and background colors. Ben would like the hover effect on every other row, just like the row striping. To create the hover effect, you use the :hover pseudo-class selector, just as you did when you created styles for link text. A few years ago, the :hover pseudo-class selector had poor browser support except when used with the anchor element, but browser support has improved in this area. The Internet Explorer and Firefox browsers both now support the hover effect for table rows. Nonetheless, test your hover effect in several contemporary browsers to confirm that it works as intended.

Because you have created row striping, you will have to create a descendent selector for the tr.stripe dependent class. Ben wants the hover effect to have white text on a black background. Because the last row has merged columns, the hover effect may appear differently in the last row in some browsers, and you may not see the hover effect across the entire row. For all other rows, the hover effect will change the appearance of the entire row as you pass the mouse pointer over any cell in it.

To create the hover effect for the table rows:

▶ **1.** Switch back to your text editor. In the embedded style sheet, position the insertion point on a blank line below the tr.stripe style.

▶ **2.** Type the following code, as shown in Figure 8-35.

```
tr:hover {
   color: white;
   background-color: black;
}

tr.stripe :hover {
   color: white;
   background-color: black;
}
```

Figure 8-35 ▶ **The code for the hover effect**

the code for the
hover effect

```
tr.stripe {
   background-color: orange;
}

tr:hover {
   color: white;
   background-color: black;
}

tr.stripe :hover {
   color: white;
   background-color: black;
}
```

▶ **3.** Save the file.

▶ **4.** Switch to your browser and refresh or reload the **filmnew.htm** page. Pass the mouse pointer over the first column and observe the hover effect, as shown in Figure 8-36.

Figure 8-36 **The table row hover effect**

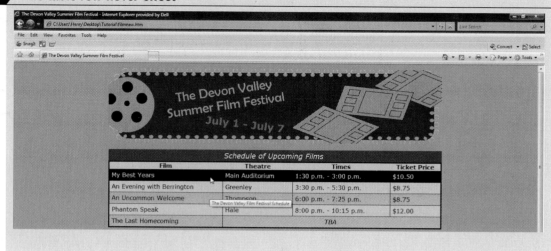

Next, you will tell Ben how to position cell contents.

Positioning a Text Block

If you will have several lines of text in a cell, you might consider creating a dependent class and using the vertical-align property with a value of "top", which positions the text at the top of the cell. By default, text aligns in the vertical middle of a cell, as shown in Figure 8-37.

Figure 8-37 **The default position for a text block**

Note that this cell has quite a bit of text. By default, text aligns in the vertical middle of the cell. To have text in the adjacent column have the same vertical alignment, apply the vertical-align property with a value of "top" to the start table row tag.	By default, text is placed in the vertical middle of the cell. The cell contents here look awkward in contrast to the cell content to its left.

However, the cell content looks better if you align all columns with text positioned at the top of the cell, as shown in Figure 8-38.

Figure 8-38 ▶ Vertical-align property with a value of top applied to table cell

Note that this cell has quite a bit of text. By default, text aligns in the vertical middle of the cell. To have text in the adjacent column have the same vertical alignment, apply the vertical-align property with a value of "top" to the start table row tag.	The "top" class was applied to the table row, so now all the cells in the row will have content that begins at the top of the cell.

To position columns of text at the top of each table cell, create a dependent class for the table row element using the following code.

```
tr.top {
   vertical-align: top;
}
```

Tip

vertical-align prop-
with a value of top is
uently used when
cells are used to
te the appearance of
spaper-style columns.

Apply the class to each row in which you want text to have a vertical-align property of top. If you want all cells in the table to have text with a particular vertical alignment, create a style for the tr element, as shown in the following code.

```
tr {
   vertical-align: top;
}
```

Now that you have shown Ben how to format table rows, you will show him how to format table columns.

Formatting Table Columns

The **column element** is used to format one or more columns, and is represented in HTML code by the <col /> tag. The column element must be closed by a space followed by a forward slash. You enter the code for the column element directly below the code for the table caption. Enter a <col /> tag for each column in the table.

erence Window | **Formatting Table Columns**

- To format table columns, enter the following code below the table caption code:
  ```
  <col />
  ```
  where *col* is the column element. Enter a <col /> element for each column in the table. If the <col/> element will format more than one column, enter span="n", where *span* is the span attribute and *n* is the number of columns to be spanned. Delete the col element for each column to be spanned.

The film schedule table has four columns, so you begin by entering four column tags below the caption tags, as shown in the following code:

```
<table>
<caption>Schedule of Upcoming Films</caption>
<col />
<col />
.<col />
<col />
```

Next, you create one or more independent classes to format the columns as you want. Then, you apply the class to the <col /> tag for the column you want to format. For example, if you wanted to create a style named "film" for the column that contains the film names, you could enter the following code in your style sheet:

```
.film {
  background-color: #efebb1;
}
```

You would then apply the class to as many columns as you want. For example, to apply the "film" class to the first column, you would enter the following code:

```
<col class="film" />
<col />
<col />
<col />
```

If you want, you can create other styles for one or more of the other columns, as shown in the following code:

```
.altborder {
   border: solid 4px navy;
}

.backimage {
   background-image: url(reels.gif);
 }
```

You would then apply the styles to one or more of the other columns, as shown in the following code. Note that not every column needs to be styled.

```
<col class="film" />
<col />
<col class="altborder" />
<col class="backimage" />
```

You can also use the **span attribute** to apply the same class to more than one column. The value for the span attribute is the number of columns to which you want to apply the style. For example, if you wanted to apply a class named "special" to the second and third columns, you would enter the following code.

```
<col />
<col class="special" span="2" />
<col />
```

Note that in the preceding code, the third <col /> tag formatted by the span has been deleted, leaving only three <col /> tags.

According to the CSS standard, the only properties you can apply to a column or column group are the background, border, width, and visibility properties. Internet Explorer, however, allows you to use other formatting properties, such as the font, color, and text properties. Other contemporary browsers conform more strictly to the CSS 2.1 standard.

In the next steps, you will create an independent class named "film," which will change the background color of cells in the first column that do not already have a color. Note, however, that the cells formatted by the tr.stripe dependent class will remain unchanged because of specificity. In other words, the tr.stripe dependent class is more specific to the table row element than the .film independent class. The order of precedence for Web table styles is shown in Figure 8-39.

Figure 8-39 ▶ **Order of precedence for table styles**

Order of Precedence for Table Styles	
Table cell (either the table data element or the table header element)	Highest precedence
Table row element	Middle precedence
Table element	Lowest precedence

As shown in the figure, styles applied to a table cell have the highest precedence, and will override any styles applied to a table row or the table element. You will show Ben how to format the first column using the col element.

To create and apply the .film independent class:

▶ **1.** Switch back to your text editor. In the embedded style sheet, position the insertion point on a blank line below the tr.stripe dependent class selector.

▶ **2.** Type the following code, as shown in Figure 8-40.

```
.film {
   background-color: #efebb1;
}
```

Figure 8-40 ▶ **The .film independent class code**

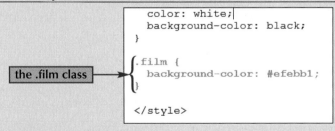

the .film class →

```
      color: white;
      background-color: black;
}

.film {
   background-color: #efebb1;
}

</style>
```

▶ **3.** In the table code, position the insertion point to the right of the end </caption> tag.

▶ **4.** Press the **Enter** key twice. On a blank line, type the following code, as shown in Figure 8-41.

```
<col class="film" />
<col />
<col />
<col />
```

Figure 8-41

The column element code

```
<table title="The Devon Valley Film Festival Schedule">
<caption>Schedule of Upcoming Films</caption>

<col class="film" />
<col />
<col />
<col />

<tr>
   <th scope="col">Film</th>
   <th scope="col">Theatre</th>
```

the col element tags; the film class is applied to the first column

▶ **5.** Save the file.

▶ **6.** Switch to your browser and refresh or reload the **filmnew.htm** page. Compare your file with the one shown in Figure 8-42 to confirm that the first, third, and fifth rows in the Film column now have a yellow background.

Figure 8-42

The table with the .film class applied

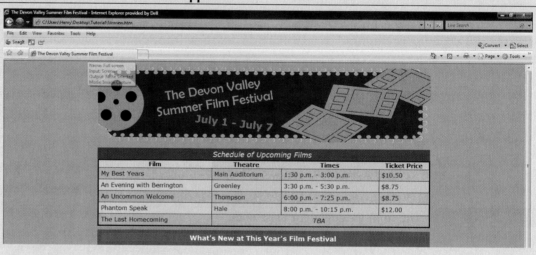

Ben would like to use the filmnew.htm CSS code in other documents that will be created at the Web site, so you will show him how to cut and paste the CSS code from the file to another file you have created—filmstyles.css, an external style sheet file.

To cut and paste the CSS code:

▶ **1.** Switch back to your text editor.

▶ **2.** On a blank line below the page title, type the following code, as shown in Figure 8-43. (You don't have to type the code on two separate lines.)

```
<link rel="stylesheet" href="filmstylesnew.css"
type="text/css" />
```

Figure 8-43   **The link code**

e link code to link
the CSS file

```
<head>
<meta http-equiv="Content-Type" content="text/html; charset=ISO-8859-1" />
<title>The Devon Valley Summer Film Festival</title>

<link rel="stylesheet" href="filmstylesnew.css" type="text/css" />

<!--
Tutorial 8
```

▶ **3.** In the embedded style sheet, delete the start `<style type="text/css">` tag and the end `</style>` tag.

▶ **4.** Select all of the CSS style code from the embedded style sheet, and then press the **Ctrl+X** keys to cut the code and place it on the Clipboard. Do not cut any HTML code.

▶ **5.** Save the **filmnew.htm** file, and then close it.

▶ **6.** In your text editor, open the **filmstyles.css** file, which is provided in your Data Files in the Tutorial.08\Tutorial folder.

▶ **7.** Enter your name and today's date in the CSS comment where noted.

▶ **8.** Position the insertion point on a blank line below the comment, and then press the **Ctrl+V** keys to paste the code, as shown in Figure 8-44 (not all of the code is shown).

Figure 8-44 | **The CSS code pasted into the filmstyles.css file**

```
filmnstylesnew.htm - Notepad
File  Edit  Format  View  Help
/*
Tutorial 8
Your Name:
Today's Date:
Filename: filmstylesnew.css
*/

#container {
   width: 900px;
   margin: 0 auto;
   border-width: 1px;
}

body {
   background-color: #d3b332;
   font-family: Verdana, sans-serif;
}

#content {
   padding: 10px;
   color: white;
   background-color: #6d6d50;
}

#footer {
   margin: 10px 0;
   border-top: solid thin black;
   border-bottom: solid thick black;
   padding: 5px;
   text-align: center;
}

a:link {
   padding: 5px;
   color: white;
   background-color: teal;
   font-weight: bold;
}

a:hover {
   padding: 5px;
   color: teal;
   background-color: white;
   font-weight: bold;
}

h3 {
   margin-top: 0;
   color: white;
   background-color: teal;
   text-align: center;
}
```

▶ **9.** Save the file as **filmstylesnew.css**, and then close the file.

Now that the code has been copied to the external style sheet and a link tag has been entered in the filmnew.htm file, you want to test the filmnew.htm file to see if the link works properly. Next, you'll validate both the HTML file and the CSS file.

To verify the link code and validate the files:

▶ **1.** Switch to your browser and refresh or reload the **filmnew.htm** page. Compare your file with the one shown in Figure 8-45 to confirm that the styles are correct.

Figure 8-45 | **The completed document**

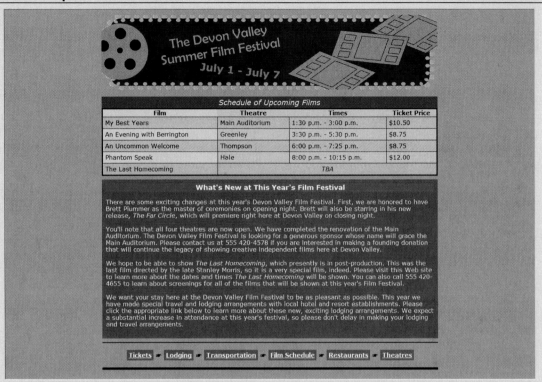

▶ **2.** In your browser, go to *http://validator.w3.org* to open the W3C validator. Validate the **filmnew.htm** file by using the Validate by File Upload method. Note any errors and correct them in your file if necessary.

▶ **3.** In your browser, navigate to *http://jigsaw.w3.org/css-validator*. Validate the **filmstylesnew.css** file by using the By file upload method. Note any errors and correct them in your file if necessary.

▶ **4.** Submit the results of the **filmnew.htm** and **filmstylesnew.css** files to your instructor, either in printed or electronic form, as requested.

▶ **5.** If you will not be completing the Review Assignments and the Case Problems, close your text editor and your browser.

In this session, you learned how to create table styles. You styled the table element to set the outside border for the table. You created styles for the table header, table data, and table row elements. You created a style to include row striping, which alternated the appearance of every other row of cells. You also learned that the col element can be used to apply several styles to a column of data.

Review | **Session 8.2 Quick Check**

1. What element controls the table width?
2. Should the table width be set as a percentage or as a pixel value?
3. What is row striping?
4. Why is row striping useful?
5. What element is used to format columns?
6. What attribute is sometimes used to apply formatting to several columns?

HTML lacks many of a word processor's features for creating and formatting tables. In the past, tables were used for page layout, but this is now discouraged, and tables are used mainly for displaying data. A good strategy for creating tables is to enter the code for the table first, using the same placeholder data in each cell. If you need to merge columns or rows, perform each merge and then view the document in the browser to observe the result. When the table code is correct, delete the placeholder data and enter the actual table data. The <table> tag begins a table, and the </table> tag ends a table. An optional table caption provides a description of the table. The tags to create a table row are <tr> and </tr>. The tags to create table data are <td> and </td>. You use the colspan attribute to merge columns and the rowspan attribute to merge rows, but these should be used carefully because of accessibility problems. The border-collapse property is used to change the default ruling of a table from a double line to a single line. You can use the float property to position a table at the left or right side of the screen. The col element can be used to apply a limited number of styles to one or more table columns.

Key Terms

border-collapse property	empty cell	scope attribute
border-spacing property	empty-cells property	span attribute
caption	frames	summary attribute
caption element	gridlines	table borders
caption-side property	key cell	table data element
cell	layout table	table element
colspan attribute	legacy code	table header element
column element	row striping	table row element
data table	rowspan attribute	

| Practice | | Review Assignments |

*time to practice
kills you learned
e tutorial using
ame case
ario.*

Data Files needed for the Review Assignments: lodge.htm, lodgelogo.gif

The sponsors of the Devon Valley Film Festival have partnered with four local hotels to provide an all-inclusive package for transportation, food, and lodging. Ben has asked for your help in developing the lodging page at the Devon Valley Film Festival Web site. Ben has already begun work on a document that has a banner and several paragraphs of promotional material, but he needs your assistance in creating the table that will be in the document body. After entering the code to create a style in your text editor, save the file, switch to your browser, refresh or reload the page, verify that you entered the style code correctly, and then switch back to your text editor and complete the next step. A preview of the Web page you will create appears in Figure 8-46.

Figure 8-46

Complete the following:

1. Use your text editor to open the **lodge.htm** file, which is provided in your Data Files in the Tutorial.08\Review folder. In the head section and below the page title, enter your name and today's date in the comment section where noted.
2. Save the file as **lodgenew.htm** in the same folder. Open the file in your browser and observe the appearance of the original file.
3. Switch back to your text editor. In the embedded style sheet, style the body element as follows:
   - Set the width to 910px.
   - Set the margins on the top and bottom to 0; set the margins on the left and right to "auto."
   - Set the background color to #a6c3a8.
   - Set the font to Verdana, a sans-serif font.
   - Set the line height to 1.5.
4. Create a grouped selector and style both h2 and h3 headings to appear with a bottom border that is solid, 4px, and navy. Center the heading text.

5. Create a grouped selector for the table and table data elements to create the following styles:

- Set the border to solid, 2px, and navy.
- Collapse the table borders.
- Set the text color to white.
- Set the background color to teal.
- Set the table text to appear in bold.

6. Below the comment in the document body, enter the code to create the following table.

Hotel	Type of Lodging	Meal Plan Available	Amenities on Site
The Devonshire Grand Hotel	Luxury	Not Included	Pool, Spa, Shopping, Tennis, Golf, Restaurants, Theatre, Art Gallery
WestWay Hotels	Standard	Included	Pool, Restaurant, Exercise Room, Lounge, Night Club
Hotels Grande	Economy	Included	Pool
Best Budgets	Budget	Included	Snack Bar

7. Save the **lodgenew.htm** file. Open the file in the browser and compare your file to Figure 8-46 to verify that your file is correct.

8. Submit the results of the preceding steps to your instructor, either in printed or electronic form, as requested.

9. If you are not completing the next assignment, close your text editor and your browser.

Apply	**Case Problem 1**

Use the skills you learned in the tutorial to create a Web page for a chain of health clubs.

Data File needed for this Case Problem: body.htm

Body by You Joan Gardner owns Body by You, a large chain of fitness centers headquartered in Alhambra, California. While most health clubs and fitness centers have adult clienteles, Body by You offers fitness classes for all ages. Each day is devoted to focusing on one particular age group. Joan is keenly interested in helping children and teens maintain proper health and fitness, and she arranges special classes for baby boomers and seniors who want to avoid a sedentary lifestyle. Joan has approached you about creating a table for her Web site. You will create table styles and apply them to a table that highlights the weekly activities at Body by You. After you complete a step to create a style, verify in your browser that the style code has been entered correctly, and then switch back to your text editor. A preview of the Web page you will create appears in Figure 8-47.

Figure 8-47

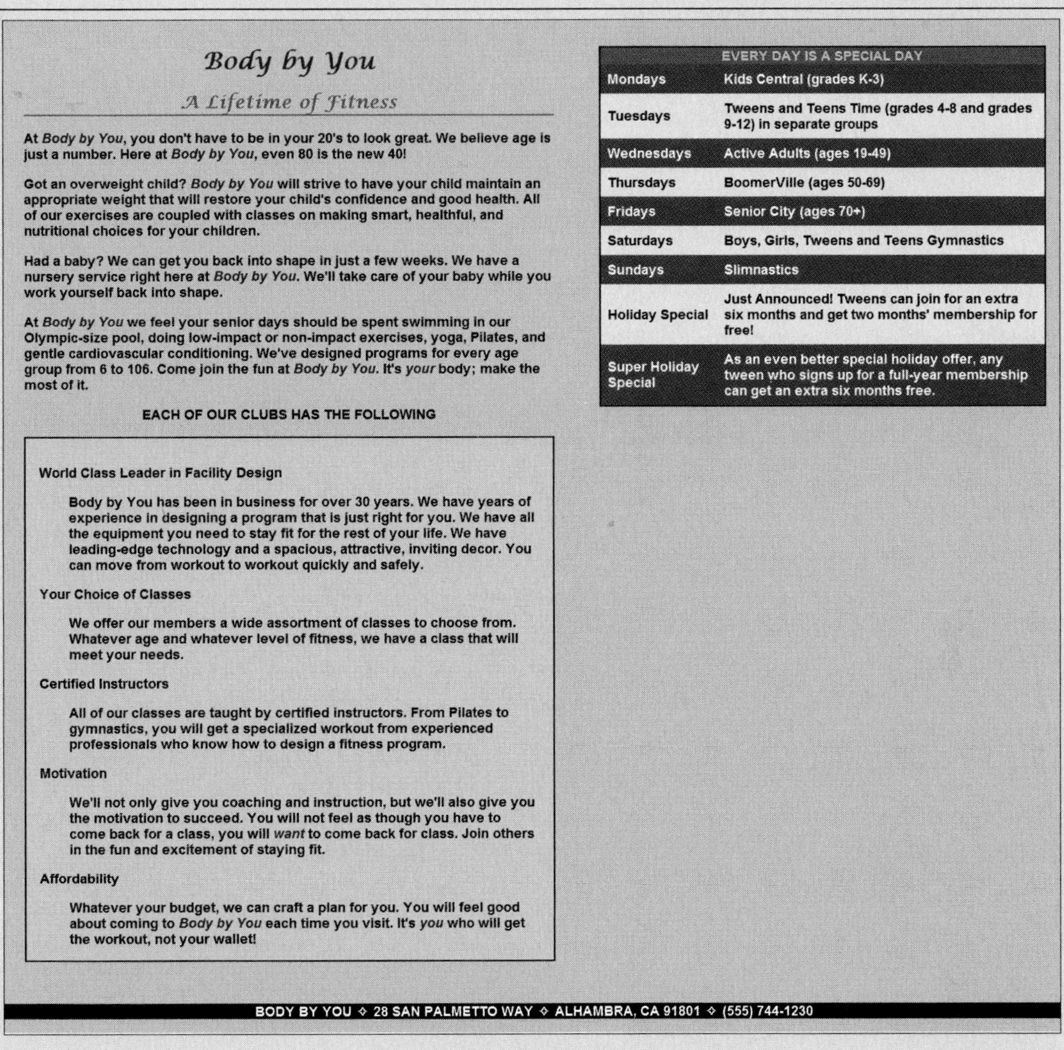

Body by You

A Lifetime of Fitness

At *Body by You*, you don't have to be in your 20's to look great. We believe age is just a number. Here at *Body by You*, even 80 is the new 40!

Got an overweight child? *Body by You* will strive to have your child maintain an appropriate weight that will restore your child's confidence and good health. All of our exercises are coupled with classes on making smart, healthful, and nutritional choices for your children.

Had a baby? We can get you back into shape in just a few weeks. We have a nursery service right here at *Body by You*. We'll take care of your baby while you work yourself back into shape.

At *Body by You* we feel your senior days should be spent swimming in our Olympic-size pool, doing low-impact or non-impact exercises, yoga, Pilates, and gentle cardiovascular conditioning. We've designed programs for every age group from 6 to 106. Come join the fun at *Body by You*. It's *your* body; make the most of it.

EACH OF OUR CLUBS HAS THE FOLLOWING

World Class Leader in Facility Design

Body by You has been in business for over 30 years. We have years of experience in designing a program that is just right for you. We have all the equipment you need to stay fit for the rest of your life. We have leading-edge technology and a spacious, attractive, inviting decor. You can move from workout to workout quickly and safely.

Your Choice of Classes

We offer our members a wide assortment of classes to choose from. Whatever age and whatever level of fitness, we have a class that will meet your needs.

Certified Instructors

All of our classes are taught by certified instructors. From Pilates to gymnastics, you will get a specialized workout from experienced professionals who know how to design a fitness program.

Motivation

We'll not only give you coaching and instruction, but we'll also give you the motivation to succeed. You will not feel as though you have to come back for a class, you will *want* to come back for class. Join others in the fun and excitement of staying fit.

Affordability

Whatever your budget, we can craft a plan for you. You will feel good about coming to *Body by You* each time you visit. It's *you* who will get the workout, not your wallet!

EVERY DAY IS A SPECIAL DAY	
Mondays	Kids Central (grades K-3)
Tuesdays	Tweens and Teens Time (grades 4-8 and grades 9-12) in separate groups
Wednesdays	Active Adults (ages 19-49)
Thursdays	BoomerVille (ages 50-69)
Fridays	Senior City (ages 70+)
Saturdays	Boys, Girls, Tweens and Teens Gymnastics
Sundays	Slimnastics
Holiday Special	Just Announced! Tweens can join for an extra six months and get two months' membership for free!
Super Holiday Special	As an even better special holiday offer, any tween who signs up for a full-year membership can get an extra six months free.

BODY BY YOU ◇ 28 SAN PALMETTO WAY ◇ ALHAMBRA, CA 91801 ◇ (555) 744-1230

Complete the following:

1. Use your text editor to open the **body.htm** file, which is provided in your Data Files in the Tutorial.08\Case1 folder. In the head section and below the page title, enter your name and today's date in the comment section where noted.
2. Save the file as **bodynew.htm** in the same folder. Open the file in your browser and observe the appearance of the original file.
3. Switch back to your text editor. In the embedded style sheet and below the CSS comment "enter table styles below," style the #table id selector to have a width of 45% and to float "right."
4. Style the table element to have the following styles:
   - Set the margin to 1em.
   - Set the table borders to appear as solid, thin, and black.
   - Collapse the table borders.
5. Style the table data element to have padding of 0.5em.

6. Style the table header element to have the following styles:
   - The text should appear in a text color of #ede568 and a background color of #626d71.
   - The text should appear in uppercase.
7. Style the table row element to have text appear in black on a background color of #dff3ef.
8. Create a dependent class named "stripe" for the table row element. Style the stripe dependent class to have text appear in white with a background color of #2a5e73.
9. In the body of the document and below the comment "enter the table code below," enter the code to create the following table. The first row ("Every Day is a Special Day") should be a table header row that spans both columns.

Every Day is a Special Day	
Mondays	Kids Central (grades K-3)
Tuesdays	Tweens and Teens Time (grades 4-8 and grades 9-12) in separate groups
Wednesdays	Active Adults (ages 19-49)
Thursdays	BoomerVille (ages 50-69)
Fridays	Senior City (ages 70+)
Saturdays	Boys, Girls, Tweens and Teens Gymnastics
Sundays	Slimnastics
Holiday Special	Just Announced! Tweens can join for an extra six months and get two months' membership for free!
Super Holiday Special	As an even better special holiday offer, any tween who signs up for a full-year membership can get an extra six months free.

10. After you have completed the table, apply the "stripe" class to the Mondays, Wednesdays, Fridays, Sundays, and Super Holiday Special rows.
11. Save the **bodynew.htm** file. Switch to your browser and refresh or reload the page. Compare your file to Figure 8-47 to verify that your file is correct.
12. Submit the results of the preceding steps to your instructor, either in printed or electronic form, as requested.
13. If you are not completing the next assignment, close your text editor and your browser.

Apply	**Case Problem 2**

Use what you've learned and expand your skills to create and style a Web page for a used car dealership.

Data Files needed for this Case Problem: berst.htm, berstlogo.gif

Berst Used Cars Berst Used Cars is one of the largest used-car dealerships in suburban Milwaukee, Wisconsin. In 50 years, Berst Used Cars has grown from a ten-car lot in downtown Milwaukee to a 500-car lot in the suburbs. Berst sells only late-model, low-mileage cars, and its customers have been quite happy with the cars they have purchased there. Fred Berst, the owner, has approached you about updating the Berst Web site. In particular, he wants a Web site that highlights some of the special cars that are on sale. You have already created several styles for the berst.htm file, which will be used for the home page, and you have created a banner image, berstlogo.gif. You will now work on creating styles for the table and entering the table data. After you complete a step to create a style, verify in your browser that the style code has been entered correctly, and then switch back to your text editor. A preview of the Web page you will create appears in Figure 8-48.

Figure 8-48   **Berst Used Cars Best Deals**

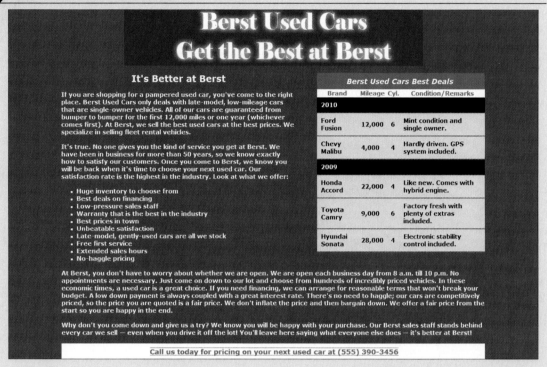

Complete the following:

1. Use your text editor to open the **berst.htm** file, which is provided in your Data Files in the Tutorial.08\Case2 folder. In the head section and below the page title, enter your name and today's date in the comment section where noted.

2. Save the file as **berstnew.htm** in the same folder. Open the file in your browser and observe the appearance of the original file.

3. Switch back to your text editor. In the code for the embedded style sheet and below the comment to "enter table styles below," style the table element as follows:
   - Set the width to 40%.
   - Set the margin on the left to 5%.
   - Collapse the table borders.
   - Float the table "right."

4. Style the table data element as follows:
   - Set the bottom border to be dotted, 2px, and navy.
   - Add padding of 10px on all sides.
   - Set the text color to black.
   - Set the background color to #deefce.
   - Set the font weight to bold.

5. Style the table header element to have a text color of teal and a background color of white.

6. Create a dependent class named "year" for the table data element. Style this dependent class to have text appear in white on a black background.

7. Style the caption element as follows:
   - Add padding of 0.5em on all sides.
   - Set the text color to white.
   - Set the background color to teal.
   - Set the font weight to bold.
   - Set the font style to italic.
   - Set the font size to 1.2em.

8. In the document body and below the comment "enter the code for the data table below," create the following data table. Please note:
   - "Berst Used Cars Best Deals" is the caption text.
   - Format the first row of the table as a table header row.
   - Merge columns for the 2010 and 2009 rows.
   - Apply the "year" class to the start table data tag for the 2010 and 2009 rows.

Brand	Mileage	Cyl.	Condition/Remarks
2010			
Ford Fusion	12,000	6	Mint condition and single owner.
Chevy Malibu	4,000	4	Hardly driven. GPS system included.
2009			
Honda Accord	22,000	4	Like new. Comes with hybrid engine.
Toyota Camry	9,000	6	Factory fresh with plenty of extras included.
Hyundai Sonata	28,000	4	Electronic stability control included.

9. Save the **berstnew.htm** file.
10. Switch to your browser and refresh or reload the page. Compare your file to Figure 8-48 to verify that your file is correct.
11. Submit the results of the **berstnew.htm** file to your instructor, either in printed or electronic form, as requested.
12. If you are not completing the next assignment, close your text editor and your browser.

Challenge | **Case Problem 3**

Use the skills you learned in the tutorial to create and style a Web page for the Education Department at a community college.

Data Files needed for this Case Problem: admit.htm, back.png, baxter.htm

Baxter Lake Community College   Baxter Lake Community College is a small, public college in eastern Colorado. The college grants a two-year Associates Degree in Education; nearly all the graduates transfer to four-year public or private institutions to obtain a full four-year Bachelor's Degree in Education. Dr. Anandami Greer, the chair of the Education Department, has approached you about updating the department's home page. Dr. Greer wants the page to focus on the department's philosophy of education. She wants to ensure that Baxter Lake Community College is attracting students who believe in a similar philosophy. After you complete a step to create a style, verify in your browser that the style code has been entered correctly, and then switch back to your text editor. A preview of the Web page you will create appears in Figure 8-49.

Figure 8-49

Baxter Lake Community College
The College for Education

Our Philosophy of Teaching

The faculty are dedicated to creating a learning environment that fosters academic achievement and mutual respect for the rights, ideas, and opinions of others. These are the primary methodologies employed:

Use a Variety of Teaching Methods

We do not presuppose that all students have the same learning styles. Some students learn through memorizing or through explanation or demonstration; others, by reading and drawing their own conclusions. For example, these are some common learning styles:

- Preference for learning alone, in small groups, or in large groups.
- Preference for observation vs. participation.
- Preference for immersion.
- Use of visuals.

Cognizant of the differences in student learning styles and being aware that each student acquires information differently, we take learning differences into account by varying the methods and approaches used. An eclectic teaching methodology must, therefore, prevail – to teach one way is the wrong way. Common principles followed here include:

- Breaking the subject matter into its smallest components (granularized instruction).
- Modify the teaching level to "fit" the class/students.
- Rearrange as need be, and then present material in the logical progression that begins with the simple and ends with the more complex.
- Add variety in all aspects of instruction; using lecture, group discussion, simulation, and modeling.

Fall Semester Academic Calendar	
Date	**Activity or Event**
August 31 - Monday	Classes Begin
October 12 - Monday	No Classes - Columbus Day
November 25 - November 28 Wednesday - Saturday	No Classes - Thanksgiving
December 14 - Monday	Last day of classes
December 15-19 (Tuesday-Saturday)	Final Exams

Encourage Student-Teacher Dialogue

Faculty make every effort to provide time for discussion of class problems. There is a student-teacher dialogue. The students, therefore, work in partnership with the professor to clarify, explain, and better organize the content of the course. By discussing common problems with the students before the lesson begins, students see that others make errors and that making errors should not lead to a lessening of self-esteem. Instead, they learn that it is normal to occasionally encounter difficulty and there are strategies that can be used to overcome these difficulties.

Maintain Good Student Rapport

Faculty strive at all times to encourage thinking as opposed to memorization. Memorization is required only when necessary. Instead, students are taught cognitive problem solving. When these students enter the business workforce, they will be required to exhibit creativity, to show the ability to solve problems, and to demonstrate sound decision making. Because of these impending job requirements, students must learn how to extrapolate what has been learned in the classroom so that they can apply their current learning to new situations. Students learn not to be teacher-dependent for the right answers because they can apply a transfer of existing learning that will give them the 'knowledge tools' for solving future problems.

Establish Fair, Measurable, and Attainable Goals

Each student knows what is expected of him or her and the time and manner of evaluation. Evaluation represents a fair, semester-long sample of a student's work, taking into account that a student's ability on a given day in a certain subject can be prone to negative outside variables — illness, family problems, fatigue, etc. Testing is done in moderation, and the results of each question in each exam are analyzed to improve instruction. Student feedback is used to improve future exams to reduce the number of questions that may be deemed by the students to be ambiguous or peripheral. The fairness and clarity of each question is always under review.

Motivate Students to Learn

Faculty are generous with deserved praise for a job well done; as a result, students get a sense of achievement, belonging, and a feeling of satisfaction.

Students are constantly reminded of the relevance of the day's lesson to future work goals. Students are told what they are going to learn today and why it is important. The proper amount of practice is provided, and the students perform an abbreviated example of the lesson. This practical application of instruction reinforces productive behavior that promotes learning and effects retention. Until the student has applied what has been taught, neither the student nor the teacher can really be certain that there has been successful instruction on the part of the teacher and complete learning on the part of the student.

Maintain a Well-Managed Classroom Environment

The classroom itself represents a planned, organized atmosphere. A work-oriented feeling prevails in the class right from the beginning. This self-directed activity is the pattern expected by a prospective employer; thus, the students are learning good job habits as well. Student anxiety is low because openness is the norm. Faculty try to maintain a positive, nonthreatening, humanistic climate at all times.

Do You Want to be in Our Program?

If the answer is yes, please contact our Admissions Office.

Visit the National Education Association Web site.

Back to Top

Complete the following:

1. Use your text editor to open the **baxter.htm** file, which is provided in your Data Files in the Tutorial.08\Case3 folder. In the head section and below the page title, enter your name and today's date in the comment section where noted.

2. Save the file as **baxternew.htm** in the same folder. Open the file in your browser and observe the appearance of the original file.

3. Switch back to your text editor. Style the body element as follows:
   - Set the background color to #f1ecdf.
   - Set the font size to 1.2em.
   - Set the font family to Times (a serif font).

4. Style the h1 selector as follows:
   - Using the background shorthand property, use the back.png image as a background image. Repeat the image horizontally.
   - Center the h1 text.

5. Style the anchor ("a") element so that link text appears in maroon and in a font size of 1.1em.

6. Style the a:hover pseudo-class selector so that when the mouse passes over a link, the link text has padding of 4px and appears as white text on a navy background.

7. Create an independent class named "clear" that clears elements on both the left and the right.

8. Apply the "clear" class to the start h3 tag before the "Maintain Good Student Rapport" heading.

9. Style the table element as follows:
   - Set the width to 50%.
   - Set the margins to be 2px on the top, 10px on the right, 8px on the bottom, and 0 on the left.
   - Create a border that is solid, thin, and navy.
   - Collapse the table borders.
   - Float the table "left."

10. Create a grouped selector for the table data and table header elements. These elements should appear with a border that is solid, thin, and black. Also add padding of 4px to these elements.

11. Style the caption element as follows:
    - Add padding of 4px to all sides.
    - Set the font weight to bold.
    - Set the font style to italic.
    - Set the text color to white.
    - Set the background color to green.

⊕ EXPLORE 12. Create a dependent class named "date" for the col element. Style the date class as follows:
    - Set the text color to white.
    - Set the background color to #735a28.

13. Apply the date class to the first <col /> element. (The <col /> element is just below the caption element in the table.)

⊕ EXPLORE 14. Apply the scope attribute with a value of "col" to the two start table header tags in the table.

15. In the start <h1> tag, enter the code for an id named "top."

16. In the start table tag, create a title for the table. Use "Baxter Community College Academic Calendar" as the title text.

17. Scroll to the bottom of the page. Using the words "Admissions Office" as the link text, create a link to the admit.htm file, which is provided in your Data Files in the Tutorial.08\Case3 folder.

18. Using the words "National Education Association" as the link text, create a link to the National Education Association Web site at *www.nea.org*.

19. Using the words "Back to Top" as the link text, create a link to the id named "top."

20. Save the **baxternew.htm** file. Switch to your browser and refresh or reload the page. Compare your file to Figure 8-49 to verify that your file is correct.

21. In your browser, test all links.

22. In your browser, go to *http://validator.w3.org* to open the W3C validator. Validate the **baxternew.htm** file by using the Validate by File Upload method. Note any errors and correct them in your file if necessary.

23. In your browser, go to *http://jigsaw.w3.org/css-validator*. Validate the **baxternew.htm** file by using the By file upload method. Note any errors and correct them in your file if necessary.

24. Submit the results of the **baxternew.htm** file to your instructor, either in printed or electronic form, as requested.

25. If you are not completing the next assignment, close your text editor and your browser.

| Create | **Case Problem 4** |

te a Web page to
our personal
nology.

Data File needed for this Case Problem: personal.htm

Your Personal Chronology Use what you have learned about creating and styling tables to create a personal chronology of your life. Create a two-column table. The first column should list important dates in your life, and the second column should list the important events that occurred on those dates. List at least 10 important dates and events in your life.

Complete the following:

1. Use your text editor to open the **personal.htm** file, which is provided in your Data Files in the Tutorial.08\Case4 folder. In the head section, give your page an appropriate title. Below the page title, enter your name and today's date in the comment section where noted.

2. Save the file as **personalnew.htm** in the same folder.

3. Within the tags for the embedded style sheet, format the body element with the text size, font, color, and background color of your choice.

4. Create styles for the table, td, th, and caption elements. Create a dependent class for the td element to stripe a row with a different format.

5. Create a two-column data table that shows examples of the following:
   * a caption
   * a table header
   * colspan or rowspan
   * row striping

6. Save the **personalnew.htm** file.

7. Open your browser and go to *http://validator.w3.org*. Use the Validate by File Upload method to check the **personalnew.htm** document and ensure that the HTML code is correct. If necessary, correct any errors detected by the validation.

8. In your browser, go to *http://jigsaw.w3.org/css-validator*. Use the By file upload method to check the **personalnew.htm** file and ensure that the CSS code is correct. If necessary, correct any errors detected by the validation.

9. Submit the results of the **personalnew.htm** file to your instructor, either in printed or electronic form, as requested.

10. Close your text editor and your browser. Close all open windows.

Review | Quick Check Answers

Session 8.1

1. A data table is used to arrange data in columns and rows.
2. The title should be a brief description of the table. The title appears as a ScreenTip when the user points to the table.
3. The caption briefly describes a table's purpose. By default, it appears in the browser above the table. The caption is an optional part of the table.
4. any element, such as text, a list, images, or links
5. A table header will make text in the cell centered and bold.
6. colspan
7. the cell in which the code to merge cells is entered

Session 8.2

1. table
2. a percentage value is preferable
3. alternating the background color of every other row
4. it makes the rows more readable
5. col
6. span

Ending Data Files

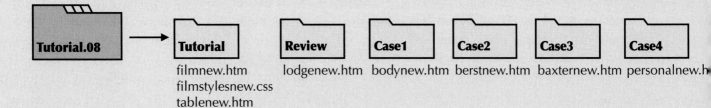

Tutorial.08 → **Tutorial**

Tutorial
filmnew.htm
filmstylesnew.css
tablenew.htm

Review
lodgenew.htm

Case1
bodynew.htm

Case2
berstnew.htm

Case3
baxternew.htm

Case4
personalnew.h

Tutorial 9

Creating Forms

Using Forms to Gather Input

Case | Fashion Squared^2

Fashion Squared^2 is a clothing company that markets its merchandise to professional men and women. The company specializes in business attire, such as men's and women's suits, dresses, shirts and blouses, ties and scarves, belts, and leather dress shoes. Fashion Squared^2 also partners with other companies to sell upscale leisurewear, swimwear, and hiking gear. The company relies on purchasing overstocks to keep its prices competitive. Based in New Orleans, Louisiana, Fashion Squared^2 began operating 20 years ago as a mail-order catalog company. The company enjoyed immediate success, but over the last few years, Fashion Squared^2 has seen declining sales, and the cost of printing and distributing catalogs has risen sharply. Competitors that market their products on the Web are increasingly taking customers away from Fashion Squared^2, so the company is considering moving most—if not all—of its business to the Web as well. Marie Rutland, the marketing director at Fashion Squared^2, has asked for your help in creating and designing several pages for the company's new Web site. She has begun work on a file named squared.htm, which contains general information about Fashion Squared^2. She also wants a Web form that people can use to enter the information needed to complete an online transaction.

Starting Data Files

Tutorial.09 →

Tutorial
squared.htm
squaredlogo.gif
squarednewstyles.css

Review
account.htm
accountnewstyles.css
squaredlogo.gif

Case1
award.htm
awardlogo.gif
awardnewstyles.css

Case2
check.gif
food.htm
foodlogo.gif
foodnewstyles.css
no.gif

Case3
hall.gif
hall.htm
hallnewstyles.css

Case4
survey.htm
surveylogo.gif

Session 9.1

How Data Is Collected and Processed

Prior to taking a course in HTML, you might not have had much experience in creating Web pages, but you certainly have worked with various kinds of forms. You have most likely completed forms—either paper forms or Web forms—to apply for college, financial aid, or a job. In addition, you have probably shopped or completed a survey online, entering and submitting data in your browser to do so. An HTML **form** is a collection of HTML elements used to gather data that a user enters online.

You use HTML to create the form, but the form does not process any of the data. When a user clicks a form's Submit button to send the data, you need a **form handler**—software that runs on a Web file server and processes the form. In a simple program, the form handler software may do nothing more than transfer the data to a database on the server. On the other hand, the form handler software may perform complex data manipulations.

For example, if you fill out a form online to purchase an item, click the Submit button, and then receive a response, such as a confirmation page, here's what happens to make the transaction possible:

1. The form in which you entered the purchase data was created by a Web developer or designer using HTML code.
2. After entering data into the form, you click the Submit button to send the data.
3. The browser sends the data to a Web server, a computer that receives the data.
4. Software on the server processes the data in the form and then retains the data in a database.
5. The results of the processing are entered into a new Web page that contains information—in this case, an order confirmation.
6. The server sends the confirmation page to the browser.
7. The browser gets the page and displays it for you to read.

Tip

The folder on a Web server that stores CGI scripts is a CGI bin. However, if you use Apache, there is no CGI bin. By default, all scripts go in the www folder.

In this process, the form handler runs a **script**, a short series of programming instructions. **Scripting languages** are used to create a series of instructions that transfer the data to the form handler on your PC or on a file server. Scripting languages commonly used with HTML forms include Perl, ASP, PHP, ColdFusion, and JavaScript. Web scripts are often called CGI scripts because **CGI** (Common Gateway Interface) is a standard for communicating with Web servers.

The data sent to the server is stored electronically in a **database**, an organized collection of data. Database software (such as Microsoft Access) is used to store and manipulate the data. A **field** represents a single kind of data in the database. For example, a field could be a person's first name, a date, or an invoice number. Each field has a name, such as "firstname," "lastname," or "date." When you design your HTML form, you need to know these field names because you enter them in your forms code. The HTML form serves only to collect the data; it does not perform any of the functions of a database program, such as organizing data, sorting data, or searching for and retrieving information.

The HTML **form element** serves as the container for all of the elements in a form. You use HTML code to create **form controls**, which are objects found in any window or dialog box, including text boxes, radio buttons, and check boxes. As you create the form for Marie, you'll learn how to determine which form controls you need and how to lay them out on a form.

Marie has already created a file of promotional information about Fashion Squared[2], and she has created numerous styles to format the Web page. You will open the file, enter a comment, and then save the file with a new filename.

To open Marie's file:

▶ **1.** In your text editor, open the **squared.htm** file, which is located in the Tutorial.09\ Tutorial folder included with your Data Files. In the head section and below the page title, enter your name and today's date in the comment section where noted.

▶ **2.** Save the file as **squarednew.htm** in the same folder.

▶ **3.** Open the **squarednew.htm** file in your browser. Figure 9-1 shows Marie's original file.

Figure 9-1 ▶ Marie's original file

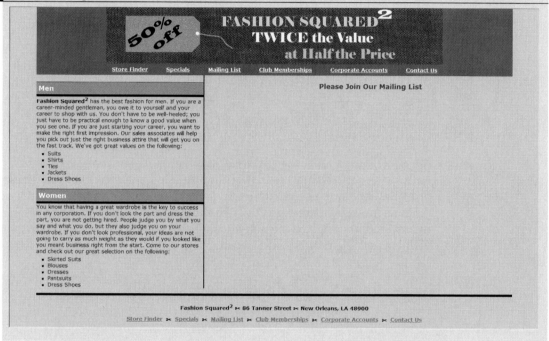

Next, you'll show Marie how to enter the code for the form element.

Creating the Form

Every form begins with the start <form> tag and ends with the closing </form> tag, which must be within the document <body></body> tags. The form tag has several attributes and values, including a unique id (identifier) for the form. You can use any value you want for the id attribute, but it makes sense to specify a value that describes the information the form gathers or is similar to the name of the database that will receive the data. In this instance, you will use an id value of "mailing" because the purpose of the form is to gather customer names for a mailing list.

erence Window | Creating the Form Element

• To create a form, enter the following code:

```
<form id="idvalue" method="methodtype" action="script_url"></form>
```
where *idvalue* is the name of the form, *methodtype* is either `get` or `post`, and *script_url* is the location on the file server where the script will be run when the form is submitted.

Tip

A Web page can have more than one form.

The code for the start <form> tag would be entered in the document body, as shown below.

```
<form id="mailing">
```

The **action attribute** identifies the location on the server where you will send the data. It also identifies the script that will run when the user clicks the Submit button to send the data collected by the form. The **method attribute**, which follows the action attribute, tells the server how to submit the form information. The two values for the method attribute are get and post. The default get method sends the data in the form directly to the server by appending the data to the URL. Because browsers limit the length of a Web address query string using the get method (each browser has a different limit), it is less secure than the post method. Therefore, the post method is used more often to submit form data. Using the post method, the browser contacts the server, and then the data in the form is sent to the server. The code for the start form tag would look similar to the following:

```
<form id="mailing"
action="http://someonesserver.com/cgi-bin/my_transfer_script"
method="post">
```

Because you don't have access to a form handler, you will enter just the code for the form in the squarednew.htm file without sending any data to the server. You will not enter a value for the action attribute; instead, you will enter placeholder code so the document will validate correctly. **Placeholder code** is one or more sets of quotation marks used to designate the attribute values. You will show Marie how to enter the form element and its attributes and values.

To enter the form element code:

▶ **1.** Switch back to your text editor.

▶ **2.** In the body of the document, scroll down almost to the bottom of the page and locate the comment "enter the form code below." Below the comment, type the following code, as shown in Figure 9-2.

```
<form id="mailing" action="">
```

▶ **3.** Press the **Enter** key four times.

▶ **4.** Type the closing **</form>** tag.

Figure 9-2 ▶ **The form element code**

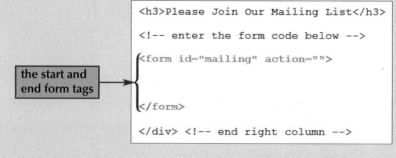

```
<h3>Please Join Our Mailing List</h3>

<!-- enter the form code below -->

<form id="mailing" action="">



</form>

</div> <!-- end right column -->
```

the start and end form tags

▶ **5.** Save the file.

You can format a form element the same way you format any HTML element. To see the boundary of the form, you will create a border. You will also create styles for margin, padding, and the font size. Each group of form controls will appear within a div, so you will create a descendant selector for the div element. Div elements are not required in a form, but using them has several advantages. First, you can style the div element to clear past other controls in the form, which ensures that no form element will be placed on top of another. Also, by using div elements, you won't have to populate your form with <p></p> tags because several form elements must always be inside a block-level element, such as the p or div element. Last, you can create a style for a div element to call attention to a particular part of the form or to position the form element within the form.

To style the form and the div elements:

▶ **1.** In your text editor, scroll up to the embedded style sheet, and position the insertion point on a blank line after the start `<style type="text/css">` code.

▶ **2.** Type the following code, as shown in Figure 9-3.

```
form {
   margin-top: 1em;
   border: solid 2px navy;
   padding: 1em;
   font-size: 16px;
}

form div {
   margin: 0;
   padding: 0.5em 0 0 0;
   clear: both;
}
```

Figure 9-3   **The code to style the form element**

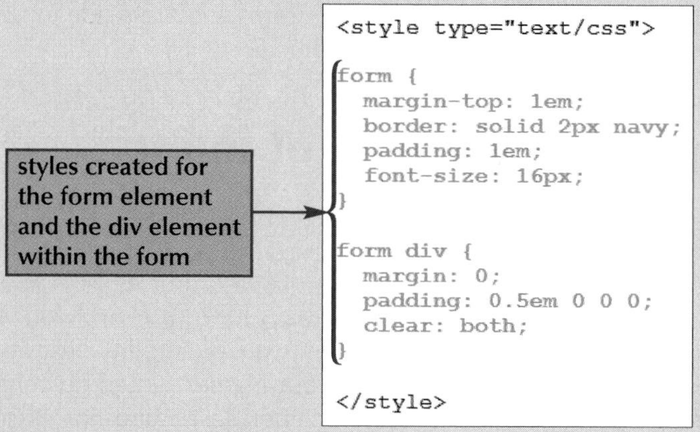

```
<style type="text/css">

form {
   margin-top: 1em;
   border: solid 2px navy;
   padding: 1em;
   font-size: 16px;
}

form div {
   margin: 0;
   padding: 0.5em 0 0 0;
   clear: both;
}

</style>
```

styles created for the form element and the div element within the form

▶ **3.** Save the file.

▶ **4.** Switch to your browser and refresh or reload the **squarednew.htm** file. Verify that the form has a solid, 2px-wide navy border, as shown in Figure 9-4.

Figure 9-4 | **The form in the browser**

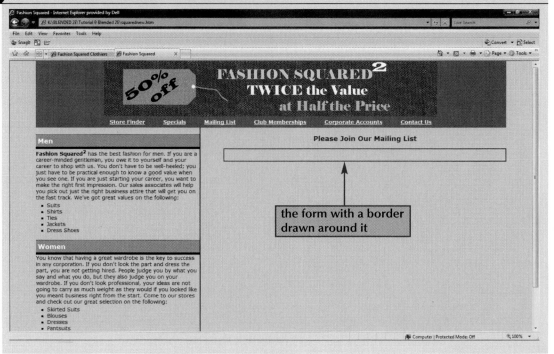

Now that you have set the style for the form, you are ready to show Marie how to add form controls so the form data can be collected.

Determining the Type of Input

Recall that a field represents a single piece of data. The user enters data into each field in the form based on **prompting text**—a short description that suggests what data belongs in a certain field. Examples of prompting text would be "Last Name," "Choose an item," or "Zip Code." You want data entry to be easy for a user, and you want the user to enter correct data in the form, so the prompting text needs to be clear and specific. For example, prompting text such as "Enter your Name" would be confusing to the user. Should users enter their full names, first names, last names, or titles—and in what order? The **label element** is used to display prompting text on the screen. You should always use the label element with the "for" attribute because the value of the "for" attribute helps screen readers associate the prompting text with the value for the form control.

Controlling Label Placement on Forms

When designing your forms, you need to decide where to position the label text. In general, you have three options, each of which has benefits and tradeoffs. The first option is to use top alignment, in which you place the label text above the text field. This option is good for shorter forms because it uses two lines for every field; however, in a very long form, top alignment would require users to scroll down too much.

The second option is to align the labels flush left. Left-aligned labels are the easiest to read because the user's eye naturally views the left edge of the screen first. The disadvantage of left alignment is that it creates some white space between the label and the form element, which might slow down some users as they enter data.

The third option is to right-align the labels, which creates the closest connection between the label text and the form control. The disadvantage is that right alignment is more difficult to read, and could also slow some users. However, the most commonly used option is to right-align the labels, so you will use right alignment for Marie's form.

The **input element** is used to determine the type of data your control will collect, such as text or data from clicking a radio button or selecting a check box. The label element is used together with the input element. The label element uses the **for attribute**, which associates the label with the id value in the input element. The **label text** is the text that appears between the start <label> and end </label> tags. In this instance, the label text is "First Name"; the user would see these words next to the field as the prompting text in the browser. The code for the label element would look like the following:

```
<label for="firstname">First Name</label>
```

The **type attribute** determines the specific type of form object that is created. The input element is an empty element (it doesn't mark up any content), so its code must be closed with a space and forward slash. You enter the input element code below the label element code, as shown in the following example.

```
<label for="firstname">First Name</label>
<input type="text" name="firstname" id="firstname" />
```

Tip

field name or id in form should also ch the case used in database. For nple, *zipcode* and *CODE* could be con- red two different names.

Note that the input element uses both the name attribute and the id attribute. Currently, you must still use the name attribute in the input element code so that the data can be recognized by older browsers and different computer software platforms. To make it easier to enter data into the database, the name or id attribute should have the same name as the field name in the database that will receive the data.

Creating Text Boxes

Use the **text box** control to gather **alphanumeric data** (letters or numbers) from a single line in a form. Later, you will learn about another form control used when more than one line of data needs to be input. Use the type attribute with a value of text to create a one-line text box.

Reference Window | **Creating Text Boxes**

- To create a text box, use the following code:
  ```
  <input type="texttype" name="name" id="id" value="initialvalue"
  size="sizevalue" maxlength="maxvalue" />
  ```
  where *texttype* is either *text* or *password*, *initialvalue* is the default data that appears in the field, *sizevalue* is the width of the box in characters, and *maxvalue* is the maximum number of characters that a user can type in the field.

Tip

The default width for a text box is 20.

Text boxes are also used to create a **password field**, a text field in which the input is masked on the screen. As the user enters data in a password field, stars or bullets appear in the text box to disguise the numbers or letters the user is actually typing. If you want the text field to be a password field, change the value of the type attribute to password.

The **size attribute** and its value are used to control the text box width. The size attribute value determines the width of the box in characters. If you assign a high number of characters as the width, the user could continue typing characters beyond the end of the text box, and the field would still accept input as the data scrolled to the right. Also, the width is correct only if you style the field to accept text in a monospace font, such as Courier or Courier New. The **maxlength attribute** and its value set a limit on the number of characters a user can type in a text box. For example, if you set the maxlength to a value of 25, then the text box will not continue to scroll and will stop accepting input after the 25th character has been entered. An example of the size and maxlength attributes is shown in the following code.

```
<input type="text" name="firstname" id="firstname" size="15"
maxlength="15" />
```

If you want the text box to display a value by default, use the "value" attribute and assign the value you expect most users to enter. Recall that you want users to complete the form as quickly and easily as possible, so only use a default value if you are sure that the overwhelming majority of users will enter it. Otherwise, users will have to delete the value and enter a new one, which wastes time.

Organizing Form Controls

Although the Fashion Squared[2] form is fairly simple, and doesn't require much organization, it's always a good coding practice to increase accessibility by organizing the form controls in related groups. For example, in this tutorial, you will organize the text boxes into one related group, and then organize radio buttons and check boxes into their own groups. Two elements are used together to organize form controls. The **fieldset element** groups a series of related form elements. By default, the fieldset element creates a 1px border around the elements you have grouped in the fieldset. The **legend element** creates caption text for the fieldset. The **legend text** is entered between the legend tags and appears in the legend caption in the browser. By default, the caption appears in the upper-left corner of the fieldset border. The code for these two elements would look similar to the following code.

```
<fieldset><legend>Descriptive Caption Text Goes Here</legend>
. . . the form code to be grouped would be entered here . . .
</fieldset>
```

Figure 9-5 shows a fieldset and a legend in Internet Explorer. Each browser modifies the appearance of these elements, but you can style both elements to make their appearance more consistent among browsers.

Figure 9-5 | **A fieldset and a legend**

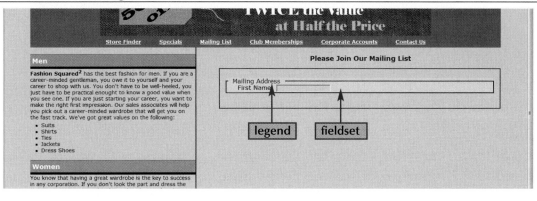

Tip

ake legend text over-
he fieldset, you can
the legend element
ave negative top or
om margins.

The appearance of the border and the legend text can differ depending on the browser, so you should check them in several contemporary browsers to make sure their appearance is satisfactory. If necessary, style the fieldset and the legend elements to add padding or create margin space around the legend text. Internet Explorer, for example, places the legend text inside the fieldset, whereas the Firefox browser places the legend outside the fieldset.

Tip

sets are also known
roup boxes."

erence Window | **Organizing Form Elements**

Tip

your legend text to
words that briefly
ribe the fieldset.
legends clutter the
and slow down
ser.

- To organize form elements using the fieldset and legend tags, enter the following code:

```
<fieldset id="description"><legend>legendtext</legend>
form_elements
</fieldset>
```

  where *description* is a description of the fieldset content, *legendtext* is the text for the legend, and *form_elements* are the controls you want to group together.

Before you enter the code for the form elements, you want to show Marie how to create styles that align and format the form elements. You will use the label element to align the content of the form. You will create a width for the label text, float the contents left, and align the label text on the right. By using CSS to align the form elements, you do not have to use older methods for alignment, such as tables or absolute positioning, both of which can hinder accessibility. You will also aid accessibility by creating a background color for the text fields, which will make the fields stand out from the form color.

To create styles for the form elements:

▶ **1.** Switch back to your text editor. In the embedded style sheet, position the insertion point on a blank line after the form div descendant selector code.

▶ **2.** Type the following code, as shown in Figure 9-6.

```
label {
    width: 120px;
    margin-right: 15px;
    color: black;
    float: left;
    text-align: right;
}

input.text {
    background-color: #f1e8c8;
}
```

```
legend {
  color: navy;
  padding: 0 10px;
}

fieldset {
  margin-bottom: 1em;
  border: solid 2px black;
  background-color: #e9edda;
}
```

Figure 9-6 | **The form elements styles code**

the label, input, legend, and fieldset styles code →

```
form div {
  margin: 0;
  padding: 0.5em 0 0 0;
  clear: both;
}

label {
  width: 120px;
  margin-right: 15px;
  color: black;
  float: left;
  text-align: right;
}

input.text {
  background-color: #f1e8c8;
}

legend {
  color: navy;
  padding: 0 10px;
}

fieldset {
  margin-bottom: 1em;
  border: solid 2px black;
  background-color: #e9edda;
}

</style>
```

▶ **3.** Save the file.

InSight | Creating Placeholder Code

When entering the code for a form, you will find the basic code structure repetitive. A good strategy is to enter the code for one control, such as a text field, then save the file and open it in the browser. If you are satisfied that the code is correct, copy and paste it below the correct code. In the pasted code, delete all of the attribute values and create placeholder code—a pair of quotation marks to designate the attribute values:

```
<label for=""></label>
<input type="text" name="" id="" size="" />
```

Copy and paste the code as many times as necessary for the text fields you need to create. After you have created enough copies of the placeholder code, enter the appropriate values between the quotation marks.

If you wanted the label elements to appear above the fields, rather than to their left, you would remove the declarations for width, margin, float, and text alignment for the label element style. Instead, you would use the declaration display: block to make the labels appear above the field. You will now show Marie how to enter the code for the first text box.

To enter the code for the first text box:

▶ **1.** In your text editor, scroll down; in the document body, position the insertion point on a blank line after the start form tag code.

▶ **2.** Type the following code, as shown in Figure 9-7.

```
<div>

<fieldset><legend>Mailing Address</legend>

<label for="firstname">First Name</label>
<input type="text" name="firstname" id="firstname"
class="text" /><br />
```

Figure 9-7 **The label and the input code for the first text box**

```
<h3>Please Join Our Mailing List</h3>

<!-- enter the form code below -->

<form id="mailing" action="">

<div>

<fieldset><legend>Mailing Address</legend>

<label for="firstname">First Name</label>
<input type="text" name="firstname" id="firstname" class="text" /><br />

</form>

</div> <!-- end right column -->

<div id="footer">
<p>Fashion Squared<sup>2</sup> &#9986; 86 Tanner Street &#9986; New
Orleans, LA 48900</p>
```

e code for the label
d the first text box →

▶ **3.** Press the **Enter** key four times.

▶ **4.** Type the following code, as shown in Figure 9-8. Be sure to press the **Enter** key twice after you type the end </fieldset> tag.

```
</fieldset>

</div> <!-- end text boxes -->
```

Figure 9-8 **The end fieldset and end div tags**

```
<label for="firstname">First Name</label>
<input type="text" name="firstname" id="firstname" class="text" /><br />


</fieldset>

</div> <!-- end text boxes -->

</form>
```

e end fieldset and
d div tags are added →

▶ **5.** Save the file.

6. Switch to your browser and refresh or reload the **squarednew.htm** file. Verify that the fieldset, legend, and First Name text box appear correctly, as shown in Figure 9-9.

Figure 9-9 | **The First Name text box in the browser**

Now that the first text box has been entered, you will show Marie how to enter the code for the remaining text boxes in this fieldset.

To enter the code for the remaining text boxes:

1. Switch back to your text editor. Position the insertion point on a blank line above the end </fieldset> tag.

2. Type the following code, as shown in Figure 9-10.

```
<label for="lastname">Last Name</label>
<input type="text" name="lastname" id="lastname"
class="text" /><br />

<label for="address">Address</label>
<input type="text" name="address" id="address"
class="text" /><br />

<label for="city">City</label>
<input type="text" name="city" id="city" class="text"
size="20" /><br />

<label for="state">State</label>
<input type="text" name="state" id="state" class="text"
size="2" /><br />

<label for="zip">Zip Code</label>
<input type="text" name="zip" id="zip" class="text"
size="5" /><br />
```

Figure 9-10   **The code for the remaining text boxes**

```
<fieldset><legend>Mailing Address</legend>

<label for="firstname">First Name</label>
<input type="text" name="firstname" id="firstname" class="text" /><br />

<label for="lastname">Last Name</label>
<input type="text" name="lastname" id="lastname" class="text" /><br />

<label for="address">Address</label>
<input type="text" name="address" id="address" class="text" /><br />

<label for="city">City</label>
<input type="text" name="city" id="city" class="text" size="20" /><br />

<label for="state">State</label>
<input type="text" name="state" id="state" class="text" size="2" /><br />

<label for="zip">Zip Code</label>
<input type="text" name="zip" id="zip" class="text" size="5" /><br />

</fieldset>
```

e code for the
maining text boxes

> **3.** Save the file.

> **4.** Switch to your browser and refresh or reload the **squarednew.htm** file. Verify that
> the text boxes in the fieldset appear correctly, as shown in Figure 9-11.

Figure 9-11   **The text boxes in the browser**

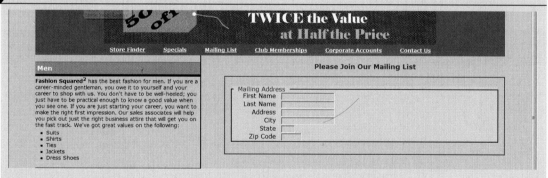

> **5.** If you will not be completing the next session, close your text editor and your
> browser.

In this session, you learned that HTML is used to create Web forms. Scripts are used to
transfer the data in a form to a database. Text boxes are used when you want the user to
enter text. You can control the size of the text box as it is displayed on the screen. You
can also set the maximum number of characters that a user can enter in a text box. You
can make a text box into a password field by changing the value of the input type to
password. Use prompting text to suggest what a user should enter in a given field. In the
next session, you will see how form controls are used to make selections.

Review | **Session 9.1 Quick Check**

1. What is a database?

2. What tags are used to start and end forms?

3. What input type would you use to create a text box?

4. What does the maxlength attribute do?

5. Is it possible to display more characters than are specified by the maxlength attribute?

6. What input type would you use to create a password field?

Session 9.2

Creating Radio Buttons

So far, you have used text boxes to input alphanumeric text. A **radio button** is a form control from which you can at most make only a single choice from a list of options. Although you can create any number of options for a particular field, you shouldn't overwhelm the user with too many choices; as a good coding practice, use two to five radio buttons for a given field. The input type for a radio button is radio. Name the radio button to correspond to the appropriate field name in the database. Note that the label element precedes the code for each radio button. The id value should always match the value of the "for" attribute in the label element code. The value for the value attribute is the data sent to the appropriate field in the database. The code for a group of two radio buttons would look similar to the following code.

> ### Tip
>
> Ensure that the value and label of each option button are coded correctly so that when the user makes a choice, the correct value is passed to the form handler.

```
<label for="male">Male</label>
<input type="radio" name="gender" id="male" value="male" /><br />
<label for="female">Female</label>
<input type="radio" name="gender" id="female" value="female" /><br />
```

Reference Window | **Creating Radio Buttons**

- To create radio buttons, enter the following code for each one:
  ```
  <input type="radio" name="name" id="id" value="field_data" />
  ```
  where *radio* is the value of the type attribute, *name* identifies the corresponding field in the database, *id* associates the field with the "for" attribute in the label element, and *field_data* is the data that will be sent to the appropriate field in the database if the button is selected.
- To specify that a radio button is checked by default, add the attribute and value of `checked="checked"` to the input tag code.

> ### Tip
>
> Radio buttons are also called option buttons.

Note that the value for the name attribute (in the preceding example, gender) must remain the same for each input tag. The value binds all radio buttons with the same name value as one selection.

If your group of radio buttons is working properly, a user can make only one choice from the group. If you test your form and notice that you can make more than one choice from a group of radio buttons, check the accuracy of the values you typed for the name attribute. The values for each name attribute must be identical. In particular, check the values for typographical errors and missing quotes.

A primary advantage of using radio buttons in your form is that the user does not have to type any data. When the Web form designer can control the input from the user, the possibilities for user errors are reduced. Error-free data is also known as **clean data**. To further ensure clean data, you should add code that checks a radio button by default, so that a value is returned even if the user fails to make a choice. Use the **checked attribute** to establish a default choice. Enter the checked attribute with a value of checked. In the following example, male is the default choice.

```
<label for="male">Male</label>
<input type="radio" name="gender" id="male"
value="male" checked="checked" /><br />

<label for="female">Female</label>
<input type="radio" name="gender" id="female"
value="female" /><br />
```

You will now show Marie how to enter the radio button code for users to indicate their gender in the form.

To enter the code for the radio buttons:

▶ **1.** If necessary, open your browser and text editor, and then open the **squarednew.htm** file in both. In your text editor, position the insertion point on a blank line below the end </div> tag and comment for the text boxes code.

▶ **2.** Type the following code, as shown in Figure 9-12.

```
<div>

<fieldset id="gender"><legend>Gender</legend>

<label for="male">Male</label>
<input type="radio" name="gender" id="male"
value="male" /><br />

<label for="female">Female</label>
<input type="radio" name="gender" id="female"
value="female" /><br />

</fieldset>

</div> <!-- end radio buttons -->
```

| Figure 9-12 | The radio button code |

```
</fieldset>

</div> <!-- end text boxes -->

<div>

<fieldset id="gender"><legend>Gender</legend>

<label for="male">Male</label>
<input type="radio" name="gender" id="male" value="male" /><br />

<label for="female">Female</label>
<input type="radio" name="gender" id="female" value="female" /><br />

</fieldset>

</div> <!-- end radio buttons -->

</form>

</div> <!-- end right column -->
```

the radio button code

▶ **3.** Save the file.

▶ **4.** Switch to your browser and refresh or reload the **squarednew.htm** file. Verify that the radio buttons appear correctly, as shown in Figure 9-13.

Figure 9-13 | **The radio buttons in the browser**

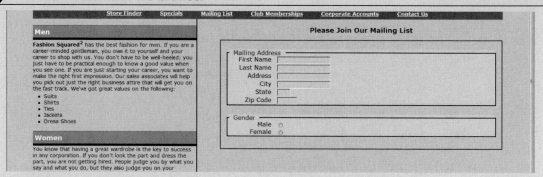

Another way to give the user a group of choices is to create check boxes, which you'll show Marie how to do next.

Creating Check Boxes

A **check box** is a form control that allows a user to choose one or more items from a list of items. The input type for a check box is checkbox. You can include any number of check boxes in a group, but as with radio buttons, don't overwhelm the user with too many choices. Also, check boxes take up space in the browser window, so if you have more than 10 choices in one group, consider creating additional check box groups.

Name the check box to correspond to the field name in the database that will receive the data if the user clicks that check box. The check box code would look like the code in the following example.

```
<label for="sportswear">Sportswear</label>
<input type="checkbox" name="special" id="sportswear"
value="sportswear" /><br />
```

Recall that you can have a radio button selected by default. Similarly, you can have a check box checked by default, again using the checked attribute with a value of checked, as shown in the following code.

```
<label for="sportswear">Sportswear</label>
<input type="checkbox" name="special" id="sportswear" value="sportswear"
checked="checked" /><br />
```

As with radio buttons, the name attribute must have the same value for each check box in the group. You will now show Marie how to enter the code for the check boxes. She wants users to be able to select which catalogs they want mailed to them. Because she wants people to be able to request more than just one catalog, check boxes are perfect for this field. Fashion Squared[2] is promoting its sportswear catalog, so you will make that check box checked by default.

To enter the code for the check boxes:

▶ **1.** Switch back to your text editor. Position the insertion point on a blank line below the end </div> tag and comment for the radio button code.

▶ **2.** Type the following code, as shown in Figure 9-14.

```
<div>

<fieldset><legend>Special Catalogs Requested (check all that
apply)</legend>

<label for="sportswear">Sportswear</label>
<input type="checkbox" name="sales" id="sportswear"
value="sportswear" checked="checked" /><br />

<label for="swimwear">Swimwear</label>
<input type="checkbox" name="sales" id="swimwear"
value="swimwear" /><br />

<label for="hiking">Hiking</label>
<input type="checkbox" name="sales" id="hiking"
value="hiking" /><br />

<label for="formal">Formal Attire</label>
<input type="checkbox" name="sales" id="formal"
value="formal" /><br />

<label for="accessories">Accessories</label>
<input type="checkbox" name="sales" id="accessories"
value="accessories" />

</fieldset>
</div> <!-- end check boxes -->
```

Figure 9-14 ▶ **The check box code**

the code for the
check boxes →

```
</fieldset>

</div> <!-- end radio buttons -->

<div>

<fieldset><legend>Special Catalogs Requested (check all that apply)
</legend>

<label for="sportswear">Sportswear</label>
<input type="checkbox" name="sales" id="sportswear" value="sportswear"
checked="checked" /><br />

<label for="swimwear">Swimwear</label>
<input type="checkbox" name="sales" id="swimwear" value="swimwear" /><br />

<label for="hiking">Hiking</label>
<input type="checkbox" name="sales" id="hiking" value="hiking" /><br />

<label for="formal">Formal Attire</label>
<input type="checkbox" name="sales" id="formal" value="formal" /><br />

<label for="accessories">Accessories</label>
<input type="checkbox" name="sales" id="accessories" value="accessories" />

</fieldset>

</div> <!-- end check boxes -->

</form>
```

▶ **3.** Save the file.

▶ **4.** Switch to your browser and refresh or reload the **squarednew.htm** file. Verify that the check boxes appear correctly, as shown in Figure 9-15.

Figure 9-15 ▶ **The check boxes in the browser**

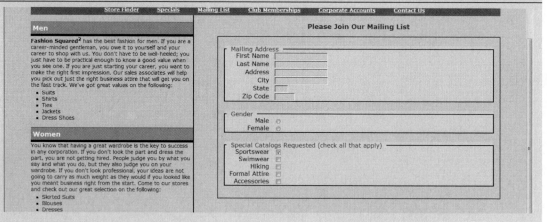

Besides selecting check boxes and radio buttons, users can also select items by clicking them in a list. You'll show Marie how to include these types of controls next.

Creating a Selection List

A **selection list**, also known as a **list box**, is a form control that allows a user to choose from a list of items; all the items in the list are shown. A **drop-down list box** displays only one item in a selection list; the user clicks a list arrow to display the remaining contents of the list and make a selection. Drop-down list boxes are useful when you want to conserve screen space; for example, if you need to have a list box that contains the names of the 50 states, you want the user to see that list only when the user clicks the list arrow.

ference Window | Creating a Selection List

- To create a selection list, enter the following code:

```
<select name="name" id="name">
<option value="value1">optiontext</option>
<option value="value2">optiontext2</option>
</select>
```

  where *name* identifies a field in the database, *id* identifies the value for the "for" attribute in the label element, and *value1* and *value2* are choices in the option list.
- To allow more than one item in the list to appear in the browser, use `size="number"`, where *number* is the number of items you want to display in the selection list. The default size value of 1 creates a drop-down list in which only one choice is visible.
- To allow the user to select more than one choice, use `multiple="multiple"` in the select tag code.
- To make an option the default choice, use `selected="selected"` in the option tag code.

You use the **select element** to create the selection list, and enter **option elements** to define each menu choice within a selection list. The option element's value attribute and its value determine the data that will be sent to the form handler. The **option text** is the text that appears in the browser as a choice in the selection list. You enter the option text between the start <option> and end </option> tags. The following code shows a sample selection list:

```
<label for="county">County</label><br />
<select name="county" id="county" size="1">
  <option value="Dershemer">Dershemer</option>
  <option value="Hastings">Hastings</option>
  <option value="Lester">Lester</option>
  <option value="Morris">Morris</option>
  <option value="Warren">Warren</option>
  <option value="none">none from this list</option>
</select>
```

You've already used the size attribute with text boxes. For selection lists, the size attribute indicates the number of items that are initially shown in the selection box. By default, the size attribute has a value of 1, so only one item appears, which creates a drop-down list box.

InSight | Creating Hidden Fields

You can use hidden fields to retain data already entered in a form as a user moves from page to page filling out additional data. This older method is not often used in form design today. When the user clicks the Back button in the browser, the information in the hidden fields is displayed so the user doesn't have to fill out the form from scratch. The following sample code shows how to define a hidden field:

```
<input type="hidden" name="collect" id="collect"
value="formhandlerscript.com" />
```

Above all, never create a form with an input type of "hidden" and include sensitive information such as a password hidden in it. Passing hidden values in a form is achieved most commonly today by using scripting languages, such as JavaScript.

You have already used the checked attribute with radio buttons and check boxes. Similarly, to make an option in a selection list selected by default, use the **selected attribute** with a value of "selected," as shown in the following code.

```
<option value="Lester" selected="selected">Lester</option>
```

The **multiple attribute** and its value of "multiple" allows the user to select nonadjacent items in a list using CTRL+click or to choose adjacent options in the list using SHIFT+click. The multiple attribute and value are entered in the start select tag, as shown in the following code.

```
<select name="county" id="county" multiple="multiple">
```

An **option group** is a set of options within a selection list. You use the **optgroup element** and the <optgroup></optgroup> tags to create option groups. The **label attribute** serves as the heading for the option group; the value you assign to the attribute will appear in bold when the selection list appears in the browser. The code for an option group would look similar to the following code.

```
<select name="purchase" id="purchase">
<optgroup label="Petites">
  <option value="4p">4P</option>
  <option value="6p">6P</option>
  <option value="8p">8P</option>
</optgroup>

<optgroup label="Misses">
  <option value="6">6</option>
  <option value="8">8</option>
  <option value="10">10</option>
</optgroup>
</select>
```

Figure 9-16 shows how the option group would appear in the browser.

Figure 9-16 ▷ **Option groups in the browser**

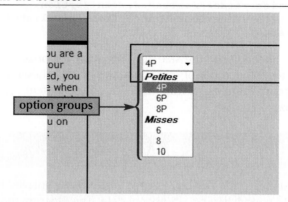

People who fill out Marie's form will need to indicate their county of residence. You've decided to use a selection list for this. Before you show Marie how to create the selection list, you will create a style for the select element so that the text appears in navy.

To style the selection list:

▶ **1.** Switch back to your text editor, scroll up to the embedded style sheet, and position the insertion point on a blank line below the fieldset element style.

▶ **2.** Type the following code, as shown in Figure 9-17.

```
select {
  color: navy;
}
```

Figure 9-17   **The selection list style code**

```
fieldset {
  margin-bottom: 1em;
  border: solid 2px black;
  background-color: #e9edda;
}

select {
  color: navy;
}

</style>

</head>
```

the style for the
select element →

▶ **3.** Save the file.

Now that the selection element has been styled, you will show Marie how to enter the code for the selection list.

To enter the code for the selection list:

▶ **1.** In your text editor, scroll down; in the document body, position the insertion point on a blank line below the end </div> tag and comment for the check boxes code. Indent the code for the option tags by two spaces, as if you were entering list items.

▶ **2.** Type the following code, as shown in Figure 9-18.

```
<div>

<label for="county" class="left">County</label><br />
<select name="county" id="county">
  <option value="Dershemer">Dershemer</option>
  <option value="Hastings">Hastings</option>
  <option value="Lester" selected="selected">Lester</option>
  <option value="Morris">Morris</option>
  <option value="Warren">Warren</option>
  <option value="none">none from this list</option>
</select>

</div> <!-- end selection list -->
```

Figure 9-18	The selection list code

```
</fieldset>

</div> <!-- end check boxes -->

<div>

<label for="county" class="left">County</label><br />
<select name="county" id="county">
   <option value="Dershemer">Dershemer</option>
   <option value="Hastings">Hastings</option>
   <option value="Lester" selected="selected">Lester</option>
   <option value="Morris">Morris</option>
   <option value="Warren">Warren</option>
   <option value="none">none from this list</option>
</select>

</div> <!-- end selection list -->

</form>
```

the code for the selection list

3. Save the file.

4. Switch to your browser and refresh or reload the **squarednew.htm** file. Click the drop-down list arrow to verify that the selection list appears correctly, as shown in Figure 9-19. (Lester should be selected.)

Figure 9-19	The selection list in the browser

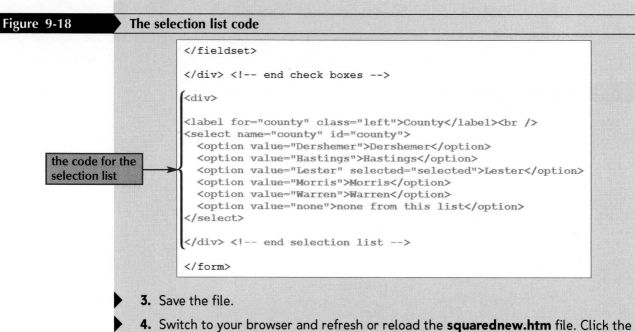

To let users enter comments or feedback, you'll show Marie how to create a text area next.

Creating a Text Area

Recall that you used a text box to create a single-line field for alphanumeric input. A **text area** is a control that allows users to enter more than one line of alphanumeric input. The **textarea element** is used to create a multiline text field. Marie wants to add a text area to obtain customer feedback about Fashion Squared[2]'s products and services.

Reference Window | **Creating Text Areas**

- To create a text area, enter the following code:
  ```
  <textarea name="name" id="id" rows="height_value"
  cols="width_value"></textarea>
  ```
  where *name* identifies the field in the database associated with the text area, *id* associates this field with the "for" attribute value in the label element, *height_value* is the number of rows, and *width_value* is the character width of the text area expressed as a number.

Tip

HTML code, a text area ways expressed as one d: *textarea*.

    Text areas allow users to enter comments that suggest how to improve a particular service or the form itself, or provide other feedback. You must specify a width and a height for the text area using the **cols attribute** and **rows attribute**, respectively. By default, a text area has a width of 19 characters and a height of 2 rows.

    The code for a text area would look similar to the following code.

```
<textarea name="name" id="id" cols="40" rows="6"></textarea>
```

Optionally, you could include some default text in the text area. Enter the default text between the code for the start and end textarea tags, as shown in the following example:

```
<textarea name="name" id="id" cols="40" rows="6">Your comments,
please.</textarea>
```

You will now show Marie how to create a text area. First, you will create a style for the textarea element so that a border appears around the text area. You will also create a dependent class for the label element so that its text appears with a text alignment of left.

To style the textarea element and create the dependent class:

  ▶ **1.** Switch back to your text editor, scroll up to the embedded style sheet, and position the insertion point on a blank line below the select element style.

  ▶ **2.** Type the following code, as shown in Figure 9-20.

```
textarea {
  border: solid 2px navy;
}

label.left {
  text-align: left;
  color: navy;
}
```

Figure 9-20 | **The textarea and dependent class code**

```
select {
  color: navy;
}

textarea {
  border: solid 2px navy;
}

label.left {
  text-align: left;
  color: navy;
}

</style>
```

code for the text area
and the label code

3. Save the file.

Now that the styles have been created, you will show Marie how to add the text area to obtain customer feedback.

To enter the code for the text area:

1. In your text editor, scroll down; in the document body, position the insertion point on a blank line below the end </div> tag and comment for the selection list code.

2. Type the following code, as shown in Figure 9-21.

```
<div>

<label for="comments" class="left">Comments</label>
<textarea name="comments" id="comments" rows="10"
cols="60"></textarea>

</div> <!-- end text area -->
```

Figure 9-21 | **The textarea code**

```
</div> <!-- end selection list -->

<div>

<label for="comments" class="left">Comments</label>
<textarea name="comments" id="comments" rows="10" cols="60"></textarea>

</div> <!-- end text area -->

</form>

</div> <!-- end right column -->
```

code for the text area

3. Save the file.

4. Switch to your browser and refresh or reload the **squarednew.htm** file. If necessary, scroll down and verify that the text area appears correctly, as shown in Figure 9-22.

Figure 9-22 The text area in the browser

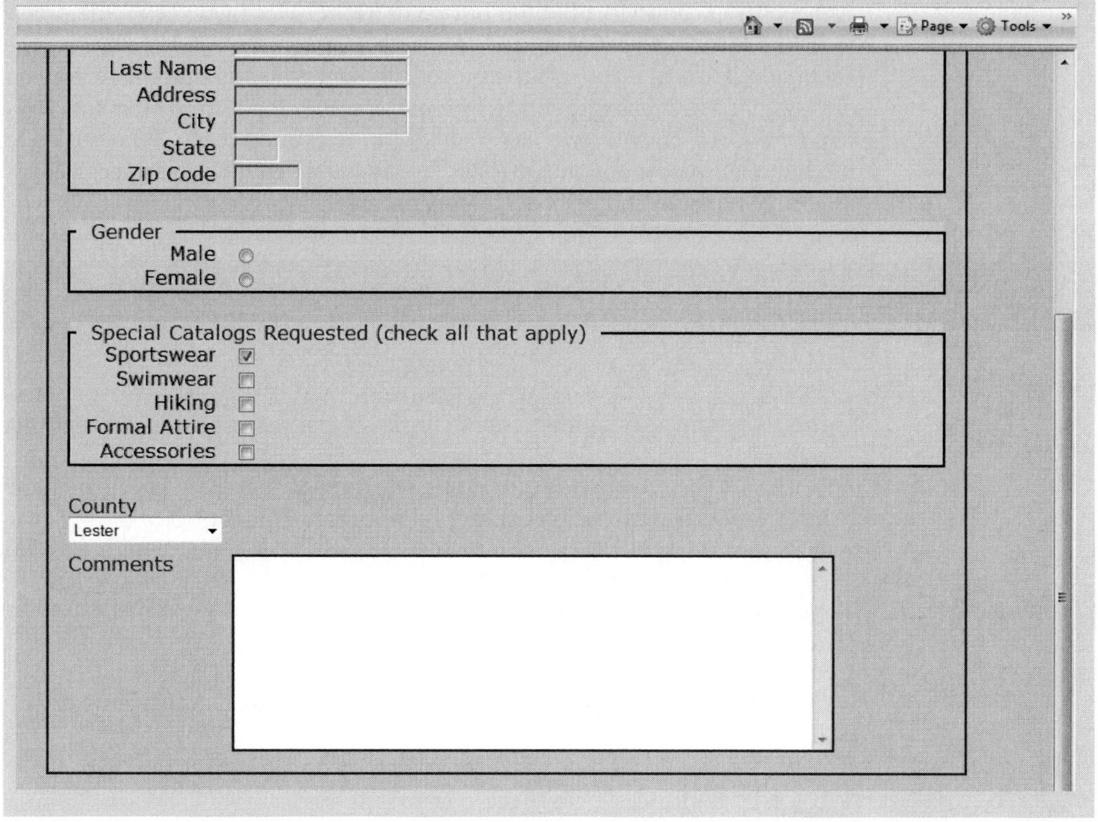

Last, you will show Marie how the user can submit data to the form handler.

Submitting Data

Tip

mand buttons have
tly different default
and shapes in differ-
browsers.

After a user enters all the data in the form, the data must be submitted to the form handler. You also might want to allow the user to clear the data and cancel the operation, although for an online transaction, you want the user to complete the transaction. A **command button** is a form control used to execute or reject a user action. A **Submit button** is used to submit the form data to the specified action location; a **Reset button** clears or resets the form fields to the default values so you can cancel the input in the form and start over.

In the code for the Submit or Reset button, the value attribute determines what text appears on the button in the browser. In the following example, the words "Send Information" will appear on the Submit button when the form is viewed in the browser.

```
<input type="submit" value="Send Information" />
```

The following code could be used to create a Reset button. The word "Cancel" would appear on the button.

```
<input type="reset" value="Cancel" />
```

Although you can style a Submit button or Reset button, you can't add a background image to it. The **button element** is used to create a button control. Unlike the Submit or Reset command buttons, if you use the button element, you *can* place an image on the button or use an image as a background for the button. With the button element, you can set a button to submit data, clear a form, create a link, or execute a script. When using an image with the button, create a dependent class for the image element selector, include margin space around the image, and position the image vertically.

Reference Window | **Creating a Button**

- To create a button, enter the following code:
  ```
  <button type="buttontype">buttontext</button>
  ```
  where *buttontype* is either submit or reset, and *buttontext* is the text that appears on the button.
- Optionally, you can include an image with alternate text, assign a value to the vertical-align property, and assign values to the width and height properties.
- If you are using an image with text, you can make the image appear to the left or the right of the button text.
- You can also use a background image for the button.

The following examples show you how to style the button element:

```
button {
  padding-top: 0.1em;
  margin-left: 2em;
  font-weight: bold;
  color: black;
  background-color: orange;
}

button.image {
  margin-right: 1em;
  vertical-align: middle;
}
```

In the HTML code in the body of the document, the first button uses an image for a Submit button:

```
<button type="submit">
  <img src="check.gif" alt="checked image" />Submit Order
</button>
```

In the second button, an image is used as a link:

```
<button type="button" class="image">
  <a href="somepage.htm"><img src="leftarrow.gif" alt="left
arrow image" />Previous</a>
</button>
```

Tip

Submit buttons and Reset buttons don't require label elements because their descriptions are contained in their value attributes.

You will show Marie how to create a style for the Submit button. Depending on your browser and browser version, the size, shape, and background color may appear differently.

To style the Submit button:

▶ **1.** Switch back to your text editor, scroll up to the embedded style sheet, and position the insertion point on a blank line below the end label.left dependent style.

▶ **2.** Type the following code, as shown in Figure 9-23.

```
input.button {
  color: navy;
  text-transform: uppercase;
  font-weight: bold;
  padding: 4px;
}
```

Figure 9-23 ▷ **The input dependent class code**

```
label.left {
  text-align: left;
  color: navy;
}

input.button {
  color: navy;
  text-transform: uppercase;
  font-weight: bold;
  padding: 4px;
}

</style>

</head>

<body>
```

the code to style the button

▶ **3.** Save the file.

Now that the styles have been created, you will show Marie how to add a Submit button to send the data to the form handler. You will also help Marie add a Reset button.

To enter the code for the Submit and Reset buttons:

▶ **1.** In your text editor, scroll down; in the document body, position the insertion point on a blank line below the end </div> tag and comment for the text area code.

▶ **2.** Type the following code, as shown in Figure 9-24.

```
<div>

<input type="submit" value="Send Information"
class="button" /> <input type="reset" value="Cancel"
class="button" />

</div> <!-- end command buttons -->
```

Figure 9-24 | **The Submit and Reset button code**

the code for the submit and reset buttons

```
<label for="comments" class="left">Comments</label>
<textarea name="comments" id="comments" rows="10" cols="60"></textarea>
</div> <!-- end text area -->

<div>
<input type="submit" value="Send Information" class="button" />
<input type="reset" value="Cancel" class="button" />

</div> <!-- end command buttons -->

</form>

</div> <!-- end right column -->
```

▶ **3.** Save the file.

▶ **4.** Switch to your browser and refresh or reload the **squarednew.htm** file. If necessary, scroll down to verify that the Submit and Reset buttons appear correctly, as shown in Figure 9-25.

Figure 9-25 | **The Submit and Reset buttons in the browser**

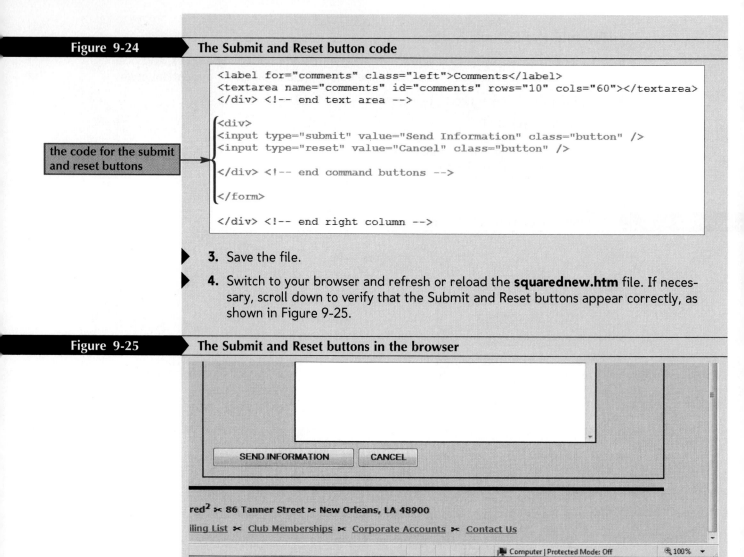

Figure 9-26 shows the completed file.

Figure 9-26 | The completed file in the browser

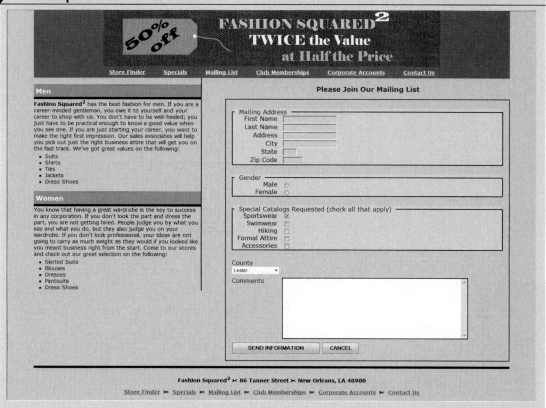

> **5.** Submit the results of the **squarednew.htm** file to your instructor, either in printed or electronic form, as requested.

> **6.** If you are not completing the Review Assignments or the Case Problems, close your text editor and your browser.

In this session, you learned that form controls allow the user to select from one or more options. Radio buttons require the user to select one choice from a list of options. Check boxes allow users to select one or more items from a list of choices. You can create option groups to divide a drop-down list into logical sets of choices. A text area is a multiple-line text box that is commonly used to obtain user feedback or comments. Submit and Reset buttons are command buttons used to submit or reject the data collected in the form.

Review | **Session 9.2 Quick Check**

1. What form control allows a user to make at most one choice from a group of options?

2. What form control allows a user to make several choices from a group of options?

3. What attribute and value preselects a choice in a group of options for either radio buttons or check boxes?

4. What element is used to create a list of options?

5. What form control creates a button that sends data to a database?

6. What form control creates a button that erases the entries in all the fields?

After you have created a form for data input, the form data must be processed using a PHP or CGI script, and then the data must be entered into a database using the script. The <form> and </form>tags start and end the form. You can use more than one set of <form> tags in the body of a document. The method attribute is used to run a script. The <input> tag is used to create a variety of form objects. Text boxes are areas of the screen in which the user can input text. The size and maxlength attributes control the size of the text box and how many characters are accepted for input. The password attribute creates a password field. The <textarea> tag creates a multiple-line text entry field. Radio buttons are used to select only one item from a list of choices. Check boxes are used to select one or more items from a list of choices. The <select> tag creates a menu, and the <option> tags are used to identify the menu items. The Submit button is used to send the form data to the specified action location, such as a CGI file. The Reset button is used to clear the form fields. You can use the <button> tag to set a style for the buttons. You can organize the form elements by using the <fieldset> tag and the <legend> tags.

Key Terms

action attribute	form handler	prompting text
alphanumeric data	input element	radio button
button element	label attribute	Reset button
CGI	label element	rows attribute
check box	label text	script
checked attribute	legend element	scripting language
clean data	legend text	select element
cols attribute	list box	selected attribute
command button	maxlength attribute	selection list
database	method attribute	size attribute
drop-down list box	multiple attribute	Submit button
field	optgroup element	text area
fieldset element	option element	text box
for attribute	option group	textarea element
form	option text	type attribute
form control	password field	
form element	placeholder code	

Practice | **Review Assignments**

*time to practice
kills you learned
e tutorial using
ame case
ario.*

Data Files needed for the Review Assignments: account.htm, accountnewstyles.css, squaredlogo.gif

Marie has asked for your help in creating a new page at the Fashion Squared[2] Web site, where new customers could fill out a form to create an account. The form would consist of text fields, a text area, and command buttons. After each step, save the file, switch to your browser, refresh or reload the page, verify that you entered the style code correctly, and then switch back to your text editor and complete the next step. A preview of the Web page you will create appears in Figure 9-27.

Figure 9-27

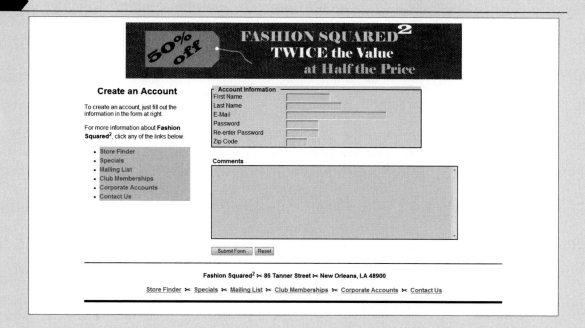

Complete the following:

1. Use your text editor to open the **account.htm** file, which is provided in your Data Files in the Tutorial.09\Review folder. In the head section and below the page title, enter your name and today's date in the comment section where noted.

2. Save the file as **accountnew.htm** in the same folder. Open the file in your browser and observe the appearance of the original file.

3. Switch back to your text editor. In the body of the document and below the comment to "enter the form code below," enter the start form tag. Within the start form tag, enter the code for the id attribute with a value of account. Enter the action attribute like this: action="" (with an empty value enclosed in quotes).

4. Enter the code for the start fieldset tag. After the start fieldset tag, create a legend for the fieldset. Use "Account Information" as the legend text.

5. Create six input tags and enter the code for six text fields using the data in the following table. Enter a break tag after the code for each input tag.

Label for value	Label text	Input type	Name attribute value	Id attribute value	Class	Size
firstname	First Name	text	firstname	firstname	text	15
lastname	Last Name	text	lastname	lastname	text	20
email	E-Mail	text	email	email	text	40
password	Password	password	password	password	text	10
password2	Re-enter Password	password	password2	password2	text	10
zip	Zip Code	text	zip	zip	text	5

6. Enter an end </fieldset> tag on a blank line after the last input tag.

7. On a blank line below the end </fieldset> tag for the text fields and the comment to "enter text area code below," complete the following:
   - Enter the code for the start label tag.
   - In the start label tag, enter "comments" as the value for the "for" attribute.
   - Apply the "left" class to the label.
   - Type "Comments" as the label text.
   - Enter the code for the end </label> tag.

8. On a new line and between the existing set of <p></p> tags, enter the code for a text area. Complete the following:
   - The text area name and id value is comments.
   - The text area has 12 rows and 80 columns.
   - Enter the end </textarea> tag.

9. On a new line and between a set of <p></p> tags, enter the code for a Submit button. The value for the Submit button is Submit Form.

10. To the right of the code for the Submit button (and on the same line), enter the code for a Reset button. The value of the Reset button is Reset.

11. On a new line and above the </div> tag for the <!-- end right column --> code, enter the end </form> tag.

12. Save the **accountnew.htm** file. Switch to your browser and refresh or reload the page. Compare your file to Figure 9-27 to verify that your file is correct.

13. Submit the results of the preceding steps to your instructor, either in printed or electronic form, as requested.

14. If you are not completing the next assignment, close your text editor and your browser.

Apply | **Case Problem 1**

what you've
ed and expand
skills to create
style a Web page
cable television
on.

Data Files needed for this Case Problem: award.htm, awardlogo.gif, awardnewstyles.css

WKZ Hollywood   WKZ is a cable television station broadcasting from Hollywood, California. WKZ prides itself as being the best source for news about pop culture and the world of entertainment. The Academy Awards will be presented next week, and Brett Michaels, station manager at WKZ, has asked you to create a form to collect users' opinions about which actors and movies should win the top five Oscars. You will create a form with a series of radio buttons and command buttons. A preview of the Web page you will create appears in Figure 9-28.

Figure 9-28

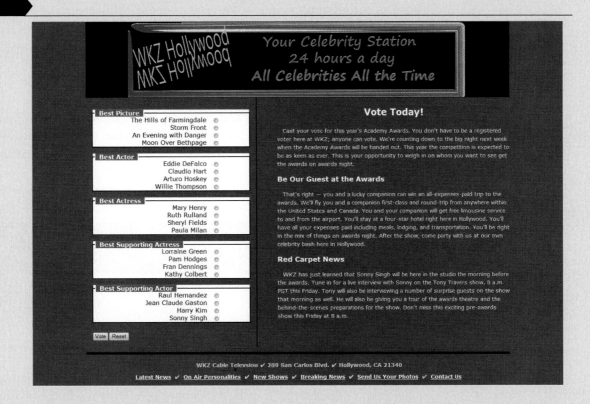

Complete the following:

1. Use your text editor to open the **award.htm** file, which is provided in your Data Files in the Tutorial.09\Case1 folder. In the head section and below the page title, enter your name and today's date in the comment section where noted.

2. Save the file as **awardnew.htm** in the same folder. Open the file in your browser and observe the appearance of the original file.

3. Switch back to your text editor. On a blank line in the document body and below the fieldset tags for "Best Picture," complete the following:
   - Enter the code for the start and end label tags.
   - The value for the "for" attribute is "hills."
   - The label text is "The Hills of Farmingdale."
     Note: Do not follow the end </label> element with a <br /> tag.

4. On a blank line below the label tags, complete the following:
   - Enter the input and type value for a radio button.
   - The value for the name attribute is "picture."

- The value for the id and value attributes is "hills."
- Follow the radio button code with a <br /> tag, and then press the Enter key once.

5. Save the file. Switch to your browser and refresh or reload the **awardnew.htm** file. Verify that the radio button appears correctly in the browser.

6. Copy the two lines of code you have entered so far, along with the blank line following the code. On a blank line below the existing radio button code, paste a copy of the code and the blank line.

7. In the copied code, create code with placeholder values (`""`) so you can make a template from which you can repeatedly copy the code to create more radio buttons. Complete the following:
    - Delete the existing value for the "for" attribute ("hills") so that the code appears as placeholder code, like this: `for=""`
    - Delete the label text, "The Hills of Farmingdale," between the start and end label tags.
    - Delete the values for the name, id, and value attributes, so that the code appears as placeholder code, like this: `name="" id="" value=""`

8. Select the two lines of label tag and input tag code that hold the placeholder values and select the <br /> tag that follows the input tag code. Copy the code.

9. On a blank line below the placeholder code you just created, paste two copies of the placeholder code.

10. Insert the values shown in the following table into the placeholder code as indicated.

Label for value	Label text	Input type	Name value	Id value	Value value
storm	Storm Front	radio	picture	storm	storm
danger	An Evening with Danger	radio	picture	danger	danger
moon	Moon Over Bethpage	radio	picture	moon	moon

11. Save the file. Switch to your browser and refresh or reload the **awardnew.htm** file. Verify that the radio buttons for Best Picture appear correctly in the browser.

12. Complete the following steps for each of the remaining four fieldsets.
    a. Copy the placeholder code four times.
    b. Enter the following values for the name attribute for each of the four remaining fieldset groups of radio buttons:

Fieldset	Value for the Name Attribute
Best Actor	actor
Best Actress	actress
Best Supporting Actress	suppactress
Best Supporting Actor	suppactor

    c. The values for the "for," id, and value attributes are the last names of the nominees, as shown in Figure 9-28.
    d. The text for each label will be the first and last names of the nominees, as shown in Figure 9-28.

13. Save the **awardnew.htm** file.

14. Switch to your browser and refresh or reload the page. Compare your file to Figure 9-28 to verify that your file is correct.

15. Submit the results of the **awardnew.htm** file to your instructor, either in printed or electronic form, as requested.

16. If you are not completing the next assignment, close your text editor and your browser.

Apply | **Case Problem 2**

*he skills you
ed in the tutorial
ate a Web page
food supplier.*

Data Files needed for this Case Problem: check.gif, food.htm, foodlogo.gif, foodnewstyles.css, no.gif

OnLoin Meat and Poultry Foods   OnLoin Meat and Poultry Foods supplies many of the nation's finest restaurants with top-quality meats and poultry. The company also has begun selling its products to individual customers on the Web. The company uses its national distribution channels to ship its products within hours after receiving orders. Gus Tyrell, the chief marketing manager, has asked you to create a new form for ordering OnLoin products. A preview of the Web page you will create appears in Figure 9-29.

Figure 9-29

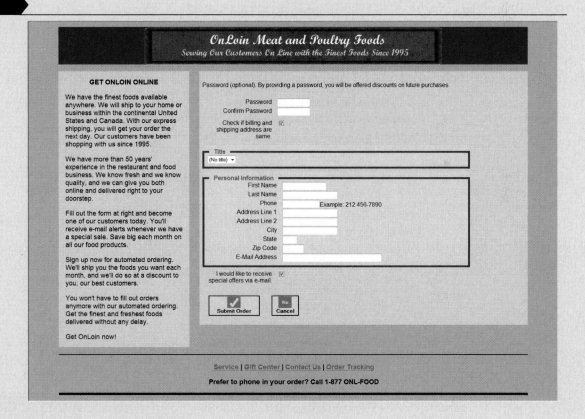

Complete the following:

1. Use your text editor to open the **food.htm** file, which is provided in your Data Files in the Tutorial.09\Case2 folder. In the head section and below the page title, enter your name and today's date in the comment section where noted.

2. Save the file as **foodnew.htm** in the same folder. Open the file in your browser and observe the appearance of the original file.

3. Switch back to your text editor. In the embedded style sheet, style the form element as follows:
   - Set the margin on the bottom to 1em.
   - Add padding of 0.5em on all sides.
   - Set the background color to #efe8ce.
   - Set the font size to 16px.

4. Create a dependent style for the form element so that the div element has the following styles:
   - Set the margin to 0 on all sides.
   - Add padding on the top of 0.5em.
   - Set the clear property to have a value of both.

5. Create a style for the label element as follows:
   - Set the width to 180px.
   - Set the margin to 0 on the top, 15px on the right, 0 on the bottom, and 4px on the left.
   - Set the text color to black.
   - Set the float property to have a value of left.
   - Align the label text right.

6. Create a style for the legend element as follows:
   - Add padding of 0 on the top and bottom and 10px on the left and right.
   - Set the text color to green.
   - Make the legend text bold.

7. Create a style for the fieldset element as follows:
   - Set the width to 80%.
   - Set the margin on the bottom to 1em.
   - Create a border that is solid, 5px, and maroon.
   - Add padding of 0.5em on all sides.
   - Set the background color to #e9edda.

8. Create a style for the button element as follows:
   - Set the margin to 1em on all sides.
   - Create a border that is solid, thin, and black.
   - Set the text color to black.
   - Set the background color to yellow.
   - Make the button text bold.

9. In the body of the document and below the comment "password fields are below," use the following table to create two password fields. Enter a <br /> tag after the input code for the first password.

Label for value	Label text	Input type	Name attribute value	Id attribute value	Size	Maxlength
password	Password	password	password	password	10	10
password2	Confirm Password	password	password2	password2	10	10

10. On a blank line in the body of the document and below the comment "first check box is below," enter the start and end label tags. The value for the "for" attribute is shipping. The label text is "Check if billing and shipping address are same."

11. On a blank line below the label tags, enter the code for a check box. The value for both the name and id attributes is shipping. Make this check box checked by default.

12. On a blank line below the comment "selection list is below," enter the code to create a selection list with four options. The select tag name and id attribute values are "title." Refer to the following table to enter the option element values and the option text.

Option element value	Option text
no	(No title)
mr	Mr.
mrs	Mrs.
ms	Ms.

13. Below the comment "text boxes are below," enter the code for nine text boxes. Refer to the following table to enter the label values and input values. Insert a <br /> tag after each input element tag. After the input element code for Phone, enter the example text, as shown in the preview figure.

Label for value	Label text	Input type	Name attribute value	Id attribute value	Size	Maxlength
firstname	First Name	text	firstname	firstname	15	-
lastname	Last Name	text	lastname	lastname	20	-
phone	Phone	text	phone	phone	12	12
address1	Address Line 1	text	address1	address1	20	-
address2	Address Line 2	text	address2	address2	20	-
city	City	text	city	city	20	-
state	State	text	state	state	2	2
zip	Zip Code	text	zip	zip	5	5
email	E-Mail Address	text	email	email	40	40

14. Below the comment "second check box is below," enter the start and end label tags on a blank line. The value for the "for" attribute is offers. The label text is "I would like to receive special offers via e-mail." On a blank line below the label tags, enter the code for a check box. The value for both the name and id attributes is offers. Make this check box checked by default.

⊕ EXPLORE 15. Below the comment "buttons are below," enter the code for two button elements. (Use the button element to create these two buttons.) The first button will be used to submit the data, and the second button will be a Reset button to clear the form. The Submit button uses an image named check.gif. The button text is Submit Order. The Reset button uses an image named no.gif. The button text is Cancel.

16. Save the **foodnew.htm** file. Switch to your browser and refresh or reload the page. Compare your file to Figure 9-29 to verify that your file is correct.

17. Submit the results of the preceding steps to your instructor, either in printed or electronic form, as requested.

18. If you are not completing the next assignment, close your text editor and your browser.

Challenge | Case Problem 3

Use the skills you learned in the tutorial to create and style a Web page for a catering service.

Data Files needed for this Case Problem: hall.gif, hall.htm, hallnewstyles.css

LaFleur Caterers   LaFleur Caterers is a large catering hall in Benson Falls, Montana that specializes in arranging events for 50 to 500 people. LaFleur makes all the arrangements for invitations, flowers, limousines, portrait photography, videography, live or recorded music, and tuxedo and gown rentals. LaFleur also arranges weddings, including honeymoon plans, wait staff, personal bridal attendants, directional cards, coat checks, and gazebo garden ceremonies. Brenda McNair, the new manager of LaFleur Caterers, has asked you to create a Web-based form that allows customers to choose from the services available. A preview of the Web page you will create appears in Figure 9-30.

Figure 9-30

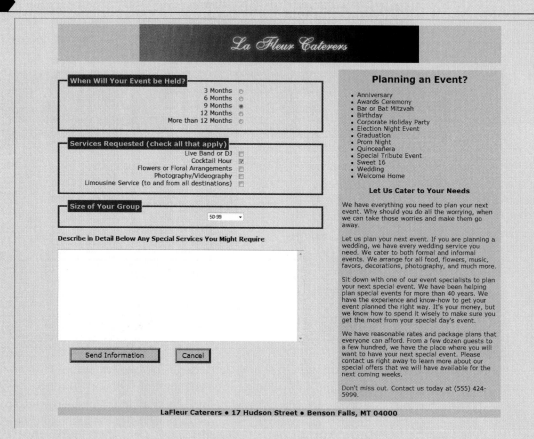

Complete the following:

1. Use your text editor to open the **hall.htm** file, which is provided in your Data Files in the Tutorial.09\Case3 folder. In the head section and below the page title, enter your name and today's date in the comment section where noted.
2. Save the file as **hallnew.htm** in the same folder. Open the file in your browser and observe the appearance of the original file.

3. Switch back to your text editor. In the embedded style sheet, style the fieldset element to have a border that is maroon, solid, and medium. Add padding of 1em to all sides.

4. Style the legend element as follows:
   - Add padding of 5px on all sides.
   - Set the text color to #f3da0c.
   - Set the background color to maroon.
   - Set the font weight to bold.
   - Set the font size to 1.1em.

5. Style the button element as follows:
   - Set the margin to 1em on the top, 0.5em on the right, 0 on the bottom, and 2em on the left.
   - Create a border on all sides that is silver, outset, and thick.
   - Set the text color to black.
   - Set the background color to #f3da0c.
   - Set the font size to 1.1em.
   - Set the font family to the Verdana (sans-serif) font.

6. Style the label element as follows:
   - Set the width to 450px.
   - Set the margin on the right to 15px.
   - Set the text color to black.
   - Set the value for the float property to left.
   - Align the text right.

7. Style the select element to have a left margin of 385px.

8. In the body of the document and below the first set of fieldset tags with the legend "When Will Your Event be Held?," enter the code for five labels and five radio buttons. Use the following table to determine the values for each label and each radio button. (Make the choice for "9 Months" checked by default.) Each input tag except the last one should be followed with a <br /> tag.

Label for	Label text	Input type	Name value	Id value	Value
three	3 Months	radio	date	three	3
six	6 Months	radio	date	six	6
nine	9 Months	radio	date	nine	9
twelve	12 Months	radio	date	twelve	12
greater	More than 12 Months	radio	date	greater	13

9. Below the fieldset with the legend "Services Requested (check all that apply)," enter the code for five check boxes. Use the following table to determine the values for each label and each radio button. (Make the choice for "Cocktail Hour" checked by default.) Each input tag except the last one should be followed with a <br /> tag.

Label for	Label text	Input type	Name value	Id value	Value
band	Live Band or DJ	checkbox	service	band	band
cocktail	Cocktail Hour	checkbox	service	cocktail	cocktail
flowers	Flowers or Floral Arrangements	checkbox	service	flowers	flowers
photo	Photography/Videography	checkbox	service	photo	photo
limo	Limousine Service (to and from all destinations)	checkbox	service	limo	limo

10. On a blank line below the fieldset with the legend "Size of Your Group," enter the code for a selection list. In the start select tag, enter "size" as the value for both the name and the id attributes. Use the following table to determine the values for each option. (Make the option for "50-99" selected by default.)

Option value	Option text
10	10-19
20	20-29
30	30-49
50	50-99
100	100-249
250	250-499
500	500 or more

11. Position the insertion point below the sentence that begins "Describe in Detail Below any Special ...". On a blank line, enter the code for a text area that has 15 rows and 80 columns.

⊕ EXPLORE
12. Use the button element (not the input element) to create two buttons. The first button will be a Submit button with "Send Information" as the button text. The second button will be a Reset button with "Cancel" as the button text.

13. Save the **hallnew.htm** file. Switch to your browser and refresh or reload the page. Compare your file to Figure 9-30 to verify that your file is correct.

14. In your browser, go to *http://validator.w3.org* to open the W3C validator. Validate the **hallnew.htm** file by using the Validate by File Upload method. Note any errors and correct them in your file if necessary.

15. In your browser, navigate to *http://jigsaw.w3.org/css-validator*. Validate the **hallnew.htm** file by using the By file upload method. Note any errors and correct them in your file if necessary. Note any errors in the code for the embedded style sheet. You can ignore the warning "File not found: import file://localhost/hallnewstyles.css: Operation not permitted," which pertains to the linked style sheet.

16. Submit the results of the **hallnew.htm** file to your instructor, either in printed or electronic form, as requested.

17. If you are not completing the next assignment, close your text editor and your browser.

| Create | | **Case Problem 4** |

ate a Web page to
ry students about
on campus.

Data Files needed for this Case Problem: survey.htm, surveylogo.gif

Student Life Survey Brad Tillman, the director of campus life at Sterling College, has asked you to design an online form that surveys students about their college experience. Possible survey topics include the following:

- Appearance and availability of campus housing
- Classroom and student center facilities
- Course availability
- Course relevance to major
- Parking issues
- Registration issues
- Satisfaction with and availability of campus activities
- Satisfaction with campus services such as admissions, the bursar, and the registrar
- Satisfaction with courses
- Scholarship availability
- Tuition costs

Complete the following:

1. Use your text editor to open the **survey.htm** file, which is provided in your Data Files in the Tutorial.09\Case4 folder. In the head section, give your page an appropriate title. Below the page title, enter your name and today's date in the comment section where noted.
2. Save the file as **surveynew.htm** in the same folder.
3. Within the embedded style sheet, in addition to the existing styles, format the body element with the text size, font, color, and background color of your choice.
4. In the document body and within the form element tags, enter code for your survey that includes examples of each of the following:
   a. three or more text fields
   b. one password field
   c. at least one group of radio buttons (make one of the radio buttons selected by default)
   d. at least one group of check boxes (make one of the boxes checked by default)
   e. a fieldset (set a style for this element)
   f. a legend (set a style for this element)
   g. a selection list (make one of the options selected by default)
   h. a text area
   i. Submit and Reset buttons
   Also make appropriate use of the label element and the "for" attribute.
5. Save the **surveynew.htm** file. Switch to your browser and refresh or reload the page. Verify that all styles work correctly.
6. Open your browser and go to *http://validator.w3.org*. Use the Validate by File Upload method to check the **surveynew.htm** document and ensure that the HTML code is correct. If necessary, correct any errors detected by the validation.
7. In your browser, go to *http://jigsaw.w3.org/css-validator*. Use the By file upload method to check the **surveynew.htm** file and ensure that the CSS code is correct. If necessary, correct any errors detected by the validation.
8. Submit the results of the **surveynew.htm** file to your instructor, either in printed or electronic form, as requested.
9. Close your text editor and your browser. Close all open windows.

Review | **Quick Check Answers**

Session 9.1

1. an organized collection of data
2. <form> </form>
3. text
4. restricts the input in a text field or password field to a set number of characters
5. yes, depending on the font used
6. password

Session 9.2

1. radio
2. checkbox
3. checked="checked"
4. the select element
5. submit
6. reset

Ending Data Files

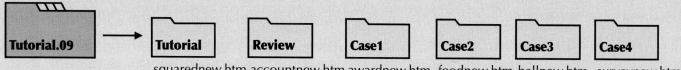

Tutorial.09 → Tutorial   Review   Case1   Case2   Case3   Case4

squarednew.htm accountnew.htm awardnew.htm foodnew.htm hallnew.htm surveynew.htm

Reality Check

Now that you have learned how to create Web pages, it's time to create Web pages for your personal use. Today most job applicants submit résumés to companies using the Web. To differentiate yourself from other job candidates who might be submitting their résumés as word-processing documents, you can send your résumé as an HTML file.

In this exercise, the Web site for the résumé should consist of at least two pages. One should contain the résumé, and the other should contain an image file, other supplementary material, or a cover page. Your Web pages do not have to be about yourself—they can describe any person, living or dead, or even a fictional character. You might create a résumé to help Mark Twain apply for a job as a newspaper columnist, to help Thomas Edison apply for a job as an inventor, or to help Eleanor Roosevelt apply for a job in government. The job can be at a real or fictional company.

The contents of your Web pages must be original work—something that you create yourself specifically for this project. Your Web pages should meet the requirements of your campus acceptable computer use policy and should not be offensive. The home page file can have either a fixed or liquid layout, but the layout should illustrate the design principles you learned in this text.

Note: Be sure *not* to include sensitive information about yourself in the Web pages you create and submit to your instructor for this exercise. Later, you can update the Web pages with more personal information.

1. Using an embedded style sheet to format your home page, create a Web page that has the following components:
   - An anchor at the top of the page (used for a link to the bottom of the page)
   - A link at the bottom of the page back to the anchor at the top
   - At least two section headings of different sizes (such as <h1> or <h2>)
   - Examples of bold text and italic text
   - At least five paragraphs of text
   - At least one image that is not a link
   - At least one image that is a link
   - A link to another page
   - At least three external links to appropriate Web sites
   - An ordered or unordered list (change the list style type or use a list style image)
   - The <div> </div> tags and a class applied to the <div> tag
   - A table with a minimum of three columns and three rows, including a colspan or a rowspan
   - An independent class that changes the appearance of text to 1.2em, italic, and red. Apply this independent class to several words on your résumé.
2. Style and use the following elements in your Web pages:
   - <h1>, <h2>, or <h3>
   - <em>
   - <strong>
   - <p>
   - a:link
   - a:visited
   - a:hover

3. Save your file with a name of *yourlastname*_resume.htm. Save all other files using a similar naming convention.

4. Submit your completed file and printouts to your instructor as requested.

Using Multimedia on a Web Page

Appendix

The term **multimedia** describes anything that includes sound, video, and animation. Multimedia is used extensively on the Web, particularly at news and information sites. Clearly, however, the popularity of sites such as *www.youtube.com* shows that anyone can use multimedia on the Web.

Although HTML and image files are usually small, multimedia files tend to be very large. These files also have a large **bandwidth**—a measurement of the amount of data and the speed at which the data can be sent over communications lines. During the early days of the Internet, most users went online using a **dial-up connection** via standard phone lines. Dial-up connections are slow to transmit data and have a low bandwidth, so to make their Web sites load quickly, most Web designers didn't use much multimedia on their sites. To download a multimedia file rapidly, your computer needs to have a **broadband** connection—a high-bandwidth communication line, such as a cable or fiber-optic line. Today, the majority of Internet users have a broadband connection, whether at work or at home.

The difference between dial-up and broadband connections is crucial when it comes to **streaming media**, which are multimedia files that can begin playing without first having to be downloaded in their entirety. Internet users who still have a dial-up phone connection can use only **nonstreaming media**—multimedia files that are downloaded completely before they can be played. As a Web site designer, you can choose to store streaming media files on your own server, but if your site depends on such files, you should probably sign up for a **hosted streaming media plan** with a company that has dedicated servers used solely for high-volume streaming media.

If you have a high-speed broadband connection, you can enjoy many multimedia features of the Internet. For example, **podcasting** is the use of sound files to record and then play audio commentary. You can find podcasts everywhere on the Web, but particularly on news and information sites. **Blogs** (Web logs) are personal diaries or commentaries posted on the Web. **Video blogs** are sites whose content is presented with video files.

Starting Data Files

There are no starting Data Files needed for this Appendix.

Understanding Plug-Ins and Players

As a Web page designer, you obviously want all visitors to your Web site to be able to view its multimedia content. However, the ability to present multimedia is not built in to Web browsers; they were designed only to present text and images. To play multimedia content, a browser needs a **plug-in** (or **add-on**), which is any software that adds functionality to a program. A **player** is a plug-in program designed to play multimedia files. The most popular players are Adobe Flash, Apple QuickTime, Microsoft Silverlight, Real Media, and Windows Media.

The procedure for seeing which players are installed on your computer depends on the browser you use. In the Mozilla Firefox browser, click Tools from the menu bar, and then click Add-ons; if necessary, click Plugins. In Microsoft Internet Explorer, click Tools from the menu bar, click Manage Add-ons, and then click Enable or Disable Add-ons.

If a player was not installed on your computer when you purchased it, the player must be downloaded from the vendor's Web site. For example, to view a Flash movie, you must have the Flash player installed on your computer. If you try to view a multimedia file without having the necessary player installed, the browser will display an alert and prompt you to go to the Web site where you can download and then install the player. Players also need to be updated periodically as newer versions are introduced.

As a Web page designer, you determine which type of player can play the multimedia files on your Web page. To assist the visitors to your Web site, use the following guidelines when selecting multimedia formats:

- Don't require the most recent version of a player or plug-in and don't require a less popular player; the user probably doesn't have it installed.
- Don't make the visitor guess; show what file format your multimedia file uses.
- Offer several versions of the same multimedia file. For example, offer the file in both the Apple QuickTime and Flash player formats.
- Provide links to download the player, especially if your file can only be viewed by using the most recent version.

Understanding Multimedia File Formats

Multimedia files are created in several different types of file formats, as there is no universally accepted format for audio, video, or animation. The filename extension, such as .swf or .avi, identifies the file format. Some of the formats were designed for personal computers, and others were created for the Apple computer. **Cross-platform** formats run on both types of computers. There are several popular audio file formats:

- **MIDI** (Musical Instrument Digital Interface) is a format for sending audio between electronic music devices like synthesizers and PC sound cards. MIDI files can record only musical notes. MIDI files are extremely small, so they are ideal for Internet transmission. The file extension for MIDI files is .mid or .midi.
- The **RealAudio** format was developed by Real Media. Sound files stored in the RealAudio format have the extension .rm or .ram.
- The **AU** format was originally designed to support low-bandwidth systems. AU sound files have the extension .au.
- The **AIFF** (Audio Interchange File Format) was developed by Apple, and is supported only on the Apple platform. AIFF sound files have the extension .aif or .aiff.
- The **SND** (Sound) format was also developed by Apple for the Apple platform. SND sound files have the extension .snd.
- The **WAVE** format was developed together by IBM and Microsoft, and is supported by all computers running the Windows operating system. WAVE sound files have the extension .wav.

- The **MP3** file format was developed by the Moving Pictures Experts Group (MPEG). This file format also supports video. Today, MP3 is perhaps the most popular sound format for recorded music. MP3 files have the extension .mp3.

Similarly, video files can be stored in a variety of file formats. Video formats include those that involve animation, such as Adobe Flash. There are several popular video file formats:

- The **MPEG** (Moving Pictures Expert Group) format is one of the most popular on the Internet. MPEG is supported cross-platform and by all contemporary browsers. Videos stored in the MPEG format have the extension .mpg or .mpeg. Most videos posted on the Internet today are in the MPEG-4 format or a subset of it.
- The **AVI** (Audio Video Interleave) format was developed by Microsoft, and is supported by all computers running Microsoft Windows. AVI video files have the extension .avi.
- The **Windows Media** format was also developed by Microsoft, and is supported by all computers running Windows. Windows Media video files have the extension .wmv.
- The **QuickTime** format was developed by Apple. To play QuickTime movies, you need the QuickTime player and the appropriate plug-in. QuickTime video files have the extension .mov.
- The **RealVideo** format was developed by Real Media. RealVideo files have the extension .rm or .ram.
- The **Shockwave/Flash** format is developed by Adobe. The Flash player is installed when you install most contemporary browsers, such as Firefox or Internet Explorer. Videos stored in the Shockwave/Flash format have the extension .swf.

Placing Multimedia on Your Web Pages

You have three options for placing multimedia on your Web pages. You can use the HTML **object element**, the nonstandard **embed element**, or you can combine the two methods. Many video sharing sites, like YouTube, use the embed element, even though it is nonstandard. If you use the embed tag in your code, your document will not validate in HTML 4.01. However, the embed element has been added to HTML 5.0, so you can use it even though your files may not validate.

Using the Object Element

The object element was designed to embed a variety of data types, images, and other file types (such as PDF documents). The type attribute and its value describe the data type. The value for the type attribute is often a **MIME** (Multipurpose Internet Extension) value. For example, the MIME type for a WAV sound file is audio/wav. The **width** and **height** attributes determine the width and height of the object in the browser.

```
<object
    data="moviename.swf"
    type="application/x-shockwave-flash"
    width="400"
    height="400">
</object>
```

Besides the data and type attributes, several attributes and values should always be included in the start object tag regardless of the player. For example, the **classid attribute** identifies which plug-in should be loaded. The class id is a combination of letters, numbers, and hyphens that identifies a system registry entry and assigns a unique number for each player. The class id tells the operating system which player to use to access the multimedia file. All class ids begin with "clsid:" and are followed by a series of alphanumeric characters grouped in the following five quantities of digits: 8 – 4 – 4 – 4 – 12.

The values for the classid attribute for several popular players are shown in Figure A-1:

Figure A-1 | **Values for the classid attribute for several players**

Windows Media	clsid:22D6F312-B0F6-11D0-94AB-0080C74C7E95
RealMedia	clsid:CFCDAA03-8BE4-11cf-B84B-0020AFBBCCFA
Apple QuickTime	clsid:02BF25D5-8C17-4B23-BC80-D3488ABDDC6B
MPEG-4 (with QuickTime)	clsid:02BF25D5-8C17-4B23-BC80-D3488ABDDC6B
Flash	clsid:D27CDB6E-AE6D-11cf-96B8-444553540000

The class id code would be entered as shown in the following example:

```
<object
    data="moviename.swf"
    type="application/x-shockwave-flash"
    classid="clsid:D27CDB6E-AE6D-11cf-96B8-444553540000"
    width="400"
    height="400">
        <param name="src" value="moviename.swf" />
</object>
```

The **codebase attribute** identifies the URL where you can go to download the plug-in if it is not already installed on the computer. (The pluginspage attribute performs the same function when you use the embed tag.) Generally, these installation files have the filename extension of .cab, as in the following example, where the URL points to the location of the most recent version of the Flash player.

```
<object
    data="moviename.swf"
    type="application/x-shockwave-flash"
    classid="clsid:D27CDB6E-AE6D-11cf-96B8-444553540000"
    codebase="http://fpdownload.macromedia.com/pub/
        shockwave/cabs/flash/swflash.cab#version=7,0,0,0"
    width="400"
    height="400">
</object>
```

Figure A-2 lists the attributes and descriptions for the object element.

Figure A-2 | **Attributes and descriptions for the object element**

Attribute	Description
data	The source of the multimedia file
type	The type of multimedia and the filename extension
autostart	A value of true will play the multimedia file automatically and a value of false will not
controller	Determines whether the play, pause, stop, and rewind buttons appear on the player
height	The height of the element in pixels or as a percentage
width	The width of the element in pixels or as a percentage
standby	The text that will be displayed while the object is loading

Using the Parameter Element

The object element works together with the **param** (parameter) **element**, which uses both the name and value attributes. **Parameters** define the characteristics of the object; an object can have multiple parameters. The parameter element can be used only within the start and end object tags. The parameter element is an empty element and should be ended with a space and forward slash. Besides the src parameter, which identifies the file to be played, you should always include the autoplay and controller parameters. The **autoplay parameter** determines when the media file starts to play. Set the value to true to make the media file play automatically or false to make the user click a control to start the media file. Generally, you should set the autoplay value to false so that visitors to your Web site have the option of playing the multimedia file or not. Not everyone has a broadband connection, and few people enjoy having their browsing interrupted while a media file plays. The **controller parameter** determines whether the player controls are visible. Set the value to false or true depending on whether you want to display the control buttons. Generally, you should set the value to true so that the user can control the playback of the media. The width attribute determines how many of the controls you can view. The code to embed a Flash video using the object and param elements would be similar to the following example, where moviename is the filename. Indenting the code is optional, but it helps readability.

```
<object
    data="moviename.swf"
    type="application/x-shockwave-flash"
    classid="clsid:D27CDB6E-AE6D-11cf-96B8-444553540000"
    codebase="http://fpdownload.macromedia.com/pub/
      shockwave/cabs/flash/swflash.cab#version=7,0,0,0"
    width="400"
    height="400">
      <param name="src" value="moviename.swf" />
      <param name="autoplay" value="false" />
      <param name="controller" value="true" />
</object>
```

Each player has its own long list of parameters, some of which are required. For example, to view the parameters and values for the Apple QuickTime player, go to *www.apple.com/ quicktime/tutorials/*. To view parameters for the Adobe Flash player, go to *http://kb2.adobe.com/cps/127/tn_12701.html*.

Figure A-3 lists the attributes and descriptions for the param element.

Figure A-3	Attributes and descriptions for the param element

Attribute	Description
name	Identifies the kind of property
value	Sets the value of the named property

Using the Embed Element

Not all contemporary browsers use the object element in the same manner, so the embed element can be nested within the object element. If the browser has trouble interpreting the object element code, it will read and execute the code within the embed element. The embed tag uses the src attribute to identify the multimedia file that will play when the user clicks the file link. The src, width, and height attributes are required for the embed element. Figure A-4 lists the attributes and descriptions for the embed element.

Figure A-4   **Attributes and descriptions for the embed element**

Attribute	Description
autoplay	Determines whether a multimedia file starts automatically; values can be either true or false
controller	Determines whether the play, pause, stop, and rewind buttons appear on the player
loop	Determines whether the multimedia file should play more than once
src	Determines the source of the multimedia file
width, height	Specifies the size of the player

The following example shows how the embed element code can be nested within the object element code. The values for the autoplay and controller attributes should be the same as those in the object element.

```
<object width="400" height="400" classid="clsid:02BF25D5-8C17-
4B23-BC80-D3488ABDDC6B"
codebase="http://www.apple.com/qtactivex/qtplugin.cab">

  <param name="src" value="build.mov" />
  <param name="autoplay" value="false" />
  <param name="controller" value="true" />

<embed src="build.mov" width="400" height="400" autoplay="false"
controller="true"
pluginspage="http://www.apple.com/quicktime/download/">
</embed>

</object>
```

Creating Video for YouTube

YouTube was launched in December 2005 as a start-up venture by three youthful entrepreneurs. From the outset, YouTube enjoyed phenomenal success, and it was purchased by Google only one year later for more than $1 billion. The site allows anyone to upload, watch, and share videos. Before YouTube, videos were expensive to create and there was no public portal to display amateur work on the Web. Today, YouTube accounts for more than one-third of the videos viewed on the Web. It serves as an important Web site for sales, marketing, training, education, communication, and just plain fun. All YouTube videos are in the MPEG-4 file format using the H.264 codec. A **codec** encodes a data stream or signal for transmission or decodes it for playback or editing.

Creating Video Content

You don't need expensive technology to record video; some high-definition cameras now cost less than $200. Many handheld camcorders, also known as **pocket camcorders**, can record in MPEG-4 format. Popular pocket camcorders include Pure Digital's Flip model and Creative Labs' Vado model. Other companies, such as Kodak and Sony, also sell popular handheld camcorders. These devices come bundled with software for managing and editing video clips. Despite their small size, most camcorders have a built-in hard drive capable of storing several hours of video. A built-in USB device allows easy connection to a personal or laptop computer, as shown in Figure A-5.

Figure A-5   A pocket camcorder

     Whether you shoot a video of yourself, friends, or a business presentation for work, use the following guidelines:

- You can use a standard quality, high-quality, or high-definition camera. YouTube accepts videos from any of these cameras, although most submissions are from high-definition models.
- Unless you are shooting live action and need to pan from location to location, use a tripod for the camera to ensure steady video. You can use tripods even with pocket camcorders.
- Make sure the subject of the video is clearly visible. If you are shooting the video indoors, make sure there is sufficient lighting. Provide additional lighting if necessary. If you shoot the video outdoors, be wary of both bright sun and shade.
- Don't overuse the zoom feature; it can distract the viewer. Zoom in only if you need to show an important small detail. Zoom out for panoramic views outdoors. In both cases, zoom slowly.
- Write a script for what you have to say and rehearse it before you shoot the video.
- Ensure that the sound is audible. It makes little sense to shoot a great video if you can't hear the characters or narration. Buy an external microphone if necessary.
- Prepare the set. Make sure there are no distractions and that the set is quiet. An unexpected knock on the door or a ringing cell phone can ruin your video.
- For lengthy video that has only one narrator, use two cameras—one that shows the narrator from the waist up and one zoomed in on just the face. Then combine the two movies, alternating every minute or so between the two views.
- If you are shooting a video for work, wear appropriate business attire.

Creating a YouTube Account

Before you can create a YouTube account, you need a valid e-mail address. For privacy purposes and to prevent unwanted e-mail, you might consider creating a separate e-mail account just for YouTube.

To create a YouTube account:

▶   **1.** Start your browser and go to *www.youtube.com*.

▶   **2.** In the upper-right corner of the YouTube home page, click the **Sign Up** link. The page shown in Figure A-6 appears. (Only the top portion of the page is shown in Figure A-6.)

Figure A-6 ▶ The "Get started with your account" page

3. After filling in the form, click the **I accept** button. The page shown in Figure A-7 appears.

Figure A-7 ▶ The "Do you already have a Google Account" page

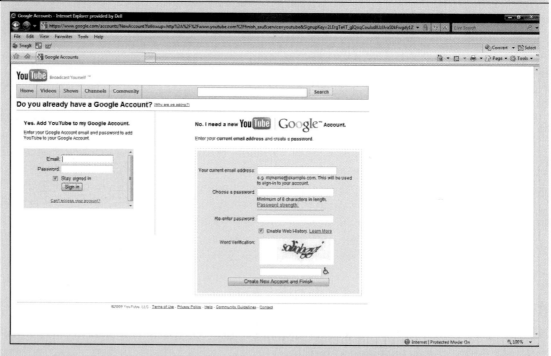

4. Fill out the form and then click the **Create New Account and Finish** button. Your account will be created.

Uploading Video

Currently, YouTube does not accept videos that are longer than 10 minutes or that have a file size greater than 2 gigabytes. As the technology of the Internet and video recordings change, so will these restrictions. YouTube accepts video files from most digital cameras, camcorders, and cell phones in the .AVI, .MOV, .WMV, and .MPG file formats. YouTube has some recommendations about the video you upload, as shown in Figure A-8.

| Figure A-8 | Recommended formats for YouTube video and audio |

Video	
Resolution	**Recommended: 1280 × 720 (16 × 9 HD) and 640 × 480 (4:3 SD)** There is no required minimum resolution—in general, the higher the resolution, the better. HD resolution is preferred. For older content, lower resolution is unavoidable.
Bit rate	Because bit rate is highly dependent on codec, there is no recommended or minimum value. Videos should be optimized for resolution, aspect ratio, and frame rate rather than bit rate.
Frame rate	The frame rate of the original video should be maintained without resampling. In particular, pull-down and other frame rate resampling techniques are strongly discouraged.
Codec	H.264, MPEG-2, or MPEG-4 preferred
Audio	
Codec	MP3 or AAC preferred
Sampling rate	44.1 kHz
Channels	2 (stereo)

When uploading videos to YouTube, make sure your content abides by the following ethical considerations:

- Your content should not be offensive, disparaging, or harmful. It should be lawful and respectful of the rights and feelings of others.
- You should submit original content. Don't use anyone else's work without signed, written permission of the content creator.
- Read and follow the YouTube instructions for Copyright Tips, Community Guidelines, and Terms of Use.

Although you can record and upload a video directly from a Webcam, you should usually view and edit your video before you upload it. To delete a video after you have uploaded it, click your account name in the upper-right corner of any YouTube page, and then click Account to access any videos you have uploaded. Click the Delete button to delete the selected video.

To upload a video to YouTube:

▶ **1.** Assemble the videos you want to upload on your computer desktop or in a folder on your hard drive or flash drive.

▶ **2.** Start your browser and go to *www.youtube.com*. If necessary, sign in to your account.

▶ **3.** Click the **Upload** button in the upper-right corner of any YouTube page. The Video File Upload page appears, as shown in Figure A-9.

Figure A-9	The Video File Upload page

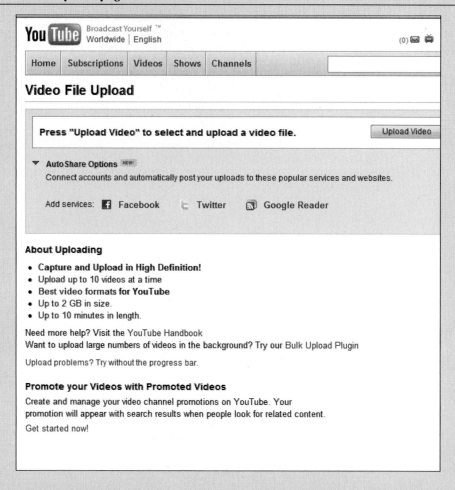

4. Click the **Upload Video** button. On your flash drive or hard drive, browse to find the video file you want to upload to the site.

5. Double-click the filename to start the uploading process. The upload time depends on whether you have a high-bandwidth or low-bandwidth connection to the Internet.

6. When a second Video File Upload page appears (see Figure A-10), enter as much information as you want about your video in the relevant fields, including Title, Description, Tags, and Category. (The Tags are the keywords that describe your video.) The more information you include on this page about your video, the easier it will be for users to find your video, and the faster your video will start playing once it is found.

Figure A-10 The second Video File Upload page

7. Click the **Save Changes** button to save your descriptive information for the video file.

A third Video File Upload page appears, confirming the success of the upload, as shown in Figure A-11.

Figure A-11 — **The confirmation page**

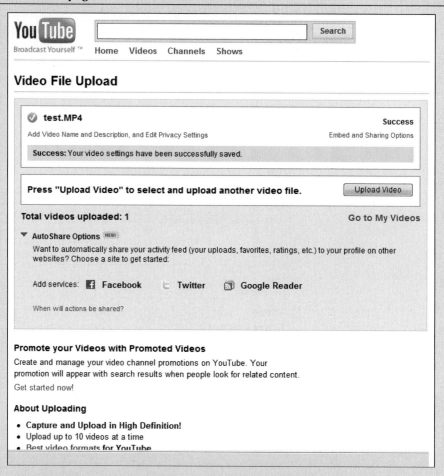

8. Click **Go to My Videos**. The My Account/My Videos page appears, as shown in Figure A-12.

Figure A-12 — **The My Account/My Videos page**

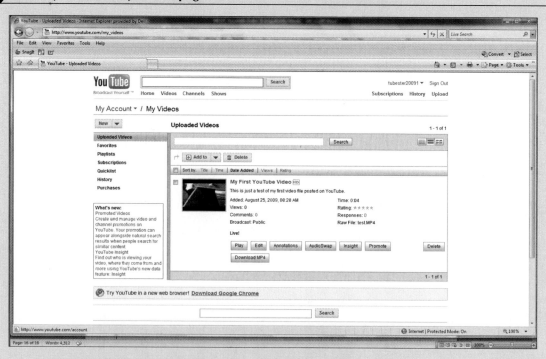

Using HTML 5.0 for Multimedia

The use of audio and video on the Web is thriving, but the content is almost all proprietary. For example, the Adobe Flash and Apple QuickTime players play only their own files. Other formats, such as MPEG, are restricted by patents. Currently, markup that successfully embeds content in one browser may not work in another. The World Wide Web Consortium has proposed two new elements for HTML 5.0—the video element and the audio element. HTML 5.0 should be made available as a final recommendation in September 2010 or shortly thereafter. The goal is to make embedding video and audio as easy as embedding an image on a Web page. The code to embed a video on a page is similar to the following code snippet. Note the similarity between this code and the code you used earlier in the book to insert an image on a Web page.

```
<video src="http://www.cafeaulait.org/birds/sora.mov" />
```

For accessibility purposes, the audio and video elements can contain additional markup that describes the audio and video content. For even greater accessibility, some browser vendors, such as Firefox, are trying to add closed captioning for video.

Currently, all contemporary browsers support the new HTML 5 audio and video elements, except for Internet Explorer 8 and earlier versions. The video and audio elements replace the object and embed elements and all of their attributes and values. The new elements are designed to be cross-browser compatible, but an industry-standard format does not yet exist for video and audio encodings. Most of the issues involved are not technical—the technology already exists. The issues are primarily legal, involving patents, royalties, and restrictions.

The code for the video tag would look like the following example. Note that text can be placed within the video tag so that the user is alerted if the browser does not support the video element.

```
<video src="http://www.somebodyswebsite.com/videos/myvideo.wmv">
Your browser does not support the video tag.
</video>
```

The video element takes the attributes and values shown in Figure A-13. The final recommendation of HTML 5 may change this list of attributes.

Figure A-13 ▶ **Video element attributes and values**

Attribute	Value	Purpose
autoplay	true I false	The value of true will cause the video to play automatically.
controls	true I false	The value of true shows the user some controls, such as a Play button.
end	a numeric value	By default, the video plays until the end. However, you can define where the video stream should stop playing; this feature is useful if you want to show a brief clip of the video.
height	a pixel value	Sets the height of the video player.
loop	a numeric value	Sets the number of times to loop (or repeat) the video.
poster	a URL	The location of an image to show before the video is ready to play (useful for users with low bandwidth).
src	a URL	The location of the video to play (similar to the src attribute for an image file).
width	a pixel value	Sets the width of the video player. The greater the width, the more controls will be visible.

The code for the audio tag would look like the following example. Note that for accessibility purposes, you should place the text for the audio between the start and end audio tags, in case the user's browser does not support the audio element.

```
<audio src="http://www.somebodyswebsite.com/audios/myaudio.mp3">

<p>Four score and seven years ago our fathers brought forth on
this continent a new nation, conceived in Liberty, and dedicated
to the proposition that all men are created equal.</p>

<p>Now we are engaged in a great civil war, testing whether that
nation, or any nation, so conceived and so dedicated, can long
endure. We are met on a great battle-field of that war. We have
come to dedicate a portion of that field, as a final resting
place for those who here gave their lives that that nation might
live. It is altogether fitting and proper that we should do
this.</p>

</audio>
```

The audio element takes the attributes and values shown in Figure A-14. The final recommendation of HTML 5 may change this list of attributes.

Figure A-14   **Audio element attributes and values**

Attribute	Value	Purpose
autoplay	true | false	The value of true will cause the audio to play automatically.
controls	true | false	The value of true shows the user some controls, such as a Play button.
loop	a numeric value	The number of times to loop the audio.
src	url	The location of the audio to play (similar to the src attribute for an image file).

Character Entities

Appendix

| Figure B-1 | Punctuation and special characters |

Named Reference	Displays As	Number Reference	Description
&acute;	´	&#180;	acute accent
&amp;	&	&#38;	ampersand
&brvbar;	¦	&#166;	piping symbol
&bull;	•	&#8226;	bullet
&cedil;	¸	&#184;	cedilla
&cent;	¢	&#162;	cent sign
&circ;	ˆ	&#710;	modifier letter circumflex accent
&clubs;	♣	&#9827;	black club suit = shamrock
&copy;	©	&#169;	copyright sign
&curren;	¤	&#164;	currency sign
&dagger;	†	&#8224;	dagger
&Dagger;	‡	&#8225;	double dagger
&diams;	◆	&#9830;	black diamond suit
&euro;	€	&#8364;	euro sign
&frasl;	/	&#8260;	fraction slash
&gt;	>	&#62;	greater-than sign
&hearts;	♥	&#9829;	black heart suit = valentine
&hellip;	…	&#8230;	horizontal ellipsis
&iexcl;	¡	&#161;	inverted exclamation mark
&iquest;	¿	&#191;	inverted question mark
&laquo;	«	&#171;	left-pointing double angle quotation mark

Starting Data Files

There are no starting Data Files needed for this Appendix.

Figure B-1   **Punctuation and special characters (continued)**

Named Reference	Displays As	Number Reference	Description
&ldquo;	"	&#8220;	left double quotation mark
&loz;	◇	&#9674;	lozenge
&lsaquo;	‹	&#8249;	single left-pointing angle quotation mark
&lsquo;	'	&#8216;	left single quotation mark
&lt;	<	&#60;	less-than sign
&macr;	¯	&#175;	macron
&mdash;	—	&#8212;	em dash
&middot;	·	&#183;	middle dot
&ndash;	–	&#8211;	en dash
&not;	¬	&#172;	not sign
&oline;	‾	&#8254;	overline
&ordf;	ª	&#170;	feminine ordinal indicator
&ordm;	º	&#186;	masculine ordinal indicator
&para;	¶	&#182;	paragraph sign
&permil;	‰	&#8240;	per mille sign
&pound;	£	&#163;	pound sign
&prime;	′	&#8242;	feet
&Prime;	″	&#8243;	inches
&quot;	"	&#34;	quotation mark
&raquo;	»	&#187;	right-pointing double angle quotation mark
&rdquo;	"	&#8221;	right double quotation mark
&reg;	®	&#174;	registered trademark sign
&rsaquo;	›	&#8250;	single right-pointing angle quotation mark
&rsquo;	'	&#8217;	right single quotation mark
&sbquo;	‚	&#8218;	single low-9 quotation mark
&sect;	§	&#167;	section sign
&spades;	♠	&#9824;	black spade suit
&sup1;	¹	&#185;	superscript one
&tilde;	˜	&#732;	small tilde
&trade;	™	&#8482;	trademark sign
&yen;	¥	&#165;	yen sign

Figure B-2 ▸ Math and scientific characters

Named Reference	Displays As	Number Reference	Description
&and;	∧	&#8743;	logical wedge
&ang;	∠	&#8736;	angle
&asymp;	≈	&#8776;	almost equal to
&cap;	∩	&#8745;	intersection
&cong;	≅	&#8773;	approximately equal to
&cup;	∪	&#8746;	union
&deg;	°	&#176;	degree sign
&divide;	÷	&#247;	division sign
&empty;	∅	&#8709;	empty set
&equiv;	≡	&#8801;	identical to
&exist;	∃	&#8707;	there exists
&fnof;	ƒ	&#402;	latin small f with hook
&forall;	∀	&#8704;	for all
&frac12;	½	&#189;	fraction one half
&frac14;	¼	&#188;	fraction one quarter
&frac34;	¾	&#190;	fraction three quarters
&ge;	≥	&#8805;	greater-than or equal to
&infin;	∞	&#8734;	infinity
&int;	∫	&#8747;	integral
&isin;	∈	&#8712;	element of
&lang;	⟨	&#9001;	left-pointing angle bracket
&lceil;	⌈	&#8968;	left ceiling
&le;	≤	&#8804;	less-than or equal to
&lfloor;	⌊	&#8970;	left floor
&micro;	µ	&#181;	micro sign
&minus;	−	&#8722;	minus sign
&nabla;	∇	&#8711;	backward difference
&ne;	≠	&#8800;	not equal to
&ni;	∋	&#8715;	contains as member
&notin;	∉	&#8713;	not an element of
&nsub;	⊄	&#8836;	not a subset of
&oplus;	⊕	&#8853;	circled plus
&or;	∨	&#8744;	logical
&otimes;	⊗	&#8855;	circled times
&part;	∂	&#8706;	partial differential
&perp;	⊥	&#8869;	perpendicular to
&plusmn;	±	&#177;	plus or minus sign
&prop;	∝	&#8733;	proportional to
&radic;	√	&#8730;	square root (radical sign)
&rang;	⟩	&#9002;	right-pointing angle bracket

Figure B-2 ▸ Math and scientific characters (continued)

Named Reference	Displays As	Number Reference	Description
&rceil;	⌉	&#8969;	right ceiling
&rfloor;	⌋	&#8971;	right floor
&sdot;	·	&#8901;	dot operator
&sim;	~	&#8764;	tilde operator
&sub;	⊂	&#8834;	subset of
&sube;	⊆	&#8838;	subset of or equal to
&sum;	Σ	&#8721;	n-ary summation
&sup;	⊃	&#8835;	superset of
&sup2;	2	&#178;	superscripted two
&sup3;	3	&#179;	superscripted three
&supe;	⊇	&#8839;	superset of or equal to
&there4;	∴	&#8756;	therefore
&times;	×	&#215;	multiplication sign

Figure B-3 ▸ Arrow shapes

Named Reference	Displays As	Number Reference	Description
&crarr;	↵	&#8629;	downward arrow with corner leftward
&darr;	↓	&#8595;	downward arrow
&dArr;	⇓	&#8659;	downward double arrow
&harr;	↔	&#8596;	left right arrow
&hArr;	⇔	&#8660;	left right double arrow
&larr;	←	&#8592;	leftward arrow
&lArr;	⇐	&#8656;	leftward double arrow
&rarr;	→	&#8594;	rightward arrow
&rArr;	⇒	&#8658;	rightward double arrow
&uarr;	↑	&#8593;	upward arrow
&uArr;	⇑	&#8657;	upward double arrow

Appendix C

HTML 4.01 Elements

Appendix

The following table lists the HTML 4.01 elements by name and provides a description of each.

Name	Description
a	Anchor
abbr	Abbreviated form
acronym	Abbreviated form
address	By convention, the italicized address of the Web site or Webmaster
area	Client-side image map area
b	Bold text
base	Designates a default target
blockquote	Block-level element for a long quotation
body	Document body
br	Forced line break
button	Button
caption	Table caption
center	Center text (deprecated)
cite	Citation
code	Computer code
col	Table column
colgroup	Table column group
dd	Definition description
div	Generic block-style container
dl	Definition list
dt	Definition term
em	Emphasis
fieldset	Form control group

Name	Description
form	Interactive form
frame	Identifies window frame document
frameset	Window division
h1	Heading level 1
h2	Heading level 2
h3	Heading level 3
h4	Heading level 4
h5	Heading level 5
h6	Heading level 6
head	Document head
hr	Horizontal rule
html	Document root element
iframe	Inline frame
img	Embedded image
input	Form control
kbd	Monospace type
label	Form field label text
legend	Fieldset legend
li	List item
link	A media-independent link
map	Client-side image map
meta	Generic meta information
noframes	Designates substitute text for frames
object	Generic embedded object

Starting Data Files

There are no starting Data Files needed for this Appendix.

Name	Description
ol	Ordered list
optgroup	Option group
option	Selectable choice
p	Paragraph
pre	Preformatted text
q	Short, inline quotation
samp	Sample program output
select	Option selector
span	Generic inline container
strong	Strong emphasis (bold)
style	Style information
sub	Subscript
sup	Superscript

Name	Description
table	Document table
tbody	Table body
td	Table data cell
textarea	Multiline text field
tfoot	Table footer
th	Table header cell
thead	Table header
title	Document title
tr	Table row
tt	Teletype (monospaced text)
u	Underlined text (deprecated)
ul	Unordered list
var	Variable

CSS 2.1 Properties and Values

Appendix

The following table lists the CSS 2.1 properties and the values available for each property. In the Values column, the default value is shown in bold. The Group column lists the group to which the property belongs.

Property	Description	Values	Group
background	Shorthand property for setting all background properties	background-attachment background-color background-image background-position background-repeat	background
background-attachment	Sets the position of a background image as fixed or scrolls as the insertion point moves down the page	fixed **scroll**	background
background-color	Sets the background color of an element	rgb value hex value short hex value named value **transparent**	background
background-image	Sets an image as the background	url(filename) **none**	background
background-position	Sets the position of a background image	top left top center top right center left **center center** center right bottom left bottom center bottom right x% y%	background

Starting Data Files

There are no starting Data Files needed for this Appendix.

Property	Description	Values	Group
background-repeat	Determines whether a background image will be repeated	**repeat** repeat-x repeat-y no-repeat	background
border	The shorthand property for setting all of the border properties	border-width border-style border-color	border
border-bottom	The shorthand property for setting all of the properties for the bottom border	border-bottom-width border-style border-color	border
border-bottom-color	Sets the color of the bottom border	border-color	border
border-bottom-style	Sets the style for the bottom border	border-style	border
border-bottom-width	Sets the width for the bottom border	thin **medium** thick length (in ems)	border
border-collapse	Determines whether a table border has a single or double rule	collapse **separate**	table
border-color	Sets the color for all four borders	rgb value hex value short hex value named value	border
border-left	The shorthand property for setting all of the properties for the left border	border-left-width border-style border-color	border
border-left-color	Sets the color for the left border	border-color	border
border-left-style	Sets the style for the left border	border-style	border
border-left-width	Sets the width for the left border	thin **medium** thick length (in ems)	border
border-right	The shorthand property for setting all of the properties for the right border	border-right-width border-style border-color	border
border-right-color	Sets the color for the right border	border-color	border
border-right-style	Sets the style for the right border	border-style	border
border-right-width	Sets the width for the right border	thin **medium** thick length (in ems)	border
border-style	Sets the style of the four borders	**none** hidden dotted dashed double groove inset outset ridge solid	border

Property	Description	Values	Group
border-top	The shorthand property for setting all of the properties for the top border	border-top-width border-style border-color	border
border-top-color	Sets the color for the top border	border-color	border
border-top-style	Sets the style for the top border	border-style	border
border-top-width	Sets the width for the top border	thin **medium** thick length (in ems)	border
border-width	A shorthand property for setting the width of the four borders in one declaration; can have from one to four values	thin **medium** thick length (in ems)	border
bottom	Determines how far from the bottom edge an element is from its parent element	**auto** length (in ems) %	positioning
caption-side	Determines the position of the table caption	**top** bottom left right	table
clear	Positions an element below another element	left right both none	classification
color	Determines text color	color in RGB, hex, short hex, or named values	text
display	Sets how and if an element is to be displayed	block inline list-item **none**	classification
empty-cells	Determines whether to show a table without content in a table	**hide** show	table
float	Positions an element in relation to another element	left right **none**	classification
font	The shorthand property for setting all of the properties for a font	font-style font-variant font-weight font-size/line-height font-family	font
font-family	A list of font family names from specific to generic	font-family name generic-family name	font
font-size	Sets the size for the font	xx-small x-small small medium large x-large xx-large smaller pt values em values	font

Property	Description	Values	Group
font-style	Sets the style for the font	**normal** italic oblique	font
font-variant	Displays text in small caps or in a normal font	**normal** small-caps	font
font-weight	Sets the weight of a font	**normal** bold bolder lighter 100 200 300 400 500 600 700 800 900	font
height	Sets the height of an element	**auto** length (in ems) %	dimension
left	Determines how far from the left edge an element is from its parent element	**auto** length (in ems) %	positioning
letter-spacing	Increases or decreases the space between characters	**normal** length (in ems)	text
line-height	Determines the white space between lines	**normal** number length (in ems) %	text
list-style	The shorthand property for setting all of the list-style properties	list-style-type list-style-position list-style-image	list
list-style-image	Sets an image to be used as a list-style marker	**none** url	list
list-style-position	Determines where the list-item marker will be positioned	inside **outside**	list
list-style-type	Determines the type of the list-item marker	circle decimal decimal-leading-zero **disc** lower-alpha lower-roman none square upper-alpha upper-roman	list
margin	The shorthand property for setting the margin properties	margin-top margin-right margin-bottom margin-left	margin
margin-bottom	Sets the bottom margin for an element	auto length (in ems) %	margin

Property	Description	Values	Group
margin-left	Sets the left margin for an element	auto length (in ems) %	margin
margin-right	Sets the right margin for an element	auto length (in ems) %	margin
margin-top	Sets the top margin for an element	auto length (in ems) %	margin
overflow	Determines the visibility of an element should content not fit into its container	auto hidden scroll **visible**	positioning
padding	The shorthand property for setting all of the padding properties	padding-top padding-right padding-bottom padding-left	padding
padding-bottom	Sets the bottom padding for an element	length (in ems) %	padding
padding-left	Sets the left padding for an element	length (in ems) %	padding
padding-right	Sets the right padding for an element	length (in ems) %	padding
padding-top	Sets the top padding for an element	length (in ems) %	padding
position	Positions an element	**static** relative absolute fixed	classification
position	Positions an element	absolute fixed relative **static**	positioning
right	Determines how far from the right edge an element is from its parent element	**auto** length (in ems) %	positioning
text-align	Aligns the text in an element horizontally	center justify **left** right	text
text-decoration	Adds a line above, through, or under text	line-through overline **none** underline	text
text-indent	Indents the first line of text in an element	length (in ems) %	text
text-transform	Determines the capitalization of text	capitalize lowercase **none** uppercase	text

Property	Description	Values	Group
top	Determines how far from the top edge an element is from its parent element	**auto** length (in ems) %	positioning
vertical-align	Sets the vertical alignment of an element	**baseline** bottom middle sub super text-bottom text-top top length %	positioning
visibility	Determines whether an element is visible	collapse hidden **visible**	classification
width	Sets the width of an element	**auto** % length (in ems)	dimension
word-spacing	Increases or decreases the space between words	**normal** length (in ems)	text
z-index	Determines the stacking order of an element (the greater the number, the higher the element is in the stack)	**auto** number	positioning

Pseudo-Classes

Pseudo-Class	Purpose
:active	Determines the style when a link is clicked
:focus	Determines the style when a link has the focus
:hover	Determines the style for mouse-over effect
:link	Determines the style for links that have not yet been visited
:visited	Determines the style for links that have been visited

Pseudo-Elements

Pseudo-Element	Purpose
:first-letter	Formats just the first letter of a word
:first-line	Formats just the first line of a paragraph
:before	Inserts white space before an element
:after	Inserts white space after an element

Glossary/Index